T0136970

Lecture Notes in Electrical Engineering

Volume 848

Series Editors

Leopoldo Angrisani, Department of Electrical and Information Technologies Engineering, University of Napoli Federico II, Naples, Italy

Marco Arteaga, Departament de Control y Robótica, Universidad Nacional Autónoma de México, Coyoacán, Mexico

Bijaya Ketan Panigrahi, Electrical Engineering, Indian Institute of Technology Delhi, New Delhi, Delhi, India

Samarjit Chakraborty, Fakultät für Elektrotechnik und Informationstechnik, TU München, Munich, Germany

Jiming Chen, Zhejiang University, Hangzhou, Zhejiang, China

Shanben Chen, Materials Science and Engineering, Shanghai Jiao Tong University, Shanghai, China

Tan Kay Chen, Department of Electrical and Computer Engineering, National University of Singapore, Singapore, Singapore

Rüdiger Dillmann, Humanoids and Intelligent Systems Laboratory, Karlsruhe Institute for Technology, Karlsruhe, Germany

Haibin Duan, Beijing University of Aeronautics and Astronautics, Beijing, China

Gianluigi Ferrari, Università di Parma, Parma, Italy

Manuel Ferre, Centre for Automation and Robotics CAR (UPM-CSIC), Universidad Politécnica de Madrid, Madrid, Spain

Sandra Hirche, Department of Electrical Engineering and Information Science, Technische Universität München, Munich, Germany

Faryar Jabbari, Department of Mechanical and Aerospace Engineering, University of California, Irvine, CA, USA

Limin Jia, State Key Laboratory of Rail Traffic Control and Safety, Beijing Jiaotong University, Beijing, China

Janusz Kacprzyk, Systems Research Institute, Polish Academy of Sciences, Warsaw, Poland

Alaa Khamis, German University in Egypt El Tagamoa El Khames, New Cairo City, Egypt

Torsten Kroeger, Stanford University, Stanford, CA, USA

Yong Li, Hunan University, Changsha, Hunan, China

Qilian Liang, Department of Electrical Engineering, University of Texas at Arlington, Arlington, TX, USA

Ferran Martín, Departament d'Enginyeria Electrònica, Universitat Autònoma de Barcelona, Bellaterra, Barcelona, Spain

Tan Cher Ming, College of Engineering, Nanyang Technological University, Singapore, Singapore

Wolfgang Minker, Institute of Information Technology, University of Ulm, Ulm, Germany

Pradeep Misra, Department of Electrical Engineering, Wright State University, Dayton, OH, USA

Sebastian Möller, Quality and Usability Laboratory, TU Berlin, Berlin, Germany

Subhas Mukhopadhyay, School of Engineering & Advanced Technology, Massey University, Palmerston North, Manawatu-Wanganui, New Zealand

Cun-Zheng Ning, Electrical Engineering, Arizona State University, Tempe, AZ, USA

Toyoaki Nishida, Graduate School of Informatics, Kyoto University, Kyoto, Japan

Federica Pascucci, Dipartimento di Ingegneria, Università degli Studi "Roma Tre", Rome, Italy

Yong Qin, State Key Laboratory of Rail Traffic Control and Safety, Beijing Jiaotong University, Beijing, China

Gan Woon Seng, School of Electrical & Electronic Engineering, Nanyang Technological University, Singapore, Singapore

Joachim Speidel, Institute of Telecommunications, Universität Stuttgart, Stuttgart, Germany

Germano Veiga, Campus da FEUP, INESC Porto, Porto, Portugal

Haitao Wu, Academy of Opto-electronics, Chinese Academy of Sciences, Beijing, China

Walter Zamboni, DIEM - Università degli studi di Salerno, Fisciano, Salerno, Italy

Junjie James Zhang, Charlotte, NC, USA

The book series *Lecture Notes in Electrical Engineering* (LNEE) publishes the latest developments in Electrical Engineering - quickly, informally and in high quality. While original research reported in proceedings and monographs has traditionally formed the core of LNEE, we also encourage authors to submit books devoted to supporting student education and professional training in the various fields and applications areas of electrical engineering. The series cover classical and emerging topics concerning:

- Communication Engineering, Information Theory and Networks
- Electronics Engineering and Microelectronics
- Signal, Image and Speech Processing
- Wireless and Mobile Communication
- Circuits and Systems
- Energy Systems, Power Electronics and Electrical Machines
- Electro-optical Engineering
- Instrumentation Engineering
- Avionics Engineering
- Control Systems
- Internet-of-Things and Cybersecurity
- Biomedical Devices, MEMS and NEMS

For general information about this book series, comments or suggestions, please contact leontina.dicecco@springer.com.

To submit a proposal or request further information, please contact the Publishing Editor in your country:

China

Jasmine Dou, Editor (jasmine.dou@springer.com)

India, Japan, Rest of Asia

Swati Meherishi, Editorial Director (Swati.Meherishi@springer.com)

Southeast Asia, Australia, New Zealand

Ramesh Nath Premnath, Editor (ramesh.premnath@springernature.com)

USA, Canada:

Michael Luby, Senior Editor (michael.luby@springer.com)

All other Countries:

Leontina Di Cecco, Senior Editor (leontina.dicecco@springer.com)

** This series is indexed by EI Compendex and Scopus databases. **

More information about this series at https://link.springer.com/bookseries/7818

Udai Pratap Rao · Sankita J. Patel · Pethuru Raj ·
Andrea Visconti

Editors

Security, Privacy and Data Analytics

Select Proceedings of ISPDA 2021

 Springer

Editors
Udai Pratap Rao
Department of Computer Science
and Engineering
Sardar Vallabhbhai National Institute
of Technology
Surat, Gujarat, India

Sankita J. Patel
Department of Computer Science
and Engineering
Sardar Vallabhbhai National Institute
of Technology
Surat, Gujarat, India

Pethuru Raj
Reliance Jio Platforms Ltd.
Bangalore, Karnataka, India

Andrea Visconti
Department of Computer Science
University of Milan
Milan, Milano, Italy

ISSN 1876-1100   ISSN 1876-1119 (electronic)
Lecture Notes in Electrical Engineering
ISBN 978-981-16-9091-4   ISBN 978-981-16-9089-1 (eBook)
https://doi.org/10.1007/978-981-16-9089-1

© The Editor(s) (if applicable) and The Author(s), under exclusive license to Springer Nature
Singapore Pte Ltd. 2022
This work is subject to copyright. All rights are solely and exclusively licensed by the Publisher, whether
the whole or part of the material is concerned, specifically the rights of translation, reprinting, reuse
of illustrations, recitation, broadcasting, reproduction on microfilms or in any other physical way, and
transmission or information storage and retrieval, electronic adaptation, computer software, or by similar
or dissimilar methodology now known or hereafter developed.
The use of general descriptive names, registered names, trademarks, service marks, etc. in this publication
does not imply, even in the absence of a specific statement, that such names are exempt from the relevant
protective laws and regulations and therefore free for general use.
The publisher, the authors and the editors are safe to assume that the advice and information in this book
are believed to be true and accurate at the date of publication. Neither the publisher nor the authors or
the editors give a warranty, expressed or implied, with respect to the material contained herein or for any
errors or omissions that may have been made. The publisher remains neutral with regard to jurisdictional
claims in published maps and institutional affiliations.

This Springer imprint is published by the registered company Springer Nature Singapore Pte Ltd.
The registered company address is: 152 Beach Road, #21-01/04 Gateway East, Singapore 189721,
Singapore

Contents

About the Editors

Udai Pratap Rao is an IEEE Senior member and has been associated with the Department of Computer Science and Engineering, Sardar Vallabhbhai National Institute of Technology (SVNIT) Surat, India since 2007. He received a Ph.D. degree from SVNIT, in 2014. His research interests include information security and privacy, privacy in location-based service, big data privacy, security and trust management in online social networks, security and privacy in the internet of things and cyber-physical systems, distributed computing. He has published about 65 papers extensively in journals and refereed conference proceedings. He has supervised 03 Ph.D. thesis in the fields of data privacy and security. He is currently the PI of the research project funded by IHUB NTIHAC Foundation, IITK under the aegis of NM-ICPS, Department of Science and Technology, Government of India. He also acted as the Chief Investigator of the project "Information Security Education and Awareness Project Phase II" from July 2018 to Dec 2019, funded by the Ministry of Electronics and Information Technology (MeitY) Govt. of India. He has edited a book entitled "Blockchain for Information Security and Privacy" published by CRC Press, Taylor and Francis Group. He serves as a reviewer of many peer-reviewed journals.

Sankita J. Patel received her Ph.D. from S. V. National Institute of Technology (SVNIT), Surat, in 2015. She is presently an Assistant Professor with the Department of Computer Science and Engineering at SVNIT, Surat. Her research interests focus on applied research in information security and privacy in various domains like the internet of things, cyber-physical systems, online social networks, data analytics, cloud computing, big data, etc. She has co-authored several papers in refereed journals and conference proceedings.

Pethuru Raj is a chief architect and vice president in the Jio Cloud Services division of Reliance Jio Platforms Ltd. Bangalore. He has over 20 years of IT industry experience and 08 years of research experience. He completed his Ph.D. degree at Anna University, Chennai, and continued with the UGC-sponsored postdoctoral research in the Department of Computer Science and Automation, Indian Institute of Science (IISc), Bangalore. He was granted a couple of international research fellowships

(JSPS and JST) to work as a research scientist for 3.5 years in two leading Japanese universities. He has published over 30 research papers in peer-reviewed journals, authored/edited 20 books and contributed 35 book chapters for various technology books edited by highly acclaimed and accomplished professors and professionals. His research interests focus on emerging technologies such as the internet of things, artificial intelligence, big and fast data analytics, blockchain, digital twins, cloud-native computing, edge/fog clouds, reliability engineering, microservices architecture and event-driven architecture (EDA).

Andrea Visconti received his Ph.D. from Università degli Studi di Milano, in 2005. He has been a contract professor at Università degli Studi dell'Insubria (2005), Università degli Studi di Trento (2015–2018), and guest researcher to NIST (Feb 2012). Since 2006, he holds a tenured position as an assistant professor of Computer Science at the Università Degli Studi di Milano. His research interests focus on cryptography, coding theory and information security, both theoretical and applied. He is a co-author of about 50 papers. He has served as a guest co-editor for special issues on the Internet of Things (Elsevier) and Security and Communication Networks (Wiley/Hindawi). Currently, he is a Topic Editor of Mathematics (MDPI) and Associate Editor of the Iran Journal of Computer Science (Springer). Dr. Visconti leads the Crypto and Coding Theory group (CLUB) at Università Degli Studi di Milano.

NITG Chain: A Scalable, Private and Permissioned Blockchain with Proof of Reputation Consensus Method

Alok Jaiswal, Sheetal Chandel, Ajit Muzumdar, Chirag Modi, Madhu G. M., and C. Vyjayanthi

1 Introduction

Blockchain technology has grown for various IT applications. It can be defined as the append only distributed database that is practically immutable, maintained by decentralized P2P network using consensus method, cryptography and back referencing blocks to order and validate the transactions [1]. In contrast to traditional databases, blockchain offers data immutability, data transparency, user anonymity, trust among the untrusted entities, decentralization etc. Bitcoin [2] is the first popular implementation of blockchain for financial application. Since then, other blockchains such as Ethereum, various Hyperledger project solutions, IOTA, Ripple, R3. Corda, Hashgraph etc. have been popularized. Blockchain is explored in various markets such as B2C, B2B, online trading, auctioning, energy, e-KYC etc. In addition, it is evolved by integrating smart contracts as business logic. As per the deployment and access scope, there are mainly three types of blockchains viz; public, private and consortium. Public blockchains are open to all nodes for read and write. The widely used public blockchains are Bitcoin and Ethereum. The public blockchains are more secure and fully decentralized as the transaction validation and confirmation is done by a large number of nodes in the network. However, scalability and blockchain forks are major issue [3]. In private blockchain, a node requires a permission to take

A. Jaiswal (✉) · S. Chandel · A. Muzumdar · C. Modi · M. G. M. · C. Vyjayanthi
National Institute of Technology Goa, Farmagudi, Ponda 403401, Goa, India
e-mail: ajitmuzumdar@nitgoa.ac.in

C. Modi
e-mail: cnmodi@nitgoa.ac.in

M. G. M.
e-mail: madhugm@nitgoa.ac.in

C. Vyjayanthi
e-mail: c.vyjayanthi@nitgoa.ac.in

© The Author(s), under exclusive license to Springer Nature Singapore Pte Ltd. 2022
U. P. Rao et al. (eds.), *Security, Privacy and Data Analytics*, Lecture Notes
in Electrical Engineering 848, https://doi.org/10.1007/978-981-16-9089-1_1

part in the blockchain network. Here, a write permission is given to the authorized nodes only, whereas read permission may be public or restricted. Here, data security and trust are dependent on the credibility of the authorized nodes. In consortium blockchain, the data write operation is performed by a pre-selected set of nodes from multiple organizations, while read permission may be public or restricted. As like a private blockchain, the data security and trust are dependent on the credibility of the selected nodes.

Although blockchain has high potential in various applications, it faces the problem of scalability due to the underlying computationally expensive consensus methods such as Poof of Work (PoW), Proof of Stake (PoS) etc. [4]. With the increasing number of nodes, the transaction throughput is decreasing as a large number of nodes are involved in transaction validation and confirmation. Although these consensus methods help in improving the trust among the untrusted entities in the blockchain network, they pose the scalability issue. In literature, researchers have proposed on-chain and off-chain solutions [5, 6] to address the scalability issue in blockchain. However, still there is a room for further improving the scalability and security of the blockchain.

In this paper, we design NITG Chain (NITGoa Chain) with the improved scalability and security. It is a private and permissioned blockchain which can be more suitable for business to business applications such as trading, asset management etc. Here, a node needs a permission from the existing nodes to participate in the blockchain network. It applies Proof of Reputation (PoR) consensus method for appending the block in NITG Chain. Here, the block mining is performed by only the dedicated nodes (authorized nodes) which have high reputation and selected by each organization. A block created by any authorized node is verified by other authority nodes along with underlying transactions, and that block is appended to NITG Chain after receiving and verifying the confirmation from 2/3 of authority nodes. The selection of authority node for block creation is done based on its liveliness and reputation. Thus, NITG Chain achieves fairness among the nodes for block creation. In addition, it ensures reliability, security from blockchain fork and affordable throughput and scalability. The functional and performance validation of NITG Chain is done using a testbed at NIT Goa by applying different size of transactions and blocks. From the experimental results, it is observed that NITG Chain achieves throughput 712 *tps* on average, while generating a block of transaction at an interval of 10 s.

In following, Sect. 2 discusses background on blockchain followed by the existing solutions to improve the scalability of blockchain. A detailed discussion of the NITG Chain is given in Sect. 3, while the experimental results and analysis of the NITG Chain is given in Sect. 4. Section 5 concludes our work with references at the end.

2 Background and Related Work

A common workflow of blockchain in peer to peer network is depicted in Fig. 1. Here, a transaction initiator broadcasts a transaction into peer to peer network of blockchain after digitally signing it. After receiving a number of transactions, each node starts creating a block of transactions by applying Proof of Work (PoW) [2]. A node which is successful of mining a block broadcasts that block in peer to peer network for the validation. After receiving the confirmation from a majority of nodes (51% nodes), each node updates their copy of the blockchain by appending that block.

In contracts to distributed database, blockchain establishes the trust among the nodes through consensus. However, scalability and fault tolerance of blockchains depend on underlying consensus method. A summary of the existing consensus methods is given in Table 1.

To address the scalability problem in blockchain, different solutions such as on-chain and off-chain including side chain and child-chain have been reported. On-chain solutions attempt to increase the block size, reduce the transaction size or sharding to improve the scalability. Big block and Bitcoin Unlimited [18] are the examples of the increased block size. Here, more number of transactions can be confirmed in a single run of the blockchain update. However, the block propagation speed decreases, which may result into blockchain forking. In Bitcoin's Segregated Witness (Segwit) [19], the signatures and transactions are separated. The witness data structure stores the signatures. This helps to address the problem of transaction malleability. Here, the size of transactions is reduced to increase the throughput. As like in the distributed databases, sharding in blockchain attempts to group nodes into different shards, and thus, allowing parallel processing of the transactions. Elastico [20], OmniLedger [21], RapidChain [22], Zilliqa [23], Harmony [24] and Monoxide [25] are applying the blockchain sharding. However, sharding causes the data integrity issue, if an attacker can have control over shards.

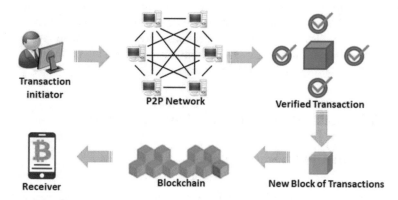

Fig. 1 A common workflow of blockchain [7]

Table 1 Summary of the existing consensus methods

Consensus	Applicable blockchain/DLT	Node identity	Block mining	Scalability	Fault tolerance
PoW [2]	Bitcoin	Permissionless	R	Low	50%
PoS [8]	Ethereum	Permissionless	D	Medium	$3f + 1$
PBFT [9]	Hyperledger	Permissioned	R	Medium	$3f + 1$
DPoS [10]	Bitshares	Permissioned	D	High	$3f + 1$ to $2f + 1$
FBA [11]	Ripple and Stellar	Permissioned	D	High	$5f + 1$ to $3f + 1$
PoAu [12]	None	Permissioned	D	High	$3f + 1$
PoET [13]	Intel's Sawtooth	Permissionless	R	High	$2c + 1$
PoAc [14]	None	Permissionless	R	Low	50%
PoB [15]	None	Permissionless	R	Low	50%
PoC [16]	Zcash	Permissionless	R	Low	50%
PoR [17]	None	Permissioned	D	High	$3f + 1$

R Random, D Deterministic, c number of nodes, f Byzantine faults

In off-chain solutions, the transaction processing is performed outside the chain for the frequent transactions. Typical solutions under this category are payment channels [26, 27], side chain [28] and Child chain [6]. Bitcoin's Lightning network [26] and Ethereum's Raiden network [27] have adopted the payment channel (off-chain) to process frequent transactions, and thus, reducing the number of transactions to be processed at main chain. This helps to improve the throughput and reduce the transaction fees. However, it may affect the ecosystem due to the reduced transaction fees and profit to miners. The goal of side chain is to transfer the cryptocurrencies among different blockchains. For example, the exchange of cryptocurrencies among different blockchains. The typical example of side chain is Pegged Sidechain [28]. Child chain follows the parent-child structure, in which transaction processing is performed at child chain, while parent chain maintains the record of the confirmed transactions. Plasma [6] follows the parent-child structure for transaction processing and record maintenance. A summary of the existing solutions to improve blockchain scalability is given in Table 2. As per our observation, there is a need of re-investigating or extending the existing consensus methods (on-chain solutions) to improve the throughput, scalability and security in blockchain.

3 NITG Chain: Proposed Blockchain Framework

3.1 Objective and Design Goals

The main objective is to design a scalable and secured private blockchain with the improved throughput for business to business applications. The proposed framework should achieve higher throughput in context of different size of transactions and block.

Table 2 Summary of the existing solutions to blockchain scalability

Category	Solutions	Advantages	Limitations
On-Chain	Increasing the block size [5, 18]	Improved throughput	Blockchain forking
	Reducing the transaction size [19]	Improved throughput	Causes fungibility
	Sharding [20–25]	Parallel processing	1% attack
Off-Chain	Payment channel [26, 27]	Reduced transaction fee and waiting time	Can affect the token ecosystems
	Side chain [28]	Allows to exchange cryptocurrencies among different chains	Difficult to control different cryptocurrencies due to their price differences
	Child chain [6]	Parent-child chain structure to improve the throughput	Complexity increases for parent-child verification

3.2 Design of the NITG Chain Framework

The design of NITG Chain is given in Fig. 2. Here, the created transactions are transmitted to all the peers (i.e. connected nodes to the transaction initiator) in peer-to-peer network. Further, these peers transmit such transactions to their peers and thus, all the created transactions are propagated in whole network for verification. Each node in P2P network has a list of all the verified transactions which are created in a particular time. The verification of transactions helps to remove any malicious transaction. In NITG Chain, only authorized nodes verify and validate the transactions. At a time, only one authorized node creates a block of such verified transactions and checks for other live authority nodes to make an active list. The active list of the authorized nodes is sorted as per their reputation score calculated over the period of time and appended to the block. The generated block by an authorized node is signed using the elliptic curve cryptography based digital signature algorithm. This generated block is broadcasted in the network for the verification. Block verification is performed by each authorized node in order to introduce valid block in the network. Upon verification, each authorized node broadcasts the signed confirmation transaction containing the block's hash value. Then, this block is added to blockchain by each node after receiving the confirmation from 2/3 of authority nodes. For the next block creation, the next authorized node is selected from the active list. Thus, all the authorized nodes have a fair chance of mining the block. In general, NITG Chain performs new node insertion, transaction flow, transaction verification, creating an active list of the authorized nodes, block creation, verification, and confirmation, time synchronization and API service. In following, a detailed discussion on these activities is given.

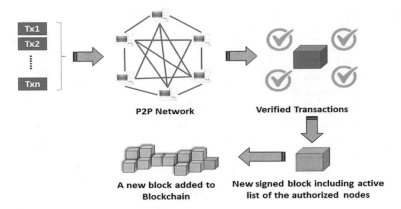

Fig. 2 Design of the NITG Chain framework

3.2.1 New Node Insertion in Network

When a new node wishes to participate in NITG chain, it broadcasts its public key to all the peers. A new node insertion in NITG chain is performed through 5-way handshaking and mutual authentication. A new node first sends a request to the existing node for adding it to the existing node's peer list, as shown in Fig. 3. In response, the existing node adds this node to its peer list and returns a node ID. Further, this new node sends a request for getting the existing node's peer list. The existing node sends its peer list to the new node. New node adds the returned peers to its peer list. Finally, a new node becomes a part of the network. For a new node insertion, following messages are involved.

1. $N \to P$: *na* //Request to add in peer list
2. $P \to N$: (*na, nb, ID*)E_{kP} //Return Node ID (Existing node adds this new node to its peer list and returns a node ID)
3. $N \to P$: (*na, nb*)E_{kN} //Request for peer list (New node sends request for the existing node's peer list)
4. $P \to N$: (*na, nb, PL*)E_{kP} //Returns peer list
5. $N \to P$: (*nb, PL*)E_{kN} //Add peers to peer list (New node adds the returned peers to its peer list and acknowledges the same)

Here, N is a new node and P is the existing peer node. *na* and *nb* are nonces of new node and peer node respectively. E_{kN} and E_{kP} are the private keys of new node and peer node respectively for signing the messages using elliptic curve cryptography. After 5-way handshaking process, all the peers add mapping of new node ID to its public key to their local cache. All further communication with this new node uses this public key.

3.2.2 Transaction Flow and Verification

The transactions created by the users are transmitted to all the nodes in the network. For this, we are applying Breadth First Search (BFS), where a node creates a transaction, it is transmitted to all its peers. Further, those peer nodes transmit that transaction to their peers as maintained in their peer list and so on. At the end, all nodes in the network receive the created transaction. Like this, each node in the network has a list of all the transactions created during time interval t. However, there may be malicious nodes which can spread the forged transactions into the network. To prevent this, the propagated transactions are verified before packaging them into the block. In NITG Chain, authorized nodes verify the transaction by checking its attributes, digital signature of sender, balance and size of the data field. Such verified transactions are collected as valid transactions for block creation.

3.2.3 Active List of the Authorized and Reputed Nodes

Each authorized node maintains a list of authorized nodes along with their reputation score calculated during time interval T. To know whether the authorized nodes are active or not, the current authorized node sends a ping request message to all other authorized nodes, as shown in Fig. 4. If it gets reply from a list of authority node, it adds that node to the active list. At the end, all the available authority nodes are identified for next block creations, as shown in Fig. 5. Consider, one of the authorized nodes is not available or crashed to send a reply. In this case, a crashed node will not be added to the active list of the authorized node. Thus, the next authorized and reputed node (potential miner) waits for a fixed time slice (2 s) and then it creates

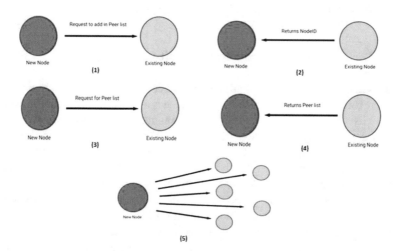

Fig. 3 New node insertion process in NITG Chain

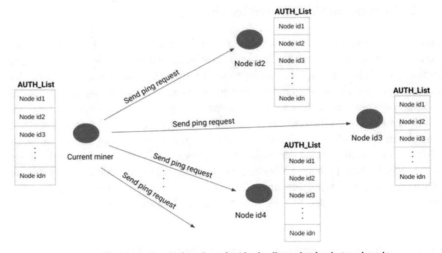

Ping request to each node and authority list maintained at each node

Fig. 4 Checking liveliness of the authorized nodes in NITG Chain

the block itself. This helps to achieve the reliability of the network and fast creation of block. For each of the authority nodes which have not participated in creating the recent m blocks, the reputation score is calculated based on their liveliness and participation in creating the recent blocks. Thus, reputation score of each node is determined as the number of times a node has generated valid blocks with respect to a chance given to that node for block creation. For this, an authorized node traverse the blockchain. Like this, all the authority nodes maintain a list of the other authority nodes and their reputation score and keeps updating it.

3.2.4 Block Creation, Verification and Confirmation

An authorized node verifies the transactions and collects them as valid transactions during the time t, as discussed earlier. It then creates a block (please refer Fig. 6) with the active list of the authorized nodes with their reputation score, as discussed earlier. Here, all the authority nodes are sorted and added to the active list of the authority nodes. This active list along with the reputation score of each node is appended in the current block so that the next authority node (potential node to create the next block) can be found from the current active list. This helps to secure the reputation score. Therefore, the active list determines the next miner automatically. If an immediate node crashes, the next potential miner waits for a fixed time slice (2 s) and then it creates the block itself and thus, making the network reliable, more decentralized and solving the problem of monopoly attack. It then signs the block using its private

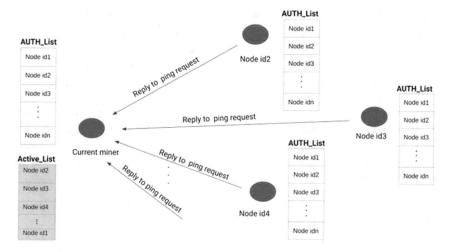

Fig. 5 Creating an active list of the authorized and reputed nodes in NITG Chain

key and appends signature to the block. Finally, the created block is broadcasted for the verification.

Block verification is done by each authority node in order to introduce valid block in the network. Here, each authority node checks the presence of the block creator in the authority list. If present, then the signature of that node is verified. If the creator node is an authority node, the signature of each transaction using the signer's public key is verified. Then, each authority node creates a confirmation transaction

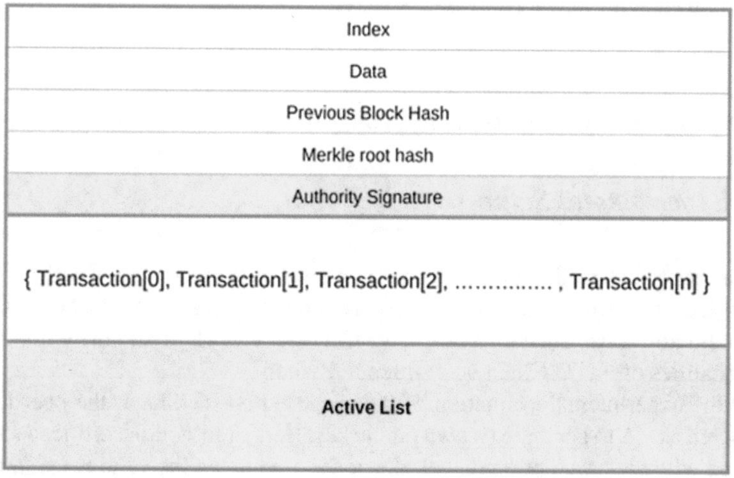

Index
Data
Previous Block Hash
Merkle root hash
Authority Signature
{ Transaction[0], Transaction[1], Transaction[2], ... , Transaction[n] }
Active List

Fig. 6 Block format in NITG Chain

containing the hash value of the created block and signs it using its private key. Such transaction is broadcasted into the network as a confirmation of the block.

Block confirmation is done by authority nodes in the network in order to append the created block to their copy of the chain. Each node waits for the confirmation from 2/3 of the authority nodes. If confirmation from 2/3 of the authority nodes are received, the confirmation transaction's fields viz; signature and hash of the block are verified. If signature and block hash is valid for the confirmation transaction from 2/3 of authority nodes, that block is appended to the node's chain. Thus, to add a block in NITG Chain, a confirmation from at least 2/3 of authority nodes is required. This helps to reduce the verification cost as each node in the network do not require to verify the block.

3.2.5 Time Synchronized Block Generation

After each fixed duration, a new block is created automatically and added to the chain. This new block contains all the transactions which are committed in particular time t. In NITG Chain, we have kept a time slice of 10 s for the next block generation and to append it to the chain.

3.2.6 API Service to Interact with NITG Chain

Many low storage devices like IOT sensors, mobile phones, etc. are unable to interact with the blockchain due to their storage and computing limit. We have developed an API service through which such devices can interact with the NITG Chain. To build an API, we have used Express.js and Node.js. The network communication is enabled through protocols like HTTPS/HTTP.

4 Experimental Results and Analysis

4.1 Experimental Setup

For the functional validation of the NITG Chain, a small-scale testbed is created at NIT Goa by setting up three servers as shown in Fig. 7. We have considered three validator nodes such as VM1.1, VM2.1 and VM3.1 as authority nodes. The functionalities of NITG Chain are written in Python.

For the experimental evaluation of the proposed NITG Chain, the peer itself is considered as CA to generate its own public key. Here, transaction certificates are not provided with the assumption that all the nodes are having the valid keys. In future, the role of CA can be implemented for the real time deployment. Each node generates a preloaded transaction (please refer Fig. 8). In Fig. 8, "vk" is the public key of the

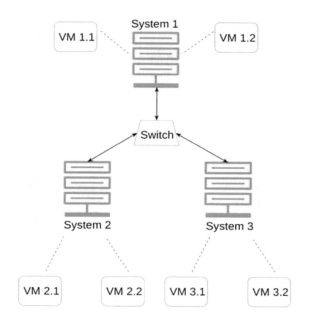

Fig. 7 Experimental setup for functional and performance validation of NITG Chain

{

"nonce":0,

"from_account":'7e2e44bddbd60e50d53f328d61d2f731058851ce9c06e34bd35
ea3b77b0a39f2',

"to_account":'fbfeec63c97591f8bf182a95d8a914e20dc9691dff4e59c8060f70516
6bd99a9',

"amount": 1233,

"vk": 'c46064f3ef5327e74a3ac514443503fbac5e50437f2f046eeea17a4d25581
38c43e919a3ea5815ea254483c1eccfec6b44b9569586fd4d038eb15a50867dec3d',

"data": '"a":"sdfsdfsdf","b":"sdfsdf"',

"sig":'38757f8cff5554949a83cd3d9df0ab91f447bfb6ef800d6257cdca00bc259ee
68b1193a64e8df223645385e9f21de7196a475b6e3e19704e27c1a7ebe5e8d7aa',

"timestamp":1591549899.9142396,

}

Fig. 8 Pre-loaded transaction on each node

sender, "sig" is the signature of the transaction signed by a sender, "form account" is the id of the sender and "to account" is the receiver's id. The transactions are automatically generated using a script running on all the nodes. For the performance evaluation, NITG Chain is evaluated in terms of throughput on different size of transactions and blocks.

4.2   Results and Analysis

During performance evaluation, the transactions are automatically generated by all the nodes and the authority nodes have followed the defined consensus rules to create the block in the time interval of 10 s. We have applied different size of the transactions with different payload sizes (1–4096 bytes) and evaluated the throughput of NITG Chain. Figure 9 shows the transaction throughput of NITG Chain with varying size of the payload. From the results, it is observed that the NITG Chain confirms more than 690 transactions per second, if the transaction payload size is up to 1000 bytes.

In addition, a range of blocks with varying number of transactions are applied to NITG Chain to test its performance. Such blocks are sent in the network by a randomly selected node. The performance results of NITG Chain in the context of different size of the blocks are shown in Fig. 10. It is observed that NITG Chain has throughput more than 545 transactions per second, while adding up to 500 transactions per block.

Although performance results of NITG Chain are derived in a limited resource environment, these results are more encouraging to use NITG Chain in large scale network as it requires less computation for performing the transactions. As per our observation, NITG Chain addresses the problems of blockchain forks and scalability at an affordable level. In NITG Chain, a block created by an authority node is verified by other authority nodes and it requires confirmation from at least 2/3 of other authority nodes to append it in blockchain. There is no chance of having another

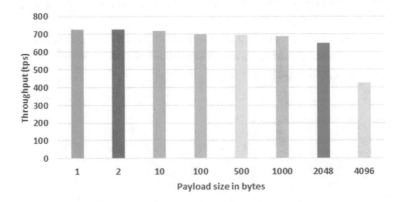

Fig. 9 Throughput of NITG Chain with different payload size (in bytes)

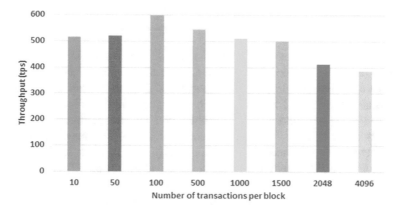

Fig. 10 Throughput of NITG Chain with different size of block

Table 3 Comparison of NITG Chain with the existing well-known blockchains

Platform/type	Consensus method	Smart contract support	Anonymity	Average throughput (tps)	Block generation interval
Bitcoin [2]/Permissionless	PoW	No	Yes	3.5	10 min
Ethereum [8]/Permissionless or Permisioned	PoS/PoW	Yes	No	15	20–30 s
Zcash [16]/Pemissionless	PoW	No	Yes	23	1.25 min
Ripple [29]/Pemissionless	RPCSA	No	No	1300	3.84 s
Hyperledger [9]/Permisioned	BFT	Yes	No	3500	Customizable
Litecoin [30]/Permissionless	PoW	No	No	56	2.5 min
NITG Chain/Permissioned	PoR	Under development	Yes	712	10 s

confirmed block in the network at same time as each authority node signs only one block at a time, and thus, it addresses the problem of blockchain forks. It assumes that at least 2/3 of reputed authority nodes behave honestly. Table 3 shows a comparison of NITG Chain with the existing well-known blockchains.

5 Conclusions

Blockchain has high potential in future IT based domains. In this paper, we have designed and implemented NITG Chain, a scalable, private and permissioned blockchain for business to business applications. It applies a proof of reputation consensus, in which the liveliness of authority nodes and their reputation are considered to select an authority node for block creation. In addition, each authority node gets a fair chance of mining the block. This helps to achieve the reliability of the network. The verification of block, underlying transactions and confirmation transaction from 2/3 of authority nodes helps to address the problem of blockchain fork as well as scalability. From the experimental results, it is observed that NITG Chain has throughput 712 *tps* on average, while applying different size of payload and blocks. The experimental results are very encouraging to use NITG Chain for large scale business to business applications, in which the authority node can be selected from each of the participating organizations. In future, NITG Chain will be further investigated to support the smart contracts and to offer on-chain data privacy.

Acknowledgements This work is part of a research project titled "Developing Smart Controller for Optimum Utilization of Energy and Trustworthy Management in a Micro Grid Environment (IMP/2019/000251)" with funding support under IMPacting Research INnovation and Technlogy-2C.1 (IMPRINT-2C.1) by Science and Engineering Research Board, Department of Science and Technology, Government of India.

References

1. Muzumdar A, Modi C, Madhu G, Vyjayanthi C (2021) A trustworthy and incentivized smart grid energy trading framework using distributed ledger and smart contracts. J Netw Comput Appl 103(074):183–184
2. Nakamoto S (2008) Bitcoin: a peer-to-peer electronic cash system. http://www.bitcoin.org/bitcoin.pdf
3. Conti M, Sandeep Kumar E, Lal C, Ruj S (2018) A survey on security and privacy issues of bitcoin. IEEE Commun Surv Tutor 20(4):3416–3452
4. Andoni M, Robu V, Flynn D, Abram S, Geach D, Jenkins D, McCallum P, Peacock A (2019) Blockchain technology in the energy sector: a systematic review of challenges and opportunities. Renew Sustain Energy Rev 100:143–174
5. Jeff G (2015) Making decentralized economic policy. http://gtf.org/garzik/bitcoin/BIP100-blocksizechangeproposal.pdf
6. Poon J, Buterin V (2017) Plasma: scalable autonomous smart contracts. https://www.plasma.io/plasma.pdf
7. Swathi P, Modi C, Patel D (2019) Preventing sybil attack in blockchain using distributed behavior monitoring of miners. In: 10th international conference on computing, communication and networking technologies, pp 1–6
8. Proof-of-stake (pos) (2021). https://ethereum.org/en/developers/docs/consensus-mechanisms/pos/
9. Hyperledger architecture, vol 1 (2017). https://www.hyperledger.org
10. Delegated proof of stake (dpos) (2021). https://how.bitshares.works/en/master/technology/dpos.html

11. Mazieres D (2016) The stellar consensus protocol: a federated model for internet-level consensus. https://www.stellar.org/papers/stellar-consensus-protocol
12. Proof of authority (2021). https://github.com/paritytech/parity/wiki/Proof-of-Authority-Chains
13. Poet 1.0 specification (2021). https://sawtooth.hyperledger.org/docs/core/releases/1.0/architecture/poet.html
14. Bentov I, Lee C, Mizrahi A, Rosenfeld M (2014) Proof of activity: extending bitcoin's proof of work via proof of stake [extended abstract]y. SIGMETRICS Perform Eval Rev 42(3):34–37
15. Karantias K, Kiayias A, Zindros D (2019) Proof-of-burn. https://eprint.iacr.org/2019/1096.pdf
16. Hopwood D, Bowe S, Hornby T, Wilcox N (2021) Zcash protocol specification. https://zips.z.cash/protocol/protocol.pdf
17. Zhuang Q, Liu Y, Chen L, Ai Z (2019) Proof of reputation: a reputation-based consensus protocol for blockchain based systems. In: Proceedings of the 2019 international electronics communication conference, IECC '19, pp 131–138
18. Bitcoin unlimited (2021). https://www.bitcoinunlimited.info/
19. Eric L, Johnson L, Pieter W (2015) Segregated witness. https://github.com/bitcoin/bips/blob/master/bip-0141.mediawiki
20. Luu L, Narayanan V, Zheng C, Baweja K, Gilbert S, Saxena P (2016) A secure sharding protocol for open blockchains. In: Proceedings of the 2016 ACM SIGSAC conference on computer and communications security, CCS '16, pp 17–30
21. Kokoris-Kogias E, Jovanovic P, Gasser L, Gailly N, Syta E, Ford B (2018) Omniledger: a secure, scale-out, decentralized ledger via sharding. In: 2018 IEEE symposium on security and privacy (SP), pp 583–598
22. Zamani M, Movahedi M, Raykova M (2018) Rapidchain: scaling blockchain via full sharding. In: Proceedings of the 2018 ACM SIGSAC conference on computer and communications security, CCS '18, pp 931–948
23. Team Z (2017) The zilliqa technical whitepaper. https://docs.zilliqa.com/whitepaper.pdf
24. Harmony (2021). https://www.harmony.one/
25. Wang J, Wang H (2019) Monoxide: scale out blockchains with asynchronous consensus zones. In: 16th USENIX symposium on networked systems design and implementation (NSDI 19), pp 95–112
26. Poon J, Dryja T (2016) The bitcoin lightning network: scalable offchain instant payments, draft version 0.5. https://lightning.network/lightning-network-paper.pdf
27. Raiden network (2021). https://raiden.network/
28. Back A, Corallo M, Dashjr L, Friedenbach M, Maxwell G, Miller A, Poelstra A, Timón J, Wuille P (2014) Enabling blockchain innovations with pegged sidechains. https://blockstream.com/sidechains.pdf
29. Ripplenet (2021). https://ripple.com/
30. Litecoin (2021). https://litecoin.com/en/

Safeguarding GeoLocation for Social Media with Local Differential Privacy and L-Diversity

Jhanvi Uday and Mohona Ghosh

1 Introduction

The major evolution of the last decade is the usage of social media. The platform is used by almost half of the world [1]. These platforms have a humongous amount of data. Social Media is an essential driver in various fields such as industry, entertainment, research, crisis management and politics, for acquiring and spreading knowledge. The data content is posts, friends list, images, videos and Geolocation. The Geolocation coordinates of a place can be fetched by who-is, thereby security remains a major concern. Even if the query does not log the information of Geolocation, the server has the information. So, to provide additional privacy, *Differential Privacy* comes into the picture.

1.1 Differential Privacy and Its Types

Differential privacy (DP) is a model of cyber security which focuses on sharing aggregate data about users collected over time, without sharing the personally identifiable information of the user. It will let you learn the pattern present there in users' population without getting insights about individual the users' identity. Implementation of differential privacy is generally done by injecting noise to the data set to make it less exact [2]. Making it imprecise will not only provide security to an individual user, but also guarantee better utility of a data set.

There are two types of DP, i.e., Local Differential Privacy (Local DP) and Global Differential Privacy (Global DP) as shown in Fig. 1. The only difference between both of them is the place where noise is being added.

J. Uday · M. Ghosh (✉)
Indira Gandhi Delhi Technical University for Women, Kashmere Gate, New Delhi 110006, India
e-mail: mohonaghosh@igdtuw.ac.in

© The Author(s), under exclusive license to Springer Nature Singapore Pte Ltd. 2022
U. P. Rao et al. (eds.), *Security, Privacy and Data Analytics*, Lecture Notes
in Electrical Engineering 848, https://doi.org/10.1007/978-981-16-9089-1_2

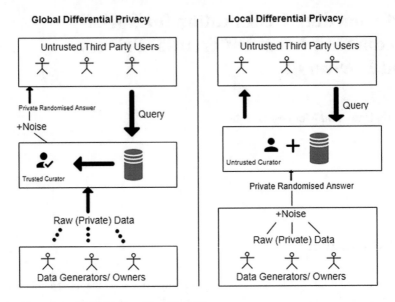

Fig. 1 Illustration of Global DP and Local DP [3]

1.2 Anonymity Techniques

Database security comes hand in hand with privacy preservation. It is mainly achieved by security management, database encryption and access control [4]. To some extent, these steps will safeguard the database's protection, for example, the direct disclosure of confidential information such as identification card numbers, home addresses, health information and so on but they are unable to avoid such indirect access to the data using federation logic. So, for these reasons, data anonymity is a crucial part to achieve privacy preservation. Thereby, most famous anonymity techniques, i.e., *K-anonymity* and *l-diversity* come into picture.

K-anonymity is a useful paradigm for preserving privacy when publishing data that can be applied in a variety of ways [5]. The basic idea is to transform any portion of the original data, such as by generalisation, compression, or other means, and then ensure that the transformed data cannot be combined with other data to reveal any personal privacy information. Local generalisation is common among them due to its low knowledge loss [5]. When the same set of quasi sensitive features of k different users are clubbed together, it is said to be $k - 1$ anonymity, e.g.,: if zip, age, nationality which are quasi sensitive features of 4 different users are same, so it is $4 - 1 = 3$-anonymity as shown in Fig. 2. Applying K-anonymity to the sanitised data is not sufficient enough as data is still prone to few attacks, namely—Linkage attacks, Homogeneity attack and Background Knowledge attack [5]. So, applying l-diverse technique to these data sets can bring immunity from these attacks.

	Non sensitive			Sensitive
	Zip code	Age	Nationality	Spots
1	1305*	<=40	*	Bakery
4	1305*	<=40	*	Cyber Cafe
9	1305*	<=40	*	Hospital
10	1305*	<=40	*	Hospital
5	1485*	>40	*	Hospital
6	1485*	>40	*	Bakery
7	1485*	>40	*	Cyber Cafe
8	1485*	>40	*	Cyber Cafe
2	1306*	<=40	*	Bakery
3	1306*	<=40	*	Cyber Cafe
11	1306*	<=40	*	Hospital
12	1306*	<=40	*	Hospital

Fig. 2 3-diverse social networking data

l-diversity is a mechanism for publishing data about people while keeping the amount of confidential information about them to a minimum [6]. With the same set of quasi sensitive features (zip code, age, nationality), having different sensitive features (means diversion in sensitive column) is called l-diversion, for example, 3 different values of sensitive information, i.e., Bakery, Cyber Cafe and Hospital (as shown in Fig. 2), so, it is 3-diversion. l-diversified data is already l-anonymous.

Contribution: The contributions are as follows:

1. We have compared Local DP and Global DP in terms of the amount of noise added to make sanitised data into perturbed data.
2. We have shown that Local DP is better than Global DP in terms of security but the amount of noise added is more. To countermeasure the extra noise, we have curtailed a very small portion of data which is a feasible trade off.
3. Use of K-anonymity and l-diversity is also shown which makes the data more secure and provides better utility.
4. Every experimental calculation is done on Gowalla data set which is a real-world geolocation data set of social media
5. Experiments are proven with the help of parameters like Hellinger Distance, Privacy Score and Mondrian Partitions. For spot categories, the Hellinger distance reduced from 324 to 299 ensuring better utility of the data. For latitude and longitude its increasing, ensuring data is more exposed, thus indicating resistance to Background knowledge attack and Homogeneity Attack.

The paper structure is as follows. In Sect. 2, i.e., Preliminaries, we introduce few basic terms which will be used throughout the paper. In Sect. 3, i.e., Motivation, we focus on the reason we have worked on this subject. In Sect. 4, i.e., Related work, we present the work done by other researchers in this field. In Sect. 5, i.e., The Proposed technique, we provide the details about the implementation of Local DP for collection of data and l-diversity for anonymizing the sensitive location on the Geolocation data. In Sect. 6, i.e., Results, we present privacy scores calculated and graphical plots which that applying l-diversity on Differential private data is better than applying l-diversity on Sanitised data. In Sect. 7, we provide the conclusion and future scope of the paper.

2   Preliminaries

In this section, we will introduce few important notations and terms which will be used in the entire work.

- **Differential Privacy**: The definition Differential Privacy states that a randomised algorithm F gives ε-differential privacy if for all data sets D0 and D1 differing on at most a single row and for any output $S \subseteq Range(F)$ [7, 8]

$$Pr[F(D0) \subseteq S] \le e^{''} \times Pr[F(D1) \subseteq S] \tag{1}$$

  The definition is a measure of the amount of privacy query F can afford. If algorithm F satisfies the above inequality, it is said to achieve ε-differential privacy protection. Here ε is the measure of privacy loss, which generally a researcher can change to manage the trade off between accuracy and privacy. The major task of Differential Privacy is to maintain the balance between maximising accuracy (more data utility can be a measure for accuracy) and privacy loss (notation ε, value minimum 0.01 should be chosen). This trade off between ε and accuracy can be maintained by differentially private algorithms. This flexibility is the major property here. When we take $\varepsilon = 0$, it leads to full privacy but no utility, but for higher values of ε, it gives low privacy but good utility. Applying Local DP to the data set adds more noise in comparison to Global DP because noise is added at individual level [9].
- **Epsilon** ε: It is a measure of privacy loss in Differential Privacy. This parameter helps to maintain the trade off between accuracy and utility of the data. In [10] ε is taken as 1 and in [11] it is in range of 0.005–15, and in most of the cases, it ranges from 0.1 to 1 and we have considered 0.1 for our experiment. We have taken 0.1 because the lesser the epsilon, the lesser the privacy loss, thereby better privacy is provided.
- **Sensitivity**: Sensitivity tells us how much noise is added. If we have a query function f: $D \rightarrow R^d$, where data is input and output of function is d-dimensional real vector, so for any adjacent data set

$$\Delta f = max_{D,D'} \parallel f(D) - f(D') \parallel_1 \tag{2}$$

  where f is the sensitivity of the function and Δ f denotes the maximum value of change of output results. $\parallel$ f(D)–f(D') $\parallel$ is 1-order norm distance between adjacent data.
- **Noise Scale**: The scale of noise with which our data set will be calibrated is known as scale. The noise scale will be calibrated to

$$scale = \Delta f / \varepsilon \qquad (3)$$

- **Quasi Sensitive Feature**: Groups of attributes that can be combined with external data to uniquely reidentify an individual. Ex: Zip code, age and nationality with reference to Fig. 2.
- **Sensitive Feature**: Attributes which we do not want to expose are known as Sensitive features, for example, salary, disease, spot travelled, etc.

3   Motivation

In Global DP, noise is added to the **output** of the database [3]. The noise is introduced just one time, at the end of the operation, until it is shared with the third party. The data curator or the central aggregator contributes noise to the performance of a database query. Thereby, **a trustworthy database curator** is needed, as the database has all the access to real sanitised data. In addition, the global model collects all data in one location. It raises the possibility of catastrophic failure such as if the aggregator is compromised and all of the data is leaked.

Unlike Global DP, in Local Differential Privacy (Local DP), noise is added to the device level only [3]. Individuals may add noise to data at the device level only. The user **does not have to trust the data curator** or database owner to properly use his or her data. The total noise, however, is much greater because each user must add noise to their own data. To get better results large data sets are used. It is one of the main reasons we have focussed on Local DP for privacy.

In addition to this, we showcase two attacks which is by not resistant using K-anonymous data. The attacks are *homogeneity attack* and *background knowledge attack*.

3.1   Homogeneity Attack

Alice and Bob are neighbours. Bob paid a visit to a place. Alice has seen Bob near a food court and she wants to know the exact shop Bob visited that day. Alice discovers the 3-anonymous table of the visitor record of a food court. She knows that one of the records in this table contains Bob's information. Since Alice is Bob's neighbour, she knows the age (38) and pin code (13051) of Bob (as seen in Fig. 3). Therefore, Alice knows that Bob paid visit to a Bakery Shop. Such kind of an attack is known as homogeneity attack.

Learning 1: K-anonymous table make groups that can expose information due to lack of diversity in sensitive attribute [6].

	Non sensitive			Sensitive
	Zip code	Age	Nationality	Spots
1	1305*	<40	*	Bakery
4	1305*	<40	*	Bakery
9	1305*	<40	*	Bakery
10	1305*	<40	*	Bakery
5	1485*	>40	*	Hospital
6	1485*	>40	*	Cyber Cafe
7	1485*	>40	*	Bakery
8	1485*	>40	*	Hospital
2	1306*	=40	*	Cyber Café
3	1306*	=40	*	Cyber Café
11	1306*	=40	*	Hospital
12	1306*	=40	*	Cyber Café

Fig. 3 3-anonymous social networking data

3.2   Background Knowledge Attack

An attacker can use background knowledge to know sensitive information. Alice has a friend Eve who has visited the same food court as Bob and whose record is present in Fig. 3. Alice has knowledge of Age (44) and zip code (1485) of Eve. Additionally, Alice knows that Eve's work is related to computers. Thereby, it is confirmed that Eve works in Cyber Cafe (as seen in Fig. 3). Such kind of an attack is known as the background knowledge attack.

Learning 2 : K-anonymity is not immune to background knowledge attacks [6].

4   Related Work

We have very extensive literature related to location privacy preserving mechanism (LPPM). LPPM generally uses perturbation methods such as Cell merging, Location precision reduction, Spatial cloaking and Anonymity [12]. Most widely used anonymity techniques are K-anonymity [13–15], l-diversity [6] and t-closeness [16]. Sweeney [17] worked on K-anonymity and proposed it as a way of communicating plain text data without revealing personal or sensitive information about people. The idea behind K-anonymity is to leverage the concept of bucketization to produce k groups of data (equivalence classes) such that there are at least k-1 tuples with the same quasi-identifier values for each tuple. Sweeney's work sparked a slew of strategies targeted at improving performance and avoiding inferential attacks, such as [18–20]. Various schemes of basic l-diversity is proposed such as [18, 19, 21, 22] to tackle the inferential attacks. For applying these two techniques, algorithms such as Mondrian [23], Incognito [24], UArgus [25], Datafly [26], etc., are available, but the most widely used and more effective is the Mondrian Algorithm [23].

There are some models which are based on Differential privacy (DP). DP uses the noise addition method to provide privacy. Functional Mechanism (FM) is one of them in which privacy is protected by an objective function of ε-differential privacy disturbance optimization problem. The combination of MCMC (Markov Chain Monte Carlo) and privacy preserving mining algorithm (Diff-FPM), also provides high availability of data and high privacy at the same time [10]. The algorithm implemented in DiffP-C4.5 and DiffGen blends differential privacy with decision trees and other data structures to maintain a balance between the privacy of data and availability [27]. A tree model which is built on multilevel location information for high value and low density of location data also maintains differential privacy and utility of the Geolocation data [10]. In most of the work, Global DP is used. Global DP is widely used because it adds less noise to the data set which makes data less noisy and of better utility. The problem with Global DP is that they require a trusted curator to calculate noise and then it is sent to the third party users.

In most of the works listed above, individual privacy preservation method is used, which means either differential privacy is used or anonymity technique is used. Incorporating differential privacy with the anonymity algorithm technique is merely used to preserve privacy. If used, firstly anonymity is induced and then the anonymized data is made differential private. This model has the limitation that the adversary can crack the accurate inferences about sensitive information of the user [9]. This occurs most often when the data contains established associations, or when the published data set reveals at least one previously unknown association between a sensitive value and the values of other attributes. Secondly, there are no comparison of implementation of noise addition to Global DP and Local DP on the Geolocation data to preserve privacy and most of the work carried out is with the Global DP only.

In our work, we investigate the effectiveness of implementing Local DP on geolocation data which has not been evaluated so far. It is also one of the techniques used to implement noise in [9]. It has an advantage over all the existing techniques that we need not trust the curator or data aggregator to implement noise. People involved in the study themselves add noise to their data before sending it to the curator. This is the reason also that Local DP adds more noise to the database and our work is the first one to implement this on the location data set.

Definition 1 (*Local Differential Privacy*) An algorithm π satisfies ε—local differential privacy, where $\varepsilon \geq 0$, if and only if for any input u and v, we have

$$\forall y \in Range(\pi) : Pr[\pi(u) = y] \leq e \in Pr[\pi(v') = y], \tag{4}$$

where Range π denotes the set of all possible outputs of the algorithm π.

5 Proposed Technique

5.1 Our Contribution

We have mainly focussed on two research gaps here which are mentioned in the above sections. Firstly, we have compared the noise addition of Local DP and Global DP techniques on data sets, which can quantify the amount of noise added. We have also shown the effectiveness of Local DP in comparison to Global DP. Secondly, we have implemented Local Differential Privacy which will add noise individually to the Geolocation data set. This noise is Laplacian noise. The perturbed data is collected and then anonymity techniques, i.e., K-anonymity and l-diversity are applied to the data sets to preserve the privacy of sensitive location involved.

This technique is followed because applying only Local DP will add the noise to the data sets, but in a probabilistic sense, they were close enough [9]. The closeness of data set does not make the data immune to linkage and background attacks. The adversary can track the pattern or sensitive location based on the correlation of closeness of data set. So, to make data sets immune to these attacks, anonymity, diversity through generalisation method is implemented.

Our contribution is well illustrated by the diagram below. The data generators have their data in the device itself. They have full control over the device's data. Now before collecting, We have implemented Local DP on the data so as to ensure that noisy data travels through the network and the same is getting stored. There is no leakage of Sanitised data from the device in the experiments. After the implementation of noise, we apply K-anonymity and l-diversity to the data to make the data utility higher. In this, we have used Mondrian Partitions and Generalisation to have a better utility, Then we are storing the data in the database, where there is no need for a trusted curator. When a third party queries, the perturbed data is fetched without any delay.

5.2 Data Set

The data set which we have considered is Gowalla data set. It is a location-based social networking website where users share their locations by checking-in. We have considered 2724891 rows with 12 features namely id, created at, Longitude, Latitude, photos count, check ins count, users count, radius meters, highlights count, items count, max items count, spot categories, where we have worked on **latitude, longitude and spot categories only**. The latitude and longitude is a quasi sensitive feature for us, whereas spot categories are sensitive features.

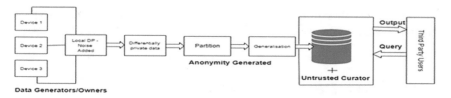

Fig. 4 Implementation of Local DP and anonymity

5.3 *Execution*

With reference to Fig. 4, We have firstly implemented Local DP in order to collect perturbed data set from the users. For Experiment purpose, We have taken 1,00,000 rows for all 12 features and then divided the data set into 7 parts. Since, there was 7 categories of the spot, we have divided the data into 7 parts. Then we have calculated noise scale for all the parts of the data individually, and noise is calibrated to the data set. Lastly, it is merged for further anonymity operation. Refer Sect. 2, for the parameters used for noise generation (Fig. 5).

After getting Perturbed data set, we need to introduce 3-anonymity and 3-diversity to our data set so as the data would not expose the sensitive pattern. We have chosen 3-anonymity and 3-diversity because it is the minimum k and l we can choose, in order to prevent definite database linkages. Choosing 2-anonymity or 2-diversity is not a safe option because there is either or situation for every row. If there would have been 2-anonymity, the attacker could say that either the person paid visit to a exact spot or not. We have used Mondrian Algorithm for our experiment. It divides the original data into smaller and smaller classes using a greedy search algorithm. The algorithm assumes that all attributes have been translated to numerical or categorical values and that the 'span' of a given attribute 'Xi' can be measured. After spanning, according to the span, we can put values to the generalised anonymous group. But, it may happen that for a k-anonymous group, all the sensitive features are same. Then,

```
#Implementing Laplace
sensitivity = 1
epsilon = 0.1 #measure of privacy loss
location =0
noise_scale=sensitivity/epsilon
Laplacian_noise = np.random.laplace(location,noise_scale,data)
DifferentiallyPdata = sanitised_data + Laplacian_noise
```

Fig. 5 Steps to generate noise

for diversifying only sensitive feature, the l-diversity is applied to this K-anonymous data set to make it immune to attacks.

6 Experiment Design and Results

The experiment was executed in python language 3.5 on jupyter notebook 6.1.4, for which the system configuration was 8 GB RAM, 2.3 GHz Intel Core i5-2410M, Hard drive capacity is 500 GB, 5,400 rpm and having Windows 10 Home OS.

After implementing the Local DP and Global DP on a part of Gowalla data set, we have shown the noise addition in the below Table 1.

In recent times, the focus is shifted from Global DP to Local DP. With the table shown above, we have compared for noise injection when Global DP and Local DP is implemented on complete data. We found that Global DP adds less noise in comparison to Local DP. So, to keep the noise level almost equal to Global Differential Privacy when Local DP implemented, We have cut down the data part and used **99.91%** of the data only. Implementation of Local DP on 99.91% of the data is the first smallest perturbed data set in comparison to 100% perturbed data (a, b) when Global DP is implemented. So, we can say that by keeping approximately same noise, a little less data (0.09% less), we are providing better utility in comparison to Global DP because Local DP eliminates the need for a data curator and the gathering of precise private data. Since, the noise is implemented at device level only, there is all perturbed data in the hands of curator. The curator also does not have the clue of private and sanitised data of the user. This is the major advantage over Global DP because Global DP have access to sanitised data. For sanitised data handling, they need a trusted curator.

So, Local DP on 99.91% of data have better utility and better privacy than Global DP on 100% of data.

For illustrating the result of implementing Local DP for data privacy and then anonymity algorithm to tackle background knowledge attack and linkage attack, we have considered 5000 rows of the data set having feature Latitude, Longitude and spot categories. Since the data is noisy and not accurate, there can be no comparison with already exposed data in the market. When no comparison can be done, no more exposure of data will take place if differential privacy is in place, thus preventing the mentioned attacks. Also, a few utility metric which help us to prove the experiment.

6.1 *Hellinger Distance*

In Hellinger Distance, each feature value in the original data set is compared to the perturbed version of that value in the corresponding position in some cases [28]. A probabilistic analogue of the Euclidean distance is the Hellinger distance. As a metric, its symmetry is an important feature. When you require a distance function

Table 1 Analysis of Noise for Local and Global DP

DP, % of Data	NoisyLat	NoisyLong	RowsConsidered	(a)-Latdiff	(b)-Longdiff
GDP, 100 %	102213527.21(a)	−61710056.00(b)	27,24,891	–	–
LDP, 100 %	102254208.24	−61695233.10	27,24,891	−40681.03	−14822.90
LDP, 99.95 %	101722247.88	−61656236.8	27,23,529	491279.329	−53819.2
LDP, 99.92 %	102220779.71	−61750074.00	27,22,711	−7252.5	40018.0
LDP, 99.91 %	102208432.65	−61747465.24	27,22,439	5094.559	37409.24
LDP, 99.90 %	102165603.54	−61711297.60	27,22,166	47923.66	1241.60
LDP, 99.80 %	102045679.82	−61711297.60	27,19,441	167847.39	9671.09
LDP, 99.00 %	101281687.77	−61587309.40	26,97,642	931839.43	−122746.0

Table 2 Hellinger distance comparison with sanitised data

S. no	Feature of comparison	(a)	(b)
1	Latitude	60.81	85.43
2	Longitude	147.62	167.88
3	Spot categories	324.52	299

Note (a)—Hellinger distance between Sanitised and 3-div implemented data; (b)—Hellinger distance between Sanitised and 3-div + Local DP implemented data

with specific features to make your proof plausible, these mathematical properties come in handy. In practise, one could find that one metric offers nicer or better results for a certain activity than another, for example, the table below shows the Hellinger distance between sanitised data when only 3-div is implemented and when Local DP and 3-div are implemented on data set.

Table 2 says, that the Hellinger distance between sanitised spot category and (c)'s spot category is less than (b)'s spot category, which says that similarity with sanitised data is more with (c) rather than (b), which ensures better utility. However, latitude and longitude of (c) has higher Hellinger distance which shows it is more exposed towards anonymity, which ensures lesser utility. Lesser utility means it will very less likely to be compared with sanitised data, and thereby lesser prone to attacks.

6.2 Privacy Score

The privacy score is a metric that says about the amount of privacy the technique is providing. For calculating privacy score, we have pipe lined Standard Scalar, PCA and Logistic Regression to be implemented on a data set as a metric. The meta parameters for PCA is 2, and for logistic regression, the solver is taken as 'lbfgs'. We have taken 5000 rows of each sanitised data and 3-diverse implemented data and calculated the privacy score.

Privacy score is the amount of privacy provided with this technique. The privacy score of 3-diversify implemented on sanitised data is 4.79% and the privacy score of Local DP along with 3-diversity implemented data is 5.27%. Both the privacy score obtained is **not appreciable**, but in comparison to 3-diverse data, the privacy score of Local DP and 3-diverse data is better.

6.3 Mondrian Partitions

Mondrian Algorithm uses Partition and Aggregation for anonymity.

It generates number of partitions for a data set to pool all the data into certain group to anonymise the quasi sensitive identifier first, that number of partition is

Table 3 Number of partitions by mondrian

S.no	Dataset type	3-anonymity partitions	3-diversity partitions
1	Sanitised dataset	32333	32301
2	Noisy data set	32768	32701

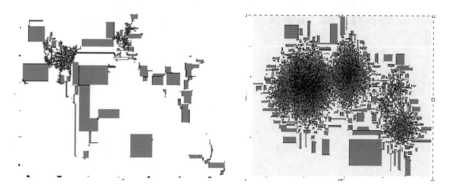

Fig. 6 Plot of latitude and longitude for sanitised and noisy data

used as a utility metric. The partition is done on the basis of similarity of quasi sensitive identifier of data set. For the analysis, we have used 1,00,000 rows and all the columns of each sanitised and noisy data set. We have shown more number of partitions, which means better anonymity is done. For noisy data set (Local DP implemented on Sanitised data set), it is apparent that 32701 partitions are done which is greater than sanitised data when 3-anonymity and 3-diversity is applied.

The above figure shows that for Sanitised data set, the major spot categories are confined to a very small area, whereas for noisy data set, the spot category is expanded. Expanding the sensitive identifier like spot category ensures that better anonymity is introduced and it is less likely to be exposed. In addition to better anonymity, better privacy is also there as it is collected by Local DP.

So with the proposed technique, we are providing better utility and privacy score. The more number of partition to spot categories as shown in Table 3, more anonymity is provided to latitude and longitude as shown in Fig. 6, our approach provides a solution to background knowledge attack and linkage attacks.

7 Conclusion and Future Work

After the comparison of noisy and sanitised data on the different metric, we find that the above discussed solution is providing better utility and privacy. Local DP proves to be a better approach as it does not compromise on the privacy of the data. There is no need for trusted curator, and even in the network, the noisy data travels.

Since the above technique is a solution to background knowledge attacks and linkage attacks only, we must work on techniques which provide solution to more recent attacks also. We must focus on techniques which provide better utility and privacy overall. We can also work on the amalgamation of 2–3 anonymity concepts and apply it on the data to see the results.

We can also work in the direction of personalised differential privacy, where each individual's privacy and the privacy of users who are involved in the study is taken care of.

8 Appendices

1. The data set link is: https://www.yongliu.org/datasets/
2. Drive link: https://drive.google.com/file/d/0BzpKyxX1dqTYRTFVYTd1UG81ZXc/view
3. The Mondrian Algorithm: https://github.com/qiyuangong/Mondrian
4. K-anonymity and l-diversity: https://github.com/Nuclearstar/K-anonymity

References

1. https://www.globenewswire.com/news-release/2020/07/21/2064947/0/en/More-than-half-of-the-people-on-Earth-now-use-social-media.html
2. Sarathy R, Muralidhar K (2011) Evaluating Laplace noise addition to satisfy differential privacy for numeric data. Trans Data Priv 4(1):1–17
3. https://medium.com/@shaistha24/global-vs-local-differential-privacy-56b45eb22168
4. Wu PF, Zhang YQ (2006) Summary of database security. Comput Eng (in Chinese) 32(12):85–88
5. Ni S, Xie M, Qian Q (2017) Clustering based K-anonymity algorithm for privacy preservation. IJ Netw Secur 19(6):1062–1071
6. Machanavajjhala A, Kifer D, Gehrke J, Venkitasubramaniam M (2007) l-diversity: privacy beyond K-anonymity. ACM Trans Knowl Discov Data (TKDD) 1(1):3-es
7. Dwork C, Roth A (2014) The algorithmic foundations of differential privacy. Found Trends Theor Comput Sci 9(3–4):211–407
8. Li Y, Cao X, Yuan Y, Wang G (2019) PrivSem: protecting location privacy using semantic and differential privacy. World Wide Web 22(6):2407–2436
9. Cormode G, Jha S, Kulkarni T, Li N, Srivastava D, Wang T (2018) Privacy at scale: local differential privacy in practice. In: Proceedings of the 2018 international conference on management of data, pp 1655–1658
10. Yin C, Xi J, Sun R, Wang J (2017) Location privacy protection based on differential privacy strategy for big data in industrial internet of things. IEEE Trans Ind Inf 14(8):3628–3636
11. Xiao Y, Xiong L, Zhang S, Cao Y (2017) Loclok: location cloaking with differential privacy via hidden markov model. Proc VLDB Endow 10(12):1901–1904
12. Xiao Y, Xiong L (2015) Protecting locations with differential privacy under temporal correlations. In: Proceedings of the 22nd ACM SIGSAC conference on computer and communications security, pp 1298–1309

13. Aggarwal CC (2005) On K-anonymity and the curse of dimensionality. In: Proceedings of the 31st international conference on very large data bases, VLDB 2005, pp 901–909. VLDB Endowment
14. Bayardo RJ, Agrawal R (2005) Data privacy through optimal K-anonymization. In: 21st international conference on data engineering (ICDE 2005), pp 217–228
15. Iyengar VS (2002) Transforming data to satisfy privacy constraints. In: Proceedings of the eighth ACM SIGKDD international conference on knowledge discovery and data mining, KDD 2002, pp 279-288. ACM, New York
16. Li N, Li T, Venkatasubramanian S (2007) t-closeness: privacy beyond K-anonymity and l-diversity. In: 2007 IEEE 23rd international conference on data engineering, pp 106–115
17. Sweeney L (2002) K-anonymity: a model for protecting privacy. Int J Uncertain Fuzz Knowl-Based Syst 10(5):557–570
18. Dewri R, Ray I, Ray I, Whitley D (2011) Exploring privacy versus data quality tradeoffs in anonymization techniques using multi-objective optimization. J Comput Secur 19(5):935–974
19. Dewri R, Whitley D, Ray I, Ray I (2009) A multi-objective approach to data sharing with privacy constraints and preference based objectives. In: Proceedings of the 11th annual conference on genetic and evolutionary computation, GECCO 2009, pp 1499–1506. ACM, New York
20. Last M, Tassa T, Zhmudyak A, Shmueli E (2014) Improving accuracy of classification models induced from anonymized datasets. Inf Sci 256:138–161. Business intelligence in risk management
21. Xu J, Wang W, Pei J, Wang X, Shi B, Fu AWC (2006) Utility-based anonymization using local recoding. In: Proceedings of the 12th ACM SIGKDD international conference on knowledge discovery and data mining, KDD 2006, pp 785–790. ACM, New York
22. Xiao X, Yi K, Tao Y (2010) The hardness and approximation algorithms for ldiversity. In: Proceedings of the 13th international conference on extending database technology, EDBT 2010, pp 135–146. ACM, New York
23. Calle AM, Chen YC, Hao Z, Comparing K-anonymity and ε-differential privacy effectiveness for social media
24. LeFevre K, DeWitt DJ, Ramakrishnan R (2005) Incognito: efficient full-domain K-anonymity. In: Proceedings of the 2005 ACM SIGMOD international conference on management of data (Sigmod'05), pp 49–60, Baltimore, Maryland, USA, June 2005
25. Xiao XK, Tao YF (2006) Anatomy: simple and effective privacy preservation. In: Proceedings of the 32nd international conference on very large data bases (VLDB'06), pp 139–150, Seoul, Korea, Sept 2006
26. Sweeney L (2001) Computational disclosure control - a primer on data privacy protection. PhD Thesis, Massachusetts Institute of Technology, Cambridge, MA, USA, May 2001
27. Zeng C, Naughton JF, Cai JY (2012) On differentially private frequent itemset mining. VLDB J: Very Large Data Bases: Publ VLDB Endow 6(1):25
28. Sei Y, Okumura H, Takenouchi T, Ohsuga A (2017) Anonymization of sensitive quasi-identifiers for l-diversity and t-closeness. IEEE Trans Depend Sec Comput 16(4):580–593

Detection of False Data Injection Cyber-Attack in Smart Grid by Convolutional Neural Network-Based Deep Learning Technique

Anupam Khan

1 Introduction

Electric Power Grid is composed of the major components like generation, transmission, and distribution system. It is evolving to smart grid with the aid of Industrial Internet of Things (IIoT) [1] technologies. The smart entities are connected to the grid via advanced Information and communication technology (ICT) [2] infrastructures, thus improving the grid performance and reliability. At the same time, these ICT systems bring the vulnerability of cyber-attack. Though the Operational Technology (OT) network is recommended to be in "air-gap" from Information Technology (IT), the trend shows the contrary [3]. This exposes the smart power grid to both external and internal threats [4, 5].

The attacks on smart grid might be classified into several types, the most common of them is FDIA. In this case, the attacker targets to compromise state estimates (SE), which disrupts the distribution process, resulting in financial loss, and even devastating outcomes. A Covert Cyber-attack is a sophisticated attack. The systems inputs are changed as well as system outputs; thus the influence of the attacker is disguised [6]. Energy theft is also a kind of attack in smart grid system done by consumers/non-consumers by modifying/bypassing the smart meter or tapping the line [7]. Moreover, a DoS (Denial-of-Service) attack can hamper smart grid operation [8].

Very recently, ten Indian Power Sector organizations across India came under RedEcho cyber-attack [9] by Chinese attackers, which caused power outage in Mumbai in October 2020 [10]. Just before that Lazarus group from North Korea attacked Kudan Kulam Nuclear Power Plant [11] in September 2019. So it is of utmost urgency to enact defense mechanisms.

A. Khan (✉)
IT Cell, Damodar Valley Corporation, Kolkata, India
e-mail: anupam.khan@dvc.gov.in

© The Author(s), under exclusive license to Springer Nature Singapore Pte Ltd. 2022
U. P. Rao et al. (eds.), *Security, Privacy and Data Analytics*, Lecture Notes
in Electrical Engineering 848, https://doi.org/10.1007/978-981-16-9089-1_3

1.1 Problem Statement

The control system of a Smart Power Grid does critically depend on the State Estimation (SE) values, which are calculated from the measurement values obtained
from the smart meters installed throughout the power grid. These smart meters bring
vulnerability to the system through the internet connection, making the system at
risk of cyber-attacks, such as FDIA. Adversaries launch these attacks to compromise
raw measurement or state estimates. Conventionally, these attacks are detected using
a threshold-based detection system. However, these legacy systems can easily be
fooled if the attacker has some knowledge of the topology. These types of attacks are
often called stealthy FDI attack. So, we need a robust algorithm that can overcome this
shortcoming of the legacy threshold-based detection system and be also able to detect
stealthy FDI attack. The problem statement is to create such an algorithm/system.

1.2 Solution Proposed

The control system of a Smart Power Grid does critically depend on the State Estimation (SE) values, which are calculated from the measurement values obtained
from the smart meters installed throughout the power grid. These smart meters bring
vulnerability to the system through the internet connection, making the system at
risk of cyber-attacks, such as FDIA. Adversaries launch these attacks to compromise
raw measurement or state estimates. Conventionally, these attacks are detected using
threshold-based detection system. However, these legacy systems can easily be fooled
if the attacker has some knowledge of the topology. These types of attacks are often
called stealthy FDI attack. So, we need a robust algorithm that can overcome this
shortcoming of the legacy threshold-based detection system and be also able to detect
stealthy FDI attack. The problem statement is to create such an algorithm/system.

1.3 Contributions

A CNN-based Deep Learning model is prepared which provides the best performance
for detection of FDIA. Tuning of model configurations and hyper-parameters are done
to provide the best performance. The effectiveness of the model is tested on a dataset
which is related to IEEE 14 bus. In addition to that some other ML and DL-based
models are configured such as SVM, ANN, and LightGBM and their performance
is tested on same dataset. As the results are compared, CNN-based Deep Learning
model performs better than these other models.

1.4 Outline of Paper

This paper starts with an introduction, which containing the problem statement, proposed solution in brief, and authors contribution. In part II, similar works for detection of FDI attack are briefly discussed. Part III contains a detailed discussion of the problem domain. The overview of ML and DL techniques used are briefly described in Part IV. The experiments performed are discussed in part V, and their results are presented in Part VI. Part VII concludes the paper with brief discussion on future scope of work. The references are mentioned at the end of the paper.

2 Related Works

False Data Injection attack in Power Grid was first analyzed by Liu et al. [12]. In continuation of that Rahman et el. [13] studied FDIA against nonlinear SE in smart grid.

To deal with FDIA, threshold-based statistical approaches were proposed initially [14]. Those methods were unable to handle stealthy FDI attacks.

Machine learning-based systems were started being used to tackle the shortcomings. Esmalifalak et al. [15] devised two ML models performing FDIA detection. One was based on Gaussian semi-supervised ML, and the other was based on deviation analysis algorithm. Wang et al. [16] devised a method of detecting FDIA in large-scale smart grid. They used a Margin Setting Algorithm (MSA) for processing of large amount domain-specific smart grid data. A method proposed by Chakhchoukh et al. [17] consisted of FDIA detection based on density ratio estimation (DRE). It doesn't need attack model or supervision.

Deep learning-based models are also used for detection of FDIA as those methods became popular in other fields. Wang et al. [18] used Stacked Auto-Encoders as feature extractor followed by logistic regression as predictor.

Deep Learning-based model is also used for prediction purpose. Ashrafuzzaman et al. [19] proposed a ANN algorithm to detect stealthy FDIA. Niu et al. [20] worked on dynamic FDIA and proposed a Long Short Term Memory (LSTM) model. Wang et al. [21] worked on locational detection of FDIA using Deep Learning tech.

As mentioned from the review literature, there is hardly any method to detect stealthy FDI attack on measurement data using CNN-based Deep learning techniques. **Sample Heading (Third Level). Only two levels of headings should be numbered. Lower level headings remain unnumbered; they are formatted as run-in headings.**

3   Problem Domain Discussion

A power system is comprised of generation, transmission, and distribution system. A smart power grid is controlled by centralized control and monitoring system. Throughout the power grid, smart meters are deployed to obtain the measurements regarding the grid-like Real and Reactive Power, Current value of Transmission lines; real and reactive power injection, voltage magnitude to the bus, the phase angles as recorded by Phase Measurement Units (PMU). These measurements are used for calculating the State Estimation (SE) of the system. These SE values are utilized for centralized monitoring and control of smart grid system.

The deduction of state estimation values can be done from the measurement values as per the following:

$$Z = HX + e \tag{1}$$

Here

Z: Measurement vector.

H: Jacobian Matrix.

It consists of the system configuration.

e.g., Network topology.

e: the measurement error.

An attacker can take control of a measuring equipment and send erroneous data. Attacker may also intrude in the data transmission network and perform man-in-the-middle attack for providing erroneous measurement values (Fig. 1).

Thus, by changing the measurement, the state estimation value is changed. This change does not change the residue values, so by performing the residual test, the attack detection is not feasible.

Linear state estimation is obtained from the equation below

$$\hat{x} = (H^T W H)^{-1} H^T W z \tag{2}$$

Here

H: Jacobian Matrix.

W: Covariance Matrix.

z: Measurement values.

Now, if we set $z\_a = z + Hc$, where c is some changes, we get

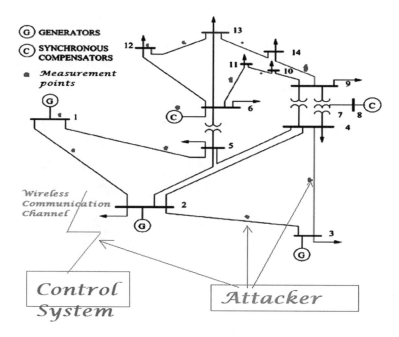

Fig. 1 FDIA in a smart grid

$$\hat{x}_a = \left(H^T W H\right)^{-1} H^T W (z + Hc)$$
$$= \left(H^T W H\right)^{-1} H^T W z + \left(H^T W H\right)^{-1} H^T W H c$$
$$= \hat{x} + c \tag{3}$$

Thus, we get new state estimation value as the original estimated value plus some changes. This is how the False Data Injection Attack works. If an attacker knows the impedances of a cart, i.e., a closed loop of the transmission line, a FDIA can be initiated by him. The changes are compared with a threshold value (δ) for detection of the attack in conventional detection system. However, attackers having the knowledge of system topology can attack the system where the change (c) value is lesser than the threshold (δ). This type of FDIA is stealthy FDIA and detection based on threshold is incapable of detecting it.

4 Overview of Techniques Used

Different DL and ML-based techniques applied in solving FDIA detection problem are discussed as follows:

Fig. 2 Support Vector
Machine

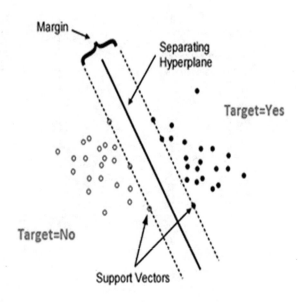

4.1 Support Vector Machine

SVM is a ML algorithm which is used for classification and regression purpose [22, 23]. SVM works by creating decision boundary aka hyperplane between classes. During training, the SVM selects the hyperplane with maximum margin. Margin is the distance between the support vectors, i.e., the nearest data points of the hyperplane. SVM uses a function called kernel which transfers the input to greater dimension where it can be separated. The SVM operation is shown in Fig. 2.

Once trained, SVM categorizes any unknown input to one category based on the hyperplane.

4.2 Light Gradient Boosting Machine

LightGBM, a gradient boosting framework, based on tree structures, was proposed by Microsoft [24, 25]. LightGBM grows tree vertically, i.e., leaf-wise unlike level-wise growth of similar methods. It selects the leaf having maximum delta loss for growing (Figs. 3 and 4).

Since its inception a couple of years back, it became highly popular among the researchers as well as ML practitioners due to its speed, and performance. LightGBM is very effective in dealing with large dataset, and needs less amount of memory. Though in case of small dataset, it is likely to over-fit.

Fig. 3 Leaf wise tree growth of LightGBM

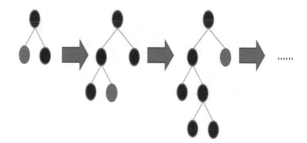

Fig. 4 Artificial neural network

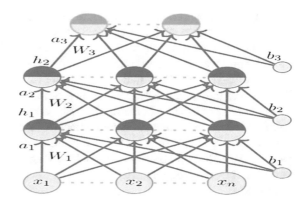

4.3 Artificial Neural Network (ANN)

ANN is very basic approximation of human nervous system [26]. There are a number of neurons placed in distinct layers. Single or multiple hidden layers are placed between an input and an output layers. Each neuron is interconnected to every neighboring layers' neuron through weights.

First, an ANN is required to be trained with training dataset, containing inputs and outputs.

During the training phase, the weights are updated. There are two steps. First, the Feedforward, where the output is calculated from the input using the weights. Then the error is calculated based on difference of calculated output from actual value. Second is Backpropagation. In this step, weights are updated based on the gradient of the error. The two stages are run for a number of iterations or until the error is reduced below a curtained predetermined value.

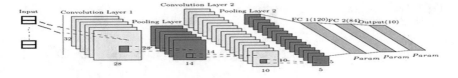

Fig. 5 A convolution neural network model

4.4 Convolutional Neural Network (CNN)

CNN [27, 28] is majorly used for images. In CNN, the spatial information surrounding an image is captured which is very important for finding pattern in images (Fig. 5).

The layers forming a CNN are Convolution, Pooling, and Fully Connected layer. Convolution layer comprises a no. of Kernels whose weights are updated during training of CNN [29]. Convolution Kernels are followed by Rectified Linear Unit (ReLU), and they produce the feature map of the input image [30]. Max-pooling operation takes the maximum of all the pixel values over a window size, and it is useful to reduce the computation requirement of the model. The feature map thus obtained after a number of convolution-relu-maxpool layers is flattened and input to fully connected layer for obtaining output [31]. Based on this basic structure of CNN, a number of Deep Learning models are built by researchers, e.g., ResNet, DenseNet, and ResNext.

5 Proposed Approach and Experiments Done

5.1 Data

The data used for this work is related to IEEE 14 bus (transmission) [32]. It is shown in the (Fig. 6):

This system has 11 loads and 5 generators. There are 14 bus and 17 transmission lines in the system. The dataset used in this experiment is obtained is "Power System Attack Datasets" from "Mississippi State University and Oak Ridge National Laboratory" [33]. The dataset contains 78,377 sets of measurement data. Each dataset contains 128 feature, and one label mentioning Attack or Normal. First some statistical data analysis on dataset is done. A boxplot analysis shows the outlier present in the data as shown in Fig. 7.

And from the histogram image, the distribution of the dataset is obtained as shown in Fig. 8.

As checked, the dataset contains outliers and data those are of bad values. Those data are discarded from the dataset before actual training is started. The final dataset contains 72,073 rows of measurement data.

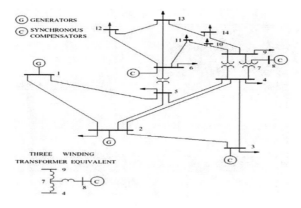

Fig. 6 IEEE 14 bus

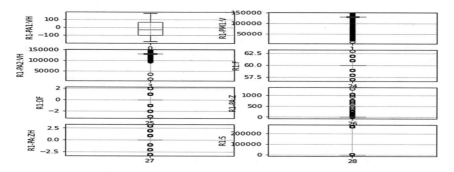

Fig. 7 Boxplot of FDIA dataset

This dataset is split into three sets—training, validation, and test sets. The training dataset contains 64% data, validation set contains 16% data, and the test set contains 20% of data. The models are trained with the test set and their performance is checked against the validation test. The models are changed by doing hyper-parameter tuning so that the performance metrics against the validation set is optimized. Finally, the performance of the model is checked against the previously unseen test data.

5.2 Models Configuration and Hyper-Parameters

The algorithm of the experiment can be formed as shown in Fig. 9. A no. of SVM configuration using different kernel types, e.g., rbf, polynomial and sigmoid kernels, as well as different c values (regularization parameters) and different gamma values are created, trained with the training data and tested against the test data. Similarly, a no. of LightGBM models are created by varying the parameters like boosting type,

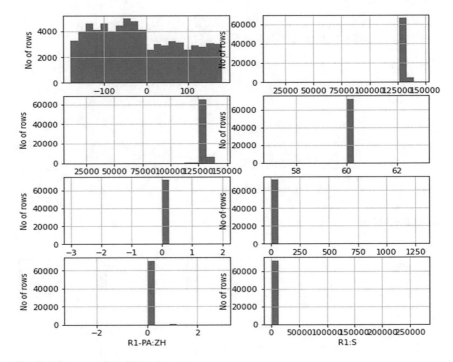

Fig. 8 Histogram of the FDIA dataset

no. of leaves, and learning rate; those are trained and tested against the data. For both these algorithms, the model with the best performance is kept.

ANN models are configured by varying the no. of hidden layers. A no. of ANN configurations using 4, 8, and 12 no. of hidden layers are checked.

As per performance, the ANN with 12 no. of hidden dense layers is selected. ReLU activation is applied for the hidden layers. For output layer, sigmoid activation function is used. Four no. of dropout layers are used in between the hidden layers to train the model well against the sparse data. For optimization, SGD optimizer is used.

For detection of FDIA, a no. of CNN models is created. The models are configured with varying no of convolution layers, different activation and optimization function, and tuned with different learning rate, and convolution layers with different no. of parameters.

For the optimum performance CNN model, the configuration started with a sequential layer, followed by four no. of one-dimensional convolution layers and ended with a dense layer. For the convolution layers, ReLU activation is employed. Final dense layer, which is included for flattening, gets sigmoid activation. A learning rate reducing mechanism is introduced on monitoring the validation loss. Adam optimizer is used, a batch size of 128 is taken, and the training is done over 200 epochs (Figs. 10 and 11).

Fig. 9 Algorithm for
detection of FDIA

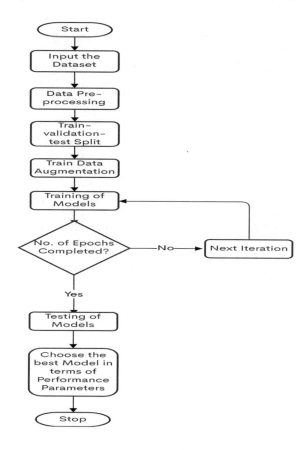

Using this model, we can prepare a system for detection of FDIA. The block
diagram is given in Fig. 12.

6 Results

As the models are trained, the loss and accuracy versus the epochs for ANN and
CNN model are shown in Figs. 13 and 14.

Results regarding testing of models are obtained in form of confusion matrix.
Performance of algorithms is obtained against test data by several metrics such as
accuracy, sensitivity, recall, F1 score, and specificity [34]. Results for all the models
are given in Table 1.

The comparison of performance in terms of the parameter can be visualized in
the chart as per Fig. 15:

```
Model: "sequential_4"
```

Layer (type)	Output Shape	Param #
dense_12 (Dense)	(None, 32)	4128
dense_13 (Dense)	(None, 64)	2112
dense_14 (Dense)	(None, 128)	8320
dropout (Dropout)	(None, 128)	0
dense_15 (Dense)	(None, 512)	66048
dense_16 (Dense)	(None, 1024)	525312
dense_17 (Dense)	(None, 512)	524800
dropout_1 (Dropout)	(None, 512)	0
dense_18 (Dense)	(None, 512)	262656
dense_19 (Dense)	(None, 1024)	525312
dense_20 (Dense)	(None, 512)	524800
dropout_2 (Dropout)	(None, 512)	0
dense_21 (Dense)	(None, 128)	65664
dense_22 (Dense)	(None, 64)	8256
dense_23 (Dense)	(None, 32)	2080
dropout_3 (Dropout)	(None, 32)	0
dense_24 (Dense)	(None, 1)	33

```
Total params: 2,519,521
Trainable params: 2,519,521
Non-trainable params: 0
```

Fig. 10 Configuration of ANN algorithm

Fig. 11 Convolutional neural network (CNN)

```
Model: "sequential_3"
```

Layer (type)	Output Shape	Param #
conv1d_4 (Conv1D)	(None, 124, 128)	768
conv1d_5 (Conv1D)	(None, 122, 256)	98560
conv1d_6 (Conv1D)	(None, 120, 128)	98432
conv1d_7 (Conv1D)	(None, 118, 128)	49280
flatten_1 (Flatten)	(None, 15104)	0
dense_1 (Dense)	(None, 1)	15105

```
Total params: 262,145
Trainable params: 262,145
Non-trainable params: 0
```

7 Conclusion and Future Scope of Work

In smart grid, false data injection attack might be very critical and this cyber-attack can create disaster that is not detected and handled timely. The ML and DL methods are described and tested, and the CNN-based model is found to perform well in

Fig. 12 CNN-based FDIA detection system

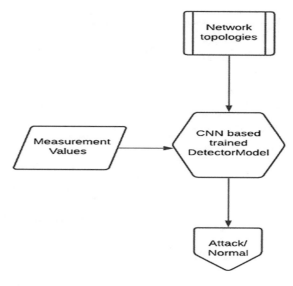

Fig. 13 Loss, Accuracy versus epoch: ANN

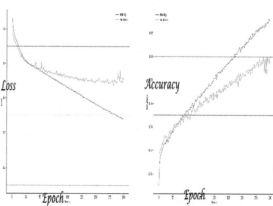

Fig. 14 Loss, accuracy versus epoch: CNN

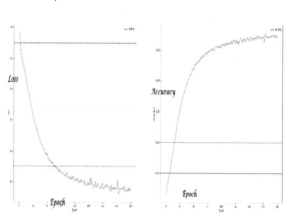

Table 1 Performance of models for detection of FDIA

Performance table

Metrics\Model	SVM	ANN	LightGBM	CNN
Accuracy (%)	76	81	91	92
Precision (%)	32	56	80	82
Recall (%)	67	71	88	89
Specificity (%)	77	84	92	93
F1 Score	43	63	84	85

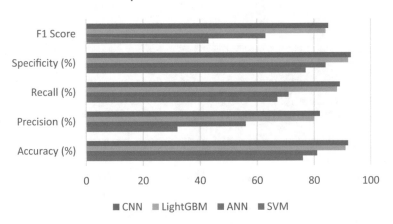

Fig. 15 Comparison of ML and DL models in terms of Performance matrices

detection of the FDIA. The next step of this is to implement this algorithm in real system; before that it is needed to be checked in real dataset as this is checked only against simulated data based on IEEE 14 bus system. The Latest Deep Learning methods based on transfer learning might also be tried to improve its performance when tested against real-world data. Once done, it is likely to resolve a very critical infrastructure problem.

References

1. Wang S, Bi S, Zhang YA (2020) Locational detection of the false data injection attack in a smart grid: a multilabel classification approach. IEEE Internet Things J 7(9):8218–8227. https://doi.org/10.1109/jiot.2020.2983911.Author F, Author S (2016) Title of a proceedings paper. In: Editor F, Editor S (eds) Conference 2016, LNCS, vol 9999, pp 1–13. Springer, Heidelberg
2. Gai K, Xu K, Lu Z, Qiu M, Zhu L (2019) Fusion of cognitive wireless networks and edge computing. IEEE Wirel Commun 26(3):69–75

3. The 'Air gap' between IT & OT is disappearing, & we're not ready to manage the risk. (26 Feb 2019). Infosecurity Magazine. https://www.infosecurity-magazine.com/infosec/air-gap-between-it-and-ot-1-1-1-1/
4. McLaughlin S, Konstantinou C, Wang X, Davi L, Sadeghi A, Maniatakos M, Karri R (2016) The cybersecurity landscape in industrial control systems. Proc IEEE 104(5):1039–1057. https://doi.org/10.1109/jproc.2015.2512235
5. Haque NI, Shahriar MH, Dastgir MG, Debnath A, Parvez I, Sarwat A, Rahman MA (2020) Machine learning in generation, detection, and mitigation of cyberattacks in smart grid: a survey. arXiv:2010.00661
6. Schellenberger C, Zhang P (2017) Detection of covert attacks on cyber-physical systems by extending the system dynamics with an auxiliary system. In: 2017 IEEE 56th annual conference on decision and control (CDC). IEEE, pp 1374–1379
7. Ford V, Siraj A, Eberle W (2014) Smart grid energy fraud detection using artificial neural networks. In: 2014 IEEE symposium on computational intelligence applications in smart grid (CIASG). IEEE, pp 1–6
8. Vijayanand R, Devaraj D, Kannapiran B (2019) A novel deep learning based intrusion detection system for smart meter communication network. In: 2019 IEEE international conference on intelligent techniques in control, optimization and signal processing (INCOS). IEEE, pp 1–3
9. Dutta S (2021) Cyber attacks on power grid: 10 power assets, Mumbai, Tamil Nadu ports came under RedEcho cyberattack|India business news—Times of India. The Times of India. https://timesofindia.indiatimes.com/business/india-business/10-power-assets-mumbai-tamil-nadu-ports-came-under-redecho-cyberattack/articleshow/81337328.cms. Accessed 5 Mar 2021
10. Maharashtra cyber police suspects cyber attack behind Mumbai power outage. (2021) Hindustan Times. https://www.hindustantimes.com/cities/mumbai-news/maharashtra-cyber-police-suspects-cyber-attack-behind-mumbai-power-outage-101614654439868.html. Accessed 2 Mar 2021
11. Decoding motives behind the Kudankulam intrusion (2019) Hindustan Times. https://www.hindustantimes.com/analysis/decoding-motives-behind-the-kudankulam-intrusion/story-c3odQAUqOT1nDgjOMFQRPK.html. Accessed 22 Nov 2019
12. Liu Y, Ning P, Reiter MK (2011) False data injection attacks against state estimation in electric power grids. ACM Trans Inf Syst Secur 14(1):1–33. https://doi.org/10.1145/1952982.1952995
13. Rahman MA, Mohsenian-Rad H (2013) False data injection attacks against nonlinear state estimation in smart power grids. In: 2013 IEEE power & energy society general meeting. https://doi.org/10.1109/pesmg.2013.6672638
14. Chakhchoukh Y, Liu S, Sugiyama M, Ishii H (2016) Statistical outlier detection for diagnosis of cyber attacks in power state estimation. In: 2016 IEEE power and energy society general meeting (PESGM). https://doi.org/10.1109/pesmg.2016.7741572
15. Esmalifalak M, Liu L, Nguyen N, Zheng R, Han Z (2017) Detecting stealthy false data injection using machine learning in smart grid. IEEE Syst J 11(3):1644–1652. https://doi.org/10.1109/jsyst.2014.2341597
16. Wang Y, Amin MM, Fu J, Moussa HB (2017) A novel data analytical approach for false data injection cyber-physical attack mitigation in smart grids. IEEE Access 5:26022–26033
17. Chakhchoukh Y, Liu S, Sugiyama M, Ishii H (2016) Statistical outlier detection for diagnosis of cyber attacks in power state estimation. In: 2016 IEEE power and energy society general meeting (PESGM). IEEE, pp 1–5
18. Wang H, Ruan J, Wang G, Zhou B, Liu Y, Fu X, Peng J (2018) Deep learning-based interval state estimation of AC smart grids against sparse cyber attacks. IEEE Trans Industr Inf 14(11):4766–4778
19. Ashrafuzzaman M, Chakhchoukh Y, Jillepalli AA, Tosic PT, de Leon DC, Sheldon FT, Johnson BK (2018) Detecting stealthy false data injection attacks in power grids using deep learning. In: 2018 14th international wireless communications & mobile computing conference (IWCMC). IEEE, pp 219–225

20. Niu X, Li J, Sun J, Tomsovic K (2019) Dynamic detection of false data injection attack in smart grid using deep learning. In: 2019 IEEE power & energy society innovative smart grid technologies conference (ISGT). IEEE, pp 1–6

21. Wang S, Bi S, Zhang YJA (2020) Locational detection of the false data injection attack in a smart grid: a multilabel classification approach. IEEE Int Things J 7(9):8218–8227

22. Suthaharan S (2016) Support vector machine. In: Machine learning models and algorithms for big data classification. Springer, Boston, MA, pp 207–235

23. Prashant111 (2020) SVM classifier tutorial. Kaggle: Your Machine Learning and Data Science Community. https://www.kaggle.com/prashant111/svm-classifier-tutorial?scriptVersionId=30116289. Accessed 13 Mar 2020

24. Ke G, Meng Q, Finley T, Wang T, Chen W, Ma W, Liu TY (2017) Lightgbm: a highly efficient gradient boosting decision tree. Adv Neural Inf Process Syst 30:3146–3154

25. Prashant111 (2020) LightGBM classifier in Python. Kaggle: Your Machine Learning and Data Science Community. https://www.kaggle.com/prashant111/lightgbm-classifier-in-python. Accessed 21 July 2020

26. Wasserman PD, Schwartz T (1988) Neural networks. II. What are they and why is everybody so interested in them now? In: IEEE Expert, vol 3, no 1. Spring, pp 10–15

27. Saha, Sumit (2018) A comprehensive guide to convolutional neural networks—the ELI5 Way. Medium, Towards Data Science, 15 Dec 2018, https://towardsdatascience.com/a-comprehensive-guide-to-convolutional-neural-networks-the-eli5-way-3bd2b1164a53

28. Bhandare A, Bhide M, Gokhale P, Chandavarkar R (2016) Applications of convolutional neural networks. Int J Comput Sci Inf Technol 7(5):2206–2215

29. Szegedy C, Liu W, Jia Y, Sermanet P, Reed S, Anguelov D, Erhan D, Vanhoucke V, Rabinovich A (2015) Going deeper with convolutions. In: 2015 IEEE conference on computer vision and pattern recognition (CVPR). https://doi.org/10.1109/cvpr.2015.7298594

30. Study of Reducing Computational Complexity of CNNs by Ranking the Features According to Their Importance—Department of Electrical Engineering Department of Electrical Engineering—Indian Institute of Technology Madras, http://www.ee.iitm.ac.in/event/study-of-reducing- computational-complexity-of-cnns-by-ranking-the- features-according-to-their-importance. Accessed 2 May 2019

31. Khapra MM, CS7015 (Deep Learning): Convolutional Neural Networks, LeNet, AlexNet, ZF-Net, VGGNet, GoogLeNet and ResNet. https://www.cse.iitm.ac.in/~miteshk/CS7015/Slides/Teaching/pdf/Lecture11.pdf

32. University of Washington, Power System Test Case Archive. http://www.ee.washington.edu/research/pstca/.

33. http://www.ece.uah.edu/~thm0009/icsdatasets/PowerSystem_Dataset_README.pdf

34. Confusion matrix (2004) Wikipedia, the free encyclopedia. https://en.wikipedia.org/wiki/Confusion_matrix. Accessed 15 June 2021

Democratic Aftermarket for Domain Names

Hrishabh Sharma, Ujjwal Kumar, Amruta Mulay, Rishabh Kumar,
and Sankita J. Patel

1 Introduction

With the development of Blockchain Technology, we observe that the world is considerably shifting toward decentralization. The users demand actual control over their data and information. Therefore, efforts are being taken to eliminate the brokers/mediators and the centralized entities present in different use cases. The Secondary Market of Domain Names is one of such areas that demands decentralization for precluding the idea of a broker system. The rapid increase in the growth of Internet users has attributed to an exponential growth in the ownership of domain names. Domainers belonging to different categories have recognized the importance of unique and appealing domain names, engendering a competitive secondary marketplace for domain names. This provides an incentive for the proposed model to focus on the rapidly growing secondary market of domain names along with the entities involved and implement a Blockchain-based system over this legacy system to permit the potential sellers who own a domain and their respective buyers to communicate directly without the need of a broker as a mediator. The overall objective lies in making the system more reliable, transparent, independent, and reducing the commission rates, thus providing a smooth service to the domain buyers/sellers.

In the present-day market of Domain Names, the middlemen are responsible for providing the services for buying and selling these domain names. The middlemen act as the centralized entities that play the role of trading the ownership of domain names and the monetary worth associated with it between the buyers and sellers. Consequently, the buyers are given access to the domain name they pay for, while the sellers settle down with the agreed price. The main concern here is that the brokers charge a commission rate for the service they provide to both these parties. In this paper, we propose a novel decentralized service for domain buyers and sellers using

H. Sharma (✉) · U. Kumar · A. Mulay · R. Kumar · S. J. Patel
Sardar Vallabhbhai National Institute of Technology, Surat 395007, Gujarat, India
e-mail: sjp@coed.svnit.ac.in

© The Author(s), under exclusive license to Springer Nature Singapore Pte Ltd. 2022   49
U. P. Rao et al. (eds.), *Security, Privacy and Data Analytics*, Lecture Notes
in Electrical Engineering 848, https://doi.org/10.1007/978-981-16-9089-1_4

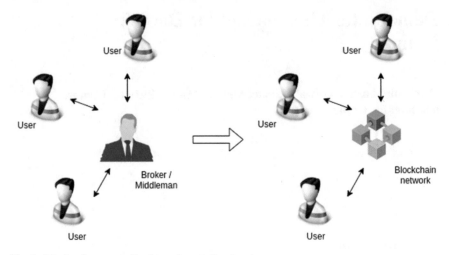

Fig. 1 Moving from centralized to a decentralized system

Blockchain technology. In the proposed system, the brokers are eliminated, allowing the buyers and sellers to communicate directly. This system provides transparency as well as reduced commission rates, thus giving benefits to both parties.

The main aim is to provide the decentralized service based on Blockchain Technology, as depicted in Fig. 1. This recommended system is safer as compared to the centralized domain name market, and avoids various attacks caused due to the broker's existence like phishing attacks, click-baits, masquerade attacks, overpricing, etc. If economically feasible, this proposed service can supplant other domain escrow services that the domain name registrars provide. The scope for applying this service is not circumscribed only to companies or organizations but can be broadened to almost everyone on the Internet.

The major contributions of our work are as follows:

- We eliminate the unfairness involved in the present domain aftermarket to develop a competitive and fair market of domain selling and buying through a Decentralized Ethereum application.
- We present the detailed system architecture in the form of algorithms, sequence, and entity diagrams.
- We discuss the economic feasibility and the reduction of commissions through the proposed approach.

2 Background

In this section, we discuss the background of how domain transfer takes place with a centralized entity involved. This will create a clear image to understand where and what entities should be replaced to transform into a decentralized model. The prominent members who are actively participating in the centralized model of Domain Name Transfer are as follows [1]:

- **Registry/Domain Name Registry:** It maintains a database of the domain names and corresponding registrant details. It also enables third-party entities to get administrative control on a domain name.
- **Registrar/Domain Name Registrar:** It is the agency responsible for managing the reservation of domain names.
- **Registrant:** This entity holds a registered domain name.
- **Buyer:** Refers to the person or party that is willing to buy a domain name presently owned by someone else.
- **Seller:** Refers to the person or party that owns a particular domain name and is interested in selling it to someone else.
- **Domain Broker Service:** Concerned with the service of transferring the domain ownership between two interested parties. They act as mediators and charge commission rates for the service they provide.

Having discussed the above main terms, the domain transfer from one registrant to another occurs in the following manner.

Initially, the domain name owner, i.e. seller, requests a change of registrant by contacting the present registrar. This registrar will request for owner's confirmation via some secured means like email verification. Once the verification process has been done, the owner initiates the transfer of the domain name to the registrar. The registrar contains the updated list of all the domain names that are available for selling. Meanwhile, the broker negotiates the price for selling that particular domain name with the owner and finds an appropriate buyer. Once both the parties have settled down with the negotiated price for buying and selling, the funds are transferred, and the domain ownership is handed over to the buyer. Here, the broker adds extra commission charges for its service, thus causing the buyer to pay more and the seller to earn less.

The current approach of the centralized model contains flaws related to the veracity between the parties involved. There may arise issues such as the broker denying fund transfer to the seller even though the buyer has made the payment and the seller has already transferred the ownership of the domain name. Another issue may be that the buyer has successfully transferred the money to the broker. In contrast, the seller has not yet completed the ownership transfer of the domain name, allowing the broker to scam with the money received from the buyer. Moreover, due to the non-transparency in the model, there is a high possibility of overpricing from the broker's side to maximize their profits. Thus, the buyer has to pay higher price money than required. In the use case that is being considered, trust needs to be established between the buyer and seller where the transaction will take place through digital currency, which the smart contract will govern. This eliminates the involvement of any centralized fiat currency.

2.1 Accessing Registry Data

The registrant data (information shared at the registration) is stored with the registrar and shared with the registry. Till May 2018, one could find the contact information (name, email address, contact number, postal address) associated with a domain name using WHOIS [2] protocol service [3]. However, this service has now been modified to bring it in line with the General Data Protection Regulation (GDPR) [4] policies (enforced in May 2018). So, at its present state, WHOIS does not provide the contact details of the registrants (postal address, email address, contact number); hence, we cannot use WHOIS for our verification process.

Nevertheless, WHOIS has now been accompanied with another service, namely Registration Data Access Protocol (RDAP) [5] which provides many features over the previous WHOIS protocol. RDAP provides differentiated access, meaning one can query RDAP service either anonymously or with some authentication.

2.2 Blockchain

Blockchain is a popular distributed database of records such that the records are stored in the form of blocks, and each block is connected to the previous block by storing its block hash. Thus, it is a chain-like linked structure formed of immutable blocks. Depending on the different architectures of the Blockchain Network, the degree of decentralization may vary; this is primarily due to the conspicuous trade-offs that will arise due to the various characteristics of Blockchain [6].

2.3 Smart Contract

Smart contracts are code stored on the blockchain which serves as a type of agreement, and contain business logic. It gets executed when certain pre-written conditions are met. Smart contracts eliminate the risk of any fraudulent activity from the participants [7].

2.4 Auction

The definition of an auction is a public sale of the property to the highest bidder. The ultimate goal of an auction sale is to obtain the best financial returns for the property owner and allow free and fair competition among bidders. The most common types of auctions are (i) Increasing price auction (English auction), (ii) Sealed-bid auction,

(iii) Decreasing price auction (Dutch auction), and (iv) Second-price auction. This paper uses English auction in its implementation [8].

According to a study, the following features of a deal help one determine if auction is the right choice to go with—

- **Buyer Profile:** The number of potential buyers should be large and familiar.
- **Process Setter's Profile:** An auction is quicker than a negotiation making it a finer mechanism when the speed is critical.
- **Contextual Factors:** Auction should always be preferred in cases where transparency and secrecy are significant factors to consider.

3 Related Work

Although there have been many pioneers for establishing aftermarket deals, all are centralized. Many domain registrars, e.g. GoDaddy, provide their domain broker service. But this comes at a fee for hiring a personal Agent ("Domain Buy Agent", as GoDaddy calls it). The "Broker Service Fee", as mentioned, there is around >8000 INR, and this cost has been doubled in the last 6 months. Once users buy their service, the negotiation with the current registrant of a domain (who may or may not be interested in selling) proceeds. If the negotiation is finalized, the buyer will have to pay the final settled price for the domain plus any commission charged by the Service Provider. GoDaddy's commission for the same is 20% of the settled price [9].

Apart from the registrar's provided domain broker services, there have been attempts to provide the aftermarket through escrow methods. "Escrow.com" [10] is one such example. Sedo.com [11] is another popular online web platform that provides services like domain acquisition and auctions for aftermarket domain selling.

To the best of our knowledge, there has not been any attempt in the literature to make the domain name aftermarket decentralized. On the other hand, this is not the case with Blockchain-based domain names. These domain names are established and managed on the Blockchain itself and use the DNS running on the Blockchain network. For example, the Ethereum Naming Service (ENS) is one of the Blockchain-based domain names which allows managing and transferring the ownership on the network itself (Ethereum Blockchain Network). Since ENS exists on Blockchain, the execution of an aftermarket is achieved natively and easily. But when we talk about domain names that exist on the existing DNS architecture, the execution requires some engineering workaround and no existing solutions exist.

4   System Architecture

In the concerned use case, the end goal is to bring trust between the buyers and sellers for the transactions in digital currency, governed by smart contracts, without any need for centralized fiat currency.

The implementation will include a web interface where sellers can list the domain for selling. While making an initial request for listing a domain for sale, the seller has to set a base price for auction on the platform. Then, interested buyers can put on their bids on the domains which they want to buy. A separate smart contract will wholly govern the auction process. During bidding, the visitors will have to transfer the bid amount to the contract address. The amount paid by the auction winner will be transferred to the seller's account after the ownership transfer of the domain. Another smart contract will govern all the data related to the listing of the domains.

4.1   Valuation of Domain Name via Auction

Association française pour le nommage Internet en coopération (AFNIC), an association that operates on French country code top-level domains (ccTLD), has suggested in one of their Issue Paper [12] that the value of a domain name is determined chiefly by factors like search engine rankings, the meaning of the name, public perception, keyword competition, and traffic analysis (and many more). Unfortunately, these factors cannot be formulated easily (at least they have not been formulated to date). Moreover, an individual/organization may prioritize these factors differently (based on their opinion), making the valuation even more difficult. Hence in our opinion, a bidding platform is the most suitable way to determine the value associated with a domain name. We have decided on an English auction type for the scenario at hand to keep the bidding process intuitive to the bidders. Furthermore, the bidding will be public (i.e. all the bidding made will be publicly visible as the bidding continues).

4.2   Choosing the Suitable Blockchain

Due to the considerable increase in the adoption of Blockchain in various use cases, it has taken different forms comprising different characteristics. Therefore, according to the use case, one must understand the different characteristics and decide on a suitable Blockchain platform. We are now surrounded by hundreds of Blockchains that differ in various characteristics. For example, they can be public or private, permissioned or permissionless, with or without Turing-complete smart contracts. So, there is "No one fit design to all" Blockchain platform [13]. After analyzing the use-case requirement, we needed Turing-complete smart contracts to smoothly govern the auction process and enable buyer-seller to use the application without permission. This narrows down our search for choosing a suitable public Blockchain network with Turing-complete smart contracts. "Ethereum" and "EOS" come into the mind with these characteristics. After performing a detailed survey plus considering the wide adoption and community support in Ethereum Network, we proceeded with our work by choosing the Ethereum Blockchain [14].

4.3 Components

The entire architecture consists of four major components: (i) The registry of domain names accessible via Registration Data Access Protocol (RDAP) [5], (ii) A server that indexes Blockchain data into information presentable to the user, (iii) The Blockchain network and its underlying database (ledger), and (iv) The smart contract where all the logic for auction and fund management resides.

The server (dApp-backend) and the domain names registry interact on the traditional client-server request model to fetch the ownership information. Another task of the dApp server is to present meaningful information fetched from the Blockchain ledger. The logic for handling the auction process and fund management is realized into a smart contract deployed on the blockchain network, which can never be tampered with once deployed. The record of all the events such as the listing of a domain, starting auction for a particular domain, bids made to a particular auction, ending of the auction and lastly, the transfer of funds is handled through the Blockchain network, which gets saved into the underlying database of Blockchain (Fig. 2).

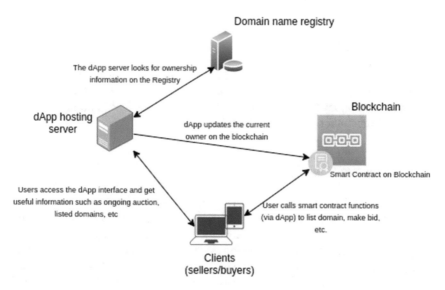

Fig. 2 System architecture—components

4.4   Implementation

This section discusses the step-by-step process that will take place to execute the use case. The activity for domain buying and selling takes place in the following sequence.

4.4.1   Domain Ownership and Email Verification

Initially, the users who are willing to sell their domain names need to fill out a form that verifies the ownership of this domain. Then, email verification can be performed using the One Time Password (OTP) approach. If the verification process is successful, we authorize this user to list their domain for the auction process. As an experimental setup of the architecture and to access the registry of authorized domain owners, the service of RDAP API can be mimicked to match the details while verifying the ownership of domain names.

4.4.2   Domain Listing for Auction

Once the final confirmation is made from the seller's side for domain selling, a Blockchain transaction will be initiated via MetaMask [15] to broadcast it on the Blockchain network. Here, the seller also associates a minimum bidding value for their domain name as the starting price for the auction process, as highlighted in Fig. 3.

4.4.3   Auction Bidding

After the seller's list is updated, the buyers can view them on a standard web interface. As shown in Fig. 4, the buyer may show interest in a particular type of domain name and want to buy it. If interested, they may select the "bid" option to initiate a Blockchain transaction creation by MetaMask.

4.4.4   Ending Auction

The sellers have the authority to end the auctions concerning their respective domain names. Once the auction has been ended, the buyers cannot bid for that particular domain name. MetaMask will report an error and restrain the buyer from initiating a transaction. Moreover, once the auction process has terminated, the highest bidder must transfer the bid amount to the smart contract address in a fixed time window. If he/she fails to do so, the auction is discarded; otherwise, the seller is supposed to transfer the ownership of the domain name. After successfully verifying the domain

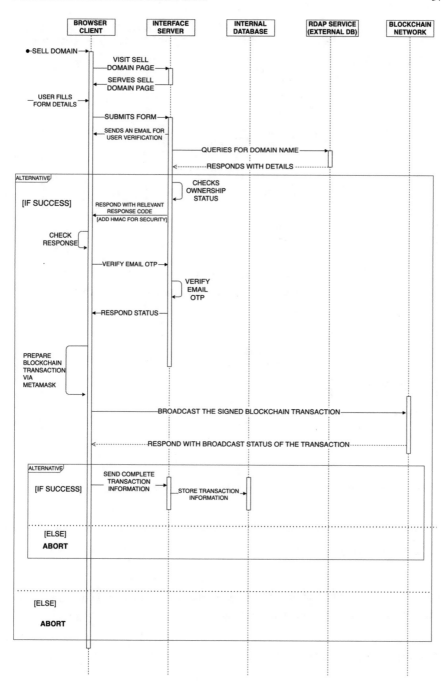

Fig. 3 Sequence diagram of listing a domain

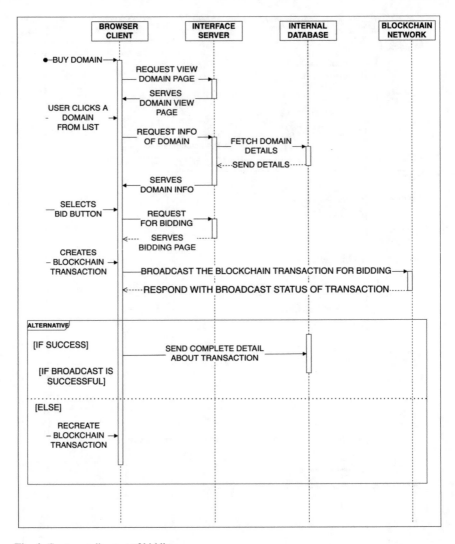

Fig. 4 Sequence diagram of bidding

ownership transfer through the dApp server, the fund settlement is initiated by the smart contract and funds are released to the seller.

5   Smart Contracts

In this paper's concerned use case, two Smart contracts will be deployed, i.e. Domain Market and Domain Auction. The Domain Market smart contract will keep track of all the domains available for sale on the blockchain platform and provide the necessary transaction functions like submitting the new domain for sale and checking the auction's status. Also, an instance of a domain auction smart contract is created and will be associated with each domain available for sale. See Code Listing 1. The domain auction contract will govern the basic auction activities like bidding in the auction, ending the auction, and receiving funds from the highest bidder.

```
1   struct Domain {
2       uint id;
3       address payable owner;
4       string domainName;
5       string contactEmail;
6       uint basePrince;
7       bool ownerVerified;
8       bool succesfullySold;
9       DomainAuction auction;
10  }
```

Listing 1 Structure of a Domain

6 Evaluation

6.1 Improvements over Current Market Scenario

Various advancements are brought by the Blockchain-based service that replaces the current Broker Services offered by various entities. The main objective has been to replace the costly, fraudulent, semi-transparent practices involved in the latter. The brokers' prominent participation in the legacy DNS causes a high probability for unfairness to occur. The Blockchain-based approach eliminates these brokers, therefore assuring no scope for fraud. Moreover, the Blockchain-based model is a decentralized system. It makes sure that the brokers do not gain a monopoly over the system and withdraw an unreasonable amount of money from either party. Since smart contracts are the coded programs implemented in the Blockchain system, this encourages trustful ownership transfer between buyers and sellers. Once any transaction has been settled between a particular buyer and seller, the details concerned with the ownership status remain unchanged and permanent in the system.

6.2 Fees Involved in a Transfer

We designed and deployed the smart contracts on the Ropsten Testnet [16] to estimate the fees incurred in a typical domain name transfer. A domain listing operation used 691,760 gas units and constituted the charges on the seller's end. The cost of listing operation varies for different lengths of domain names because we store the domain names on the Blockchain. Similarly, a long domain name (say 64 characters long)

Table 1 Cost Involved in different operations at gas price of 30 Gwei

Operation	Gas units used	Fee in ETH
Listing a domain	691760	0.0207528
Bidding	48775	0.00146325
Ending an auction	53508	0.00160524

will require 692,528 gas units for the same operation. Similarly, a bidding operation constitutes the major transaction charges from the buyer's end. Single bidding on any domain name took 48,775 gas units on average. Moreover, an explicit termination of auction consumes 53,508 gas units. Table 1 shows the cost discussed above for different operations.

6.3 Reducing the Network Transaction Fee

To make the proposed work more novel, we performed a detailed analysis of the Layer-2 Blockchain solutions based on the Ethereum blockchain. Plasma solutions helped reduce the transaction cost and provide faster transaction speed [17]. We used the Polygon (previously known as Matic) network, an adapted version of Plasma, to perform a detailed comparison in reducing the network transaction fee compared to Ethereum Network. Tables 2 and 3 show the gas used (in ETH) on Ethereum and Polygon Network for seller and buyer, respectively.

Table 2 Seller's fee on ethereum and polygon network

L*	Seller@ETH	Seller@Polygon
27	0.02235768	0.002235768
28	0.02235804	0.002235804
508	0.0332298	0.00332298

Table 3 Buyer's fee on ethereum and polygon network

L*	Buyer@ETH	Buyer@Polygon
27	0.00146326	0.000146326
28	0.00146326	0.000146326
508	0.00146326	0.000146326

*Length of the domain name added with the email address of the owner, in characters
*The Cost is estimated at Average Gas Price of 30 Gwei on Ethereum Network and 3 Gwei on Polygon Network
*All costs are indicated in terms of Ethereum (ETH) cryptocurrency

6.4   Limitations of the Architecture

Most public Blockchains today suffer from the lack of scalability, and hence any solution built using a public Blockchain network will also get a hit on the scalability side. Though the Ethereum platform currently uses the Proof-of-Work consensus mechanism, which offers 15 TPS, it will soon make a complete shift to the Proof-of-Stake consensus mechanism, which will drastically boost the TPS to a few thousand. Another central point that should be noted is that the ownership information of legacy domain names resides on off-chain databases, and Blockchain solutions have the limitation of not being able to access off-chain data directly. Bridging this gap gives the architecture a hybrid design which makes such a solution not full proof as a Blockchain network. Despite this, the proposed design offers significant trust, transparency, and no hassle of negotiation over the legacy aftermarket platforms to handle the auction process and funds.

7   Future Work

There is much scope for improvement concerning off-chain data fetching. Integrating solutions that allow accessing off-chain data more securely and seamlessly will be an ongoing task as improvement in this aspect of Blockchain technology emerges. The weakest part of the proposed architecture is the dApp server, which also fetches domain ownership information. Though the architecture achieves the secure management of funds, it fails to handle cases of breached dApp server, which poses a security threat. This security threat can be handled by allowing the affected party to raise a dispute in scenarios of unfair settlement. It can be achieved using a multi-signature Smart contract design for the Domain Auction. This smart contract will enable the affected party to raise a dispute in a given time frame so that the inaccurate fund settlements do not occur in case of a dApp server breach. The dispute settlement process will again leverage the Blockchain network of independent validators, which will aid the ownership conflict resolution. This model further requires work and analysis for its practicality.

Also, there has been the advent of Blockchain managed domain names. Therefore, the platform can be extended to include those domain names to make it more inclusive. Furthermore, the support of Blockchain-managed domain names will be much more secure and seamless than the auction of legacy domain names as the complete information will be available on-chain, thus reducing the risks of accessing off-chain data.

References

1. ICANN, Resources. https://www.icann.org/resources. Accessed 12 Sep 2021
2. ICANN, WHOIS. https://whois.icann.org/en/about-whois. Accessed 12 Sep 2021
3. Temporary Specification for gTLD Registration Data. https://www.icann.org/en/system/files/files/gtld-registration-data-temp-spec-17may18-en.pdf. Accessed 12 Sep 2021
4. What is GDPR. https://gdpr.eu/what-is-gdpr/. Accessed 12 Sep 2021
5. Registration Data Access Protocol (RDAP). https://www.icann.org/rdap. Accessed 12 Sep 2021
6. Zheng Z, Xie S, Dai H-N, Chen X, Wang H (2018) Blockchain challenges and opportunities: a survey. Int J Web Grid Serv 14:352
7. Mohanta BK, Panda SS, Jena D (2018) An overview of smart contract and use cases in blockchain technology. In: 2018 9th international conference on computing, communication and networking technologies (ICCCNT), 2018, pp 1–4. https://doi.org/10.1109/ICCCNT.2018.8494045
8. Online auction - Wikipedia. https://en.wikipedia.org/wiki/Online_auction. Accessed 12 Sep 2021
9. GoDaddy Broker Service. https://godaddy.com/domains/domain-broker. Accessed 12 Sep 2021
10. About Escrow.com. The Online Escrow service. https://www.escrow.com/why-escrowcom/about-us. Accessed 12 Sep 2021
11. Sedo company details. https://sedo.com/us/about-us/. Accessed 12 Sep 2021
12. AFNIC, The secondary market for domain names (2010) https://www.afnic.fr/medias/documents/afnic-issue-paper-secondary-market-2010-04.pdf. Accessed 12 Sep 2021
13. Kannengießer N, Lins S, Dehling T, Sunyaev A (2020) Trade-offs between distributed ledger technology characteristics. ACM Comput Surv 53(2), Article 42
14. Wood G (2014) Ethereum: a secure decentralised generalised transaction ledger, EIP-150 revision. https://gavwood.com/paper.pdf. Accessed 12 Sep 2021
15. MetaMask About. https://metamask.io/about. Accessed 12 Sep 2021
16. Networks-Ethereum. https://ethereum.org/en/developers/docs/networks/#testnets. Accessed 12 Sep 2021
17. Plasma-EthHub. https://docs.ethhub.io/ethereum-roadmap/layer-2-scaling/plasma/. Accessed 12 Sep 2021

Defect Analysis of Faulty Regions in Photovoltaic Panels Using Deep Learning Method

S. Prabhakaran, R. Annie Uthra, and J. Preetha Roselyn

1 Introduction

The statistics from the International Energy Agency (IEA) indicates that the total global Photovoltaic capacity (PV) is expected to reach 740 GW by 2022 [5]. As per the statistics collected by International Energy Agency, Solar power has been considered as the latest energy resource that grows exponentially year after year. When it comes to the overall global capacity, Photovoltaics (PV) stands third in the renewable energy sector [1]. The potential that lies behind solar power generation systems is enormous and it is considered as the most clean, eco-friendly, safe and reliable renewable resource ever utilized [2]. The classification of solar power generation systems is purely based on whether they are a part of the power generating system [4]. All Photovoltaic systems are categorized as either grid connected or self-sustained systems [4].

Solar panels need direct exposure to sunlight and operates only in open environment thus leading to exposure of extreme natural conditions like heat, cold, snow and fog [13]. Such exposures lead to damage of solar panels which proportionately stops the production of solar power or leads to poor output efficiency of the panel [3]. The solar panel has to be properly maintained at regular intervals so as to achieve higher output efficiency during conversion of solar power into electricity. The protective glass layer of the panel and the sensitive layers that lie between the protective surface have to be preserved and conserved for efficient functioning of the solar power generating systems [3, 8].

S. Prabhakaran · R. A. Uthra (✉) · J. P. Roselyn
SRM Institute of Science and Technology, Kattankulathur, TN, India
e-mail: annieu@srmist.edu.in

S. Prabhakaran
e-mail: ps8209@srmist.edu.in

J. P. Roselyn
e-mail: preethaj@srmist.edu.in

© The Author(s), under exclusive license to Springer Nature Singapore Pte Ltd. 2022
U. P. Rao et al. (eds.), *Security, Privacy and Data Analytics*, Lecture Notes
in Electrical Engineering 848, https://doi.org/10.1007/978-981-16-9089-1_5

63

Table 1 Defects versus nature of severity on solar panels

Defects/faults in solar panels	Nature and severity of damage done by defects
Broken	Damaged solar panels during manufacturing or maintenance or excessive usage
Cracks, micro-cracks	Solar panels damaged during manufacturing, transport, installation or exposure to extreme weather conditions
Dust/Snow	Accumulated over a period of time due to improper or poor maintenance
Bird droppings	Impurities on the panels as a result of droppings from birds
Hotspot	Occurs in a PV module as a result of failure in solar cells, disjoint soldering, partial shading, and discrepancy in parallel strings that are connected together
Ground faults	Exhibits an inadvertent low electric resistance path between the ground and any current carrying capacitors (CCCs)
Arc faults	Occurs as a Result of degraded connections in junction boxes, improper crimping, cracked PV modules and out of date firmware

Defects introduced during the manufacturing of solar panels have to be detected and repaired adequately [1]. The size and shape of these defects vary accordingly. Defects in solar panels such as cracks, hairline-cracks, dust, dirt and scratches are bound to occur during the manufacturing as well as deployment of solar panels [2]. Detection of the above-mentioned defects plays a crucial part in the effective functioning of the panel [15]. Innovative methods have been discovered and deployed to replace manual inspection of panels with latest automated technologies that detects these defects effectively and efficiently [2, 10]. The PV module defects thus identified promises extended lifetime of PV modules as well as increased productivity in terms of power generation [5, 9]. The various defects in PV systems are summarized in the Table 1.

Of the below-mentioned defects electrical, soldering, ground fault and line-to-line defects are not areas of concern in this paper. The defects under the scanner are defects that can be identified through images and techniques employed on those images. Broken panels, Cracks, Micro-cracks (Hairline), Dust/Snow, Bird droppings and Hotspot defects can be identified from images of solar panels taken from high-definition CCD cameras or aerial drones. The figures given above illustrates the various types of defects that occur externally on solar panels (Fig. 1).

Deep learning, Convolutional Neural networks (CNN), Multilayer Neural Networks (MNN), MMPT algorithms and Near-Infrared (NIR) systems are some of the prominent methods that are discussed in the forthcoming chapter for identification of the above-mentioned defects.

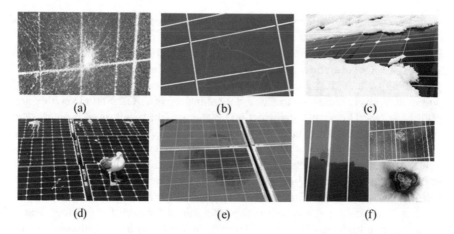

Fig. 1 Solar panels with defects—**a** Broken panel, **b** Cracked panel, **c** Panel with snow, **d** Panel with bird droppings, **e** Panel with dust, **f** Panel with hotspots

2 Related Work and Contributions

Some methods for the fault diagnosis of photovoltaic (PV) systems have been proposed. Rodriguez et al. [1] presented an inspection system called as Cell Doctor that employs ultra-modern techniques that discovers and categorizes defects in photovoltaic cells. The proposed diagnosis and therapeutic process helps in defect isolation. The automated process can be incorporated as part of the manufacturing process. A robotic arm moves the solar cells to an Electroluminescence workspace which captures the images of the panels and provides the necessary diagnostics. A combination of techniques are deployed that constitutes Principal Component Analysis, Random forest classifier, Gabor filters in tandem with various image pre-processing methods helps in identification of various defects in the PV system. A dataset of monocrystalline PV module images was used as test data. The diagnosis by Cell doctor proved to be effective and achieved an accuracy and recall of 90% for detection of cracks, area defects and interruptions. Fu et al. [2] proposed a machine vision-based detection scheme for multi-crystalline PV modules that can detect multi-crossed cracks. The periodic noise is handled effectively by an improved filtering mechanism which simultaneously retains the coherence of the crack signal. The crack features are extracted using a special mesh-shaped kernel filter that exhibits convolutional properties. The features are extracted at low contrast and in the habitation of a heterogenous background. The missing information from the mid portion of the cracks is reconstructed using the above method that relies on the orientation of mask patterns. While compared with existing mechanisms, numerical results have proved that the proposed framework is found to be extremely robust and has higher efficiency in terms of detection of cracks.

Haba et al. [3] proposed a Machine learning framework that identifies the possible deterioration of functioning of photovoltaic panels. Two key factors are considered while developing and validating the model. Data collected from the control system of the solar panels and data obtained from weather predictions were used for validation of the model. The model focusses on experimental results obtained when the solar panels are covered with snow. However, the model may be extended to other parameters such as dust, cracks and hotspots in the near future. Hwang et al. [4] proposed a novel framework that uses a combination of ART2 Neural network and Multilayer Neural Network for detecting the faults in the panels used in solar street lights. The open-circuit voltage is given as an input for the above hybrid network which helps in detecting the faults in the solar panels deployed as part of the street light. The prediction of faults using this novel method reduces the maintenance cost of the solar powered street light model. Experimental results on real time data have verified the performance of the system and proved its efficiency.

Li et al. [5] designed a pattern recognition model for identifying defects that is based on deep learning. The images are obtained with the aid of unmanned aerial vehicles (UAV). The classification of various defects in PV module is performed by Convolutional Neural networks. The various deep features of the images that are obtained aerially are extracted by CNN. When large scale PV farms are taken into consideration, the proposed deep learning model improves the quality of inspection and assessment of solar panels extensively. The proposed framework works more efficiently when compared with existing models. Kim et al. [6] developed an algorithm which detects defective solar cells using computer vision and captured out the meaningful outcome by analysing the result of the experiment. The use of UAV and the thermal camera can reduce the cost and improve the efficiency of maintenance by minimizing human labour. The defective solar cells in large solar farms can be easily detected by mapping the small and high-resolution thermal images taken from the autonomous drone flying with GPS.

Lee [7] put forward a real-time framework that involved UAVs, thermal camera and high resolution RGB camera for detecting faults in solar panels. The UAV is equipped with the thermal camera that captures the faulty areas of the panel. The high resolution RGB camera records the position of the PV modules and the array. The features detected using the thermal camera helps in identifying the failure of the photo voltaic cells. The suggested framework was tested in a solar plant to establish the practical applicability of the model. Tsanakas et al. [11] proposed a novel technique that involved thermal image processing and canny edge detector tools for diagnosis of hotspots. Thermal images of photo voltaic modules obtained during infrared thermal imaging were taken as input and the proposed hybrid technique is applied to it. The innovative hybrid approach yielded better results with detection of hotspot formations in defective solar cells. Peng Xu et al. [12] suggested a framework based on electroluminescence (EL) technology and image processing for detecting hairline cracks in PV modules. Forward bias voltage is applied to the PV modules. In the next step enormous quantity of non-equilibrium carriers is inserted into PV modules from the diffusion region which emits photons. These photons are captured by high-definition CCD cameras and an image is thus formed. The brightness of the captured image is proportional to minority carrier diffusion length and current density. If the minority carrier diffusion length is relatively low, there may be defects, which results in a relatively dark image. On analysing the EL image, it was found that hairline cracks are identified with better accuracy.

3 Preliminaries

3.1 Convolutional Neural Network

Convolutional Neural Networks has the ability to perform feature extraction. This ability is not available with normal neural networks or neural networks that are recurrent in nature. The CNN architecture has two distinct functionalities namely feature extraction and classification. Feature extraction deals with obtaining the relevant distinct section of the input and apply various levels of convolution which ultimately helps in reducing the size of the source input drastically. While reduction of size naturally involves losing the resolution of the images, convolution makes sure that the depth of the image is increased to such an extent that it makes it more accurate for the Neural network to classify the input image based on the training provided. The various key terminologies are discussed in brief as given below:

Convolution Layer: It refers to the application of numerous filters to the input solar panel images which ultimately results in the activation. The filter is applied repeatedly on the input solar panel images. The application of the filter results in a collection of activation maps referred as a feature map. The detected feature detects the defects in the solar which is indicated by the location and strengths of the feature map. The output of the convolution layer is an activation which happens as a result of the application of the kernel to the solar panel source image.

Feature Map: When the same kernel is applied repeatedly to the input solar panel image, a feature map is generated. Feature maps are used to identify the key areas of the input image. The size of the feature map can be computed as follows:

$$M_d = [I_s - K_s] + 1 \tag{1}$$

where,

M_d—Dimension of the Feature Map.

I_s—Size of the Input Pixel.

K_s—Size of the Kernel/Filter.

The architecture of a convolutional neural network for detecting defects in a faulty solar panel is provided (Fig. 2):

Stride: It controls the number of right shifts that should be applied for moving the filter over the actual image. By default, the stride for any filter is set to 1. The stride value has to be kept to a bare minimum so as to reduce loss of critical information. Stride is denoted by S. Thus, Eq. (1) can be rewritten as follows:

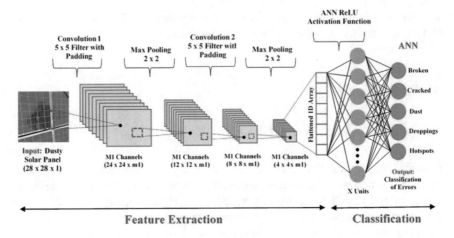

Fig. 2 CNN Architecture for feature extraction and Classification of PV module defects

$$M_d = \left[\frac{I_s - K_s}{S}\right] + 1 \tag{2}$$

For a 5×5 input matrix and a 3×3 kernel, when stride is set to 1, the dimension of the feature map will be a 3×3 matrix. For a stride value of 2, the dimension of the feature map will be a 2×2 matrix.

Padding: In order to match dimensions of the input image and the generated feature maps, padding is used. Padding adds zeros or ones on all sides of the matrix of the input image. Padding is denoted by P. After padding, Eq. (2) can be rewritten as follows:

$$M_d = \left[\frac{I_s - K_s + 2P}{S}\right] + 1 \tag{3}$$

Re-Lu: It stands for Rectified Linear activation Unit. Neural networks use this function to introduce non-linearity which forwards the output if positive or else will discard it with a zero value. The activation function is derived as follows:

$$b = max(0, a) \tag{4}$$

Since the activation function does not involve heavy computation, the model takes relatively less time to train itself.

4 DenseNet Architecture for Defect Detection in Solar Panels

DenseNet is an extended version of ResNet that helps in feature extraction and image classification. There are a few basic differences between DenseNet and ResNet which makes it more powerful and efficient. In ResNet, the shallow layers are merged with the deeper layers by additive property whereas in DenseNet it is replaced by concatenation. The difference between CNN, ResNet and DenseNet is tabulated as follows (Table 2):

The uniqueness of DenseNet is that every layer is interconnected. Feature maps of shallow layers are given as input for deeper layers of the network. Inside DenseNet, the feature maps from previous layers are concatenated with those of subsequent layers. Once the network is trained, the final prediction is made on the inputs from all activation maps available from the entire network (Fig. 3).

Even though the dimensions of the feature maps within the block are similar, the filters that are used within the blocks are unique. Batch normalization is handled by transition layers. Down-sampling between blocks are achieved using batch normalization. Growth rate refers to the increase in output channels in comparison with

Table 2 Comparative study of CNN, RESNET AND DENSENET

Type of network	Input	Output G(x)	Building block of F(x)	No of connections for L layers	Connection between layers
CNN	x	F(x)	Convolution + Relu	L	Direct
ResNet	x	F(x) + x	BatchNorm + Convolution + Relu	L	Additive (+)
DenseNet	x	[F(x), x]	BatchNorm + Convolution + Relu + Dropout (Optional)	L (L + 1)/2	Concatenation (·)

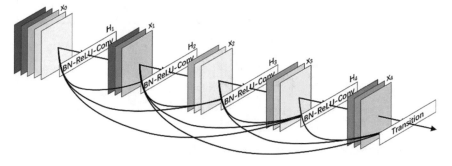

Fig. 3 A single unit of Dense Block within DenseNet

the total count of input channels. Growth rate is controlled by convolution block channels.

Batch Normalization

It refers to the process by which deep neural networks are added with additional layers to make it faster and reliable. The inputs from the previous layer are normalized by the new layer. Normalization occurs for batches of input and hence the name BatchNorm. The training epochs required for training are decreased through batch normalization which in turn stabilizes the learning process of the deep neural network. BatchNorm plays a vital role in CNN, ResNet and DenseNet.

DenseNet Architecture

DenseNet is a classic network where the composite functions are used to insert the output of earlier layers as an input into deeper layers. As the name itself implies the composite operation has 4 different functions associated with it. Each operation has a convolution layer, a pooling layer, batchNorm and a ReL unit. As mentioned earlier, there are L(L + 1)/2 direct connections in a DenseNet. Here L denotes the total count of layers in the DenseNet architecture (Fig. 4 and Table 3).

Some of the versions of DenseNet that are commonly used are DenseNet-121, DenseNet-160, DenseNet-201. The number of layers in the network is represented by the number associated with each DenseNet. The number of layers is computed as follows:

$$D_L = C_L P_L + (T_{L1} + T_{L2} + \cdots + T_{Ln}) * B_L \tag{6}$$

where,

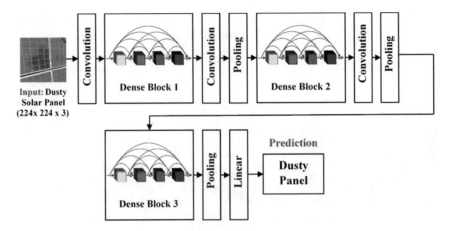

Fig. 4 DenseNet architecture for detect defection in solar panels

Table 3 Procedure for DenseNet

Procedure DenseNet
Input: *Solar panel with Defects, Training Set T and Testing Set T´*
Step 1: *Performs 2-Dimensional Convolution with 64 kernels with a stride of 2*
Step 2: *Output of 2-D Convolution given as input to Dense block*
Step 3: *Each Dense block Consists of 3 × 3 Convolution, BatchNorm, ReL Unit and transition layer. Concatenate the Skip connections within the Dense block*
Step 4: *Output of Step 3 is provided as input to 3 × 3 convolution*
Step 5: Output of Convolution is provided as input to pooling which is turn is connected to the next Desne block
Step 6: *Repeat steps 3, 4 and 5 till dense blocks are exhausted*
Step 7: Perform global average pooling before flattening the output into a 1-Dimensional array
Output: Type of defect in Solar panel is predicted with high accuracy

D_L—No of layers.

C_L—Convolution layer.

P_L—Pooling layers.

$T_{L1}, T_{L2},..., T_{Ln}$—Transition layers.

$Conv_L$—Convolution Layers.

B_L—No of Dense Blocks.

DenseNet-121 refers to a network that has five convolution and 5 pooling layers, three transition layers, one classification layer and 2 dense blocks. The total number of layers can be computed using Eq. (6).

The vanishing gradient problem is effectively handled by DenseNet. In addition, DenseNet provides certain additional features that helps in reuse of feature maps and also brings down the count of parameters drastically. The results achieved in this paper are computed using a variant of DenseNet architecture. Results have proved that the network trains with lesser datasets more effectively and the prediction of the defects in solar panels are more accurate when compared with previous versions of deep learning algorithms.

5 Experimental Results and Analysis

Experimental results are computed using TensorFlow on Windows 10 platform. TensorFlow is an open-source tool, that helps developers to build machine learning based applications. Python is used as the front-end for TensorFlow. The DenseNet architecture is initially provided with a learning rate of 0.0001 (denoted by λ).

Dataset

The PV module dataset constitutes 500 samples of 192 × 192 pixel images taken from a residential complex using high resolution cameras. Distortion issues that occur while capturing images are eliminated. The dataset is a diverse collection of photovoltaic module images that has various defects associated with it. The defects taken into consideration affects the performance of photovoltaic modules and are extrinsic in nature. Table 5 labels the dataset in accordance with the defect associated with it (Table 4).

In this paper dust and bird dropping defects are our area of concern. The proposed architecture detects these defects with high accuracy when compared to existing systems.

Qualitative Analysis

Ground Truth: The results of the model are checked again the real-world scenarios in terms of accuracy. It is carried out in the premises through physical inspections where the solar cells are located. The following table delineates the ground truth of solar panels with dust and bird droppings.

Once the test data were used to perform the classification, the predictions are evaluated on the basis of a confusion matrix. Four crucial parameters are used to calculate the performance of the DenseNet classification as given in Table 6.

Experimental results must ensure the fact that maximization of true positive and true negative values and minimization of false positive and false negative values. Based on these four values it is possible to calculate the performance of the classification by the network.

There are five important parameters as given below:

Accuracy: It is defined as the ratio between observations that are correctly predicted and the total number of observations. It is calculated using the formula given below:

$$Accuracy = \frac{TP + TN}{TP + FP + FN + TN} \tag{7}$$

Table 4 Defect-wise classification of datasets

Module type	No defects	Faded	Broken	Cracked	Droppings	Dust	Hotspots
Monocrystalline	78	84	80	93	50	65	50

Table 5 Ground truth for identification of defective panels

Defects in panels	Ground truth
No defects (Normal)	93.52
Panel with bird droppings	93.52
Dusty panel	93.52

Table 6 Classification parameters for confusion matrix

Actual classification		Predicted classification	
		Yes	No
	Yes	True positive	False negative
	No	False positive	True negative

Precision: It is defined as the ratio between positive observations that are correctly predicted and total number of positive observations predicted. It is calculated using the formula given below:

$$Precision = \frac{TP}{TP + FP} \tag{8}$$

Recall (Sensitivity): It is defined as the ratio between positive observations thar are correctly predicted and total observations. It is calculated using the formula given below:

$$Recall = \frac{TP}{TP + FN} \tag{9}$$

F1 score: It is defined as the weighted average of precision and recall. All false values are considered for calculating the score. When the distribution if classes is uneven, this parameter is more appropriate when compared to accuracy.

$$F1 = 2 * \frac{(Recall * Precision)}{(Recall + Precision)} \tag{10}$$

Specificity: It is an ML metric that identifies the quantity of negative results that are identified correctly. It is also referred to as false positive rate

$$Specificity = \frac{TN}{TN + FP} \tag{11}$$

The performance of the DenseNet model is evaluated with the help of these metrics. A Deep learning algorithm was implemented on real time data to evaluate the efficiency of the fault detection system for solar panels. The results of the application of DenseNet architecture on normal and defective solar panel are shown in Figs. 5,

Fig. 5 Solar Panels without defects—**a** Input, **b** Ground truth, **c** Predicted output, **d** Predicted accuracy

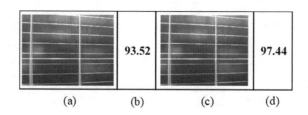

(a) (b) (c) (d)

Fig. 6 Solar panels with
dust defects—**a** Input, **b**
Ground truth, **c** Predicted
output, **d** Predicted accuracy

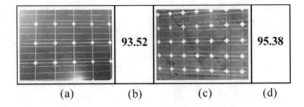

                    (a)   (b)   (c)   (d)

Fig. 7 Solar panels with
bird droppings—**a** Input, **b**
Ground truth, **c** Predicted
output, **d** Predicted accuracy

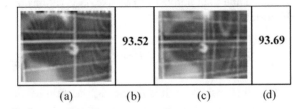

                    (a)   (b)   (c)   (d)

Table 7 Observed parametric values for performance evaluation of defects

Type of defect	Number of predictions				
	No of samples observed	TP	TN	FP	FN
No defects (Normal)	78	65	11	1	1
Panel with bird droppings	50	44	3	1	2
Dusty panel	65	57	5	1	2

6 and 7. The results compare the ground truth of the panels with their predicted accuracy.

From the results of the experiment, the following numerical results are derived. A total of 193 samples are classified. The following table denotes the distribution of predicted true and false values obtained from the confusion matrix (Table 7).

The values provided in table are used to calculate the performance of the classification made by DenseNet. These values prove that the DenseNet provides accurate prediction when compared to the ground truth (Table 8).

The prediction accuracy of DenseNet stands at 0.9744 for panels without defects, 0.94 for panels with bird droppings and 0.9538 for dusty panels. On observing the above numerical results, DenseNet achieves an average approximate prediction accuracy of 95.6 which is comparably high than the ground truth value. Precision denotes

Table 8 Performance evaluation of defective and non-defective solar panels

Type of defects/parameters	Accuracy	Precision	Recall	F1	Specificity
No defects (Normal)	0.9744	0.9848	0.9848	0.9848	0.9167
Panel with bird droppings	0.94	0.9778	0.9565	0.967	0.75
Dusty panel	0.9538	0.9828	0.9661	0.9744	0.8333

the low positives of the predictions made by the proposed model. The average precision stands at 98.18% which is highly desirable. Recall, F1 and specificity values demonstrate that DenseNet provides better predictions with relatively lower training datasets. Thus, it is evident that DenseNet is more accurate in prediction of fault in solar panels than existing deep learning models.

Performance of DenseNet Deep Learning Model

In a Deep neural network when the entire dataset is passed forward and backward once completely, it indicates that one epoch is completed. Larger datasets are segregated into smaller epoch batches since the model cannot accommodate larger datasets at one instance. It is advisable to choose optimal number of epochs during training and testing.

The accuracy and loss incurred in the training and testing the DenseNet model are represented graphically. Experiment_X_1 denotes the training data and Experiment_X_2 denotes the testing data. Figures 8 and 9 graphically represents the training and validation accuracy between training and testing data. It can be observed that there is a minimal difference is the curves between training accuracy and validation accuracy. This indicates that the model does not overfit or underfit.

Figures 10 and 11 graphically represents the training and validation losses between training and testing data. It can be observed that there is a minimal difference is the curves between training loss and validation loss. This indicates that the model performs optimally with minimum training and testing errors. Thus, DenseNet is

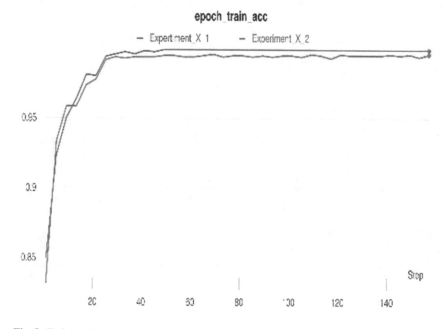

Fig. 8 Training Accuracy

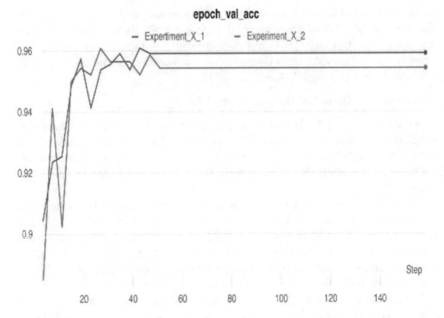

Fig. 9 Validation Accuracy

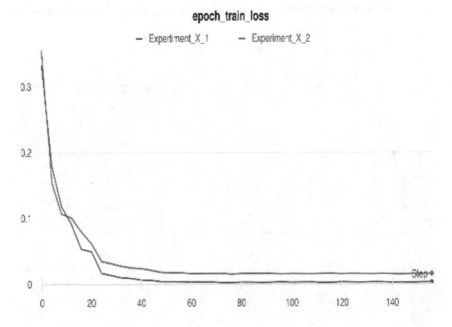

Fig. 10 Training Loss

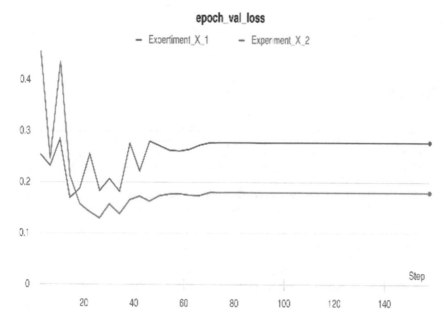

Fig. 11 Validation Loss

considered as one of the best deep learning model which can provide the best fit with minimum number of datasets used for training and validation.

6 Conclusion

The most significant and reliable source of clean energy is derived from Solar cells. Undeterred production of solar energy needs periodic detection of defects and maintenance of photovoltaic modules. This paper presents a novel extension of CNN called DenseNet for detection of defects in solar panels. DenseNet is evaluated against a real-time dataset of Photovoltaic modules from a residential complex. The architecture is equipped with 2D convolutions and Dense blocks that eventually helps in lossless feature extraction. The size and complexity of the network is drastically reduced while being more efficient in terms of prediction.

Tensorflow computations have shown enormous improvement in terms of prediction accuracy, recall and precision. Experimental results on limited datasets have proved the prediction of the DensNet model to be more accurate and robust and using the extended deep learning approach. The accuracy can still be tweaked by increasing the training dataset provided to the model. Adopting the DenseNet architecture it has been proved that it is more efficient than CNN and ResNet-50. In future the model can be extended to accommodate all possible detection of defects thus expanding the scope of the current proposal.

References

1. Rodriguez A, Gonzalez C, Fernandez A et al (2021) Automatic solar cell diagnosis and treatment. J Intell Manuf 32:1163–1172. https://doi.org/10.1007/s10845-020-01642-6
2. Fu Y, Ma X, Zhou H (2021) Automatic detection of multi-crossing crack defects in multi-crystalline solar cells based on machine vision. Mach Vis Appl 32:60. https://doi.org/10.1007/s00138-021-01183-9
3. Haba C (2019) Monitoring solar panels using machine learning techniques. In: 2019 8th international conference on modern power systems (MPS), pp 1–6. https://doi.org/10.1109/MPS.2019.8759651
4. Hwang H-R, Kim B-S, Cho T-H, Lee I-S (2019) Implementation of a fault diagnosis system using neural networks for solar panel. Int J Control Autom Syst 17. https://doi.org/10.1007/s12555-018-0153-3
5. Li X, Yang Q, Lou Z, Yan W (2019) Deep learning based module defect analysis for large-scale photovoltaic farms. IEEE Trans Energy Convers 34(1):520–529. https://doi.org/10.1109/TEC.2018.2873358
6. Kim K, Choi Y, Shim K, Jeon H, Commerford J, Matson ET (2019) Analyzing the range of angles of a solar panel to detect defective cells, using a UAV. Third IEEE Int Conf Robot Comput (IRC) 2019:471–476. https://doi.org/10.1109/IRC.2019.00099
7. Lee S, An KE, Jeon BD, Cho KY, Lee SJ, Seo D (2018) Detecting faulty solar panels based on thermal image processing. IEEE Int Conf Consum Electron (ICCE) 2018:1–2. https://doi.org/10.1109/ICCE.2018.8326228
8. Affonso C, Rossi ALD, Vieira FHA, de Carvalho ACPDLF (2017) Deep learning for biological image classification. Expert Syst Appl 85:114–122. ISSN 0957–4174, https://doi.org/10.1016/j.eswa.2017.05.039
9. Salamanca S, Merchán P, Garcia I (2017) On the detection of solar panels by image processing techniques, pp 478–483. https://doi.org/10.1109/MED.2017.7984163
10. Kogler A, Traxler P (2017) Health monitoring of large amounts of photovoltaic systems: a case study, pp 385–389. https://doi.org/10.1145/3151759.3151828
11. Tsanakas I (John), Chrysostomou D, Botsaris P, Gasteratos A (2015) Fault diagnosis of photovoltaic modules through image processing and canny edge detection on field thermographic measurements. Int J Sustain Energy 34:351–372. https://doi.org/10.1080/14786451.2013.826223
12. Xu P, Zhou W, Fei M (2014) Detection methods for micro-cracked defects of photovoltaic modules based on machine vision. In: 2014 IEEE 3rd international conference on cloud computing and intelligence systems, pp 609–613. https://doi.org/10.1109/CCIS.2014.7175807
13. Alam MK, Khan FH, Johnson J, Flicker J (2013) PV faults: overview, modeling, prevention and detection techniques. In: 2013 IEEE 14th workshop on control and modeling for power electronics (COMPEL), pp 1–7. https://doi.org/10.1109/COMPEL.2013.6626400
14. Lorenzo E, Moretón R, Luque I (2014) Dust effects on PV array performance: in-field observations with non-uniform patterns. Prog Photovolt Res Appl 22:666–670
15. Chiou Y-C, Liu J-Z, Liang Y-T (2011) Micro crack detection of multi-crystalline silicon solar wafer using machine vision techniques. Sens Rev 31:154–165. https://doi.org/10.1108/02602281111110013

Multimodal Biometric Authentication Using Watermarking Technique

C. Vensila and A. Boyed Wesley

1 Introduction

A biometric system is a biometric identity management system that is used to authenticate typical individuals. Biometric devices are now used in a variety of applications, including banks, homes, mobile phones, government protection areas, and so on. Biometric recognition systems (BIS) measure and verify biological characteristics of individuals (such as fingers, feet, hands, teeth, irises, faces, voices, gaits, retinas, ears, signatures veins, typing styles, DNA [1] and odours). Individual feature values are extracted and stored in a biometric database or biometric models for biometric identification. This database or models are used to classify individuals for checking [2].

Unimodal and multimodal BIS are two forms of BIS. Just one biometric characteristic of the human identification is used in a unimodal BIS [3]. Unimodal BIS has some disadvantages, including a maximum rate of spoofing, uniqueness, maximum error rate, noise and non-universality. Multi-modal BIS are now recommended to address the shortcomings of Uni-modal BIS, as they increase accuracy and population coverage. This method combines more features from each biometric to produce improved authentication results [4].

Face and iris biometrics, as well as face and fingerprint biometrics, are used in multimodal biometric systems. Spoofing attacks are more difficult to detect in multimodal systems [5]. The most important reason behind the multi-modal BS is to increase the recognition rate [6]. As opposed to unimodal systems, multimodal systems have minimum error rates and maximum accuracy [7]. As a result, multimodal systems have been used in a more biometric applications, including the Department of Homeland Security's US-VISIT, e-commerce, the FBI's Next Generation Identification (NGI), passports, the Indian government's UID law enforcement, smart

C. Vensila (✉) · A. B. Wesley
Department of Computer Science, Nesamony Memorial Christian College, Marthandam Affiliated to Manonmaniam Sundaranar University, Abishekapatti, Tirunelveli, TN 627012, India

© The Author(s), under exclusive license to Springer Nature Singapore Pte Ltd. 2022

U. P. Rao et al. (eds.), *Security, Privacy and Data Analytics*, Lecture Notes in Electrical Engineering 848, https://doi.org/10.1007/978-981-16-9089-1_7

cards, and visa etc,. Since the device stores numerous biometric modalities of every user, multimodal systems have a higher requirement for integrity and privacy.

In multimodal biometric systems, watermarking techniques have been used to authenticate and secure biometric data, as well as improve recognition accuracy. Watermarking is a method of safely inserting data in an image by concealing data in the spatial or transform domains. By modifying coefficients of a frequency domain image created using a transform such as the Discrete Wavelet Transform (DWT), or the Discrete Cosine Transform (DCT) data is embedded in the transform domain. In comparison to transform domain counterparts, spatial domain methods [8] can conceal data in host images imperceptibly, but they lack vigorousness and are susceptible to frequency attacks (Median, filtering, JPEG compression, blurring, JPEG compression etc.).

Transform domain approaches are resistant against frequency-based attacks because the distortions generated by the watermarks in the transform coefficients will outspread over every pixels in the spatial domain making alterations low noticeable. Watermarking of biometric images using a fusion of wavelet and Least Significant Bits (LSB) dependent watermarking approaches was suggested by Vatsa et al. [9]. Recently, watermarking strategies have been combined with evolutionary computation [10]. However, most of these approaches need the real image for watermark extraction, or the extracted watermark is of poor quality if the watermarked image is subjected to image processing attacks. In the suggested watermarking approach, Particle Swarm Optimization (PSO) is utilized to determine the optimal DCT coefficients block wise in an individual's face and finger vein image, where demographic data and the fingerprint image can be included. The extraction of Watermark does not necessitate use of the original image. The PSO goal feature is constructed as a combination of invisibility and robustness features, ensuring that the watermarked image has a good quality and that the watermark can be recovered even when the image is subjected to image processing problems. The findings of proposed method were compared to those of [11–18] in the experimental section. Higher values of numerous standard metrics illustrate the usefulness of the suggested methodology in keeping good watermarked image standard while preserving the feature set of real face, finger vein and fingerprint to be employed in multimodal biometric identification. The remainder of the article is organized as follows: Related works is explained in part 2, PSO is explained in part 3, a proposed methodology is presented in part 4, experimental data is discussed in part 5, and the article is concluded in Sect. 6.

2   Related Works

Kumar et al. [19] used PSO to develop an adaptive compound system of several biometrics to achieve the best execution performance for the essential level of safety. They have experimented with various biometric combinations (speech, face), (hand geometry, fingerprint) and (palmprint, iris). In comparison to the decision-level method, the experimental results demonstrated that the proposed score-level technique created relatively steady performance and required fewer iterations to produce superior performance.

Anzar and Sathidevi [20] suggested a PSO integration weight optimization approach based on d-prime statistics for determining the best weight factors for interrelated traits. In the score level fusion, voice biometrics and fingerprint were used. By calculating the ideal integration weight utilizing stochastic optimization approaches and Leave-One-Out Cross Validation procedures, the suggested method has lowered the False Acceptance Rate (FAR) under varied noise situations.

To safeguard biometric data, Zebbiche et al. [21] suggested a wavelet digital watermarking technique. They employed fingerprint images to conceal fingerprint minutiae points, ensuring that both hidden data and the host image were kept safe. Zebbiche et al. [22] proposed a watermarking-based technique to preserve fingerprint images by placing a watermark within the area of ridges acquired behind processing.

By masking biometric data in several images, Jain and Uludag [23] suggested an amplitude modulation based watermarking technique. Dong and Tan [24] proposed a watermarking strategy for protecting iris templates in iris identification systems by inserting them as a watermark in the cover image.

3   Particle Swarm Optimization

Particle Swarm Optimization is a computational technique to problem solving that attempts to generate a candidate solution in terms of a consistency metric iteratively. A PSO algorithm manages a swarm of particles, each of which represents a potential result. The fitness function measures the fitness values of all particles in order to optimize them, as well as the velocities that guide particle movement. Here Particle Swam Optimization is used to find best DCT coefficient block wise to be used for watermark embedding.

In the solution space, each particle keeps up with its coordinates, which are related to best result (fitness) of particles thus far, known as personal best, or prbest. Global best or glbest is the another best value that the PSO keeps up it in the particle's vicinity. The basic idea behind PSO is to iteratively accelerate every particle about its prbest and glbest positions, using a disorderly weighted acceleration w_a at every time point. At time step, let $x_{yz}(s)$ represent the location of particle i in depth $z = 1$, ..., n_x, in the search space. The following formula is used to calculate the location and acceleration of particle in the adjacent time step $s + 1$,

$$x_{yz}(s + 1) = x_{yz}(s) + v_{yz}(s + 1) \tag{1}$$

$$v_{yz}(s + 1) = w_a \times v_{yz}(s) + a_1 r_{1z}(s)[prbest_y - x_{yz}(s) + a_2 r_{2z}(t)[glbest - x_{yz}(s)] \tag{2}$$

where, v_{yz} (s) is the acceleration of particle y in depth $z = 1,...,n_x$ at time step s. x_{yz} (s) is the location of particle y in depth z at time step s, a_1 and a_2 are positive dispatch constants used to scale the beneficence of intellectual and social components respectively. r_{1z} (s), $r_{2z}(t) \sim U$ (0,1) are uniformly sampled random numbers in the range [0,1]. The personal best location prbest$_y$ related with particle y is the best location the particle has look in on because the first time step and glbest is the global best location at time step s. When a suitable result is identified or the highest number of iterations has been achieved, the process ends.

4 Proposed Technique

High performance protection systems are multi-model BS. This article introduces a new watermarking technique for the purpose of improve protection. The motivation for the proposed approach is to provide high security in multimodal biometric system and improve the performance. The proposed algorithm aims to watermark a uncolored face image and a uncolored finger vein image with a uncoloured fingerprint image and some demographic data. The suggested technique make sure-

1.   The invisibility of the watermark in the watermarked image
2.   Robustness, in the sense that the watermarked image would be of good quality even if it were subjected to image processing attack.
3.   At the receiver's end, the retrieved fingerprint, as well as watermarked face and finger vein images, are accurately identified, allowing for effective multimodal biometric authentication.

The phases of the watermarking methodology at the end of sender and the retrieval of image at the end of receiver are shown in Fig. 1. The steps are described in detail in the subsections that follow.

4.1   Image Enhancement

For image enhancement and sharpening, a High-Pass Filter (HPF) is used. When high-pitched are attenuated, the graphic quality of a picture suffers considerably and these filters emphasize fine information in the picture. Improving the image's high-frequency components, however improves the quality of image.

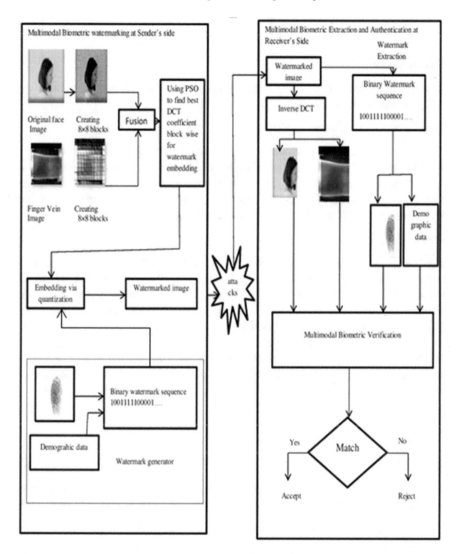

Fig. 1 Proposed Architecture of Multimodal Biometric Authentication

4.2 Extraction of Feature

This section extracts enhanced image features. Face and finger vein extraction is done using Empirical mode decomposition (EMD) feature value retrieval approach. Finger feature extraction is done using the Minutiae method.

4.3   Embedding of Watermark

Step 1: Reading images.

Take the secret demographic data and the face image F(i × j), finger vein image V(k × l), and watermark fingerprint image P(x × y).

Step 2: Watermark array generation.

The most important bit planes of an image contain the image's visual information. To get a order of bits W_m, take out four MSBs from every pixel in P and combine them. Append the demographic data to W by converting it to a binary bit sequence. The bits in W_m can be permuted for protection, and this watermark sequence of bits W_m is supposed to represent F and V. Length of W_m is denoted by len(W_m).

Step 3: Fusion.

The Fusion method joins the feature extracted values, combining two or more separate entities into new full entities. Feature level fusion (FLF) contains more biometric feature information. This FLF is used until a match is found, and it includes biometric information such as a person's face, veins, and fingerprint. Until matching, this FLF is performed, and it incorporates biometric data such as face, finger vein, and finger print. The feature level fusion is faster than the fusion of score level in terms of response time. The extracted features are concatenated by FLF. Function set concatenation increases the dimensionality of the fused feature vector. In the FLF, the following steps are followed.

- Feature vector Normalization
- Feature vector Fusion

Feature vector Normalization.

Face, finger vein, and fingerprint feature vectors are incompatible because of diversity in its own dimension and distribution. The feature vector is normalized to solve this problem.

Feature vector fusion.

The final fused vector is created by concatenating the feature vectors from the face, finger vein, and fingerprint. In Eq. (3), the Fusion vector is shown.

$$F_{vector} = [FA_1, FA_2, \ldots FA_n FV_1, FV_2, \ldots FV_n FPR_1, FPR_2, \ldots FPR_n$$
(3)

where FA_1, FA_2, ... FA_n, FV_1, FV_2, ... FV_n, and FPR_1, FPR_2, ... FPR_n are the normalized vectors of the face, finger vein, and fingerprint, respectively. Every person are identified using these fused vectors, which are saved in a database.

Step 4: Compute forward DCT.

Split the fused image into M × M sized blocks. Calculate the DCT for each image block, which is a signal decomposition technique that transfers images from the structural domain to the frequency domain. Let b be the overall blocks number. Compute the overall concealed watermark bits in every block using the formula $n = \frac{len(W)}{b}$.

Step 5: Applying PSO.

In order to achieve the optimum coefficients position for every block, some parameters for the PSO function must be set. The overall iterations can be adjusted to meet the appropriate degree of precision. Every particle in the swarm has a capacity of n since the number of coefficients required as the result in each DCT transformed block equals n. As a result, the starting population is formed by disorderly selecting n coefficients from all of the medium frequency coefficients in the block. The PSO module's goal function is then set to ensure that the worth and vigorousness of watermarked image are acceptable.

The Structural Similarity Index (SSIM), which is a generalized structure of the Universal Image Quality Index (UQI) is used to determine the worth of the watermarked image represent in Eq. (4).

$$SSIM(u, v) = \frac{(2\hat{u}\hat{v} + a_1)(2\sigma_{uv} + a_2)}{(\hat{u}^2 + \hat{v}^2 + 1)(\sigma_u^2 + \sigma_v^2 + a^2)} \tag{3}$$

where u and v are respective windows of identical size of the real and steganography images and $\hat{u}$ and $\hat{v}$ are the respective median of u and v, σ_u^2 and σ_v^2 are the respective dissimilarity of u and v, σ_{uv} is the discriminant of u and v, a_1 and a_2 are proper constants. The Human Visual System (HVS) is considered when calculating the consistency index. Normalized Correlation (NC) is used to compare the original and retrieved watermarks and represents the vigorousness of the watermarked image. It is described as:

$$NC = \frac{\sum_j w_{mj} w'_{mj}}{\sum_j w_{mj}^2} \tag{4}$$

where, W_m act as the inserted watermark and W'_m act as the retrieved watermark. The NC value can range from 0 to 1. If the NC value is nearer to one, the recovered watermark is more accurate. The NC value is evaluated after the watermarked block has been subjected to various attacks. Hence the goal function for PSO is determined as:

$$G.F = \left(1 - SSIM\left(b, b'\right)\right) + \beta(1 - NC) \tag{6}$$

where, β is a weighting constant and b and b′ are respective blocks in cover and watermarked images.

Step 6: Embedding of Watermark.

By quantizing the excellent coefficients (evaluated with PSO) in every block, the n bits from the watermark pattern P are sequentially inserted. The n bits from the watermark pattern P are consecutively inserted by quantizing the good coefficients (computed with PSO) in every block. D_c is the DCT coefficient's value and m_d be the modulus, the remainder re and the quotient Q_o respectively are given by Eq. (7)

$$Q_o = \frac{|D_c|}{m_d} \ and \ r_e = |D_c| mod \ m_d \tag{7}$$

To insert the binary data of the watermark pattern, the primary value D_c of the coefficient is altered to D'_c as follows:

If the watermark bit in the present input is set to:

$$r'_e = \frac{m_d}{4}$$

$$D_{cmin} = Q_o \times m_d + r'_e$$

$$D_{cmax} = (Q_o + 1) \times m_d + r'_e$$

If the watermark bit in the present input is set to 1:

$$r'_e = 3 \times \frac{m_d}{4}$$

$$D_{cmin} = (Q_o - 1) \times m_d + r'_e$$

$$D_{cmax} = Q_o \times m_d + r'_e$$

Let D_{cmin} and D_{cmax} be of the identical sign as Dc. Now modify Dc to Dc′

$$D'_c = \begin{cases} D_{cmin}, if(|D_{cmin} - D_c| \le |D_{cmax} - D_c|) \\ D_{cmax}, if(|D_{cmin} - D_c| > D_{cmax} - D_c|) \end{cases} \tag{8}$$

Step 7: Calculate the inverse DCT block by block.

After all of the watermark bits have been embedded, the watermarked image is created by applying inverse DCT to each image block separately.

4.4 Watermark Extraction

The reverse process can be used to extract the secret watermark fingerprint image as well as demographic data. The locations found out with PSO during the embedding phase are used in this process, and the modulus m_d is serves as the extraction key. The watermark pattern is retrieved by using the key in Eq. (9). Initially calculate the forward block by block DCT of the watermarked face and finger vein image. For every block, retrieve the coefficients based on the key. For every such coefficient D_c, let the retrieved watermark bit be W_m as:

$$W_m = \begin{cases} 1, if\,(|D_c| mod\, m_d \geq \frac{m_d}{2} \\ 0, if\,(|D_c| mod\, m_d < \frac{m_d}{2} \end{cases} \tag{9}$$

The reverse permutation transformation is applied after all the bits are merged. The fingerprint image and demographic data are created after the watermark pattern has been obtained.

5 Experimental Results

The suggested watermarking methodology was reviewed and compared to some of the most recent multimodal biometric authentication techniques [11, 12, 15], some of the most recent DCT based watermarking techniques [13, 14, 16] and some of the most recent hybrid watermarking techniques [17, 18]. The test fingerprint image dataset [25], test face images from CVL face images database [26] and test finger vein image from SDUMLA-HMT finger vein image database [27] were used in the tests. The findings are tabulated for four quality face images of size 516×516 and finger vein image as illustrate in Figs. 2a–d and 3e–h Using the suggested method, all of these images were utilized to conceal smaller fingerprint images of size 100×100, as illustrated in Fig. 4i–k, along with demographic data. The input face image and finger vein image are separated into 8×8 blocks, and PSO is applied to each block to obtain the best DCT coefficients.

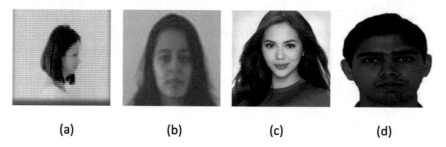

(a)　　　　　(b)　　　　　(c)　　　　　(d)

Fig. 2 Host Face images. **a** F_{11} **b** F_{12} **c** F_{13} **d** F_{14}

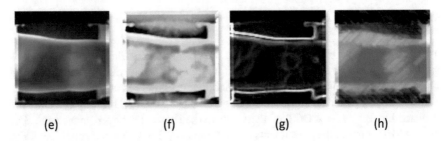

Fig. 3 Host Finger Vein images **e** V_{21} **f** V_{22} **g** V_{23} **h** V_{24}

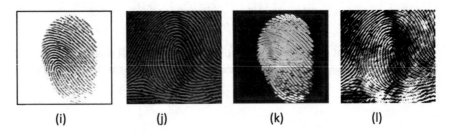

Fig. 4 Watermark fingerprints **i** I_{31} **j** I_{32} **k** I_{33} **l** I_{34}

Depending on the amount of watermark data that needs to be hidden, every block of a cover image is used to conceal 8–10 bits of the input watermark bit pattern. The value of md is set to 15 and the value of β is set to 0.5. The number of particles (ns) and the number of iterations are set to 115 and 100 respectively, in the PSO module. The value of the a1 and a2 constants in Eq. (2) are taken around about 2. The objective quantitative measurements used to analyze real and watermarked images are Structural Similarity Index (SSIM) and Peak Signal Noise Ratio (PSNR) (Eq. 4). The real and extracted watermarks are also compared using Normalized Correlation (NC) as indicated by Eq. 5. Table 1 shows the SSIM and PSNR values for cover and watermarked images for each approach. The proposed strategy clearly outperforms existing techniques due to the effectual goal function used by the PSO module and the effectual coefficient quantization carry out in the watermark embedding step. The PSNR and SSIM values for cover and watermarked images along with NC values for real and retrieved watermarks are listed in Table 2 for the suggested technique. These data are tabulated after the watermarked image has been subjected to different image processing attacks. The value of md in the embedding approach is set so that the watermarked face, finger vein image, and retrieved fingerprint image are of acceptable quality and preserve their individual features, allowing accurate verification (as specified by the NC values in Table 2).

Table 1 The quality indicator's values PSNR and SSIM were calculated by embedding the fingerprint images I_{31}, I_{32}, I_{33} and I_{34} in the matching host face images $F_{11}, F_{12}, F_{13}, F_{14}$ and Finger Vein images $V_{21}, V_{21}, V_{23}, V_{24}$ together with demographic data

Orginal image	Metrics	[11]	[12]	[13]	[14]	[15]	[16]	[17]	[18]	Proposed
F_{11} and V_{31}	PSNR	38.90	37.52	31.98	37.12	40.12	40.35	34.53	40.95	40.90
	SSIM	0.928	0.932	0.918	0.923	0.935	0.939	0.928	0.938	0.956
F_{12} and V_{32}	PSNR	39.40	38.72	32.95	37.66	40.92	40.94	32.86	40.94	40.98
	SSIM	0.939	0.940	0.911	0.932	0.957	0.960	0.925	0.956	0.965
F_{13} and V_{33}	PSNR	37.55	36.80	31.69	36.14	39.87	39.91	31.56	39.85	39.95
	SSIM	0.920	0.905	0.895	0.917	0.939	0.942	0.898	0.941	0.946
F_{14} and V_{34}	PSNR	39.20	39.31	33.88	38.02	41.31	41.32	35.63	41.35	41.39
	SSIM	0.941	0.939	0.925	0.922	0.959	0.962	0.937	0.959	0.966

Table 2 II. The quality indicator's values SSIM, NC and PSNR obtained after inserting the watermark I_{31} in the face image F_{11} and finger vein image V_{21} and exposing it to several image prcessing attacks

Attack	SSIM	NC	PSNR
Unattacked	0.9560	1.0000	41.01
Sharpen	0.8489	0.4210	32.92
Sharpen edges	0.9478	0.9756	39.99
Diffuse glow	0.8598	0.8447	35.05
Median filter	0.8521	0.4288	36.10
Unsharp mask	0.9533	0.9999	41.02
Blur	0.9290	0.9493	40.04
Salt & Pepper Noise	0.8173	0.8193	27.99

6 Conclusion

This article presents a multimodal biometric image watermarking strategy based on Particle Swarm Optimization (PSO) for concealing a fingerprint image as well as certain demographic data in the related face and finger vein images. The methodology was developed with the aim of enhancing recognition accuracy, minimizing bandwidth consumption and maintaining biometric data security and authentication. PSO chosen DCT coefficients of the face and finger Vein images were utilized to conceal fingerprint image and binarization of demographic data using the proposed approach. The performance of suggested technique was examined and compared to several previous multimodal biometric watermarking and DCT-based approaches. The improved values of quality metrics such as Structural Similarity Index (SSIM), Normalized Correlation (NC) and Peak signal noise ratio (PSNR) demonstrate the suggested technique is effective in preserving invisibility and acceptable watermarked image standard even when the amount of concealed data is large, as well as the experimental utility of biometric images.

References

1. Reid DA, Samangooei S, Chen C (2016) Soft biometrics for surveillance: an overview. In: Handbook of statistics. Elsevier, pp 327–352
2. Rathgeb C, Uhl A (2011) A survey on biometric cryptosystems and cancelable biometrics 25
3. Sanjekar PS, Patil JB (2013) An overview of multimodal biometrics. SIPIJ 4:57–64. https://doi.org/10.5121/sipij.2013.4105).
4. Kim YG, Shin KY, Lee EC, Park KR (2012) Multimodal biometric system based on the recognition of face and both Irises. Int J Adv Rob Syst 9:65
5. Ross A, Jain AK (2004) Multimodal biometrics: an overview
6. Oloyede MO, Hancke GP Unimodal and multimodal biometric sensing systems: a review. IEEE Access 4:7532–7555
7. Nagar A, Nandakumar K, Jain AK (2012) Multibiometric cryptosystems based on feature-Level fusion. IEEE Trans Inform Forensic Secur 7:255–268
8. Uludag U, Gunsel B, Ballan M (2001) A spatial method for watermarking of fingerprint images
9. Vatsa M, Singh R, Noore A (2006) Robust biometric image watermarking for fingerprint and face template protection. IEICE Electron Express 3:23–28
10. Wang Z, Sun X, Zhang D (2007) A novel watermarking scheme based on PSO algorithm
11. Ma B, Li C, Wang Y, Block (2010) Pyramid based adaptive quantization watermarking for multimodal. Biom Authentication
12. Edward S, Sumathi S, Malini RR (2011) Multimodal biometrics for authentication using DRM technique
13. Rohani M, Avanaki AN (2009) A watermarking method based on optimizing SSIM index by using PSO in DCT domain. In: 2009 14th international CSI computer conference 2009. IEEE, Tehran, Iran, pp 418–422
14. Lin SD, Shie S-C, Guo JY (2010) Improving the robustness of DCT-based image watermarking against JPEG compression. Comput Stand Interfaces 32:54–60
15. Bedi P, Bansal R (2012) Sehgal P Multimodal biometric authentication using PSO based watermarking. Procedia Technol 4:612–618
16. Bousnina N, Ghouzali S, Mikram M, Abdul W (2019) DTCWT-DCT watermarking method for multimodal biometric authentication
17. Dholu PA (2017) Multimodal biometric system using hybrid watermarking technique. Int J Eng Technol Sci Res
18. Dholu P, Suthar DAC (2018) A hybrid technique using DWT and SVD watermarking for multimodal biometric system. Int J Creative Res Thought
19. Kumar A, Kanhangad V, Zhang D (2010) A new framework for adaptive multimodal biometrics management. IEEE Trans Inform Forensic Secur (2010)
20. Anzar SM (2012) An efficient PSO optimized integration weight estimation using D-prime statistics for a multibiometric system. IJBB 2:31–42
21. Zebbiche K, Ghouti L, Khelifi F, Bouridane A (2006) Protecting fingerprint data using watermarking (2006)
22. Zebbiche K, Khelifi F, Bouridane A (2008) An efficient watermarking technique for the protection of fingerprint images. EURASIP J Inf Secur (2008)
23. Anil KJ, Uludag U (2003) Hiding biometric data. IEEE Trans Pattern Anal Mach Intell (2003)
24. Dong J, Tan T, Effects of watermarking on iris recognition performance. In: 10th International conference on control, automation, robotics and vision, pp 1156–1161. IEEE, Hanoi, Vietnam (2008)
25. BiometricsIdealTest. http://biometrics.idealtest.org/findDownloadDbByMode.do?mode=Fingerprint. Accessed 16 Apr 2021

26. Computer Vision Laboratory. http://www.lrv.fri.uni-lj.si/facedb.html. Accessed 16 Apr 2021
27. Finger Vein SDUMLA-HMT Database sample images. | Download Scientific Diagram. https://www.researchgate.net/figure/Finger-Vein-SDUMLA-HMT-Database-sample-images_fig2_341907498. Accessed 06 Sept 2021

Image Deblurring for CCTV Captured Images of Fast Moving Vehicles

Sahil Nande, Saail Ganesh, Santosh Krishnan, and Kalyani Pampattiwar

1 Introduction

Identification of vehicle owners and traffic control has become a significant problem in every country. Sometimes it becomes difficult to spot vehicle owners who violate traffic rules and drive too fast. Therefore, it is impossible to catch and punish people because the traffic personnel will not be ready to retrieve vehicle numbers from the moving vehicle because of its speed. License plate recognition is the most common technique for the vehicle identification process. Recognizing information from a digital image is efficient and reduces the work needed to be done by humans.

There is a need for an Image Deblur algorithm that can easily remove different blurs and give us a sharp noise-free image. A speed camera in the region of Durham in the United Kingdom caught over 100,000 vehicles overspeeding, and the cameras could not recognize over 25% of the drivers due to high speeds or camera shakes.

Capturing images of high-speed vehicles is an exigent task. Currently, speed cameras can take pictures with a delay of 50 ms. This delay causes blurry plates where we cannot determine the characters on these license plates, due to which most of the criminals are released.

2 Related Work

Image processing is an essential field for researching to get accurate information from the images using computer vision. We have considered various approaches to take a blurred image from different sources to get a good result in this approach.

S. Nande (✉) · S. Ganesh · S. Krishnan · K. Pampattiwar
S.I.E.S. Graduate School of Technology, Nerul, Navi Mumbai, Maharashtra, India
e-mail: saail.gurunath17@siesgst.ac.in

© The Author(s), under exclusive license to Springer Nature Singapore Pte Ltd. 2022
U. P. Rao et al. (eds.), *Security, Privacy and Data Analytics*, Lecture Notes
in Electrical Engineering 848, https://doi.org/10.1007/978-981-16-9089-1_8

Fig. 1 Classification of datasets

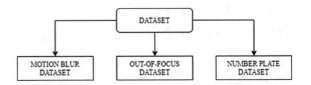

W. Yao and S. Rahardja proposed another system called dynamic threshold [1] for keyframe detection. In this real-time keyframe [2], the selection is made using a Dynamic threshold.

Chengtao Cai, An Liu, and Baolu Zhang proposed using a wiener filter [3] for deblurring the image. They analyzed the spectrum of the Fourier transform to estimate the purpose spread function of the blurred image and restore the image. The limitation in this approach is that the quality of the image was degraded after applying the filter.

Suphongsa Khetkeeree and Sompong Liangrocapart proposed a system called the Lucy Richardson [4] algorithm. The number of iterations was optimized to run the algorithm faster than the Wiener filter [3]. This system supported the modified Tikhonov regularization. The drawback of this approach is that only out-of-focus blur is considered, and the rest of all blurs are ignored.

3 Dataset

Our process begins with acquiring a large-scale dataset consisting of deblurred images and their blurred counterparts. A series of short-exposure frames are averaged from high-speed cameras such as a GoPro for generating motion-blurred images. We have a total of 3000 images for our Deblurring software [5]. For our dataset on license plate detection, we have images of cars with license plates. For the Recognition of characters from a license plate, we have images of different letters and characters (Fig. 1).

4 Proposed System Architecture

Our approach is divided into four sub-modules. The Key Frame Detection module provides its output to Image Deblurring, and the Image Deblurring module provides its output to the License plate Detection and Character Recognition module.

4.1 Key Frame Detection

The first module we use is Key Frame Detection. Katna automates the Key Frame extraction procedure and provides us with the most accurate frames from the video.

These frames given by the Katna module provide us with a compact summary of the video content. The frames are then selected based on their differences in LUV color spaces. It applies Brightness Score Filtering for the extracted frames. On the extracted frames, we use Entropy/Contrast Score Filtering. Using Image Histogram, we use K-Means Clustering of frames, and we select the best frames from the cluster based on the variance of Laplacian. The image gets repudiated if the variance falls below a certain threshold. It gives us a selected frame that contains a license plate.

4.2 Image Deblurring

We create a module that takes input as a blurry image downsampled from the input images at different sizes and produces corresponding sharp images. We approach this architecture by using a coarse-to-fine [6] strategy. We would be using U-NETS with RESNET Encoders. U-NETS encodes and decodes the images by upsampling and downsampling. Different levels of information are combined by using skip connections between feature maps. Each Resblock [6] contains two convolutional layers with the same kernel size. Decoder ResBlocks are similar to Encoder ResBlocks, but we increase the spatial and feature size while decoding (Figs. 2 and 3).

As we downsample the image and then upsample the image, we get a U-shaped structure. This provides us with the output on the expanding part of the diagram. Successive convolutions improve the detail when we double the dimensions. The original image is also added to the final ResBlocks with skips to allow final computations.

Fig. 2 Image Deblurring Architecture

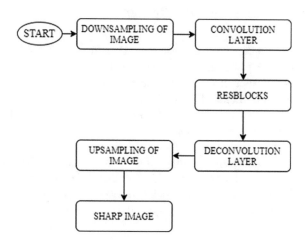

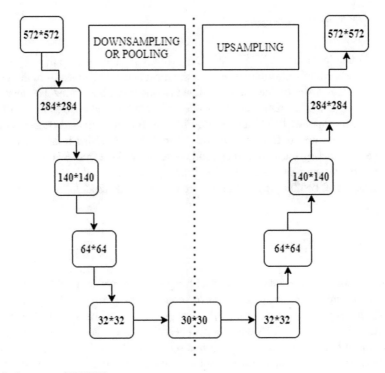

Fig. 3 Structure of U-NETS

We have restricted the image size to be of dimensions 256 * 256. The ResBlocks are separated into different groups, each group having a different feature size. We use Rectified Linear Unit(ReLU) as an activation function for all layers.

4.3 License Plate Detection

Our approach for License Plate Detection begins with preprocessing of the dataset. Our dataset consists of images that contain license plates and also have annotated coordinates of the license plates. These are the bounding boxes that we will use to train our model. They contain the coordinates of license plates for the given image. We would be using a YOLOv4 object detection model with weights we trained for License plate detection.

An object detector such as YOLOv4 takes an image as an input and compresses the features down through a CNN backbone [7]. We use our YOLOv4 model with the base of CSPDarknet53. The DenseNet separates the feature map of the base layer through a dense block and sends it on to the next stage. Object Detection then combines features formed in the backbone of Darknet53 to prepare for the detection

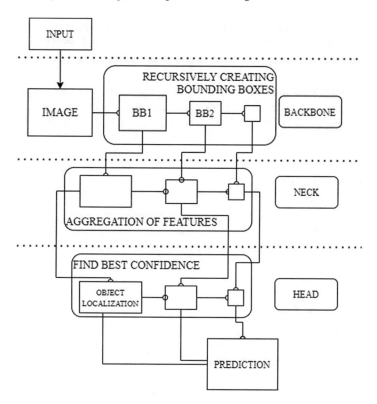

Fig. 4 License Plate Detection Architecture

step. This is called Feature Aggregation [7] and is done at the YOLOv4 neck. We use a PANet [8] for feature aggregation.

YOLOv4 also allows data augmentation without adding inference time in production. These techniques improve the accuracy and proportion of the training set to show the model to scenarios that might have otherwise been unseen. YOLOv4 is an anchor-based detection model [7]. Each anchor box calculates which bounding bo x has the very best overlap divided by non-overlap, named Intersection-Over-Union (IOU). YOLOv4 uses DropBlock Regulation [7] as an activation function (Fig. 4).

4.4 License Plate Characters Recognition

There is a two-step process for the recognition of characters from the license plate. We convert the RGB colorspace of the image to GRAY color space. As the image is now in GRAY color space, we can use the Thresholding technique to convert it to a binary image. We use Otsu's Binarization [9] with Binary Thresholding for calculating the threshold. We find the binary image using this threshold. After generating a binary image, we erode the boundaries away from the foreground objects and dilate the necessary regions. It would detect a change in image color and mark it as a contour. After finding all the contours, we construct a complete hierarchy of nested contours [9].

Character Recognition is done using a neural network model that reads images and inputs characters from the image. We train our model using AdamOptimizer [9]. We use Rectified Linear Unit (ReLU) as an activation function for all layers.

5   Implementation

Our Experiments are conducted on a PC with Intel i5 CPU and AMD Ryzen 4000 series. We have trained our model on Google Colaboratory with a hardware accelerator with 16 GB NVIDIA Tesla P100 GPU.

5.1   Key Frame Detection

For keyframe detection, we have implemented three different modules. To check the models' accuracy, we run a recorded video to see the results on threshold selection, local maxima, and Katna (Fig. 5).

As the above results are considered, it shows that the Katna modules give an accurate keyframe above all the other modules than the other two. Katna chooses a frame that gives the critical information within the image with a bit of blur. Katna

(a)Threshold   (b)Local Maxima   (c)Katna

Fig. 5 Key Frame Detection using various methods

Fig. 6 Wiener Filter Algorithm (LEFT) and Lucy Richardson Algorithm (RIGHT)

frames provide us with the foremost accurate and compact summary of the video content. Further, we use the architecture suggested in Sect. 4.1.

5.2 Image Deblurring

We tried to implement three different algorithms for the image deblurring part: Wiener filter [3], Lucy Richardson, and a Deep Learning algorithm using RESNETs (Fig. 6).

From the above results, we can conclude that our algorithm using RESNET gives the best results than the Wiener filter [3] and Lucy Richardson [4] algorithm. The Wiener filter calculates values of parameters by performing mathematical operations on Matrix. Lucy Richardson is better than the Wiener Filter in terms of runtime but is not accurate as to our neural network. The last model we would be using is U-NETS with RESNET Encoders. RESNETs is a CNN Architecture that is made up of residual blocks with skip connections. We would be using the architecture suggested in 4.2.

5.3 License Plate Detection

We design four different models for evaluating and testing which model is the best out of them. The first model we designed is using OpenCV. In the second model, we detect vehicles using a Histogram of Gradients with Linear SVM [10]. We group pixels into smaller cells. We compute all the gradient directions and group them into orientation bins. As HOG feature [10] extraction is time-consuming, we use the sliding window technique to check subregions of a frame for the license plate. The third model we used was a VGG16 model. We use a sequential model so that all the layers are arranged in a sequence. After following the VGG16 architecture, we flatten all the layers and send the data to Dense layers. We use a ReLU activation function for the same. The last model we have evaluated is the YOLOv4 architecture

Fig. 7 License plate detection (L-R): OpenCV, SVM-HOG, VGG16, YOLOv4

(a)Matching Characters to Dataset   (b)CNN

Fig. 8 License plate recognition

model. The first model detects the image with the use of masking. YOLOv4 works better than VGG16 and can detect license plates with higher accuracy than others (Fig. 7).

5.4 License Plate Recognition

We use three different models for the evaluation of Character recognition from the license plate. We first try to recognize characters by matching the characters to the dataset. We find the nearest match for the character. Our third model is a CNN architecture [9], where the dataset is queued for training in our recognition model. Further, we follow the architecture suggested in Sect. 4.4 (Figs. 8 and 9).

6 Results

See Fig. 9 and Tables 1 and 2.

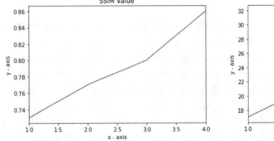

Fig. 9 SSIM and PSNR value plotting

Table 1 Image deblurring

Sr. no	Methods used	Values	
		SSIM	*PSNR*
1	Wiener filter	0.73	17.06
2	Lucy richardson	0.77	21.02
3	Blind image deconvolution [11]	0.80	26.76
4	Using RESNET(Our Model)	0.86	31.98

Table 2 License plate detection

Sr. no	Method used	Accuracy (%)
1	SVM with HOG features [12]	84.45
2	VGG16	88.71
3	YOLOv4	91.06

7 Conclusion

Different approaches were discussed and implemented in this project to get the best possible results for license plate detection. We implemented a Katna module that selects the best frame out of a video captured from a speed camera. The deblurring is done with a RESNET model train and tested to give the finest non-blurry image out of a distorted blur image. Our License Plate Detector trained on YOLOv4 crops the exact plate from an image. Thus, we have created a state-of-art project for license plate detection and recognition, which can be implemented on traffic lights and places where overspeeding is prohibited.

References

1. Yao W, Rahardja S (2010) Dynamic threshold based keyframe detection. In: 2010 5th IEEE conference on industrial electronics and applications, pp 2137–2141. https://doi.org/10.1109/ICIEA.2010.5516644
2. Singh M, Kaur A (2015) An efficient hybrid scheme for key frame extraction and text localization in video. In: 2015 International conference on advances in computing, communications and informatics (ICACCI), pp 1250–1254. https://doi.org/10.1109/ICACCI.2015.7275784
3. Cai C, Liu A, Zhang B (2016) Motion deblurring from a single image. In: 2016 IEEE 20th international conference on computer supported cooperative work in design (CSCWD), pp 406–410. https://doi.org/10.1109/CSCWD.2016.7566023
4. Khetkeeree S, Liangrocapart S (2019) Iterative image deblurring algorithm using complementary pair of filters. In: 2019 7th international electrical engineering congress (iEECON), 2019, pp 1–4. https://doi.org/10.1109/iEECON45304.2019.8939044
5. Nah S, Kim TH, Lee KM (2017) Deep multi-scale convolutional neural network for dynamic scene deblurring. IEEE conference on computer vision and pattern recognition (CVPR) 2017:257–265. https://doi.org/10.1109/CVPR.2017.35

6. Sun J, Cao W, Xu Z, Ponce J (2015) Learning a convolutional neural network for non-uniform motion blur removal. In: 2015 IEEE conference on computer vision and pattern recognition (CVPR), pp 769–777. https://doi.org/10.1109/CVPR.2015.7298677

7. Li. H, Wang P, Shen C (2017) Toward end-to-end car license plate detection and recognition with deep neural networks. IEEE Trans Intell Transp Syst. https://doi.org/10.1109/tits.2018.2847291

8. Liu S, Qi L, Qin H, Shi J, Jia J (2018) Path aggregation network for instance segmentation. IEEE/CVF conference on computer vision and pattern recognition 2018:8759–8768. https://doi.org/10.1109/CVPR.2018.00913

9. Yuan Y, Zou W, Zhao Y, Wang X, Hu X, Komodakis N (2017) A robust and efficient approach to license plate detection. IEEE Trans Image Process 26(3):1102–1114. https://doi.org/10.1109/TIP.2016.2631901

10. Khan M, Sharif M, Javed T, Akram M, Yasmin T (2017)License number plate recognition system using entropy based features selection approach with SVM. IET Image Process 12. https://doi.org/10.1049/iet-ipr.2017.0368

11. Singh et al S (2019) A novel approach for deblurring colored images using blind deconvolution algorithm. In: 2019 5th international conference on signal processing, computing and control (ISPCC), pp 108–113. https://doi.org/10.1109/ISPCC48220.2019.8988325

12. Dalal N, Triggs B (2005) Histograms of oriented gradients for human detection. In: 2005 IEEE computer society conference on computer vision and pattern recognition (CVPR'05), vol 1, pp 886–893. https://doi.org/10.1109/CVPR.2005.177

Detecting Stegomalware: Malicious Image Steganography and Its Intrusion in Windows

Vinita Verma⬤, Sunil K. Muttoo⬤, and V. B. Singh⬤

1 Introduction

Steganography, a technique to hide data within digital media, has primarily been used to communicate secret data, embed watermarks for copyright protection, etc. This practice, however, has trended into hiding the malware within digital media to evade detection. Such malware is known as stegomalware. Specifically, the popularity of seemingly innocuous digital images shows a high potential for the malicious use of image steganography. Images across the internet, social media, email attachments, or resources in the applications can be exploited to hide malicious code, configuration data, or URL to retrieve the code or other components from an external server [1]. Such images though stay undetected by intrusion detection systems or static analysis that typically lack analyzing the steganography in images and thus anything suspicious within images. Static analysis analyzes opcodes, control flow graphs, n-grams, etc., within the code without executing it. However, it fails to identify malicious components other than the code such as images and is thwarted by code obfuscation. Dynamic analysis unaffected by obfuscation executes the code to trace malign actions. This analysis is, however, un-scalable for large-scale detection being time- and resource-intensive. Alternatively, signature-based detection fails to detect unknown samples which contain new malicious patterns or signatures for every attack. These factors lead malware developers to a more secure obfuscation technique, a lucrative method of steganography, specifically image for hosting malware.

The malicious role of steganography is discussed in the McAfee 2017 report [2]. The years 2011–2017 witnessed steganographic threats [3]. According to the

V. Verma (✉) · S. K. Muttoo
Department of Computer Science, University of Delhi, Delhi, India

V. B. Singh
Department of Computer Science, Delhi College of Arts and Commerce, University of Delhi, Delhi, India

© The Author(s), under exclusive license to Springer Nature Singapore Pte Ltd. 2022
U. P. Rao et al. (eds.), *Security, Privacy and Data Analytics*, Lecture Notes in Electrical Engineering 848, https://doi.org/10.1007/978-981-16-9089-1_9

Criminal Use of Information Hiding (CUING) [4], which is an initiative launched in cooperation with Europol's European Cybercrime Centre, stegomalware with respect to the malware discovered between 2011 and 2016 hiked from 12% to 24%. A survey of node capture attack in wireless sensor networks [36] and an optimization technique [37] is presented to escalate its attacking efficiency.

The literature has discussed some methods to detect malicious image steganography. A method was proposed to find a URL [5] hidden in LSBs for all kinds of images. However, only the LSB hiding technique was considered. Anomalous data appended to GIF images [6] was detected based on locating the end of the file. DCT-based techniques [7], smart threshold, and anomaly correction were proposed against cyberattacks that exploit images and video streams, applicable for JPEG images and H.264 I-Frames. It resulted in 80% protection against cyberattacks with 25.74 dB PSNR for an aggressive attack configuration. Data gathering or kernel tracing-based [8] stegomalware detection was proposed. Its future scope, however, aims at a more programmatic approach for tracing execution patterns for stegomalware or specific covert channels. A study was performed on favicons [9], the icons associated with webpages or websites, using state-of-the-art steganalysis and features exploiting flat areas in them. It detected Vawtrak malware's steganography in favicons though steganalysis was not found the same as in natural images. It is discussed an image security technique using cryptography and steganography [38].

Many works have been discussed related to stegomalware for Android OS relative to Windows. Stegomalware for smartphones [10] was demonstrated via an app with malicious executable components within its assets. However, preliminary results of detection were not conclusive but revealed a considerable amount of data hidden in the app assets. A malicious Android application was hidden inside JPEG/PNG images [11] followed by storing the images in resources of another application to show the ease of trivial hiding methods in evading anti-malware. Our work differs from this approach in a way that the authors [11] indeed created malware by hiding malicious applications inside images while our work has used a real-world dataset of malicious images which are not just limited to containing an application but URLs, deviations from standard image format, statements comprising malicious function, etc. Moreover, no such work has been demonstrated for the Windows platform to the best of our knowledge. Steganography was used as one of the threat models [12] to implement a malign Android app to pose attacks. As follows in observation, the image chunks failing to meet file format specification are ignored by the picture viewer, thereby used to insert malicious codes. A method to detect obfuscated malware components within smartphone apps [13] was considered for stegomalware detection. It analyzes behavioral differences between the original app and the modified version with faults injected. However, the method uses a dynamic approach.

It has, therefore, been observed a lack of effective methods when it comes to locating malicious data within images. Also, relatively no such work has been found in the literature that studies or demonstrates stegomalware in Windows applications. However, this paper has addressed both issues. The remainder of the paper is structured as follows. Section 2 reviews related work. Section 3 describes the JPEG file format. Section 4 provides a methodology for the proposed tool and Sect. 5 discusses the experiment. The results are analyzed in Sect. 6. Section 7 examines the detection of stegomalware within Windows applications by available antiviruses. Section 8 concludes the paper.

2 Related Work

The first machine learning-based method to detect malicious JPEG images [14] used ten features derived from the JPEG file structure. It resulted in an FPR of 0.004, TPR of 0.951, and AUC of 99.7%. However, this method contains no mechanism to give information on the hidden malicious content or its location within images. Moreover, no analysis has been performed for the images with non-malicious data hidden which could also impact the file structure. Steganalysis based on an Artificial Immune System (AIS) [15] was proposed to detect JPEG images modified with specific steganography tools. Using haar wavelet, horizontal coefficients attained the best steganogram detection rate of 94.33% while vertical and diagonal coefficients reached an average detection rate of 85.71%. Different image entropies-based [16] a method was proposed to detect stegobot, a social network security threat that uses images on social networks to spread the malware. It attained almost 80% accuracy for the images embedded using different JPEG hiding techniques. The method needs further computations for the network-level defense of botnets with scalability an issue in the social networks. A framework identifying malicious JPEG images [17] over social networking sites consisted of three phases: (a) use of available steganalysis methods to find steganography artifacts (b) extraction of embedded data to identify file header (c) uploading that data to VirusTotal [18] to confirm the results. The method, however, has not used any real-world datasets and the hidden data may not necessarily be an application with a header part, failing the detection. Fridrich et al. [19] presented an overview of feature-based steganalysis for JPEG images and its implications for the future design of stegosystems. A method was proposed to distinguish legitimate JPEG operations [20] like compression from malicious ones. However, 'malicious' in the context of the work does not refer to an image containing malicious data, but rather an unauthentic and manipulated image.

Many steganographic threats have been observed in the wild. In July 2013, a backdoor [21] was found that compromised a site. It contained PHP functions within the JPEG header to read the header part and execute the content. Saumil Shah [22] at the 2015 Black Hat conference introduced the term 'stegosploit' referring to an image-based exploit. The exploits are embedded into JPG and PNG images with HTML and JavaScript code, producing an HTML+ image polyglot which seems an innocuous image but triggered in the victim's browser. Facebook Messenger [23] was reported in November 2016 for using JPEG images to spread Locky ransomware while in August 2017 [24], JPEG images spread the SyncCrypt ransomware. In December 2018, Trend Micro [25] reported the use of memes (JPEG) on Twitter to communicate with the malware. A LokiBot malware [26] was noted in August 2019 for an up-gradation hiding its source code in images. In December 2019, a cybersecurity company reported the use of JPEG of Taylor Swift [27] to hide MyKings crypto mining botnet.

Given the rising cyber threats via JPEG images, a comprehensive detection method is needed. The existing works on JPEG images have not exactly focused on revealing the hidden malicious data but rather finding artifacts left behind by the hiding tools or on feature-based detection which lacks this functionality to reveal the hidden content. This paper though alongside classification attempts to locate malicious content in JPEG images and produce that data as the output.

3 JPEG Format

JPEG stands for Joint Photographic Experts Group, named after a committee that created the JPEG standard in 1992. This file format is used by image capturing devices such as digital cameras and to store and transmit photographic images on the web. It is a widely used image format primarily due to its lossy compression ability. JPEG images have a file extension of .jpg/.jpeg. A JPEG image consists of a sequence of segments where each segment begins with a two-byte indicator called a marker. Every marker starts with the 0xFF byte (hexadecimal notation) followed by another byte that indicates a kind of data the respective segment holds. The markers are followed by the two bytes indicating the size of the segment-specific data that follows including two bytes for itself. Few segments though don't contain any payload and consist of just two marker bytes. A JPEG image starts with 0xFFD8 marker bytes (SOI_Start of Image), followed by the application-specific 0xFFEn markers (APPn) holding metadata where n = 0... F. The 0xFFDA marker (SOS_Start of Scan) contains the compressed image data where restart markers 0xFFD0 through 0xFFD7 inserted at regular intervals separate independent chunks of the data to allow parallel decoding. The 0xFFD9 or EOI marker denotes the end of the image. Table 1 provides JPEG-specific markers with their corresponding bytes and description.

4 Tool Proposed

We have created a tool in python (a python script) to detect malicious JPEG images. The tool is provided an input—a JPEG image. It reads the image, scanning and locating specific marker bytes and interpreting the data in respective segments to find any malicious content or deviation from the JPEG format. Based on this, it classifies the image into malicious or non-malicious. Besides classification, the tool contains the functionality of revealing the malign data found within the image along with its location as part of the output. Concerning the detection of stegomalware with respect to images, this functionality to the best of our knowledge has not been found in the available literature. It would enhance insight into the kind of malicious

Table 1 JPEG image markers

Marker	Bytes	Data	Description
SOI	0xFF 0xD8	None	Start of image
APPn	0xFF 0xEn, n = 0... F	Variable size	Application specific
COM	0xFF 0xFE	Variable size	Comment
SOF0	0xFF 0xC0	Variable size	Start of frame (Baseline JPEG)
SOF2	0xFF 0xC2	Variable size	Start of frame (Progressive JPEG)
DHT	0xFF 0xC4	Variable size	Define huffman table(s)
DQT	0xFF 0xDB	Variable size	Define quantization table(s)
RSTn	0xFF 0xDn, n = 0... 7	None	Restart
DRI	0xFF 0xDD	4 bytes	Define restart interval
SOS	0xFF 0xDA	Variable size	Start of scan
EOI	0xFF 0xD9	None	End of image

content hidden within images. The proposed tool flags an image as malicious under either of the following scenarios and non-malicious in case none of the scenarios are detected, as also illustrated in a flowchart presented in Fig. 1.

a. The tool reads and checks the starting two bytes in an input JPEG image. If the image is not found starting with the 0xFFD8 bytes (SOI marker), the image is reported as malicious for deviating from the JPEG format. It is uncommon and suspicious for an image to start with any other bytes than the SOI marker.

b. The tool locates application-specific markers by their corresponding bytes and scans the metadata that follows to find any malicious content. The corresponding ASCII code of the bytes comprising the metadata is obtained which is searched for some suspicious keywords or strings such as 'script', 'eval', and 'iframe' using a string finding function. The 'script' keyword has been used to locate a <script> tag which specifies a JavaScript file to load. Another keyword, a JavaScript function 'eval' has been searched for which is used to evaluate or execute the arguments passed to it. The argument can be any expression or one or more JavaScript statements. The 'iframe' stands for Inline Frame. Locating this tag identifies a suspicious action of embedding another document within the current HTML document. If either of the strings is found, the image is flagged as malicious.

c. The tool locates 0xFFFE bytes and searches in the respective comment segment for the suspicious strings in the same way it does for the metadata. The image is predicted as malicious upon finding either of the strings.

d. The tool searches for the bytes 0xFFD9 indicating the end of the image. If the image is found missing these bytes (EOI marker), the image raises suspicion for not following the standard JPEG format, thereby predicted as malicious.

e. The tool on locating the EOI marker, if finds any anomalous data appended to the end of the image, i.e., finding any data after the 0xFFD9 bytes, flags the image as malicious. The maliciousness of such data is identified using the same

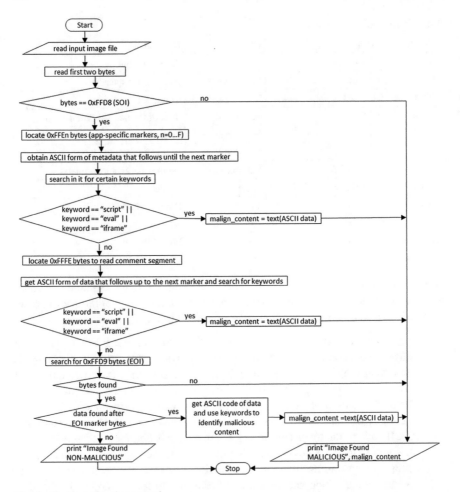

Fig. 1 Working of tool proposed

strings as used for the metadata and comment. Such trailing data is usually hard to notice for it comprises a few bytes causing a negligible change in the file size.

In cases (b), (c), and (e) as mentioned above that involve locating the hidden malign data, the tool outputs/produces the found malicious content along with its location.

5 Experiment

We have collected three types of JPEG images for the experiment: malicious, benign images hiding no data, and stego images that contain non-malicious data hidden. Though malicious images hiding malign content are also stego images, the ones hiding non-malicious data have been referred to as the stego images in the context of this paper. Therefore, stego images can be categorized into benign images for they are harmless, not containing any malware. The purpose behind using stego images is to evaluate the effectiveness of our tool in classifying the images hiding malicious and non-malicious data. Many existing works have focused on finding steganography artifacts [9, 15, 17, 19] produced by specific algorithms. However, the presence of steganography may indicate malware but it is not sufficient enough to reach conclusions since images can use steganography for legitimate purposes as well such as copyright protection. Thus, we want to ensure that the tool proposed doesn't just rely on steganography artifacts but rather inspects the content of the hidden data for detection.

We have collected about 5,893 JPEG images, containing 2,620 malicious, 3,185 benign, and 88 stego images. Malicious images have been collected from the malware repositories [28, 29]. We have analyzed VirusTotal reports for every malicious sample to ensure their maliciousness. The size of malicious images ranges from 22 bytes to 1,358 KB. Besides, 3,185 benign images have been collected from multiple sources [29–32]. These images range from 1 KB to 13,154 KB in size. Also, we have used about 40 stego images collected from our previous work [33] which used steganography, hiding non-malicious data in JPEG images with improved capacity and imperceptibility. The paper [33] aimed to protect sensitive data in PCs via hiding such data within image resources present on the systems from any malicious attempt of stealing or tampering with data. The stego images collected consist of eight images each with different embedding rates of 0.2, 0.4, 0.6, 0.8, and 1.0, and vary in size from 32 to 76 KB. These stego images depict spatial domain steganography. Therefore, to extend the evaluation, about 48 JPEG stego images have been further generated that hide non-malicious data in the transform domain. For this, we have used the F5 steganography algorithm [34], running it via Java from the command line. The size of these images lies between 5 and 175 KB. In total, 88 (40 + 48) stego images have been collected. All the benign and stego images have been analyzed using Virus-Total to verify if the files are clean. After collecting the samples, we have run the proposed tool, the python script, via command prompt in Windows for each of the 5,893 images, providing file name as the input.

6 Results

The tool proposed has analyzed every input JPEG image into malicious and non-malicious as per the procedure mentioned in Sect. 4. The stego images have been named S1, S2, and so on for convenience. Being harmless as containing non-malicious data, the stego images have been included in the dataset of benign images to produce a collective result. Running the tool on 2,620 malicious and 3,273 (3,185 + 88) benign images, we have observed and noted the results for every image. Summarizing the results, the precision, a ratio of correctly classified positive (malicious) samples to the total samples predicted as positive, obtained is 0.99. On other

Table 2 Comparative analysis of our technique with state-of-the-art techniques

Techniques	Detection rate (%)	Output the malign data found within images
Entropy-based [16]	~80	✗
AIS [15]	94.33	✗
MalJPEG [14]	94.8	✗
Proposed tool	96.16	✓

hand, recall (sensitivity) which is a ratio of correctly classified positive samples to the total positive ones, attained is 0.91. Considering both precision and recall, the F-measure of 95.50% has been obtained and an accuracy of 96.16% using our method. Other important measures that evaluate the classification performance are the False Negative Rate and the False Positive Rate. FNR is defined as a ratio of the positive samples misclassified as negative (benign) to the total positive ones. FPR is a ratio of negative samples misclassified as positive to the total negative ones. The lower the FNR and the FPR, the higher is the performance. The tool has resulted in an FNR of 0.08 and FPR of 0.001 which are fairly low. Indeed, all the stego images have been predicted as non-malicious, indicating the effectiveness of the proposed tool in distinguishing the images hiding malicious and non-malicious data. This can be attributed to the use of certain strings by the tool for locating malicious data within images. On the other hand, misclassification of malicious samples can be attributed to the presence of malware in the locations not covered by the tool such as LSBs. However, such cases are less likely since JPEG uses a lossy compression technique which can disrupt the data hidden in LSBs. The easy and more likely JPEG hiding methods consist of embedding the data in the header, comments, or at the end of the image file. Therefore, we have focused on finding the suspicious data at these locations in JPEG images.

A comparison of our result with that of state-of-the-art techniques [14–16] is presented in Table 2. Unlike our technique, the works [14–16] have used feature-based analysis for the detection of JPEG images. The table shows that our tool has relatively obtained a better detection rate with the functionality to output the malicious content found within images.

Other than the classification results, the distribution of threats in malicious images used in this paper has been explored as shown in Fig. 2. The figure shows that the majority of malicious images, i.e., around 94% contain suspicious data appended to the end of the image file. About 3% of images contained malware in the header comprising the metadata while the ones with malicious comment segments have been found with 0.04% distribution. The images found not following the standard JPEG format in terms of SOI and EOI markers, account for around 1 and 2% of the distribution, respectively.

Another observation being illustrated in Fig. 3 is regarding the presence of suspicious strings within the malicious images used. The samples have been found containing the HTML code for malicious purposes. The figure shows that about 53% of images contain the script tag enabling malicious JavaScript and PHP files

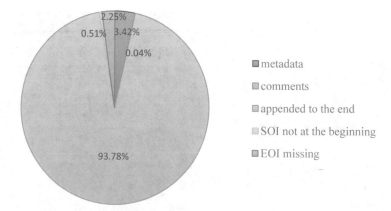

Fig. 2 Distribution of threats in malicious JPEG images

Fig. 3 Presence of suspicious strings within malicious JPEG images

and 38% comprise an iframe tag with hidden visibility while 6% contained both the tags. About 3% of images contained the JavaScript eval function for executing malicious string arguments. It could end up running malicious code on the targeted machine. An instance of the output for malicious and stego images is depicted via a screenshot provided in Fig. 4.

7 Stegomalware in Windows Applications

The applications have been found one of the convenient mechanisms for stegomalware to intrude into the systems. We have demonstrated the hiding of malicious JPEG images within Windows applications to evaluate the detection rate of several commercially available anti-malware scanners toward the stegomalware in Windows applications. Specifically, we have selected Windows operating system since to the best of our knowledge, there doesn't exist any such work or demonstration for the Windows platform relative to Android [10–13]. Concerning the hiding of malware in

Fig. 4 Screenshot representing an instance of the output of the tool proposed

apps using steganography, this is the first work highlighting this issue in Windows. Moreover, Windows has a large user base which makes it a potential target for malware attacks than others. To demonstrate, ten most frequently used Windows applications have been used. On the other hand, ten images have been randomly selected from the dataset of malicious images used in this paper. To enable hiding, a tool called Resource Tuner [35] has been used that allows editing the resources in Windows applications. We have used the ten images randomly, one each for each application, embedding and replacing the image resources within the applications used. The apps after hiding the images were scanned via VirusTotal. We intend to assess whether the applications containing stegomalware are detected by the anti-malware scanners. Figure 5 presents the number of anti-malware engines used by VirusTotal which detected these Windows applications containing malicious images

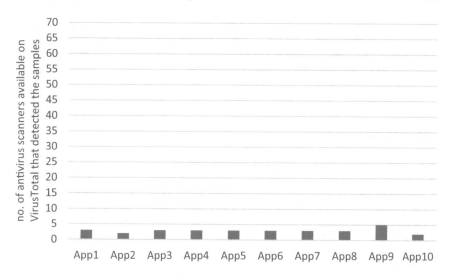

Fig. 5 Detection of Windows applications containing stegomalware

hidden. The figure shows that on average only 3 or 4 antiviruses out of over 70 scanners used by VirusTotal were able to detect such applications. This indicates the role of malicious image steganography in Windows applications to evade detection. This highlights a need for more effective Windows malware detectors since thwarting malware attacks on Windows is a formidable challenge.

8 Conclusion

This paper has proposed an effective tool to detect malicious JPEG images. Analyzing three types of JPEG images: malicious, benign, and the stego ones hiding non-malicious data, a low FNR and FPR with a better detection rate relative to state-of-the-art techniques have been attained for the 5,893 images. Indeed, the tool has classified the stego images as non-malicious, indicating the effectiveness of the tool in classifying the images hiding malicious and non-malicious data. Unlike existing works that have focused on finding steganography artifacts or used feature-based analysis which lacks revealing the hidden data, the proposed tool has attempted to locate malign data within images using certain keywords and produce that data as the output. This functionality has been found missing in the existing literature where hidden malicious data is not accessible for analysis. The proposed tool thus can be integrated with existing tools to enhance detection. Moreover, malicious images have been demonstratively hidden in Windows applications showing the role of steganography in apps to evade several antivirus scanners, indicating a need for more effective Windows malware detectors. Also, the scope of our algorithm can be extended in the future for other image formats, requiring the algorithm is modified/adapted accordingly to read format-specific data.

Acknowledgments All the authors have contributed to the work without any conflict of interest. The authors specifically thank VirusShare.com and Hybrid-Analysis.com for granting access to their malware collection. To mention, the research has not received any grant from any funding agency in the public, commercial or not-for-profit sectors.

References

1. Mazurczyk W, Caviglione L (2015) Information hiding as a challenge for malware detection. IEEE Secur Priv 13:89–93. https://doi.org/10.1109/MSP.2015.33
2. Beek C, Dinkar D, Gund Y, Lancioni G, Minihane N, Moreno F et al (2017) McAfee labs threats report: June 2017 (2017). https://www.mcafee.com/enterprise/en-in/about/newsroom/research-reports.html
3. Cabaj K, Caviglione L, Mazurczyk W, Wendzel S, Woodward A, Zander S (2018) The new threats of information hiding: the road ahead. IT Prof 20:31–39. https://doi.org/10.1109/MITP.2018.032501746
4. Mazurczyk W, Wendzel S (2017) Information hiding: challenges for forensic experts. Commun ACM 61:86–94. https://doi.org/10.1145/3158416
5. Aljamea MM, Iliopoulos CS, Samiruzzaman M (2016) Detection of URL in image steganography. In: ICC '16: proceedings of the international conference on internet of things and cloud computing. ACM, pp 1–6. https://doi.org/10.1145/2896387.2896408
6. Puchalski D, Caviglione L, Kozik R, Marzecki A, Krawczyk S, Choraś M (2020) Stegomalware detection through structural analysis of media files. In: ARES '20: proceedings of the 15th international conference on availability, reliability and security. ACM, pp 1–6. https://doi.org/10.1145/3407023.3409187
7. Amsalem Y, Puzanov A, Bedinerman A, Kutcher M, Hadar O (2015) DCT-based cyber defense techniques. In: Proceedings of the SPIE 9599, applications of digital image processing XXXVIII. SPIE. https://doi.org/10.1117/12.2187498
8. Carrega A, Caviglione L, Repetto M, Zuppelli M (2020) Programmable data gathering for detecting stegomalware. In: 2020 6th IEEE conference on network softwarization (NetSoft). IEEE, pp 422–429. https://doi.org/10.1109/NetSoft48620.2020.9165537
9. Pevny T, Kopp M, Křoustek J, Ker AD (2016) Malicons: detecting payload in favicons. In: Electronic imaging symposium, media watermarking, security, and forensics, pp 1–9. https://doi.org/10.2352/ISSN.2470-1173.2016.8.MWSF-079
10. Suarez-Tangil G, Tapiador JE, Peris-Lopez P (2014) Stegomalware: playing hide and seek with malicious components in smartphone apps. In: International conference on information security and cryptology, LNCS. Springer, Cham, pp 496–515. https://doi.org/10.1007/978-3-319-16745-9_27
11. Badhani S, Muttoo SK (2018) Evading android anti-malware by hiding malicious application inside images. Int J Syst Assur Eng Manag 9:482–493. https://doi.org/10.1007/s13198-017-0692-7
12. Cao C, Zhang Y, Liu Q, Wang K (2015) Function escalation attack. In: International conference on security and privacy in communication networks, LNICST. Springer, Cham, pp 481–497. https://doi.org/10.1007/978-3-319-23829-6_33
13. Suarez-Tangil G, Tapiador JE, Lombardi F, Pietro RD (2016) Alterdroid: differential fault analysis of obfuscated smartphone Malware. IEEE Trans Mob Comput 15:789–802. https://doi.org/10.1109/TMC.2015.2444847
14. Cohen A, Nissim N, Elovici Y (2020) MalJPEG: machine learning based solution for the detection of malicious JPEG images. IEEE Access 8:19997–20011. https://doi.org/10.1109/ACCESS.2020.2969022

15. Pérez JDJS, Rosales MS, Cruz-Cortés N (2016) Universal steganography detector based on an artificial immune system for JPEG images. In: 2016 IEEE Trustcom/BigDataSE/ISPA. IEEE, pp 1896–1903. https://doi.org/10.1109/TrustCom.2016.0290
16. Natarajan V, Sheen S, Anitha R (2012) Detection of StegoBot: a covert social network botnet. In: SecurIT '12: proceedings of the first international conference on security of internet of things. ACM, pp 36–41. https://doi.org/10.1145/2490428.2490433
17. Kunwar RS, Sharma P (2017) Framework to detect malicious codes embedded with JPEG images over social networking sites. In: 2017 international conference on innovations in information, embedded and communication systems (ICIIECS). IEEE, pp 1–4. https://doi.org/10.1109/ICIIECS.2017.8276144
18. Virus scanning website. https://www.virustotal.com
19. Fridrich J (2004) Feature-based steganalysis for JPEG images and its implications for future design of steganographic schemes. In: International workshop on information hiding, LNCS. Springer, Berlin, Heidelberg, pp 67–81. https://doi.org/10.1007/978-3-540-30114-1_6
20. Lin C-Y, Chang S-F (2001) A robust image authentication method distinguishing JPEG compression from malicious manipulation. IEEE Trans Circuits Syst Video Technol 11:153–168. https://doi.org/10.1109/76.905982
21. Cid DB (2013) Malware hidden inside JPG EXIF headers. Sucuri Blog, Website Security News. https://blog.sucuri.net/2013/07/malware-hidden-inside-jpg-exif-headers.html
22. Shah S (2015) Stegosploit—exploit delivery with steganography and polyglots. In: Briefings, Black Hat Conference. https://www.blackhat.com/eu-15/briefings.html
23. Khandelwal S (2016) Beware! Malicious JPG images on facebook messenger spreading locky ransomware. In: The hacker news, cybersecurity news and analysis. https://thehackernews.com/2016/11/facebook-locky-ransomware.html
24. Abrams L (2017) SyncCrypt ransomware hides inside JPG files, appends .KK Extension. Bleeping computer, Technology News Website. https://www.bleepingcomputer.com/news/security/synccrypt-ransomware-hides-inside-jpg-files-appends-kk-extension
25. Zahravi A (2018) Malicious memes that communicate with Malware. Trend Micro, IT security company. https://www.trendmicro.com/en_us/research/18/l/cybercriminals-use-malicious-memes-that-communicate-with-malware.html
26. Osborne C (2019) LokiBot malware now hides its source code in image files. ZDNet, Technology News Website. https://www.zdnet.com/article/lokibot-information-stealer-now-hides-malware-in-image-files
27. Szappanos G, Brandt A (2019) MyKings botnet spreads headaches, cryptominers, and Forshare malware. Sophos, cybersecurity company. https://news.sophos.com/en-us/2019/12/18/mykings-botnet-spreads-headaches-cryptominers-and-forshare-malware
28. Malware repository. https://virusshare.com
29. Malware analysis service. https://www.hybrid-analysis.com
30. Image database. http://sipi.usc.edu/database
31. Photos and Videos sharing platform. https://www.pexels.com
32. Social networking site. https://www.facebook.com
33. Verma V, Muttoo SK, Singh VB (2019) Enhanced payload and trade-off for image steganography via a novel pixel digits alteration. Multimed Tools Appl 79:7471–7490. https://doi.org/10.1007/s11042-019-08283-9
34. Westfeld A (2001) F5—a steganographic algorithm. In: International workshop on information hiding, LNCS. Springer, Berlin, Heidelberg, pp 289–302. https://doi.org/10.1007/3-540-45496-9_21
35. Visual resource editor. http://www.restuner.com
36. Butani B, Kumar Shukla P, Silakari S (2014) An exhaustive survey on physical node capture attack in WSN. Int J Comput Appl 95:32–39. https://doi.org/10.5120/16577-6265

37. Bhatt R, Maheshwary P, Shukla P, Shukla P, Shrivastava M, Changlani S (2020) Implementation of fruit fly optimization algorithm (FFOA) to escalate the attacking efficiency of node capture attack in wireless sensor networks (WSN). Comput Commun 149:134–145. https://doi.org/10.1016/j.comcom.2019.09.007
38. Kumar SA, Sinha S, Shukla P (2018) Design and development of image security technique by using cryptography and steganography: a combine approach. Int J Image, Graph Signal Process 10:13–21. https://doi.org/10.5815/ijigsp.2018.04.02

A Review on Data Integrity Verification Schemes Based on TPA and Blockchain for Secure Cloud Data Storage

S. Sudersan, V. S. Abhijith, M. Thangavel, and P. Varalakshmi

1 Introduction

Nowadays the demand for cloud-based methodologies that offer storage facilities is increasing rapidly. In addition, as information exchange has increased a lot due to the move to a complete virtual platform in every sector and domain everyone has made their way to store the data in the cloud for better access, collaboration, and reliability. However, the verification of the integrity of data in cloud storage has been challenging. In the real-world scenario the encryption algorithm, the signatures, and other mechanisms and policies ensure data privacy. But when data has moved to a remote server (i.e.) cloud storage, it is being tedious to maintain and manage them. So verification of the data and its integrity in a cloud-based system or storage has very high importance. Blockchain offers unique characteristics of resistance from tamper, a noncentralized approach, maintaining very high consistency and stability, and the ability to trace every transaction. The increase in the peer-to-peer (P2P) working on cloud storage leads to a large amount of exhaustion of the data available. Blockchain technology is decentralized, transparent, and immutable storage and a record that proves it has not been tampered [31, 35, 39]. The mechanism of agreeability or consensus ensures the state of the complete system in the blockchain. Smart Contracts are business logic or the processing logic in the Blockchain-based framework and execute the necessary conditions and instructions given based on the conditions.

S. Sudersan · V. S. Abhijith
Department of Information Technology, Thiagarajar College of Engineering, Madurai, Tamilnadu, India

M. Thangavel (✉)
School of Computing Science and Engineering, Vellore Institute of Technology, Bhopal Campus, Bhopal, India

P. Varalakshmi
Department of Computer Technology, Madras Institute of Technology, Anna University, Chennai, Tamilnadu, India

© The Author(s), under exclusive license to Springer Nature Singapore Pte Ltd. 2022   117
U. P. Rao et al. (eds.), *Security, Privacy and Data Analytics*, Lecture Notes
in Electrical Engineering 848, https://doi.org/10.1007/978-981-16-9089-1_10

Billions of users across the world store data in the cloud. However the integrity of data stored in the cloud is not guaranteed, it by nature assumed that the CSP shall not compromise on integrity, that is not, however, the case always. Several solutions emerged to ensure data integrity, one such solution is to introduce a blockchain. In this survey, we have highlighted various methods for data integrity verifications with and without Blockchain and the issues that plague them and highlighted the problems associated with Third-Party Auditors (TPAs). Several solutions to the data integrity problem have been analyzed, their pros and cons weighed. In our survey, we have also tried to find how the inclusion of blockchain can produce a much more efficient, secure, and viable solution.

2   Issues and Challenges

Many reasons stand as an issue or the cause of compromising the integrity in data storage. The errors include those that are intentional or unintentional. Errors in transfer including modifications can happen during the transfer of data from one device to another. Viruses, malware, and other vulnerabilities of the cyber world could also be an indirect chance of compromising data integrity [26]. Some other issues may include system failures and human errors. In some or for some rare chances may include the compromising of the data in the intention of providing more value to the premium consumers in the expectation of higher profit. This may happen in the case of private clouds that intend to provide better security with a pay increase. Thus with the increase in demand for the independent, remote access of data and services and the incorporation of the CSPs in gaining a high revenue with the help of the available resources and services being offered and shared over to a large community the demand for cloud storage and services has raised to a greater extent [23]. However, all these demands show a greater need and brighter side of the technology, there is still some inherent weakness called trust. A CSP can never be trusted always because of the higher chances of being motivated towards malicious events and activities. As an example, a CSP in the case of storage could analyze the usage of data in the storage and may gradually try to delete unnecessary files or information that the user has not made access to for a certain amount of time. Since there is a large spread of the data being stored and the data is scattered across multiple servers in a widespread geographical area the user is unable to inspect every data link visually especially when the size of the data is very large. Thus as a main area of concern, unauthorized physical access could be one of the major issues being faced specifically in the area of storage.

3 State of the Art

Several solutions have been proposed to solve the problem of data integrity, both involving and excluding blockchain technology.

3.1 Challenges Addressed Without Blockchain

Xiling Luo et al. [28] have proposed an integrity verification scheme or methodology based on Boneh Lynn Shacham type of signature. The proposed system has 3 entities: User, Server, and the TPA and involves 5 functions: Key Generation, Token Generation, Puzzle, Responding, and Proof checking. Operations, Key Generation, Token Generation, Puzzle, Responding, and Proof checking. The public and private keys are generated by the user by running the key generation functionality. When the user wants to check the integrity of his/her data, the user requests the TPA, which in turn creates a challenge and sends it to the CSP. The service provider in turn solves the challenge and returns the proof to the TPA. The TPA on receiving the proof provided by the CSP checks and returns the status to the user.

Shaomin Zhang et al. [44] proposed a remote integrity verification methodology using cloud computing. The proposed scheme involves 3 commodities: Owner of the data (DO), the Provider of the Cloud systems (Cloud Service Provider), Auditor on third-Party policy (Third-Party Auditor). The Provider of the Cloud systems uses the generation of key functionalities to generate secret key pairs. The data proofs are protected by random parameters. A challenge is generated by the TPA and sent to the CSP based on set equations and parameters, to which the CSP responds, which the TPA verifies for an integrity based on the verification equations.

Yuan Zhang et al. [40] have proposed a public data integrity verification mechanism for cloud storage systems. To verify the data integrity, the auditor first generates a challenge message and issues it to the cloud server. With the challenging message, the cloud server generates proof of the information and that is then sent to an auditor. After the information is received, the data integrity is verified by the auditor on checking the proof information. Based on the verification results, the auditor informs the user accordingly.

Yuan Ping et al. [4] have proposed a public data integrity verification scheme for secure cloud storage. The system model comprises Users, Cloud Service Providers (CSPs), and Third-Party Auditors (TPAs). Typical working of the system involves the user sending a verification request to the TPA, which chooses challenge information and sends the data, computes the proof, and sends it back to the third-party auditor, which it further processes by computing the sum of hash values, verifies the proof and then transmits the result to the user.

Annamalai Rajendran et al. [34] have proposed a mechanism for data integrity verification using provable identity-based data possession in cloud storage environments. The proposed integrity verification process involves partitioning the file into blocks and is stored into data and encoded using AES. The data is encrypted and uploaded to the cloud. The TPA performs the auditing process. The user requests the TPA to verify the integrity of data. The TPA performs a probabilistic check to verify the integrity of the user data. The proposed solution is implemented in a multi-storage cloud so that in case of data corruption, the data blocks can be replaced.

Yunxue Yan et al. [29] have proposed a dynamic data integrity verification scheme based on bloom's filters and lattices. The proposed scheme involves three entities: User, Cloud Service Provider (CSP), and Third-Party Auditor (TPA). Bloom's filter is a highly efficient data structure, which uses a vector to represent a set of members. The main function of Bloom's filter is to determine whether an element belongs to this collection or not. To verify the integrity of his/her data, the user sends an audit request to the TPA, which in turn generates a challenge and sends it to the CSP. The CSP on authentication accepts the challenge and generates the corresponding file signature and returns it to the TPA. The TPA verifies the proof and notifies the user accordingly.

Junfeng et al. [7] have proposed a data integrity verification scheme involving a homomorphic hash function that provides greater privacy, efficiency and handles data dynamically better than other conventional schemes. The experimental verification and the security analysis also prove that the system is completely efficient.

Filipe Apolinário et al. [30] have developed S AUDIT which is a service that performs data verification of information stored in cloud servers. The proposed system performs homomorphic verification using digital signatures to prevent retrieval of the data that is protected, especially in the case of cloud-based storage systems. Experimental evaluation reveals that the S-AUDIT-based approach is 7.1% cheaper than using other signature methods like RSA.

Shivaraj Hiremath et al. [36] provides an efficient public audit methodology using TPA to assure integrity. The analysis of the work proves that the approach is safe and the TPA takes only unit time to help to the audit of data.

3.2 Challenges Addressed with Blockchain

Muhammad Saqib Niaz et al. [43] have proposed Merkle hash tree-based techniques to ensure the integrity of outsourced data. The authors consider that there exists a methodology where the system takes the efficiency to securely transfer the data and information with the Data Owner (DO) and the clients. The transmitted information could be the public key of the DO or some hash data. The authors have used deterministic approaches based on Authenticated Data Structures (ADS) to verify the integrity of data (Merkle Hash Tree-based Integrity techniques). Merkle Hash Tree In the signature scheme each end node called leaf holds the current data block hash. Internal nodes hold the hash of the concatenated hashes of their children. In the B + tree, the node that is at the root is either considered as leaf or internal. These nodes hold only the key and not the exact information. Data stays always in the leaf nodes. Leaf nodes form some kind of linked list, which allows for the sequential traversal of the data. Data integrity schemes based on MHT have been designed by replacing B + trees in Merkle's original signature scheme. The authors have also explained MHT storage in the database and Authenticated Data Extraction (ADE) and have also performed a detailed analysis of the methodologies proposed.

PengCheng Wei et al. [8] have proposed a cloud-based integrity verification and protection mechanism using blockchain. The proposed mechanism involves a virtual agent using cloud and mobile technology. The virtual machine agent mechanism ensures reliable data storage, verification, and monitoring. The integrity protection framework involves a proxy virtual machine model and a unique hash value of the file generated by the Merkle tree, which listens for any changes on the data using smart contracts. In case of any data tampering, a warning is issued to the user.

Pei Huang et al. [9] have proposed a Collaborative Auditing Blockchain (CAB) to ensure data integrity in cloud storage systems. The proposed framework involves consists of consensus nodes, which substitute for the single TPA, in executing audit delegations and recording them. The authors have designed a new data structure ACT (Auxiliary Chain Table, which is employed by each Data Owner (DO) to provide for fast and secure data retrieval and verification. The ACT is a two-dimensional data structure. The proposed system consists of four entities: Data Owners (DO), Private Key generators (PKG), Group Managers (GMs), and Cloud Service Providers (CSPs). The PKG is responsible for setting parameters for the system and generating keys for the GM. The DO has limited computational capabilities and is responsible for generating and sending auditing challenges on-demand to the CSP and tracks changes in the ACT. The GM is designated collectively by a group of Dos, however, GMs, in general, possess more computational powers than Dos. The verification process is triggered by the DO, when it initiates an integrity request to the CSP through the GM, once the CSP authenticates and responds to the request, the CAB performs the consensus process and records the result as a block in the blockchain.

Ahsan Manzoor et al. [3] have proposed an IoT data sharing platform based on blockchain, which uses a proxy re-encryption scheme for securely transmitting the information. The proposed system involves a proxy re-encryption scheme for securely transmitting the information. The collected data is encrypted and stored in the cloud. The data is shared between sensors and data users without the involvement of TPA, using runtime smart contracts between them. The proposed scheme is efficient, secure, and fast and serves as a safe platform for trading, storing, and managing sensor data. The system has been deployed using commercially available sensors and IoT devices.

Xiaodong Yang et al. [10] have proposed a multi-cloud and multi replica auditing scheme based on blockchain. The proposed scheme involves a hash table and modification record table, which dynamically updates the results of group audits. The inherent unpredictability of blockchain is used to construct challenges, which prevents malicious TPA and cloud servers from colluding. Every audit result is recorded in the blockchain making the whole process transparent and efficient.

Dongdong Yue et al. [20] have proposed a data integrity verification methodology based on integrity in P2P remote storage based on BC (blockchain). The proposed framework involves three entities Clients, Cloud Storage Servers (CSS), Blockchain

(BC). The workflow consists of two stages viz. Preparation and verification. The first stage has 5 steps. The verification phase also includes five steps, At first, a challenge is generated by the client and sent to the CSS, which then chooses a shard to verify. Then the CSS calculates the hash digest using a hash function based on the challenge and the selected shard. Then the CSS sends the digest and the auxiliary information to the blockchain. Then using smart contracts the blockchain will compute a new hash root and compare it with the previous root. If they are equal, then the integrity of the data is validated, else the data has been compromised.

Gaetani et al. [5] proposed the methodology of a database that could help in the verification of integrity in the cloud with the help of BC. In this paper, the authors have focused on taking up a real-world concern of a SUNFISH project thereby securing the data in the cloud-based storage systems. They have detailed the research and innovation gaps and the tediousness in explaining and documenting them. They have outlined the design using an effective BC approach.

Kun Hao et al. [6] have proposed a data integrity verification mechanism based on blockchain. The proposed solution involves a blockchain model in a non-trustable environment, called Decentralized Collaborative Verification, which proposes an efficient algorithm called Decentralized Integrity Verification which includes two parts, viz., Write Block, and the Check Block.

Igor Zikratov et al. [37] detailed a blockchain-based methodology of verification of data and integrity. The proposed model involves two components viz. The user side and the server-side. The user side consists of the UI etc. The server-side handles session management, authentication, Handling of transactions, and integrity check. Information and its integrity are verified using cross-checking hashes with blockchain.

Hao Wang et al. [11] have proposed a blockchain-based fair payment auditing for public cloud storage. The proposed Non-Interactive-Provable Data Possession (NI-PPDP) scheme consists of three entities: CSP, data owner, and integrity verifier. The scheme consists of four algorithms and is divided into two phases viz. the setup and auditing phase. The setup phase consists of the key and tag generation phase. The audit phase consists of the proof generation and verification phase.

Chao Wang et al. [24] have proposed a blockchain-based audit and access control mechanism in service collaboration. The proposed solution involves a blockchain for recording the file activities of the users in sequential order. The audit process involves a sequence of steps: The first phase is the startup phase, wherein the user generates a key and broadcasts it to the CSP and auditors. In the second phase, the user computes a verifiable homomorphic digest for every data block in a file and each file is construed as an aggregation of the various homomorphic digests. Then the user stores the aggregation and the file in the audit node and cloud storage respectively. In the verification phase, proof of ownership for the data blocks in the file is requested by the audit node. Then a challenge is generated by the audit node and sent to the Cloud Storage Service Provider (CSSP). In the fourth step, the CSSP builds the data possession certificate and sends it to the audit node. Finally, the audit node verifies the result of the challenge and sends the result to the user.

Xuanmei Qin et al. [12] have proposed a blockchain-based access control scheme for secure cloud data sharing with multiple attributes. The proposed system model consists of five entities viz: Certificate Authorities (CA), Attribute Authorities (Aas), Cloud Service Providers (CSPs), Data Owner (DO), Data User (DU). The entities participating in a blockchain network, which records all transactions occurring between the different entities. The blockchain also assists in performing partially trusted computing and in effectively managing user attributes. The proposed mechanism consists of four phases: System initialization, Encryption phase, token generation phase, and decryption phase. The proposed scheme implements cross-domain management of attributes by using smart contracts and also fosters mutual trust among multiple Aas.

Huaqun Wang et al. [41] have proposed a remote data integrity verification mechanism in a cloud-dependent Health Internet of Things. The proposed Integrity Checking & Sharing (ICS) system consists of four entities: Public Cloud Server (PCS), Hospital, Patient, and Patient's authorized entry set (AuthSet). The proposed is an ensemble of seven linear time algorithms.

Lei Zhou et al. [33] have surveyed data integrity verification of the outsourced big data in the cloud environment. In this paper, the authors have reviewed the state of art DIV (data Integrity Verification) efforts to ensure the integrity of data stored in CSS (Cloud Storage Server). Overhead on the users' side. A clear and detailed classification of the forthcoming DIV approaches based on the user mode and storage type has been presented. Some open problems and challenges have been discussed and several valuable ideas have been suggested for further investigation.

Benil et al. [13] have proposed a cloud-based security scheme in E-health systems using blockchain. The proposed Elliptical Curve Certificateless Aggregate Cryptography Signature scheme (EC-ACS) scheme to protect the integrity of Electronic Health Records (EHR) stored in the Medical Cloud Server (MCS) using public auditing and verification. The patient data is encrypted using Elliptic Curve Cryptography (ECC) and the digital signature is generated using the Certificateless Aggregate Signature Scheme (CAS). The proposed scheme offers integrity, traceability, security, and efficiency.

Haiping et al. [14] developed a blockchain-based scheme for preserving the privacy and security in medical data being shared. The privacy concern towards the healthcare data is being considered now as one of the most sensitive sources of information available. The authors have clearly stated the need and concern for Zero-knowledge proof, proxy re-encryption, bilinear maps in such a model proposed. The proposed model behavior has been categorized as if or not the patient believes in the data meeting the requirements provided by the smart contracts and the perspective of the authority and commercial interests concerning the transactions between the patients and the research institutions. A series of 3 major properties have been detailed concerning providing the utmost privacy protection to the data being transacted. A step-wise mathematical proof and steps of the proposed approach give a great insight into the proposed scheme. A brief analysis of the proposed approach has been given in various contexts such as confidentiality, privacy-preserving, integrity, traceability, and a detailed evaluation regarding the procedure.

Bobo et al. [16] have proposed a model for communication that is claimed to be efficient and reliable in multi-tenant edge clouds with a blockchain-enhanced paradigm. A detailed insight into broker-based enabling. The authors provide a detailed analysis and find the ambiguities like issues in authorization and handling sensitive information like metadata. The proposed solution led to the implementation of Kafka and EOS-based solutions using BC (blockchain). An intensive analysis of the proposed solution also proves the suitability of practice by BPS.

Lei et al. [17] opened up the extension of blockchain-based platforms that help in data integrity in the domain of agriculture. The authors have specifically focussed on a platform for fish farms. The main motive of the paper has been to provide fish farmers a secure storage platform for storing the agriculture data with the help of smart contracts. The proposed methodology is implemented using the proof of concept with the help of Hyperledger fabric in the blockchain. A series of experiments were carried out for the analysis of the proposed methodology which has been demonstrated concerning the efficiency and usability of the system.

Bin et al. [38] has introduced the challenges in ensuring data integrity for IoT-based data in the cloud and have given the reason as the dynamic and inherent nature of the data. The authors also claim the inefficiency of Third-Party Auditor (TPA) based data integrity frameworks with reliability being a factor of concern. Hence the authors implement relevant protocols and a prototype system and the necessary analysis of the system has been carried out. The authors identified protocols like DOA to CSS-Y, DOA to CSS-N, DCAs to CSS-Y, DCAs to CSS-N, where DOA $\rightarrow$ Owner of the application, CSP $\rightarrow$ Providers who provision Cloud-based storage, CSS $\rightarrow$ Cloud Storage Service, DCA $\rightarrow$ Data Consumer Apps, P2PPS $\rightarrow$ p2p System, DIS $\rightarrow$ service for integrating the data, DISSC $\rightarrow$ Integrity of the data with smart control.

Haiyan Wang et al. [25] aimed at providing data integrity verification in the case of large-scale IoT data. The proposed work implements a BC (blockchain) and Bilinear scheme for Data Integrity. The performance analysis including feasibility, security, dynamicity, and complexity of the BB-DIS system to implement the verification scheme supports the achievement of data integrity. The smart contracts verification process is carried out using the SC-VERIFICATION ALGORITHM and the performance analysis has been compared with other similar models and schemes and a detailed simulation has been presented.

Huang et al. [15] proposed a blockchain-based E-Health system called BCES that helps in handling the issues of handling the manipulation of electronic health records (EHR) and that can be audited. Each query made in the EHR will be written in the Blockchain for traceability and helps in permanent storage. Time-based attributes have also been proposed in addition to the main methodology that provides a proxy-based re-encryption to achieve the grained access control of the most sensitive information. The reason for the implementation in the blockchain is the tamper resistance and the characteristics of providing traceability. The security analysis and performance evaluation of the system has been demonstrated which proves the system to be secure and efficient.

Quanyu et al. [18] utilize blockchain technology to implement a scheme that helps in providing remote data integrity for IoT. The main difference of this approach from other existing approaches is that the scheme does not involve any other third parties. The scheme proposes the usage of Lifted Elliptic Curve El-Gamal cryptography, bilinear pairing with the help of BC (blockchain) to provide batch signature verification thus protecting and securing the devices in an IoT-based system.

Jiaxing et al. [19] utilizes the blockchain-based approach to develop an auditing scheme that helps in verifying the data integrity in the case of cloud storage. The scheme is claimed to be different from other existing approaches as it consists of three participatory entities out of which only two entities are said to be predefined entities. The two predefined entities could be the data owner (DO) and the cloud service provider (CSP) and the main assumption of the system is that they don't have the possibility of trusting the other. Also, there isn't any role for the TPA. A hashtag-based methodology is also being followed. A series of experimental results have been demonstrated that could provide computation and communication.

Yuan et al. [27] proposed a verification methodology that does not require a certificate wherein procrastinating auditors using blockchain. The proposed scheme or methodology involves the auditors recording each verification result into the blockchain in the form of a transaction. The verifications are also time stamped when they are recorded in the blockchain. The paper also demonstrates rigorous security proofs and a comprehensive valuation of the performance proving the system to be efficient.

Dongdong et al. [32] developed a blockchain-based framework without the help of Third-Party Auditors for data integrity verification. The scenario has been designed to take place in a decentralized edge cloud storage environment. The Merkle tree with random challenging numbers has been employed. Hence to solve the problem of these like the limitation in the number of resources available can be solved by using certain rational sampling verification strategies as explained by the authors.

Velmurugadass et al. [21] creates a SDN. It consists of mobile-based IoT devices, open flow, and controllers based on blockchain, servers, servers for authentication (AS), an investigation. It uses an elliptic curve algorithm and is transferred to the cloud. The control system helps in maintaining the evidence and signatures based on the SHA 256 algorithm. The experimental analysis reveals that it gained better performance in response, accuracy, throughput, and security arguments.

Ren et al. [1] identifies and proposes a scheme based on identity proxy using a signature that is aggregated to enhance efficiency and reduce the space usage and bandwidth. The methodology also proves to be cost-efficient in the case of other ordinary signature schemes and the performance is also very high.

Abdullah et al. [2] present a health care management of data that helps in increasing the privacy of data using blockchain methodologies. Cryptosystems and operations are being mentioned in the encryption of data and which helps in ensuring pseudonymity. The analysis of the proposed schemes along with the data processing procedures claims to be cost-effective.

Rupa et al. [22] have proposed a blockchain-based solution to ensure the integrity and security of VC-based device data. The proposed system is implemented by deploying an IoT-based application in a vehicle monitoring system. The various device data such as technical information, vehicle reactions are stored in the cloud storage. Pentatope based Elliptic Curve Cryptography and SHA is used to ensure privacy. On security and performance analysis the proposed scheme is proved to be efficient and secure.

Shangping et al. [42] have proposed a new blockchain-based data integrity verification scheme for ensuring integrity in health records. The usage of blockchain in the proposed scheme averts the single point of failure problem and ensures fault tolerance. Compared with other existing schemes, the proposed scheme allows a safer environment for sharing the private attributes, keys, etc. of users. The scheme uses smart contracts to evaluate the integrity of the stored data. The security and performance analysis of the proposed solution proves that the scheme is secure, efficient, and feasible for commercial use.

4 Inferences of the Review

Storage, computing, and services are the main resources of cloud computing. In the advanced development of cloud computing technologies, security has been a major concern and more specifically data integrity verification. Several methodologies have been proposed with and without Third-Party Auditors (TPA). It cannot be guaranteed that the TPA would legitimately cooperate with Cloud Service Providers (CSPs) or may be subject to flattery due to some interest or for some other reasons. Moreover, there are chances of loss of confidentiality on the part of CSPs due to some special interest towards premium customers in the private cloud scenario. Even with the development and advanced computing techniques, the security and confidentiality of encryption are under serious threat. Hence, there is a necessity that feasibility should go hand in hand with technology in developing integrity. Verification service that avoids the problem of untrustworthy TPAs and CSPs. However, Blockchain has been identified to be one of the most trustworthy decentralized and transparent systems which have been thought of as a solution to the problem and to overcome the constraints of TPA thus providing authentication, data recovery, backup, and confidentiality in addition to data integrity verification. The main aim and objective are to understand the issues, specifically the proposals made in the area to solve the issues both involving blockchain and to contrast those without involving blockchain. The author aims to highlight the pros and cons involved in the use of blockchain in solving the problem. As an inference of the survey, it has been found emphasized that involving Blockchain technology in solving the problem is the best approach in solving the problem because of the series of validation networks that the blockchain has and the additional feature of data traceability and recoverability. The main problem addressed by many researchers is the loss of confidentiality when TPAs are involved even if the data has been encrypted. The validation of every transaction in the blockchain with its characteristic of being immutable that each transaction or data entered in the blockchain can never be modified or changed to an extent gives a partial solution to the problem thereby replacing the need of the TPAs. Besides, there are a lot of technologies that Blockchain follows to develop its application like the Kafka in Hyperledger fabric which is believed to bring an entire change in the existing models and constraints. With all these advancements and cons being negligible when compared the blockchain-based implementation of the data integrity service schemes proves to be a lot more trustworthy and secure since there is less involvement of the validators being able to see the transactions that they validate and traceability that if any modifications are done would be explicitly be caught. And this would develop a fear against all those illegitimate activities from the side of CSPs thus providing a safer solution to the issue concerned.

5 Conclusion and Future Scope

Even after all the advancements in security and technologies there still stands a concern of data integrity. As and when technology evolves and new methodologies are being proposed, the changes in the system being vulnerable are high. Still, loopholes are being generated every time and new methodologies are being proposed to handle them. In this paper, we have undertaken an extensive survey on the various proposals, improvements, and suggestions that could help in verifying the data integrity in cloud-based storage systems involving both blockchains versus non-blockchain-based solutions, analyzing their respective complexities, efficiency, feasibility, etc. As we have come to know through this survey, blockchain-based solutions are more efficient and secure. We intend to extend our work to building a secure system. The focus is also on the comparison of secureness in using Blockchain as a technology for ensuring data integrity-based issues, especially in cloud-based environments.

References

1. Ren Y, Leng Y, Qi J, Sharma PK, Wang J, Almakhadmeh Z, Tolba A (2021) Multiple cloud storage mechanisms based on blockchain in smart homes. Futur Gener Comput Syst 115:304–313
2. Omar A, Md, Bhuiyan, Basu A, Kiyomoto S, Rahman S (2019) Privacy-friendly platform for healthcare data in cloud-based on blockchain environment. Futur Gener Comput Syst 95C:511–521
3. Manzoor A, Braeken A, Kanhere SS, Ylianttila M, Liyanage M (2021) Proxy re-encryption enabled secure and anonymous IoT data sharing platform based on blockchain. J Netw Comput Appl 176
4. Ping Y, Zhan Y, Lu K, Wang B (2020) Public data integrity verification scheme for secure cloud storage. Information 11(9)
5. Gaetani E, Aniello L, Baldoni R, Lombardi F, Margheri A, Sassone V (2017) Blockchain-based database to ensure data integrity in cloud computing environments. ITASEC
6. Hao K, Xin J, Wang Z, Wang G (2020) Outsourced data integrity verification based on blockchain in untrusted environment. World Wide Web 23
7. Tian J, Jing X (2020) Cloud data integrity verification scheme for associated tags. Comput Secur 95

8. Wei P, Wang D, Zhao SK, Tyagi S, Kumar N (2020) Blockchain data-based cloud data integrity protection mechanism. Futur Gener Comput Syst 102:902–911
9. Huang P, Fan K, Yang H, Zhang K, Li H, Yang Y (2020) A collaborative auditing blockchain for trustworthy data integrity in cloud storage system. IEEE Access
10. Yang X, Pei X, Wang M, Li T, Wang C (2020) Multi-replica and multi-cloud data public audit scheme based on blockchain. IEEE Access
11. Wanga H, Qin H, Zhao M, Wei X, Shen H, Susilo W (2020) Blockchain-based fair payment smart contract for public cloud storage auditing. Elsevier, Information Sciences
12. Qin X, Huang Y, Yang Z, Li X (2020) A blockchain-based access control scheme with multiple attribute authorities for secure cloud data sharing. J Syst Arch 112
13. Benil T, Jasper J (2020) Cloud-based security on outsourcing using blockchain in E-health systems. Comput Netw 178
14. Huang H, Zhu P, Xiao F, Sun X, Huang Q (2020) A blockchain-based scheme for privacy-preserving and secure sharing of medical data. Comput Secur 99
15. Huang H, Sun X, Xiao F, Zhu P, Wang W (2021) Blockchain-based eHealth system for auditable EHRs manipulation in cloud environments. J Parallel Distrib Comput 148:46–57
16. Huang B, Zhang R, Lu Z, Zhang Y, Wu J, Zhan L, Hung PC (2020) BPS: a reliable and efficient pub/sub communication model with blockchain-enhanced paradigm in multi-tenant edge cloud. J Parallel Distrib Comput 143
17. Hang L, Ullah I, Kim DH (2020) A secure fish farm platform based on blockchain for agriculture data integrity. Comput Electron Agric 170
18. Zhao Q, Chen S, Liu Z, Baker T, Zhang Y (2020) Blockchain-based privacy-preserving remote data integrity checking scheme for IoT information systems. Inf Process Manag 57
19. Li J, Wu J, Jiang G, Srikanthan T (2020) Blockchain-based public auditing for big data in cloud storage. Inf Process Manag 7(6)
20. Yue D, Li R, Zhang Y, Tian W, Huang Y (2020) Blockchain-based verification framework for data integrity in edge-cloud storage. J Parallel Distrib Comput 146:1–14
21. Velmurugadass P, Dhanasekaran S, Shasi Anand S, Vasudevan V (2020) Enhancing blockchain security in cloud computing with IoT environment using ECIS and cryptography hash algorithm. Mater Today: Proc 37:2653–2659
22. Ch R, Srivastava G, Gadekallu TR, Maddikunta PK, Bhattacharya S (2020) Security and privacy of UAV data using blockchain technology. J Inf Secur Appl 55
23. Wang Y, Chen Z, Wang K, Yang Z (2019) Education cloud data integrity verification based on mapping-trie tree. In: International conference on machine learning, big data and business intelligence, vol 1, pp 155-158
24. Wang C, Chen S, Feng Z, Jiang Y, Xue X (2019) Block chain-based data audit and access control mechanism in service collaboration. In: IEEE international conference on web services, pp 214–218
25. Wang H, Zhang J (2019) Blockchain-based data integrity verification for large-scale IoT data. IEEE Access
26. Sharma P, Jindal R, Borah MD (2019)Blockchain-based integrity protection system for cloud storage. In: 4th technology innovation management and engineering science international conference (TIMES-iCON), pp 1–5
27. Zhang Y, Xu C, Lin X, Shen X (2019) Blockchain-based public integrity verification for cloud storage against procrastinating auditors. IEEE Trans Cloud Comput 9(3):923–937
28. Luo X, Zhou Z, Zhong L, Mao J, Chen C (2018) An effective integrity verification scheme of cloud data based on bls signature. Secur Commun Netw
29. Yan Y, Wu L, Gao G, Wang H, Xu W (2018) A dynamic integrity verification scheme of cloud storage data based on lattice and Bloom filter. J Inf Secur Appl 39:10–18
30. Apolinário F, Pardal M, Correia M (2018) S-audit: efficient data integrity verification for cloud storage. In: 17th IEEE international conference on trust, security and privacy in computing and communications/12th IEEE international conference on big data science and engineering, pp 465–474

31. Krithikashree L, Manisha S, Sujithra M (2018) Audit cloud: ensuring data integrity for mobile devices in cloud storage. In: 9th international conference on computing, communication and networking technologies (ICCCNT), pp 1–5
32. Yue D, Li R, Zhang Y, Tian W, Peng C (2018)Blockchain-based data integrity verification in p2p cloud storage. In: Proceedings of the IEEE 24th international conference on parallel and distributed systems (ICPADS'18), pp 561–568
33. Zhou L, Fu A, Yu S, Su M, Kuang B (2018) Data integrity verification of the outsourced big data in the cloud environment: a survey. J Netw Comput Appl
34. Rajendran A, Balasubramanian V, Mala T (2017) Integrity verification using Identity-based provable data possession in multi-storage cloud. In: International conference on computational intelligence in data science (ICCIDS), pp 1–4
35. Ferretti L, Marchetti M, Andreolini M, Colajanni M (2017) A symmetric cryptographic scheme for data integrity verification in cloud databases. Inf Sci 422
36. Hiremath S, Kunte S (2017) A novel data auditing approach to achieve data privacy and data integrity in cloud computing. In: International conference on electrical, electronics, communication, computer, and optimization techniques (ICEECCOT), pp 306–310
37. Zikratov I, Kuzmin A, Akimenko V, Niculichev V, Yalansky L (2017) Ensuring data integrity using blockchain technology. In: Proceedings of the 20th conference of open innovations association, pp 534–539
38. Liu B, Yu XL, Chen S, Xu X, Zhu L (2017) Blockchain-based data integrity service framework for IoT data. In: IEEE international conference on web services (ICWS)
39. Lin C, Shen Z, Chen Q, Sheldon FT (2016) A data integrity verification scheme in mobile cloud computing. J Netw Comput Appl 77
40. Zhang Y, Xu C, Li H, Liang X (2016) Cryptographic public verification of data integrity for cloud storage systems. IEEE Cloud Comput
41. Wang H, Li K, Ota K, Shen J (2016) Remote data integrity checking and sharing in cloud-based health internet of things. IEICE Trans Inf Syst E99.D:1966–1973
42. Wang S, Zhang D, Zhang Y (2016) Blockchain-based personal health records sharing scheme with data integrity verifiable. IEEE Access
43. Niaz MS, Saake G (2015) Merkle hash tree-based techniques for data integrity of outsourced data. In: 27th GI-workshop on foundations of databases
44. Zhang SM, Xu YC, Wang BY, Xiao J, Niu R (2014) A remote data integrity verification scheme based on cloud computing. Appl Mech Mater 9:644-650

Media House Bias Prediction Using Deep Learning Framework

Vikash Kumar, Ashish Ranjan, Md Shah Fahad, and Akshay Deepak

1 Introduction

India is the world's largest democratic country. Four pillars were constituted to safeguard this democracy, and one of the four pillars is media. The media has the ability to alter a country's perception of truth and lies. However, nowadays, diverse perspectives on a single issue exist. As per Wikipedia [1], media bias can be defined as "Selection Criteria of many story and events that are reported and how they are covered". Now, we have two mechanisms, i.e., "selective coverage and way of presenting for an issue", to describe media bias. There are different terminologies to which bias can be categorized [2].

1. Bias by spin: It happens when a story only includes one interpretation of an event or policy, to the exclusion of others. Spin incorporates tone—a reporter's subjective comments about objective facts and makes one side's ideological view look better than the other.
2. Bias by placement: It refers to the location of a story or event on a website (or in a newspaper) or in an article.
3. Bias by Selection of Sources: It includes more sources that support one view over another. This bias can also be seen when a reporter uses such phrases as "experts believe," "observers say," or "most people believe". And when a news story only presents one side, it is obviously the side which the reporter supports.

V. Kumar (✉) · A. Ranjan · M. S. Fahad · A. Deepak
National Institute of Technology, Patna, India
e-mail: vikashk.ph21.cs@nitp.ac.in

A. Ranjan
e-mail: ashish.cse16@nitp.ac.in

M. S. Fahad
e-mail: shah.cse16@nitp.ac.in

A. Deepak
e-mail: akshayd@nitp.ac.in

© The Author(s), under exclusive license to Springer Nature Singapore Pte Ltd. 2022
U. P. Rao et al. (eds.), *Security, Privacy and Data Analytics*, Lecture Notes
in Electrical Engineering 848, https://doi.org/10.1007/978-981-16-9089-1_11

4. Bias by Omission: It can be defined as leaving one side out of an article, including only one aspect of the story, aspects favoring or disapproving an individual party or person and ignoring all other aspects.
5. Bias by Labeling: It is when one party or individual is assigned extreme labels, while the other party or person is assigned mild or moderate labels.

We have used a publicly available dataset [3] for this work and three class labels, i.e., polarity score $(-1, 0, 1)$ was assigned manually by splitting the content into paragraphs. The problem was converted into a classification problem like sentiment analysis. Sentiment analysis can be defined as contextual mining of text which identifies and extracts subjective information in the source material and helps a business to understand the social sentiment of their brand, product, or service while monitoring online conversations. A lot of researchers had worked on sentiment analysis using different machine learning and deep learning techniques and classified the problem into binary and multi-class problems. Sentiment analysis can be done on text as well as image data. Sentiment analysis on textual data such as tweets data has been examined as binary and multi-class problems by using SENTA [4], different machine learning techniques [5] such as Random Forest, Support Vector Regression, Decision Trees, and Multinomial Logistic Regression and Deep Learning Techniques such as Glove-DCCN [6]. Sentiment analysis has also been done on product reviews such as Amazon products review which has been proposed by using machine learning techniques such as Random Forest and Support Vector Machine and has achieved a promising score [7].

The news articles and media reports these days cover a vast range of issues and topics ranging from social, political, and economic issues to the entertainment industry. The impact of bias news and articles of the tweets on real-time issue, "Demonetization in India", was proposed, and they show that an enormous number of people can be influenced by bias news [8]. Our work aims to determine if a media organisation and/or individual is biased, with a focus on detecting bias against a political leader and/or political party.

Media house bias can be seen in various aspects. The first is related to selective coverage, in which a country's specific events are given less attention in worldwide media. Low coverage of events connected to country-level factors unique to Africa, for example, has been studied [9]. They also indicate that non-media organisations cover a large number of events that are not covered by media organisations. Bias can be shown in the form of pictures; when we see an image in newspaper or news television, it create thoughts for that particular image or personality. Pictures shows the specific emotions, characters, ideology, and many more which has been shown [10]. They take the help of some sort of workers to rate a subset of images and determine that image can change the perception among the people for a particular personality if presented in a bias manner.

Felix Hamborg [11] made use of natural language processing and deep learning to determine the instance of bias by word choice and labeling for news articles reported on the same event and evaluate the induced frame.

Upcoming sections are structured as follows. We discuss the dataset and then propose the methodology along with the process by which a label is assigned, in Sect. 2. After this, we have discussed the results in Sect. 3, and Sect. 4 concludes the paper.

2 Proposed Methodology

A neural network model was proposed to classify the media bias into polarity value $(-1, 0, 1)$ such as done in sentiment classification. Then, the predicted results of different test data were compared with the ground truth of that test data. For pre-processing of text data, we have used different natural language techniques such as Count Vectorizer, Lemmatization, Tokenizer, and many more. Figure 1 shows the workflow diagram representation of Media house bias prediction.

2.1 Dataset

The dataset used in this work is of Indian political articles from January 2018 through December 2018, collected from over seven news portals; it consists of 15346 articles and is publicly available. Dataset descriptions are given in the form of a bar chart (see Figs. 2, 3, and 4). Sometimes, automatic annotation does not work as expected in many cases; research shows that manually annotated bias is more effective than automatic annotation [12]. After deeply examining each aspect, we manually assigned the class label by splitting the sentences into paragraphs consisting of three lines, and then each paragraph was given a polarity score. The polarity score of $(-1, 0, +1)$ represents negative bias, unbiased, and positive bias respectively. We have taken the specific ratio of (70: 30) data for the training and testing of the model.

2.2 Text Pre-processing

In Natural Language Processing (NLP), text pre-processing is the first task we all do, which includes data cleaning, removing stop words, stemming, lemmatization, and many more. We have used the NLTK library [13] for this specific task. To make this text data into a machine-understandable form, we have used count vectorizer, token vectorizer, and embedding layer from the Keras API.

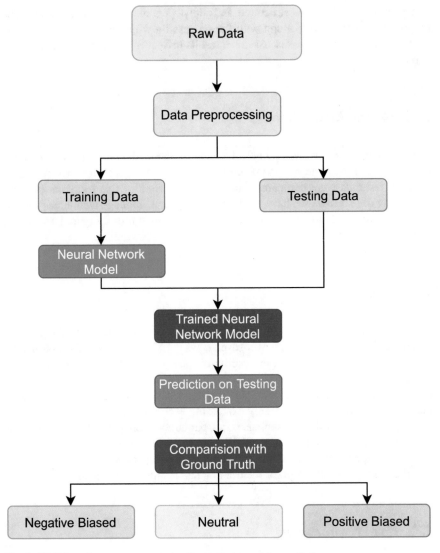

Fig. 1 Workflow diagram representation for media house bias prediction

2.3 Deep Learning Techniques

The proposed architecture (see Fig. 1) consists of Neural Network Models such as Deep Neural Network (DNN) and Long Short-Term Memory (LSTM). DNN is better than the artificial neural network (ANN) as it can extract the important features in a better way than ANN. The Neural Network Models are described below.

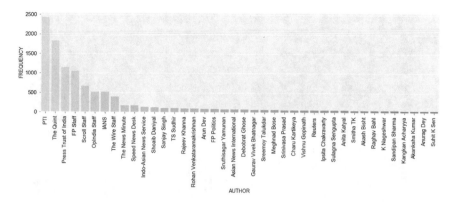

Fig. 2 Data description with respect to the author is given which shows gradual decreasing of the number of articles in which PTI has the highest number of articles and Suhit K Sen has the lowest number of articles

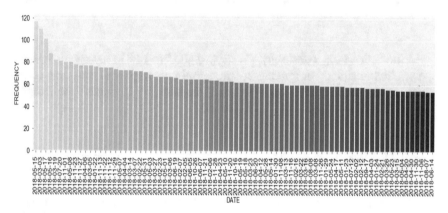

Fig. 3 Data description with respect to date is given here, and we have the highest number of articles of earlier dates and lowest number of articles with nearest date

1. **DNN**: Neural networks with a maximum of 2 hidden layers are termed as simple neural networks.

   Here, dense layers with *ReLU* activation function are used after getting the embedding vector from the embedding layer. As input, we have pre-processed articles in the form of vectors and as output we get 3 class results in the form of polarity values. *Softmax* activation function is used at the output layer. For training, Adam optimizer is used with categorical cross entropy as loss and to stop overfitting dropout $= 0.3$ is used. To get the best model, early stopping monitoring is done.

2. **LSTM**: LSTM works better for learning automatic features of the temporal data such as in Natural Language Processing task, signal *processing* [14], bio-informatics sequential data [15], and many more. Here, the sequential model consists of the LSTM layer with 128 LSTM cells used after the embedding layer.

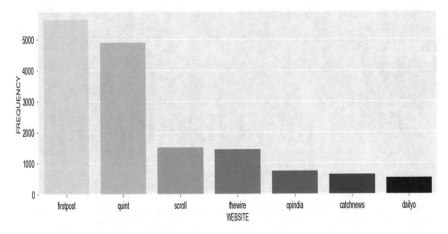

Fig. 4 Frequency of data with respect to sources are given in which Firstpost has the highest frequency and Dailyo has the lowest

For prediction task, a dense layer is stacked after the LSTM layer with Softmax activation function. For training, Adam optimizer is used with categorical cross entropy as loss. To get the best model, early stopping monitoring is done. Dropout = 0.3 is used to stop overfitting of the model.

3 Result and Comparison

As this is a different concept and have limited amount of research inputs for this specific dataset. So, we proposed two neural network models (i) DNN and (ii) LSTM. Apart from this, the deep neural network model was trained and testing of this model gives us the accuracy = 35.69 % for sentiment classification. Further, the LSTM models are trained and testing result gives accuracy = 37.99% for sentiment classification. Training accuracy of the proposed model per epoch is shown here (see Fig. 5). After epoch = 22, the accuracy remained unchanged, and the model stopped training as shown in Fig. 5. Table 1 shows the comparison between the proposed model marked as * and the base model. It shows the proposed model behaves better in terms of accuracy. Next, this trained model is used for predicting the biasness of each article.

We have proposed a neural network model which classifies an article to be negatively biased, neutral, and positively biased as sentiment classification, i.e., classification for polarity value of (−1, 0, +1), and again this model is used for testing individual articles. So, for predicting whether media houses or authors are biased toward the event or personality, three different articles were taken. So, in order to detect the media bias, firstly, the ground truth on any particular issue is determined based on the number of articles from multiple media houses and by authors. Based

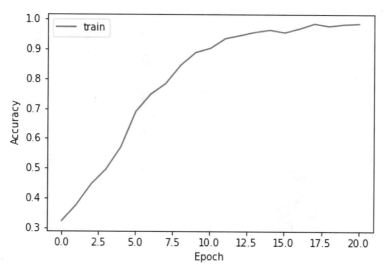

Fig. 5 Model accuracy per epoch is shown here and it shows that after 22 epochs, the training accuracy tops

Table 1 Comparison analysis with other deep learning model

S. No.	Model	Accuracy (%)
1.	LSTM [16]	32.30
2.	DNN*	35.69
3.	LSTM*	37.99

on the ground truth, it is determined whether the media houses or the author's article is biased or not on that particular issue. If any media house or author's articles are mostly biased, we conclude that it always reports in a biased manner.

So, for the first article, results are shown here (see Fig. 6). This shows the different predictions for this particular article in which Quint and Scroll are negatively biased and Firstpost is neutral against this article which is the ground truth of the given article. When the second article was evaluated, the result shows (see Fig. 7) that Scroll and Firstpost media houses are unbiased, whereas Quint is positively biased in nature for this article. Last but not the least, the third article on evaluation with this trained model, result (see Fig. 8), shows that Scroll and Quint media houses are negatively biased and Firstpost is unbiased toward this article. Now, based on these statistics, we tested which media house in general is positively biased, unbiased, or negatively biased for any type of article. So, this result shows (see Fig. 9) that Quint and Scroll are negatively biased as they are negatively biased for two articles out of three whereas Firstpost is neither negatively biased nor positively biased, i.e., it is unbiased in nature which predicts all the articles as unbiased which is similar in nature with ground truth of test articles.

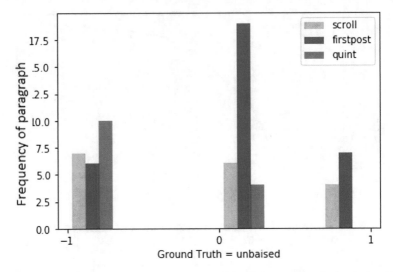

Fig. 6 Prediction of biasness by model on the first article where average calculated ground truth was zero. The result shows Scroll and Quint media houses are negatively biased and Firstpost media house is unbiased

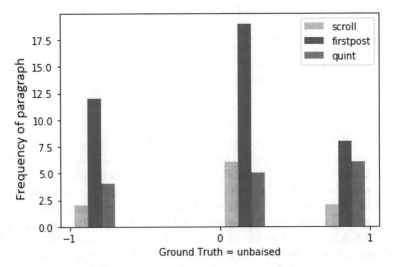

Fig. 7 Prediction of biasness by model on the second article where average calculated ground truth was zero for the article. The result shows Firstpost and Scroll media houses are neutral and Quint media house is positively biased

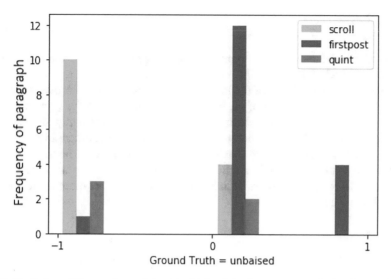

Fig. 8 Prediction of biasness by model on the third article where average calculated ground truth was zero for the article. The result shows Quint and Scroll media houses are negatively biased and Firstpost media house is positively biased

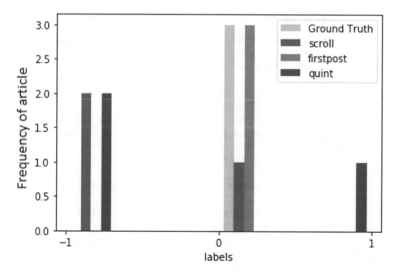

Fig. 9 Overall predicted result of the model with deviation from the ground truth. The result shows that Ground truth was Neutral for all the three articles and prediction by the model shows Scroll and Quint media houses are Negatively biased for two articles and Firstpost media house is unbiased for all the tested articles

4 Conclusion

Reasonably satisfactory results were obtained on using neural network models such as DNN and LSTM. However, the accuracy cannot be relied upon as of now because of the extremely small size of the training dataset and highly selective test dataset as compared to the vastness of the news domain. But nevertheless, an end-to-end pipeline has been developed which when supplied with sufficiently large data for training the model that can achieve great results and high accuracy in predictions. Also, other Deep Learning and Machine Learning models could be tried for better predictions of bias of individual articles. Thus, further work on this project would bequite useful in achieving extraordinary results in this field of detecting media bias which has huge potential.

References

1. Media Bias Wiki. https://en.wikipedia.org/wiki/Media_bias. Accessed 7 Jul 2021
2. Baker BH, Graham T, Kaminsky S (1994) How to identify, expose & correct liberal media bias. Media Research Center, Alexandria
3. Maxnet Homepage. https://github.com/maxent-ai/Datasets/tree/master/data/politics18. Accessed 7 Jul 2021
4. Bouazizi M, Ohtsuki T (2017) A pattern-based approach for multi-class sentiment analysis in Twitter. IEEE Access 5:20617–20639
5. Saad SE, Yang J (2019) Twitter sentiment analysis based on ordinal regression. IEEE Access 7:163677–163685
6. Jianqiang Z, Xiaolin G, Xuejun Z (2018) Deep convolution neural networks for twitter sentiment analysis. IEEE Access 6:23253–23260
7. Al Amrani Y, Lazaar M, El Kadiri KE (2018) Random forest and support vector machine based hybrid approach to sentiment analysis. In: 1st international conference on intelligent computing on data science, pp 511–520. Procedia Computer Science
8. Aggarwal S, Sinha T, Kukreti Y, Shikhar S (2020) Media bias detection and bias short term impact assessment. Array 6
9. Dietrich N, Eck K (2020) Known unknowns: media bias in the reporting of political violence. Int Interact 46(6):1043–1060
10. Peng Y (2018) Same candidates, different faces: uncovering media bias in visual portrayals of presidential candidates with computer vision. J Commun 68(5):920–941
11. Hamborg F (2020) Media bias, the social sciences, and nlp: automating frame analyses to identify bias by word choice and labeling. In: Proceedings of the 58th annual meeting of the association for computational linguistics: student research workshop, pp 79–87
12. Spinde T, Hamborg F, Donnay K, Becerra A, Gipp B (2020) Enabling news consumers to view and understand biased news coverage: a study on the perception and visualization of media bias. In: Proceedings of the ACM/IEEE joint conference on digital libraries, pp 389–392
13. Bird S, Klein E and Loper E (2009) Natural language processing with Python: analyzing text with the natural language toolkit. O'Reilly Media, Inc., Sebastopol
14. McFee B, Raffel C, Liang D, Ellis DPW, McVicar M, Battenberg E, Nieto O (2015) Librosa, "Audio and music signal analysis in python." In: Proceedings of the 14th python in science conference, vol 8, pp 18–25. Citeseer (2015)

15. Ranjan A, Fahad MdS, Fern' andez-Baca D, Deepak A, Tripathi S (2020) Deep robust framework for protein function prediction using variable-length protein sequences. IEEE/ACM Trans Comput Biol Bioinf 17(5):1648–1659
16. Baly R, Da San Martino G, Glass J, Nakov P (2020) We can detect your bias: predicting the political ideology of news articles. arXiv:2010.05338

Hindi Songs Genre Classification Using Deep Learning

Md Shah Fahad, Raushan Raj, Ashish Ranjan, and Akshay Deepak

1 Introduction

Music is like a mirror; it provides a lot of information about who you are and what you like. Companies increasingly utilize music classification to classify what they care about either to be able to make consumer recommendations (such as Spotify, Soundcloud, and other similar services) or just as a product (for example, Shazam) [1]. The first step in that direction is to identify music genres. Machine Learning algorithms are effective at extracting trends and patterns from massive amounts of data. In music analysis, the same principles are used [2, 3]. Songs are analyzed for tempo, acoustics, energy, and other factors based on their digital signatures.

Early notable works for the music genre classification include [1, 2, 4, 5]. In the paper [4], a multivariate auto-regressive feature model is introduced for music genre classification. In [5], the author proposed an ensemble method based on the deep learning (extracted using CNN) + hand-crafted features (time-domain features and frequency-domain features) for the seven-class music genre classification. In [1], a (CNN + word2vec) model is used for predicting the music genre. Most of these approaches use MFCC as the input feature for their deep learning models [1, 5]. In the paper [6], the authors proposed the method for classifying Hindi songs into four genre classes—*Classical, Folk, Ghazal,* and *Sufi.* They employed spectral features and SVM classifiers to conduct the classification. Further, in [7], the author studied and identified hand-crafted features specific to music genre classification that include mel-frequency cepstrum coefficients (MFCCs), pitch [8], dominant frequency, and chroma [9] features.

M. S. Fahad (✉) · R. Raj · A. Ranjan · A. Deepak
National Institute of Technology, Patna, India
e-mail: shah.cse16@nitp.ac.in

R. Raj
e-mail: raushanr.pg20.cs@nitp.ac.in

A. Ranjan
e-mail: ashish.cse16@nitp.ac.in

A. Deepak
e-mail: akshayd@nitp.ac.in

© The Author(s), under exclusive license to Springer Nature Singapore Pte Ltd. 2022
U. P. Rao et al. (eds.), *Security, Privacy and Data Analytics*, Lecture Notes
in Electrical Engineering 848, https://doi.org/10.1007/978-981-16-9089-1_12

The proposed framework used a convolutional neural network (CNN) alongside the long short-term memory network (LSTM) with an attention mechanism for the task of Hindi music genre classification. In this work, a convolutional neural network (CNN) [10] is used to determine the features automatically from data itself [5]. Chroma, Pitch, Mel-spectrogram [11], and MFCC are used as input to the CNN. Further, the global features are identified by using a long short-term memory network (LSTM). LSTM [12] can learn the sequential pattern of different categories of songs. Further, because each sub-part of a signal does not contribute equally, henceforth, an attention mechanism [13] is applied to weigh each sub-part. The results for the proposed framework demonstrate the effectiveness of the MFCC features for the audio genre classification.

Paper organization: The explanation of the dataset and the proposed methodology are discussed in Sect. 2. Section 3 discusses the experimental design and results. Section 4 concludes the paper.

2   Proposed Methodology

Further, this section is divided into subsections as demonstrated below. Section 2.1 describes the database. Section 2.2 discusses feature extraction. The discussion of deep learning architecture is presented in Sect. 2.3.

2.1   Dataset

The dataset is composed of 599 audio tracks of Hindi songs where each audio track is trimmed to a maximum length of 30 s. Further, each audio track is trimmed between 0.5 and 5.5 s to generate a feasible size of the input matrix. The sampling rate is 40 kHz. The genres corresponding to songs were downloaded manually taking references from popular websites, such as Spotify and Wynk. It includes six genres: Sufi, Classical, Romantic, Ghazal, Party, and Bhakti. Each genre has between 70 and 80 sound clips. The dataset is collected from various websites in which the categorization of songs is given. The distribution of samples corresponding to each genre is shown in Fig. 1.

2.2   Feature Representation

Every audio signal contains a variety of features. However, we must extract the features that are pertinent to the problem at hand. Librosa [14] is a Python module for analyzing audio signals in general, with a focus on music. In this work, chroma, pitch, mel-spectrogram, and MFCC features are used as input for the proposed framework.

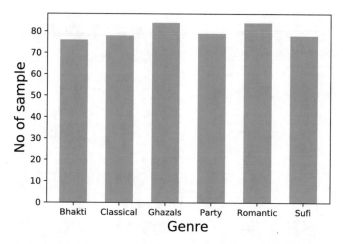

Fig. 1 Distribution of a number of audio signals of each song's genre

The audio signal is non-stationary, therefore, frequency transformation is done frame-wise with 50% overlapping. The size of a frame is the same as FFT length, i.e. 2048. The total number of frames is 391 for an audio clip. The other attributes for different representations are:

1. **Chroma**: For chroma features, 12 bins are used and an output matrix of size 431×12 is produced.
2. **Pitch**: For pitch, 1025 FFT bins are chosen, resulting into 1025 pitch and their corresponding magnitude values for each frame. A matrix of size $391 \times 1025 \times 2$ is created. [1]
3. **Mel-spectrogram** [11]: The mel-frequency cepstrum captures the properties of the signal's frequency as represented on the Mel-scale, which closely resembles the non-linearity of human hearing. For Mel-spectrogram, the frequency of a signal is represented on the Mel-scale of length 128 which is similar to the non-linear nature of the human hearing. Thus, a matrix of size 391×128 is fed to the proposed framework. Mel-spectrogram corresponding to each of the song's genre is shown in Fig. 2.
4. **MFCC**: MFCCs are often the frequently used features for several speech-related tasks [15]. For MFCC, 26 MFCC features are extracted and a matrix of size 391×26 is fed to the proposed framework. MFCC corresponding to each of the song's genres is shown in Fig. 3.

---

[1] https://librosa.org/doc/main/generated/librosa.piptrack.html

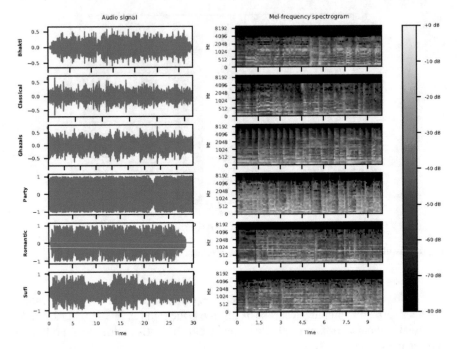

Fig. 2 Audio signal and corresponding Mel-Spectrogram of each song's genre

2.3 Proposed Framework

The proposed solution is a deep learning-based framework and consists of CNN, bi-directional LSTM, and Attention [13] layers. In contrast to shallow neural networks, deep neural networks are more specialized toward extracting the features that are more meaningful and incorporate a better learning methodology. The block diagram of the proposed framework is depicted in Fig. 3. These layers are described next:

1. **CNN**: The advantage of convolutional neural network (CNN) [10] layers is that they aid in capturing the local features by the convolution operation.

   A stack of two (convolution + batch-normalization) layers is used. The input to the first convolutional layer is a matrix representation of an audio clip. The matrix can either be a representation, for instance, Pitch, Chroma, Mel-spectrogram, and MFCC. After that, max-pooling layers are added to minimize the number of parameters. The hyper-parameters with CNN layers are as follows:

   (a) Filter-size (1st layer): 5×5
   (b) Filter-size (2nd layer): 5×5
   (c) Number of filters (1st layer): 32
   (d) Number of filters (2nd layer): 64

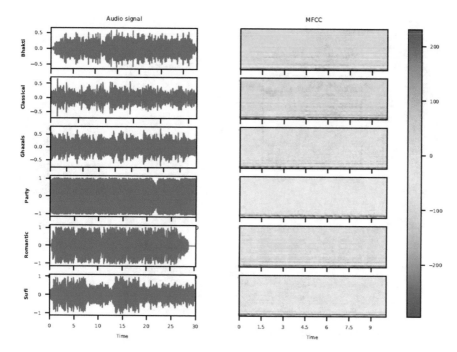

Fig. 3 Audio signal and corresponding MFCC of each song's genre

(e) Pool-size: (2 × 2).

2. **LSTM**: LSTM is popular for sequences, such as NLP, biological sequences [16], and speech signals [12, 17] and aid in learning temporal dependencies in the sequence.

   The sequential behavior underlying the features extracted from the CNN layer is learned by using the long short-term memory (LSTM) layers. The LSTM network is used in a bi-directional mode [12] and the number of hidden neuron units with the LSTM cell is taken as 32.

3. **Attention**: This helps assign different weights to the LSTM outputs, since not all the regions in a given signal play the same role. The additive attention proposed by Bahdanau et al. [13] was used for this work.

In between the CNN layer and LSTM layer is the reshape layer to transform the 3-D output to a 2-D output (suitable for the LSTM).

Further, a dense layer is stacked on top of the attention layer. The number of neurons in this layer is 20, while the activation function is taken as *ReLU*. Finally, the last layer with *Softmax* activation is used to perform the music genre classification task.

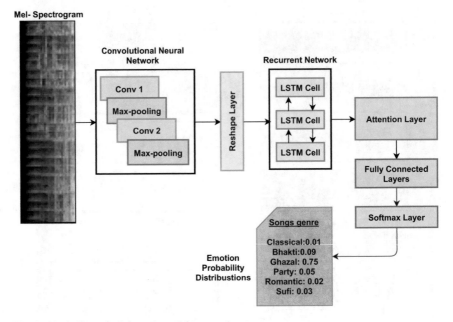

Fig. 4 Block diagram of the proposed framework

The choice of other hyper-parameters for the proposed framework is as follows (Fig. 4):

1. Loss function: categorical_cross-entropy to deal multi-class problem.
2. Optimizer: Adam.
3. Batch-size: 32.
4. Total epochs: 100.
5. Early-stopping criteria with patience: 10 epoch.

3 Experimental Design and Result Discussion

The proposed model architecture was implemented using the Keras API that is built on top of TensorFlow. The dataset is divided into training and testing sets, with 80% data (479 samples) in the training set and 20% data (120 samples) in the testing set. The training set is used for developing the model and the test set for evaluating the model.

Table 1 Precision (P), Recall (R), and F1-Score (F1) for each feature (pitch, chroma, Mel-spectrogram (Mel), and MFCC) corresponding to each genre

Feature	Metric	Bhakti	Classical	Ghazal	Party	Romantic	Sufi	Avg.
Pitch	P	0.45	0.41	0.72	0.65	0.33	0.33	0.48
	R	0.42	0.50	0.81	0.71	0.21	0.33	0.49
	F1	0.43	0.45	0.76	0.68	0.26	0.33	0.48
Chroma	P	0.32	0.41	0.62	0.58	0.32	0.44	0.44
	R	0.33	0.50	0.62	0.67	0.32	0.22	0.44
	F1	0.33	0.45	0.62	0.62	0.32	0.30	0.43
Mel	P	0.50	0.59	0.93	0.70	0.50	0.38	0.59
	R	0.58	0.59	0.88	0.76	0.42	0.33	0.59
	F1	0.54	0.59	0.90	0.73	0.46	0.35	0.59
MFCC	P	**0.70**	**0.73**	**1.00**	**0.82**	**0.52**	**0.62**	**0.73**
	R	**0.67**	**1.00**	**0.88**	**0.67**	**0.63**	**0.44**	**0.71**
	F1	**0.68**	**0.85**	**0.93**	**0.74**	**0.57**	**0.52**	**0.71**

3.1 Comparison with Respect to Different Speech Features

In this work, different speech features, namely (i) Chroma, (ii) Pitch, (iii) Mel-spectrogram, and (iv) Mel Frequency Cepstral Coefficient (MFCC) have been explored using the proposed deep learning (CNN + Bi-directional LSTM + Attention) architecture. Popular evaluation metrics such as *Precision, Recall*, and *F1-score* for each speech features (Pitch, Chroma, Mel-spectrogram, and MFCC) for different genre classes (Bhakti, Classical, Ghazal, Party, Romantic, and Sufi) are shown in Table 1.

The best precision, recall, and F1-score are obtained using MFCC features. The genre class *"Ghazal"* has the best precision, recall, and F1-score 100%, 88%, and 93%, respectively. After that, the genre classes *"Classical"*, *"Party"*, and *"Bhakti"* achieve better results order-wise. The genre class *"Sufi"* is least accurate among all the genres. It achieves only 52% F1-score. The genre class *"Sufi"* is more confused with the genre *"Bhakti"* and *"Romantic"*.

3.2 Comparison with Other State-of-the-Art Models

This includes a comparison to the other standard deep learning models, such as the standalone CNN model and the (CNN + LSTM) model, widely applicable in processing the speech signal data. Note that the LSTM model is evaluated for both; the uni-directional and the bi-directional configuration. This sort of comparison also benefits understanding the advantage of different layers with the proposed model (i.e. based on the MFCC features). The results obtained for the different models are shown in Table 2.

Table 2 Classification report with respect to different models (Uni: stands for the uni-direction LSTM; Bi: stands for the bi-direction LSTM; *indicated the proposed model)

S. no.	Models	Precision	Recall	F1-Score
1.	CNN	0.57	0.57	0.56
2.	CNN + Uni-LSTM	0.59	0.62	0.58
3.	CNN + Bi-LSTM	0.62	0.65	0.63
4.	CNN + Uni-LSTM + Attention	0.68	0.68	0.67
5.	CNN + Bi-LSTM +Attention*	**0.73**	**0.71**	**0.71**

As observed from Table 2, the results clearly suggest the strong results for the proposed model. The proposed model beats the standalone CNN-based model by a significantly huge margin, where the improvements recorded with respect to the *F1-score* is 15.0 percent. Similarly, the proposed model also outperformed the (CNN + Bi-LSTM) model by a margin of 8.0 percent. These improvements were also observed for other metrics, such as *precision* and *recall*. In addition, performances obtained for models with the uni-directional LSTM come out to be much lower when they are compared to models with the bi-directional LSTM.

The confusion matrices corresponding to different experimental models are also shown in Fig. 5 (with the CNN model), Fig. 6 (with the CNN + Uni-directional LSTM), Fig. 7 (with the CNN + Bi-directional LSTM), Fig. 8 (with the CNN + Uni-directional LSTM + Attention), and Fig. 9 (with the CNN + Bi-directional LSTM + Attention). Confusion matrix for different models indicates the best performances

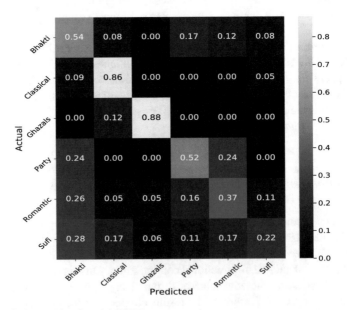

Fig. 5 Confusion matrix of model (CNN)

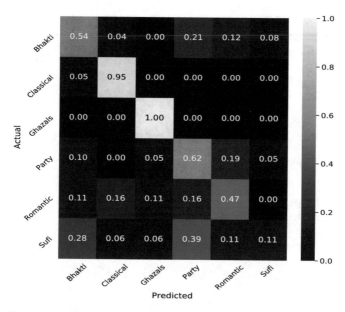

Fig. 6 Confusion matrix of model (CNN + Uni-LSTM)

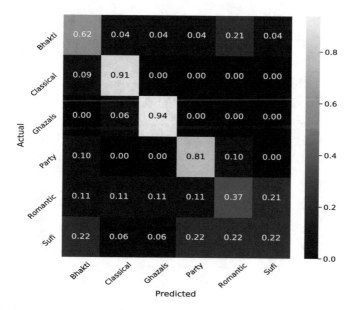

Fig. 7 Confusion matrix of model (CNN + Bi-LSTM)

for the music genre class, "*Classical*" and "*Ghazals*", while the worst performance is observed for "*Sufi*", such that a lot of them are classified under the "*Bhakti*" and the "*Romantic*" class.

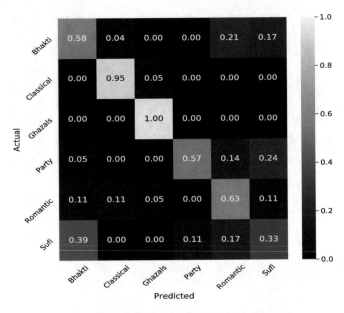

Fig. 8 Confusion matrix of model (CNN + Uni-LSTM + Attention)

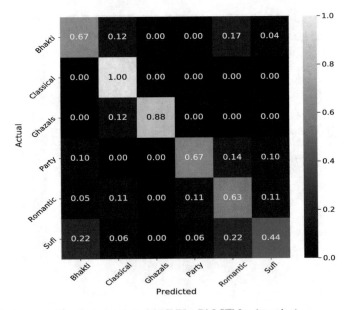

Fig. 9 Confusion matrix of proposed model (CNN + Bi-LSTM + Attention)

4 Conclusion

This work is for automatic genre identification of Hindi songs. There is no publicly available dataset. Therefore, a dataset is created for genre classification for Hindi songs. The deep learning architecture is developed to model the songs. Different features (Chroma, Pitch, Mel-spectrogram, and MFCC) are evaluated for the proposed architecture. Among all the features, MFCC produces the best F1-score of 71%.

References

1. Budhrani A, Patel A, Ribadiya S (2020) Music2vec: music genre classification and recommendation system. In: 2020 4th international conference on electronics, communication and aerospace technology (ICECA). IEEE, pp 1406–1411
2. Liang Dawen, Haijie Gu, O'Connor Brendan (2011) Music genre classification with the million song dataset. Machine Learning Department, CMU
3. Andrew Minkyu Sang (2020) Predicting musical genres using deep learning and ensembling. University of California, Los Angeles
4. Meng A, Ahrendt P, Larsen J, Kai Hansen L (2007) Temporal feature integration for music genre classification. IEEE Trans Audio Speech Lang Process 15(5):1654–1664
5. Bahuleyan H (2018) Music genre classification using machine learning techniques. arXiv:1804.01149
6. Chaudhary D, Singh NP, Singh S (2019) Genre based classification of hindi music. In: Innovations in bio-inspired computing and applications, Cham. Springer International Publishing, pp 73–82
7. Fu Z, Lu G, Ting KM, Zhang D (2010) A survey of audio-based music classification and annotation. IEEE Trans Multimed 13(2):303–319
8. Zhu Y, Kankanhalli MS (2006) Precise pitch profile feature extraction from musical audio for key detection. IEEE Trans Multimed 8(3):575–584
9. Bartsch MA, Wakefield GH (2005) Audio thumbnailing of popular music using chroma-based representations. IEEE Trans Multimed 7(1):96–104
10. Albawi S, Mohammed TA, Al-Zawi S (2017) Understanding of a convolutional neural network. In: 2017 international conference on engineering and technology (ICET). IEEE, pp 1–6
11. Khunarsa P, Lursinsap C, Raicharoen T (2010) Impulsive environment sound detection by neural classification of spectrogram and mel-frequency coefficient images. In: Advances in neural network research and applications. Springer, pp 337–346
12. Graves A, Fernández S, Schmidhuber J (2005) Bidirectional lstm networks for improved phoneme classification and recognition. In: International conference on artificial neural networks. Springer, pp 799–804
13. Bahdanau D, Cho K, Bengio Y (2014) Neural machine translation by jointly learning to align and translate. arXiv:1409.0473
14. McFee B, Raffel C, Liang D, Ellis DPW, McVicar M, Battenberg E, Nieto O (2015) librosa: audio and music signal analysis in python. In: Proceedings of the 14th python in science conference, vol 8, pp 18–25. Citeseer
15. Fahad MS, Deepak A, Pradhan G, Yadav J (2021) DNN-HMM-based speaker-adaptive emotion recognition using MFCC and epoch-based features. Circ Syst Signal Process 40(1):466–489
16. Ranjan A, Fahad MS, Fernández-Baca D, Deepak A, Tripathi S (2020) Deep robust framework for protein function prediction using variable-length protein sequences. IEEE/ACM Trans Comput Biol Bioinf 17(5):1648–1659

17. Chen Mingyi, He Xuanji, Yang Jing, Zhang Han (2018) 3-D convolutional recurrent neural networks with attention model for speech emotion recognition. IEEE Signal Process Lett
25(10):1440–1444

Multi-model Emotion Recognition Using Hybrid Framework of Deep and Machine Learning

Md Shah Fahad, Aparna Juhi, Shambhavi, Ashish Ranjan,
and Akshay Deepak

1 Introduction

Emotion is a psycho-physiological response produced by conscious and/or uncon-
scious perceptions of things and circumstances, and is linked to a variety of characteristics including mood, temperament, personality, disposition, and motivation.
Emotions are often felt and conveyed through a variety of modalities, including facial
expressions, voice, and other bio-signals. Several independent studies had been conducted for emotion recognition that uses speech [1–3], text [4], facial cues [5], and
EEG-based brain waves [6]. Emotion also influences several aspects of human communication that may include facial expression, gestures, posture, voice tone, word
choice, and breathing. Emotions are difficult to recognize since they are extremely
subjective and temporally unbound.

Emotion is better comprehended, if interpreted based on combined source of
information such as, text, speech, and human expression. This makes single mode
emotion recognition often challenging. For example, the textual modal can only
judge the emotion by means of words and phrases used during the communication.
Typically, a word can signify a different emotion. Because of the intrinsic relationship

M. S. Fahad (✉) · A. Juhi · Shambhavi · A. Ranjan · A. Deepak
National Institute of Technology, Patna, India
e-mail: shah.cse16@nitp.ac.in

A. Juhi
e-mail: aparnaj.ug18.cs@nitp.ac.in

Shambhavi
e-mail: shambhavi.ug.17.cs@nitp.ac.in

A. Ranjan
e-mail: ashish.cse16@nitp.ac.in

A. Deepak
e-mail: akshayd@nitp.ac.in

© The Author(s), under exclusive license to Springer Nature Singapore Pte Ltd. 2022
U. P. Rao et al. (eds.), *Security, Privacy and Data Analytics*, Lecture Notes
in Electrical Engineering 848, https://doi.org/10.1007/978-981-16-9089-1_13

between text, speech, and mocap (face, head, and hand rotations), modal fusion may be used to improve the performance of the emotion recognition system. The inclusion of the various sources of information is needed in order for computers to identify emotional expression in real-world scenarios.

In this paper, apart from the feature fusion, the advantages of both deep and machine learning are also merged. The existing works either used the machine learning or deep neural network to develop the multi-modal emotion recognition [7–9]. Features are extracted from a deep learning framework where no feature engineering is required. Further, machine learning algorithms are used to develop the emotion recognition model. We have laid a special focus in describing the strengths and weaknesses of current ways and have tried to establish a new methodology that consists of the following contributions:

1. Categorizing human emotions by exploiting different data modalities and their combinations.
2. Exploring the combined nature of deep and machine learning algorithms.
3. Establishing a general behavior of emotion class under classification task.

Our research work aims to explain the current use, limitations, and challenges in integrating the multi-modal data. The final emotional state in our research would be a comparison among (i) each modality and their combinations (ii) understanding the behavior of different machine learning algorithms (SVM, Decision tree, Random forest, and XGBoost).

The next is the organization about paper. The related works are discussed in Sect. 2. Section 3 describes the dataset and the proposed methodology where the processing and modeling of each modality are discussed. Section 4 discusses result and discussion. Section 5 concludes the paper.

2 Related Work

So far, investigations in emotion recognition have been largely restricted to individual modality, for example, voice emotion recognition [2–4], EEG signals [6, 10], and facial expression [5]. Multi-modal emotion categorization has lately gained popularity, and IEMOCAP remains an important dataset for this study area. In this regard, a few studies, [7, 11, 12], have attempted to demonstrate interdependence between different modalities. Soujanya et al. [12] provide the most recent state-of-the-art categorization on IEMOCAP. They utilize 3D-CNN to extract visual features, text-CNN to extract textual features, and openSMILE to extract audio features.

3 Proposed Methodology

Further, this section is divided into subsections as demonstrated below. Section 3.1 describes about the database. Section 3.2 discusses the emotion recognition framework of the proposed approach.

3.1 Dataset

IEMOCAP [13] has 12 hrs of audio-visual data, collected from ten actors (five males and five females). The recordings were done for the dialogue exchanged between a male and female actor in both scripted and improvised topics. The audio-visual data is separated into short utterances ranging from 3 to 15 s in length, which are then labeled by evaluators. Three to four examiners judge each utterance. Neutral, happiness, sad, anger, surprise, fear, disgust, frustration, enthusiasm, and others were among the ten alternatives on the rating form. To maintain consistency with previous research, we only consider four of them: anger, excited (happy), neutral, and melancholy.

Our multi-modal emotion recognition pipeline is built around these three types of data: (i) Speech, (ii) Text, and (iii) Mocap. The distribution of utterances concerning different emotions in the training and testing dataset is shown in Table 1. To restrict our work to understand the effect of different modalities, we have neglected the imbalance between the sample distribution for different emotions. This will be included in future work. We discuss these data types in detail in the following sections.

3.1.1 Speech

Speech signals contain a multitude of information, for example, frequency, amplitude, and pitch, that helps identify the emotional state of a person. Raw speech signals represent a continuous form of signal and, therefore, must be processed before being used to train the model. For this work, a filter bank of size 40 is used to extract the spectrogram information using log-fbank features. The frame-by-frame processing of the voice signal is performed with a 50 % overlap. As a result, the duration of an

Table 1 Distribution of utterances corresponding to different emotions in the training and testing data

Emotion	Training	Testing
Anger	933	170
Excitation	742	299
Neutral	1324	384
Sad	839	245

utterance determines the total number of frames in the speech. We reduce the number of frames by 500 by truncating lengthier utterances and padding shorter utterances, and each frame contains 40 features. So, a matrix of size 500×40 is built for each utterance.

3.1.2 Text

Many social media sites create a large amount of textual data including rich emotional information in this era. Nonetheless, text-based emotion information is very limited, and there are numerous limitations to identifying technical words in certain disciplines. Still, a few words are often the strong indicator for a certain emotion. For example; consider the sentence, *"This is disgusting"*. Here, the word *disgusting* strongly suggests anger emotion.

3.1.3 Mocap

For the Mocap data, we sample all feature values between the start and finish time values and divide them into 200 partitioned arrays for each separate mode such as the face, hand, and head rotation. Then, for each utterance, we average each of the 200 arrays along with the columns (165 for faces, 18 for hands, and 6 for rotation), and then concatenate them together to get a (200, 189) dimension vector. The Mocap features are similar to image because it consists of face, hand, and head rotation.

3.2 Proposed Framework

Figure 1 shows the block diagram of the proposed framework. Light green, light orange, and light violet blocks represent the speech block, text block, and mocap block, respectively. The detailed information of each block is given in Sect. 3.2.1 (speech block), Sect. 3.2.2 (text block), and Sect. 3.2.3 (Mocap block).

3.2.1 Speech Block

This block is designed to capture the important features from the speech signals. The input to the speech module is the (500×40) sized speech utterance formulated as discussed in Sect. 3.1.1.

The processing of the utterance is conducted using the "attention-based bidirectional LSTM" model.

1. **Bi-directional LSTM**: LSTM, over the decades, has established itself as a benchmark for modeling the sequences. Common examples include textual sequences,

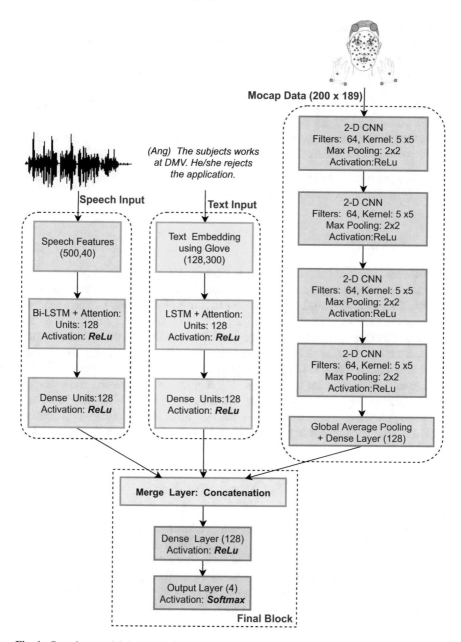

Fig. 1 Complete model demonstrating the processing and concatenation of all the three features, i.e., Speech, Text, and Mocap

biological sequences [14], speech signals [1, 15], etc. This helps detect and capture the sequential pattern information within the utterances that are relevant to emotion detection. The bi-directional property enables reading the utterances from both the direction. The number of hidden neurons with Bi-LSTM layers is taken as 128.

2. **Attention** [16]: Because every frame of an utterance does not contribute equally toward emotion, therefore, the attention mechanism to highlights emotional frame and masks the non-emotional frames is used. The attention is calculated for each frame and multiplied by the corresponding frames.

The output is the sum of all the weighted frames that are passed to the dense layer with 128 hidden units and *ReLU* activation.

3.2.2 Text Block

In this work, words are characterized using the GloVe embedding, i.e., using a 300-dimensional embedding. Because the count of words in each utterance varies in the dataset, therefore, the length of each sentence is fixed by 128 words. The maximum length of the sentence is fixed based on the observed maximum length of a sentence in the dataset. Additionally, as required zero-padding is applied for the shorter sentence.

Each utterance is thus represented by a (128×300) matrix. This matrix is passed through attention-based LSTM with a total of 128 hidden units, where *ReLU* is used as activation. Similar to the logic of attention for the speech, every word in the sentence will not contribute equally to emotion. Thus, attention-based LSTM is used which highlights the important emotional words. Here, simple uni-directional LSTM is used because the English language contains the left to right semantic of a sentence. The rest of the hyper-parameters are the same as speech emotion modeling.

3.2.3 Mocap Block

This block is composed of four layers of convolutional neural networks (CNNs) with max-pooling. Each CNN uses a kernel size of (5×5), and the number of filters is 64 for all the first three CNN layers. The max-pooling operation with pool-size of dimension (2×2) is applied after each CNN layer. The pooling operation helps to reduce the number of dimensions. Next, there is a global-average pooling layer to reduce the 2D output matrix into a 1D vector, and a dense layer of 128 hidden units is applied on a 1D vector.

3.2.4 Final Block

The outputs obtained from all of the three block, (i) speech block, (ii) text block, and (iii) mocap block, are then concatenated together as shown in Fig. 1. This gives a combined feature of a 384-dimensional vector. This 384-dimensional vector is then passed through a dense layer of hidden units 128 where *ReLU* activation is used. The last output layer which is the dense layer having a *Softmax* activation. The last layer has four neurons corresponding to the four emotions.

The other hyper-parameters are as defined follows:

1. Loss function: *categorical cross-entropy*
2. Optimizer: *Adam*
3. Batch size: 64
4. Epochs: 100

In addition, the early stopping criteria (taking patience equal to ten) is used to stop the over-fitting. The model obtained is called a *pre-trained multi-model*.

3.2.5 Utilizing the Pre-trained Model for Classification

The raw data is again passed to the *pre-trained multi-model*, as described in Fig. 2. The deep features are extracted from the dense layer of the final block. The size of the feature vector obtained from the *pre-trained multi-model* is (1×128).

Machine learning algorithms that include (i) Support vector machine (SVM) [17], (ii) Decision tree [18], (iii) Random forest [19], and (iv) XGBoost [20] are used to develop the emotion recognition model using the deep feature extracted from the *pre-trained multi-model*.

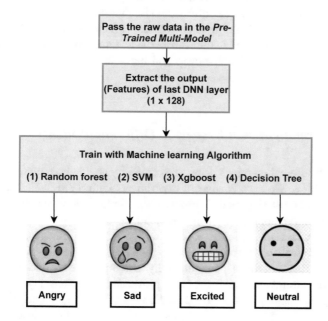

Fig. 2 Flowchart representing the final model

4 Result and Discussion

Here, we discuss the implementation and the experiments.

4.1 Implementation Details

There are 4936 utterances in total from the five different sessions. We split these utterances across two sub-datasets. The first set contains 3838 utterances (77.7%) as our training set for the final combined model, which corresponds to the first four sessions of the data with eight actors. As a test set, we use the remaining 1098 (22.2%) utterances from the fifth session. Each session has two actors (Male and Female) and no actor is repeated in any session. Thus, the experiment is validated in a speaker-independent manner. Keras is used to implement the proposed framework architecture.

4.2 Results Discussion

In this paper, a multi-modal emotion recognition model from textual, acoustics, and motion-capture (hand, head rotation, and facial expressions) on the IEMOCAP is presented. The proposed model takes advantage of different modalities to get more comprehensive and precise information for emotion classification. To get more effective features for the multi-modal emotional classification, a DNN network was put forward to learn the fused features from the text, mocap, and speech. Moreover, according to the qualities of text, mocap, and audio information, we set up a suitable model to detect features.

4.3 Performances with Respect to Different Modality

Accuracy of different emotions using each modality and their combination are presented in Table 2. We have conducted experiments with SVM [17], Decision Tree [18], Random Forest [19], and XGBoost [20]. Here, we have mentioned the best accuracy for each modality and their combination.

In most cases, random forest is showing the best performance, while for the combination consisting of (Mocap + Text) modality, XGBoost is showing the best performance. Random forest's default ability to compensate for decision tree's tendency of over-fitting to its training set is its most handy feature. When this algorithm is run using the bagging approach and random feature selection, it nearly eliminates the problem of over-fitting, which is wonderful because over-fitting leads to incorrect results. XGBoost is a scalable machine learning approach for tree boosting that pre-

Table 2 Accuracy of different emotions using each modality and their combination. Random forest, Anger, Excitation, and Neutral are abbreviated as (RF), (Ang), (Exc), and (Neu), respectively

Model/Emotion	Ang	Exc	Neu	Sad	UWA	WA	Classifier
Speech	0.74	0.14	0.49	0.56	0.48	0.53	RF
Text	0.70	0.44	0.59	0.61	0.59	0.63	RF
Mocap	0.57	0.78	0.07	0.00	0.36	0.44	RF
Mocap+Speech	0.66	0.45	0.55	0.59	0.56	0.59	RF
Mocap+Text	0.72	0.50	0.55	0.53	0.58	0.62	XGBoost
Text+Speech	0.67	0.55	**0.63**	**0.66**	0.63	0.68	RF
Speech+Text+Mocap	**0.79**	**0.58**	0.62	0.64	**0.66**	**0.71**	RF

vents over-fitting, which is popular among data scientists. So, we can conclude that ensemble machine learning algorithms (Random forest, XGBoost) achieve better accuracy than other algorithms (SVM and Decision Tree).

The best weighted-accuracy (WA) and unweighted-accuracy (UWA) are 71 and 66% obtained after combining all the three modalities (Speech + Text + Mocap). WA accuracy is the average accuracy, while UWA is termed as average class accuracy. This dataset is imbalanced, therefore UWA should be high.

4.4 Confusion Matrix Discussion

Considering the speech features alone, the confusion matrix as shown in Fig. 3a is showing the best accuracy of 74% accuracy for *anger* emotion. However, the *neutral* and *excited* are the most misclassified emotions, while *excited* emotions mostly got classified as *anger*. This happens because, in the case of *excited*, people tend to speak louder and faster, which also occurs when a person is *angry*. On the contrary, from the confusion matrix for text input as in Fig. 3b, we can see that there is less misclassification because from textual input the emotion of the person is almost clear.

The confusion matrix in Fig. 4a obtained using only Mocap features performed worst among all the independent modalities. It can be seen that the *excited* emotion is detected the best when it is compared by all the modalities and their combinations. *Neutral* and *sad* are the most misclassified emotions with *anger*. However, *neutral* and *sad* should be classified with each other due to the fact that when a person is sitting neutral, i.e., with a blank expression, then we normally classify them to be sad.

Further, when both (Speech + Mocap) data is combined, the accuracies for different emotions are improved, when compared to accuracies obtained using independent modalities, as observed from the correlation matrix as shown in Fig. 4b. Similarly, the confusion matrices as observed in Fig. 5a, b; when (Mocap + text) and (speech + text) are considered, receptively, they lead to good results. Importantly, the confu-

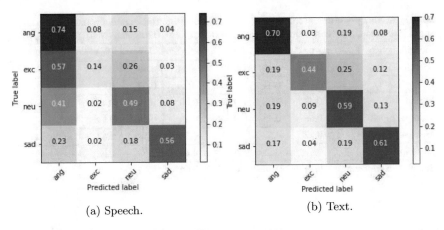

(a) Speech.

(b) Text.

Fig. 3 Confusion matrices of Speech and Text

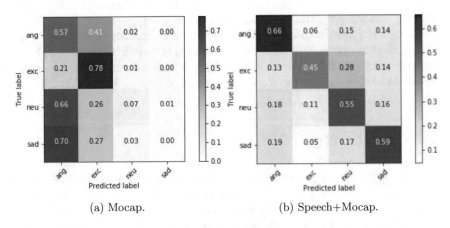

(a) Mocap.

(b) Speech+Mocap.

Fig. 4 Confusion matrices of Mocap and (Speech + Mocap)

sion matrix for the combination of mocap, speech, and text features, as is shown in Fig. 6), yields the best results. It has reduced misclassification to a greater extent and thus leads to increase in accuracy of our model.

5 Conclusion

In this work, multiple modalities such as speech, text, and mocap are to develop multi-modal emotion recognition. The best individual and combined deep learning architectures are identified to extract the features. Further, the deep features extracted from the last DNN layer are fed to the machining learning classifiers (SVM, Decision Tree, Random forest, and XGBoost). It is found that the accuracy of multi-model

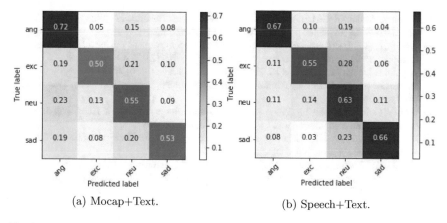

(a) Mocap+Text.   (b) Speech+Text.

Fig. 5 Confusion matrices of (Mocap + Text) and (Speech + Text)

Fig. 6 Confusion matrix of
(Speech + Text + Mocap)

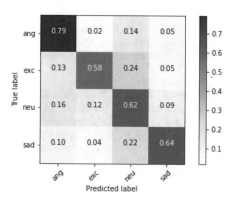

emotion recognition with three sources (speech, text, and mocap) is better than the individual or two sources of data. Most of the ensemble classifiers (Random forest and XGBoost) worked better because they prevent over-fitting and provide a generalized model.

References

1. Lee J, Tashev I (2015) High-level feature representation using recurrent neural network for speech emotion recognition. In: Sixteenth annual conference of the international speech communication association
2. Chernykh V, Prikhodko P (2017) Emotion recognition from speech with recurrent neural networks. arXiv:1701.08071
3. Neumann M, Thang Vu N (2017) Attentive convolutional neural network based speech emotion recognition: a study on the impact of input features, signal length, and acted speech. arXiv:1706.00612

4. Zhang Y, Wallace B (2015) A sensitivity analysis of (and practitioners' guide to) convolutional neural networks for sentence classification. arXiv:1510.03820
5. Bassili JN (1979) Emotion recognition: the role of facial movement and the relative importance of upper and lower areas of the face. J Pers Soc Psychol 37(11):2049
6. Tripathi S, Acharya S, Sharma RD, Mittal S, Bhattacharya S (2017) Using deep and convolutional neural networks for accurate emotion classification on deap dataset. In: Twenty-ninth IAAI conference
7. Sebe N, Cohen I, Huang TS (2005) Multimodal emotion recognition. In: Handbook of pattern recognition and computer vision. World Scientific, pp 387–409
8. Haq S, Jackson PJB (2011) Multimodal emotion recognition. In: Machine audition: principles, algorithms and systems. IGI Global, pp 398–423
9. Tzirakis P, Trigeorgis G, Nicolaou MA, Schuller BW, Zafeiriou S (2017) End-to-end multimodal emotion recognition using deep neural networks. IEEE J Sel Top Signal Process 11(8):1301–1309
10. Sreeshakthy M, Preethi J (2016) Classification of human emotion from deap eeg signal using hybrid improved neural networks with cuckoo search. BRAIN. Broad Res Artif Intell Neurosci 6(3–4):60–73
11. Schlegel K, Grandjean D, Scherer KR (2012) Emotion recognition: unidimensional ability or a set of modality-and emotion-specific skills? Pers Ind Diff 53(1):16–21
12. Poria S, Majumder N, Hazarika D, Cambria E, Gelbukh A, Hussain A (2018) Multimodal sentiment analysis: addressing key issues and setting up the baselines. IEEE Intell Syst 33(6):17–25
13. Busso C, Bulut M, Lee C-C, Kazemzadeh A, Mower E, Kim S, Chang JN, Lee S, Narayanan SS (2008) IEMOCAP: interactive emotional dyadic motion capture database. Lang Res Eval 42(4):335–359
14. Ranjan A, Fahad MS, Fernández-Baca D, Deepak A, Tripathi S (2020) Deep robust framework for protein function prediction using variable-length protein sequences. IEEE/ACM Trans Comput Biol Bioinf 17(5):1648–1659
15. Graves A, Mohamed A-R, Hinton G (2013) Speech recognition with deep recurrent neural networks. In: 2013 IEEE international conference on acoustics, speech and signal processing. IEEE, pp 6645–6649
16. Bahdanau D, Cho K, Bengio Y (2014) Neural machine translation by jointly learning to align and translate. arXiv:1409.0473
17. Noble WS (2006) What is a support vector machine? Nat Biotechnol 24(12):1565–1567
18. Brijain MR, Patel R, Kushik MR, Rana K (2014) A survey on decision tree algorithm for classification
19. Biau G, Scornet E (2016) A random forest guided tour. Test 25(2):197–227
20. Chen T, Guestrin C (2016) Xgboost: a scalable tree boosting system. In: Proceedings of the 22nd ACM SIGKDD international conference on knowledge discovery and data mining, pp 785–794

Decentralized and Secured Voting System with Blockchain Technology

Rishikesh Choudhari, M. Shivakumar, Shreyas Nandavar, Shruti Maigur, Saroja V. Siddamal, Suneeta V. Budihal, and Shrishail M. Pattanshetti

1 Introduction

A blockchain is a decentralized distributed technology with advanced features that help the security of the data and the system as a whole. In blockchain, decentralization refers to the transfer of control and decision-making from a centralized entity (individual, organization or groups) to a distributed network. It is a peer-to-peer technology where each peer indicates a node having copies of every transaction over the network which is called distributed ledger and all nodes have access to the same ledger. Therefore, it is also called "Distributed ledger technology". A distributed ledger is a database that is consensually shared and synchronized across multiple sites, institutions, geographies and accessible by multiple people that are connected over the network. It has the feature called immutability where the data remains unchanged. One cannot alter the package information and security is attained through the cryptographic hash concept.

Cryptography uses complex mathematical algorithms that are used to secure data and systems. Smart contract deploys blockchain incorporating system logic written in solidity programming language. In a blockchain network, all the blocks having the transaction details are cryptographically connected, i.e., for every transaction over the network by any connected peer, a block is created with the hash associated with it, and also it contains the hash of the previous block. Before adding a newly created block to the blockchain, it undergoes a consensus algorithm where it is validated and verified for the real transaction and later it is added to the records. Every peer in the blockchain network has a private key which is used to access the

R. Choudhari · M. Shivakumar · S. Nandavar · S. Maigur · S. V. Siddamal · S. V. Budihal (✉) · S. M. Pattanshetti
School of Electronics and Communication Engineering, KLE Technological University, Hubballi, India
e-mail: suneeta_vb@kletech.ac.in

S. V. Siddamal
e-mail: sarojavs@kletech.ac.in

© The Author(s), under exclusive license to Springer Nature Singapore Pte Ltd. 2022
U. P. Rao et al. (eds.), *Security, Privacy and Data Analytics*, Lecture Notes in Electrical Engineering 848, https://doi.org/10.1007/978-981-16-9089-1_14

transactions carried out. There can be both public and private blockchain networks depending on the requirement. Therefore, with blockchain technology the need for third parties to ensure the security and other parameters can be eliminated. The online voting system is where the voters can cast their votes without actually going to the voting booths which helps in reducing the budget for setting up the booths and in providing improved accessibility for physically challenged voters. For online voting systems, security is the main concern. Therefore, blockchain technology with its great security features can be applied in implementing the online voting system. The main challenge in implementing the e-voting system is the possible violations of election rules specified in smart contracts. The major concern is about undesirable disclosure of the intermittent voting results during the voting process. Along with scalability issues, some smart contracts contain vulnerabilities and are facing attacks.

The contributions of the proposed framework are as follows:

- The proposed framework records a single vote from a user and rejects other fraud votes.
- The proposed framework provides security against cast votes against tampering.

2 Related Work

The paper [1] signifies the security measures that are required for creating a voting system using blockchain technology. The software in creating the systems are thr Truffle framework for implementation, testing and deployment. The Ganache software helps in creating a virtual environment of a blockchain network. MetaMask is used for initiating the transaction from Ganache. The website displays the candidates who are standing for the elections and helps the user in voting and displays the results. The authentication is done through user login. Here, the security verification is carried out wherein users register using their user name and password along with user verification using face detection and proceed to cast the vote using Ethereum blockchain. Each transaction is written into smart contracts that are then implemented on the blockchain network. The private and public keys are created by the nodes before the voting program starts. The system holds all the public keys which are verified for voting. All the data from the voting is collected by every node. On completion of the process, the nodes will hold the data until the new blocks are created.

The paper [2] discusses e-voting on the concept of Consensus algorithm and Encryption. The blockchain uses a consensus algorithm that creates a unique identifier for initiating a new transaction while the new node is being created. By calculating the block header hash value, the consensus algorithm creates a new block. The new block will be added to the blockchain network when the new nodes are verified by most of the nodes. There are two techniques in the encryption algorithm. In order to encrypt and decrypt, the RSA algorithm is used. By the decomposition of large integers, complexity is increased which adds to the protection. While providing the places in a circular manner to the users, the ring structure is used. The preparation and publishing are used in the voting, first and second phase of registration and casting of votes.

The paper [3] discusses a new e-voting system which is built based on voting system protocols with blockchain technology. The system has been designed in order to obtain fundamental properties of the e-voting system as well as highlight the importance of decentralization. It allows the voter to change/update their vote within the permissible voting period. This design includes a website for online voting as the name itself suggests "e-voting". The method consists of three parts: voter, election-administrator and election process. The voter is the user who casts vote. In order to do so, the voter has to register using personal information. This information includes the user's unique id which is required to generate the public and private keys for every user. The election administrator is the system which takes care of registering the users by verifying their ids and generating the public and private keys. The election process is the last step where the voter votes for the candidate after verification.

The paper [4] discusses a systematic review approach of blockchain technology in an online voting system. First, the user is registered and verified using his voter id. After this, a 32-byte (256 bits) secret key will be generated by the system. The key acts as a secondary procedure in the verification step and also as a digital signature for the voting and is encrypted using the AES256 encryption as well as decryption algorithm. After the user is verified, select a candidate for him. While voting for the candidate, he needs to enter the key generated in the first step. The key encrypted previously will be decrypted while voting. If the encryption key is the same as the decryption key, then it is an authentic user. If it does not match, the user's vote will not be recorded, and this will be considered as a malicious act. After the vote is cast, the user's data will be recorded, and the same user will not be allowed to vote again.

The paper [5] discusses the benefits of blockchain technology, mainly the cryptographic foundations in the e-voting system. It mainly uses multichain, an open-source blockchain platform to discuss the functioning of e-voting. The system generates a strong cryptographic hash in order to protect the anonymity and integrity of the vote, for each vote transaction based on information specific to a voter. This hash is also provided to the voter using various encrypted channels as a verification method. The votes will be protected using a hash method where each data is encrypted in a block and is connected from one block to another. The user is verified using fingerprint technology and biometrics. After verification, the user is provided with a hash key to be used as a password in the user login before casting the vote. After the user logins, the user will be given a list of voting options in one column and voting choice in another column [6].

The paper [7] discussed a decentralized architecture to run and support a voting scheme that is open, fair and independently verifiable. An e-voting system is designed based on the blockchain technology to securely conduct elections and also safeguard the voter's privacy. It also discusses an idea about cancelling an already cast vote and may modify the decision. The procedure consists of 2 sides, the voter and the ballot. The voter should be verified before casting the vote. Each voter is assigned a public key. The user is verified through the public key and then allowed to vote.

Here, the voter has a choice to either vote or reject. At such time, there is an option for cancelling the vote. The next step is the ballot. In the ballot, once the voter casts his vote, the public key will be cross-verified with the data available in the ballot box and allowed to cast the vote only if the key matches or is present in the record.

The paper [8] discusses the voting system in Estonia which is developed using blockchain technology. There are five phases in the project. The first phase is the candidate registration where the account invoking a smart contract is verified to be the admin. The admin later adds the candidate. Each candidate has a name and a unique ID. The second phase is voter registration where each voter has a pre-input name and address. The voters are registered by the admin. The third phase is self-verification where the voter can check the status of the vote by putting the address. Other details like his registration and vote are also displayed. If the address does not match, the voter can complain to the admin. The fourth phase is voting which is the most important phase. The voters are verified with their details before voting.

The paper [9] discusses an electronic voting model which uses blockchain method-based distributed ledger technology where data is shared and distributed into a network. Moreover, this project uses an IoT-based system to exchange data from the e-voting system to the nodes. Raspberry Pi is used as a medium to exchange data between the EVMs. The first step is verification where each voter is assigned a private key. The user is verified through his thumbprints in the EVM. The data is transferred to the server through Raspberry Pi where the user's details are present. The server checks whether the user is a citizen. It returns back a verification key if it is true. The second step is casting vote where the voter uses his private key to vote; his vote is recorded on the server through the data sent by Pi from EVM.

The paper [10] discusses the recording of voting results using the blockchain algorithm from every place of election. This consists of a database recording e-voting system on blockchain technology. It starts with verifying a user. Each user is provided with a public key and a private key. When he wants to cast a vote, the system checks whether he is a new user in the database. If he has already voted, the system allows him to vote only to be rejected at the end. If he is a new user, the database sends a verification key back to the system. This is called "get a turn around". Then the voter is allowed to cast his vote for the desired candidate. Then the votes are broadcasted by the system in order to declare the winner.

The paper [11] discusses an effective e-voting system based on the Ethereum blockchain technology which ensures the privacy of votes on the basis of the ring signature mechanism. The ring signature mechanism is an effective method of securing the votes and maintaining the privacy of votes. In order to prevent fraud voting, each user is provided with one key pair that is the public and private keys so as to register himself as a first-time voter. There is a key manager who verifies the private key belonging to the user and allows him to cast the vote.

3 The Proposed Framework

The functional block diagram shown in Fig. 1 explains the working of the voting system. This web-based application is an interactive GUI to vote online. The user is verified to cast the vote. After voting, the system checks whether he has cast the vote. While voting, the user has to make some transactions authenticated by the MetaMask wallet exported from Ganache. The user will be able to vote only if the wallet has the required value, else a vote is not considered. After the user has voted, the vote will be recorded, and the vote button will be invisible so that the same user cannot vote twice. The system is implemented using Ganache, Truffle and MetaMask; Ganache uses the SHA-256 hashing algorithm.

The proposed framework is comprised of the following segments.

- Ethereum Virtual Machine: Blockchain-based software platform for creating a decentralized application.
- Node Package Manager with NodeJS: A javascript runtime used in the Back-end of the system.
- Truffle Framework: This software allows the user for building decentralized voting system applications on virtually simulated Ethereum Blockchain.
- Ganache: A local in-memory blockchain, which gives 10 external accounts with addresses on Ethereum.

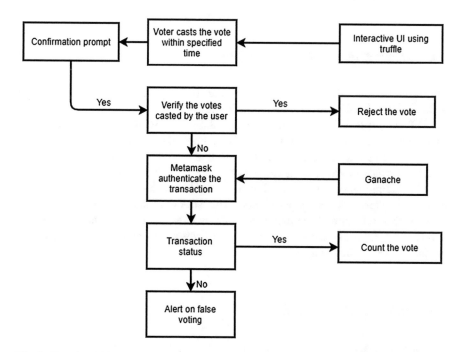

Fig. 1 Functional Block Diagram for a smart voting system using Blockchain

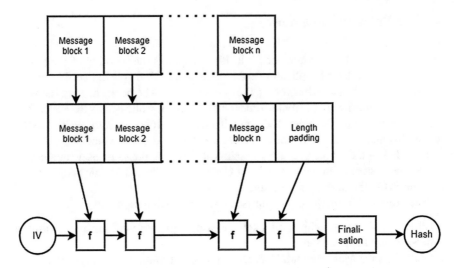

Fig. 2 SHA-256 algorithm

- MetaMask: A chrome extension that connects the Ethereum blockchain to a browser.
- Sublime: IDE/Text editor.

3.1 Cryptographic Hash Function

The SHA-256 algorithm as shown in Fig. 2 uses padding and dividing procedures to secure the block data with cryptographic hashing.

[1] Padding: Pad the input string to the multiple of 512-bit length. Uses ASCII chart to convert letters and signs to numbers. Appends 1 to the converted string of 1's and 0's. Later appends a bunch of zeroes that total whole bits to 448-bit length. Finally, appends 11000 (24) making it to a total of 512-bit length string.

[2] Dividing: Divides the padded binary into 512-bit chunks. Divides each chunk into 32-bit words (16 words per chunk). The SHA-256 algorithm is used to hash 32 bit words, 64 times. Then they are bought together to generate the result which is final. That is, SHA-256 uses 64 rounds of encryption and can even specify the number of rounds manually.

3.2 Public and Private Keys

For every user, there is a public and a private key generated. The public and private keys are similar to the user name and password which are used in the centralized

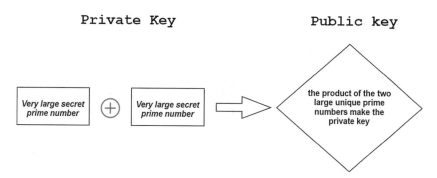

Fig. 3 Public and Private Key generation for security in blockchain technology

systems using which the user authentication takes place. In order to create a public and a private key, there is an algorithm used which is the RSA (Rivest-Shamir-Adleman) algorithm. It is a public-key cryptography system that is used for transmitting data securely. Both the public and private keys are related to each other as shown in Fig. 3, but it is not possible for someone to derive the public key from the address and cannot derive the private key by having the public key. Since the two keys are derived from the same algorithm, it is not possible for the user to change their private key once it is generated. It is strictly advised for the user to keep their private key with themselves as once it is leaked or is forgotten; it is impossible to retrieve their account and the account is permanently lost.

3.3 Mining

Mining in blockchain works by adding the transaction to the blockchain in the network. The process here is where the hash for the blocks are created which cannot be manipulated by providing protection for the entire blockchain. Mining is carried out by the miners by a fast computer which carries out the mining. The computers consume more electricity and also produce heat, hence the miners are rewarded the gas money for validating the transaction. In order to decrypt the data encoded in the blocks, it requires more computational power which will give rise to verification of the transaction. Miners solve the problem which is complex in order to find the correct hash that matches, known as proof of work. In this project, mining is carried out by the Ganache software. Ganache is a local development blockchain used to develop decentralized applications on the Ethereum blockchain. It provides 10 unblocked accounts with their addresses and private keys. It Provides 100 fake Ethers for each account. To develop a decentralized application, Blockchain needs to be simulated. For Ethereum, we need an Ethereum client like "Geth" and "Parity" Ethereum which includes setting up our own wallet, setting up miners and the network with the different nodes connected together. So, Ganache provides all these setups inbuilt and is specially designed for developers.

The main difference between Ganache and other Ethereum clients is

- With Ganache, only one node in Ethereum network is available.
- No need to set up any miner, that is, all the transactions that are sent to the Ganache will be mined instantly which is very convenient for the developer. This means it has Automining feature.
- Time it takes to mine the block is "0" s.
- Ganache is only local, not connected to the main Ethereum network.

So, a virtual environment is created using Ganache which will replicate the working of real blockchain over the main network, and we can test the working of the voting system developed in that simulated environment.

3.4 MetaMask

The MetaMask software works as a wallet that holds cryptocurrency which is transacted in the Etherum blockchain. Using this, users are able to access the virtual cryptocurrency wallet by using a browser extension that helps to be then used to interact with decentralized applications. It is one of the most famous Ethereum wallets. MetaMask serves as a kind of bridge between centralized web and decentralized Ethereum blockchain. It does not require you to run a full node to interact with Ethereum, but MetaMask connects to an Ethereum node called Infura, allowing us to run smart contracts via proxy.

The MetaMask software is a wallet to store and dispatch and also acknowledge ETH and ERC20 cryptocurrency. Any transaction in MetaMask wallet requires a minimum of 21,000 gas which mainly depends on the miners. It uses cryptocurrency community standards to generate seed phrases that can be kept as backup and is used to access the MetaMask wallet. A default account is created after registration on MetaMask and can import accounts using a private key.

3.5 Truffle

Truffle is the great development framework for Ethereum which is used to develop, test and deploy our smart contract. It is a sort of all-in-one platform for the solidity contract. With the truffle, we get instant rebuilding of assets during development. It supports console app, web app and tight integration.

3.6   Algorithm: Smart Contract

Input: *Candidateobject*
Output: *voteCount*
   Initialize candidate structure :
   struct Candidate
   int id
   string name
   int voteCount
   function vote(Candidate)
   while timeNow <= timeLimit **do**
     if (*voted*()) **then**
       exit()
     else
       Candidate.voteCount++
       voted() return *true*
     end if
   end while
   return *voteCount*

3.7   User Authentication

To verify the identity of the user or voter that is connected over the network, a feature of user authentication is added as shown in Fig. 4. The users use their private key as the credential to register and login. The concept used is the javascript object verification for verifying the users; if the user's account address (public key) and private keys are present in the object, then the user will be allowed to proceed to the voting page and if the user authentication fails the user will be prompted an error indicating the wrong credentials being entered and the user can't proceed further for the voting process.

3.8   Security Aspect in Blockchain

The main concern with blockchain technology is security of it and how it is different from the traditional centralized system. The addition of the blocks in the blockchain network takes place by adding the new blocks to the existing chain of the network after verification by the miner. Is is not possible change the contents of block because the consensus has reached the majority of the miners. All the blocks consist of three parts, data, hash of the previous block and the hash of its own block. The hash codes are created by the data from the ledger and if anyone tries to change the data in the

Fig. 4 User verification page

block, the hash code changes breaking the link of the blocks. Unauthorized users trying to hack, require enormous amount of resources such a time, processing power and money.

3.9 The Flowchart for Complete Voting System with Blockchain Technology

As shown in Fig. 5, user logins to the portal using the credentials that were previously used during the registration stage. The system checks for the user authentication whether he is an eligible citizen to vote. Once it is confirmed that he is eligible, the system allows the user to vote. The user then chooses the candidate to vote. On pressing the vote button, the user is asked for confirmation through the MetaMask confirmation slip. The system counts the user's vote only if there is enough balance.

4 Results and Discussions

The user or voter is able to cast the vote only during the specified time interval. Once the voting time is completed, one cannot cast the vote and after the set time the total vote count of the respective candidate is displayed under their respective cards.

Fig. 5 Flowchart for the
complete process of e-voting

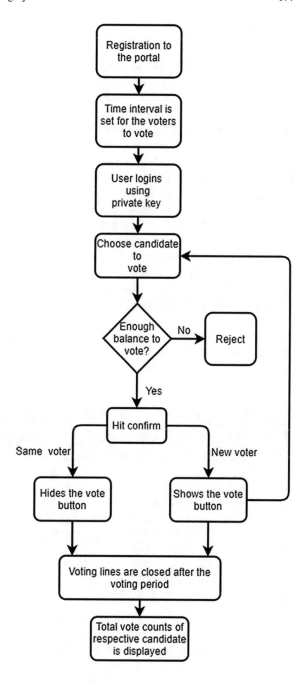

4.1 Result Analysis

As shown in Fig. 6, from the Ganache software from the first account the balance has been reduced after initiating the transaction to vote, showing that the gas balance has been deducted from the user's account. In the Ganache software, we can see that the balance has been reduced from the first account that implies the first user has voted using his account and the gas balance required to vote has been deducted from his account through the MetaMask extension.

As shown in Fig. 7, before the user votes the timer is displayed indicating the remaining duration and the user's account address is displayed. When the user wants to vote, a timer will be displayed on top. This means that the user has to vote for the desired candidate in that duration of time, else his vote will not be recorded.

After the user votes for the candidate of his/her choice, the account address and the voting button disappear indicating that the user has voted and cannot vote anymore as shown in Fig. 8. After the user votes for the desired candidate, the address of the Ganache account from which he has voted will disappear along with the vote button indicating that the voter has already voted and he cannot vote anymore. The same will be reflected in the balance cut from his account through MetaMask.

Once the user has cast the vote, the system displays a message saying "You have already voted" as shown in Fig. 9. That means a user cannot vote multiple times. Hence, no double voting is possible. Once the user casts his vote, the system displays a message saying "You have already voted". This means the same user cannot vote

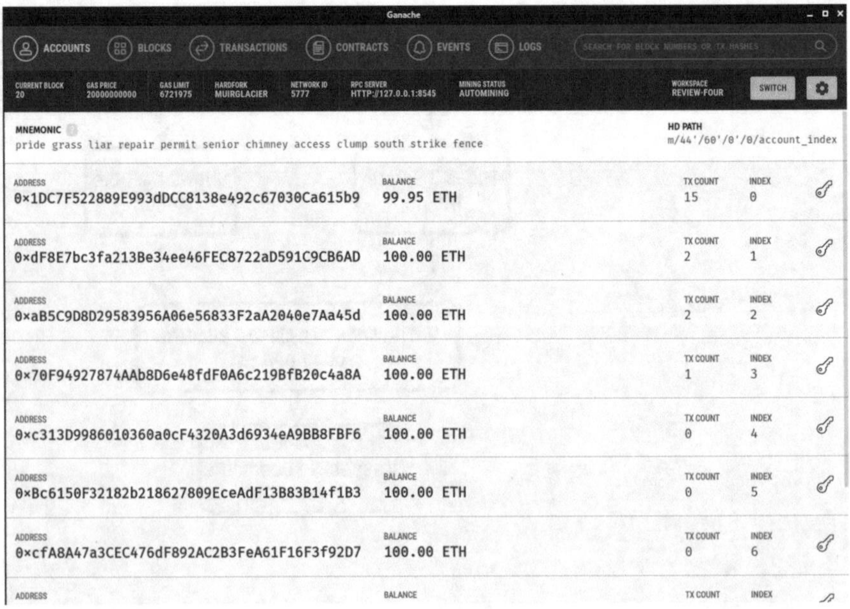

Fig. 6 Ganache software

Fig. 7 Before voting

Fig. 8 After voting

multiple times. Hence, double voting is not possible. From the security point of view, multiple votes are not counted.

After the scheduled voting time has expired, the user cannot vote anymore and the user gets a warning which says that the voting lines are closed and the number of votes are displayed for each candidate as shown in Fig. 10. Thus, the user has to vote in the given time duration. After the scheduled time expires, the votes recorded for each candidate will be displayed.

The MetaMask confirmation pictures are shown in Fig. 11: the account from which the user is voting and also the gas amount that is required to process the transaction. The MetaMask confirmation picture shows the account from which the user is voting and the gas amount required to process the transaction. The gas balance shown in

Fig. 9 Multiple vote trials by the same user

Fig. 10 After specified voting interval

the MetaMask slip will be deducted from the same account address in Ganache as shown in the MetaMask confirmation slip (Fig. 12).

When the first user votes, a new block is created in the Ganache with the unique cryptographic hash after verification. New blocks go on adding to the existing block whenever users vote. This forms a blockchain network. When the first user votes, a new block will be created in ganache with a unique cryptographic hash after verification. As new users cast their votes, new blocks go on adding to the existing block forming a blockchain network. This constitutes the blockchain technology through which voting is carried out securely.

Fig. 11 MetaMask confirmation slip

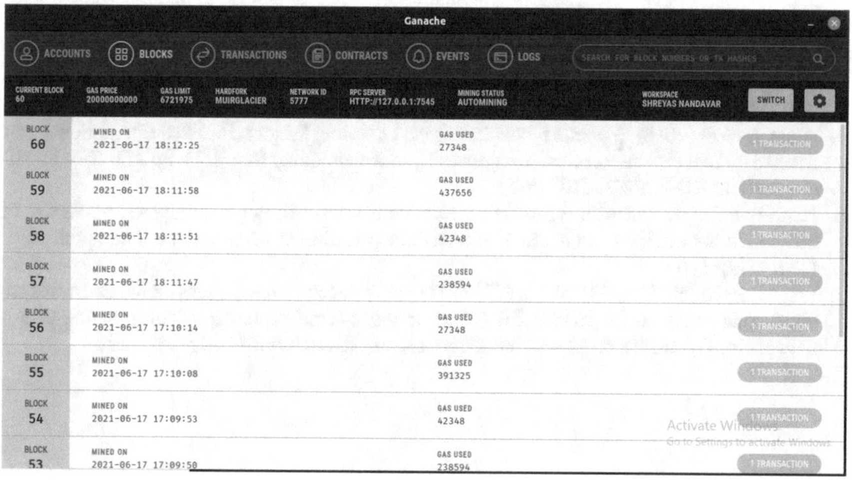

Fig. 12 Creation of blocks in Ganache

5   Conclusion

The proposed framework used Blockchain Technology to implement a user-friendly voting system. The blockchain technology with its great advantages in securing the data and the system as a whole made it possible to achieve the intended objectives. That is, each voter is able to cast the vote only once. No double voting is possible. As it includes user identity verification, no fake voters can cast their votes. The blockchain technology has a major scope in the field of cyber security. For additional security of the voting system, an extra feature of facial detection can be added at the time of registration. Also, a thumb impression can be added to the user authentication. Authentication using signature can also be implemented.

References

1. Adiputra CK, Hjort R, Sato H (2018) A proposal of blockchain-based electronic voting system. In: 2018 second world conference on smart trends in systems, security and sustainability (WorldS4), pp 22–27
2. Pawar SSD, Sarode P, Thore P (2019) Secure voting system using blockchain. Int J Eng Res Technol (IJERT) 8(11):2278–0181
3. Arshad J, Khan MM, Kashif Mehboob Khan (2018) Secure digital voting system based on blockchain technology. Int J Electron Gov Res (IJEGR) 14(1):53–62
4. Hima JK, Chaithra S, Amaresh R (2020) Electronic voting system using blockchain. Int Res J Eng Technol (IJERT) 07(7)
5. Raj AK, Garag V, Padmashree (2018) E-voting system using blockchain. Int Res J Eng Technol (IJERT) 07(5)
6. Jaiswal S et al (2021) E-voting using blockchain. Int J Eng Res Technol 10(3):2278–0181
7. Hardwick FS et al (2018) E-voting with blockchain: an E-voting protocol with decentralisation and voter privacy. In: 2018 IEEE international conference on internet of things (iThings) 2018, pp 1561–1567. https://doi.org/10.1109/Cybermatics_2018.2018.00262
8. Teja K, Shravani M, Simha CY, Kounte MR (2019) Secured voting through Blockchain technology. In: 2019 3rd international conference on trends in electronics and informatics (ICOEI), pp 1416–1419. https://doi.org/10.1109/ICOEI.2019.8862743
9. Alam A et al (2018) Towards blockchain-based e-voting system. In: 2018 international conference on innovations in science, engineering and technology (ICISET), pp 351–354. https://doi.org/10.1109/ICISET.2018.8745613
10. Hanifatunnisa R, Rahardjo B (2017) Blockchain based e-voting recording system design. In: 2017 11th international conference on telecommunication systems services and applications (TSSA), pp 1–6
11. Lai W, Hsieh Y, Hsueh C, Wu J (2018) DATE: a decentralized, anonymous, and transparent e-voting system. In: 2018 1st IEEE international conference on hot information-centric networking (HotICN), pp 24–29. https://doi.org/10.1109/HOTICN.2018.8605994

Network Traffic Classification Using Deep Autonomous Learning Approach

N. G. Bhuvaneswari Amma

1 Introduction

The exponential growth of the Internet has contributed to today's dynamic, large scale, and complex networks [8]. These networks experienced an exponential rise of traffic owing to the increased usage of smart devices and are vulnerable to attacks. Despite the recent advancements in computer networks and its security, current network protection solutions against never-ending Distributed Denial of Service (DDoS) attacks remain open challenge for the research community. These DDoS attacks target critical Internet services with the deceptive goal of making online crucial services inaccessible on time to legitimate users. As the technology advances, the frequency and size of DDoS attacks are also on the increase. This attack follows many to one structure and if the attack is initiated, the complexity and impact become proportionally high. The reason for these attacks is the availability of enormous amount of attack tools in the Internet. Even a novice can launch such attacks with the available tools [9]. Therefore, classification of network traffic is a challenge and design of an autonomous attack detection system is needed for on the fly detection of DDoS attacks in evolving large network traffic data streams [10].

Nowadays attack detection can be performed using statistical, data mining, and machine learning approaches. Among these approaches, the research community is preferring deep learning-based attack detection systems that learn the network traffic by identifying correlations in the traffic with different learning levels [7]. The deep learning techniques used for attack detection includes Convolutional Neural Network (CNN), Recurrent Neural Network (RNN), Long Short Term Memory (LSTM), auto-encoder, etc. These conventional deep learning approaches perform static and offline-based detection. In reality, the network traffic evolves as data streams, i.e., continuous arrival of traffic data which requires on the fly detection of DDoS attacks.

N. G. Bhuvaneswari Amma (✉)
Indian Institute of Information Technology Una, Himachal Pradesh 177 005, India
e-mail: bhuvaneswari@iiitu.ac.in

© The Author(s), under exclusive license to Springer Nature Singapore Pte Ltd. 2022
U. P. Rao et al. (eds.), *Security, Privacy and Data Analytics*, Lecture Notes
in Electrical Engineering 848, https://doi.org/10.1007/978-981-16-9089-1_15

183

In order to achieve this objective, incremental learning can be used which learns the evolving data as and when it arrives [6]. The incremental learning algorithms adapt to rapidly changing network environments [10]. Further, these algorithms perform well on classifying known and unknown classes of network traffic. These characteristics motivated to propose a Deep Autonomous Learning (DAL) classifier which automatically extracts and learns features to classify the network traffic data stream. The arriving new classes are learned by incorporating a generalized structure for each of the new class with the existing structure. The key contributions are listed as follows:

1. A Deep Autonomous Learning (DAL) structure to construct network traffic classification system.
2. A DAL methodology to train the network traffic classification system.
3. DAL classifier to classify the network traffic.

2   Related Works

This section discusses the existing literature related to the proposed approach. DDoS attacks shut down the targeted server or network by flooding with huge Internet traffic either partially or fully. The goal of the attacker is to disrupt the normal traffic flow to the targeted server or network. In the earlier days, the DDoS attacks were generated from a single machine and launched to a single server. Nowadays, as low security Internet of Things (IoT) devices, viz., web cameras, monitoring devices, printers, etc., evolved, these attacks were generated from single or multiple machines and launched to single or multiple servers or devices [1]. These IoT devices were compromised to form a botnet to reroute high traffic to the servers for disrupting the regular services. Therefore, the research community is on urge to design and develop network traffic classification systems.

The function of the attack detection models is to detect the known and unknown DDoS attacks and to discriminate the normal traffic from the attack traffic. If DDoS attack detection system is used, legitimate users are not denied while requesting for a service or accessing the service [11]. Recently, the DDoS attacks detection systems are designed based on deep learning techniques that accurately assign weights in stages for learning the network traffic data in each processing layer in abstract way. From the literature, it is studied that the existing deep learning approaches used for attack detection include CNN, RNN, LSTM, and auto-encoder [2, 12]. These methods are capable of handling data in fixed network capacity leading to static and offline detection of attacks. But the attackers are creating intelligent IoT botnets to generate traffic. These evolving traffic can be handled by techniques that are capable of adapting to dynamically changing network environments. To overcome this issue, Deep Autonomous Learning (DAL) can be used for DDoS attacks detection. The DAL is a continual learning algorithm in which the learning model can be constructed from scratch without an initial network model [10]. The incremental and flexible nature of DAL motivated to propose a DAL-based network classification approach.

3 Proposed DAL-Based Network Traffic Classification

DAL classifier is proposed to detect DDoS attacks by extracting the relevant features and learns the extracted features automatically by adapting to dynamically changing network environments. It consists of learning and classification modules. The learning phase learns the extracted features automatically using Fully Connected Network (FCN) with Distilled Cross Entropy (DCE) [4]. The detection phase uses the learning modules in the DAL-based attack detection except DCE computation. The architecture of the DAL traffic classification is depicted in Fig. 1. The learning module is depicted using solid lines and the classification module is depicted using dotted lines.

3.1 Network Traffic Data Representation

The network traffic dataset is denoted as $NT_D = [ntr_1, ntr_2, \ldots, ntr_k, C_m]$, where $ntr_a = [ntf_{a1}, ntf_{a2}, \ldots, ntf_{an}], 1 \leq a \leq k$, is the ath network traffic data record

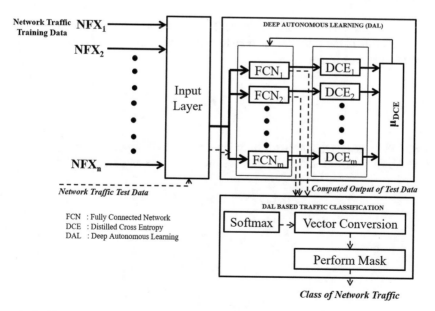

Fig. 1 Architecture of proposed DAL-based network classifier

and C_m be the class of the traffic data. The network traffic features are in the following forms: binary, continuous, and ordinal. The ordinal values are converted to numerical using ordered numbers. Furthermore, the features are normalized using min-max normalization in the range of 0–1. The raw data is normalized as follows:

$$NFX_n^k = \frac{ntf_n^k - min_{fn}}{max_{fn} - min_{fn}}, \tag{1}$$

where ntf_n^k is the data to normalize, min_{fn} is the minimum value of the feature, and max_{fn} is the maximum value of the feature. The normalized data is passed to the proposed DAL-based traffic classifier for learning and classification.

3.2 Deep Autonomous Learning

The DAL module consists of multiple Fully Connected Networks (FCNs) and the number of FCNs are based on the classes in the traffic dataset. As the traffic evolves due to the technology advancement, there is a possibility of new class of attacks to be generated. To tackle this situation, a FCN for the new class of attack needs to be added in the learning network structure. The structure of FCN is $NFX_i - 9 - 7 - 1$, where NFX_i be the number of input features. The reason behind this structure is that the extracted features are learned layer-wise with different level of abstractions. The normalized network traffic is passed to the input layer and this layer passes the traffic to the FCN.

The computation in the hidden layers (HLs) is performed by computing the product of the sum of the values of the transformed pooling layer with the corresponding weights and is as follows:

$$I_j^{HL_i} = \sum_{i=1}^{p} NFX_i \times W_{ij}^{HL_i}, \tag{2}$$

where W^{HL} is the weight vector from input layer to HL. In the HL, Rectified Linear Unit (ReLU) activation function has been utilized and computed as follows:

$$f_{RL}\left(I_j^{HL_{i+1}}\right) = max\left(I_j^{HL_i}, 0\right). \tag{3}$$

The computation in the output layer of FCNs is performed as follows:

$$O_i^c = \sum_{i=1}^{p} HL_i \times W_{jk}^{HO} + B, \tag{4}$$

where B is the Bias term which is added to place the traffic record to the suitable class. In the output layer, sigmoid activation function has been utilized and computed as follows:

$$f_{Sig}\left(O_i^c\right) = 1/(1 + exp^{-O_i^c}). \tag{5}$$

The rate of loss in the learning process is computed using Distilled Cross Entropy (DCE). The DCE provides generalization ability by distilling the knowledge gained from the model and is computed as follows:

$$DCE_l(DT_i, DO_i) = -\sum_{i=1}^{n} DT_i log\left(DO_i\right), \tag{6}$$

where $DT_i = (T_i)^{1/D}$, T_i is the target class in the training dataset and $DO_i = (O_i)^{1/D}$, O_i is the computed output, D is the distillation parameter, and l ranges from 1 to m. The training continues till the mean of DCE reaches the threshold and is computed as follows:

$$\mu_{DCE} = \frac{1}{m} DCE_l. \tag{7}$$

3.3 DAL-Based Network Traffic Classification

The DAL-based traffic classification is similar to that of the learning procedure but instead of DCE, the softmax is used to classify the type of traffic. The reason for using softmax activation function is to squash the output between 0 and 1 which is similar to sigmoid activation function but it also divides the output in such a way to make the sum of the output is equal to 1 and computed as follows:

$$f_{SM}\left(O_{ij}\right) = \frac{Exp\left(O_{ij}\right)}{\sum_{j=0}^{k} Exp\left(O_{ij}\right)}. \tag{8}$$

The output of softmax is converted to a vector and the class of the network traffic is detected using the vector value.

Table 1 Statistics of datasets

Dataset	Feature	Training data		Testing data	
		Normal	DDoS attack	Normal	DDoS attack
KDD Cup	41	97278	391458	60593	229057
NSL KDD	41	13449	9195	2152	3603
UNSW NB	48	20520	4076	56000	12264

4   Results and Discussions

Experiments were conducted on desktop PC under Windows 10 with Intel Core 2 Quad CPU Q9650 @ 3.00 GHz processor and 16 GB RAM. MATLAB R2019a was utilized for constructing the traffic classification model and also to test the proposed classifier. The datasets used for experimentation are KDD Cup, NSL KDD, and UNSW NB15. Table 1 tabulates the statistics of datasets. For experimentation, normal and DDoS attacks traffic in the benchmark datasets are only considered [3].

4.1   DCE Loss Computation in Autonomous Learning

The number of FCNs used for training in DAL module were 6 for KDD Cup, 6 for NSL KDD, and 2 for UNSW NB based on the number of classes in each of the datasets. Figure 2 depicts the DCE loss variation for different epochs. It is observed from the graphical representation that the proposed approach converges around 82th epoch for KDD Cup dataset, 78th epoch for NSL KDD dataset, and 89th epoch for UNSW NB dataset. As the number of classes in UNSW NB is small, the convergence of UNSW NB dataset becomes slow. It is observed that the DAL works better for more number of classes. The proposed classifier acts as a framework as the FCN and DCE blocks to be added for the upcoming new target classes which satisfies on the fly detection.

4.2   Performance Evaluation of Proposed DAL Classifier

The performance of the proposed classifier is evaluated using the following metrics: True Positive Rate (TPR), False Positive Rate (FPR), Accuracy, Loss Rate, and Area Under the Curve (AUC) [9]. The performance metrics are tabulated in Table 2. It is noted from table that the achievement of accuracy 99.62% for KDD Cup dataset, 99.77% for NSL KDD dataset, and 97.16% for UNSW NB dataset with the loss rate of 0.38% for KDD Cup dataset, 0.23% for NSL KDD dataset, and 2.84% dataset for UNSW NB dataset using the proposed DAL approach.

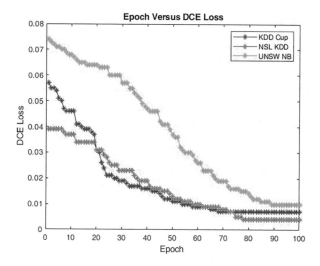

Fig. 2 Epoch versus DCE loss

Table 2 Performance metrics of proposed approach

Dataset	Performance metrics				
	FPR(%)	TPR(%)	Accuracy (%)	Loss rate(%)	AUC(%)
KDD Cup	0.12	99.55	99.62	0.38	99.71
NSL KDD	0.19	99.75	99.77	0.23	99.78
UNSW NB	2.71	96.53	97.16	2.84	96.91

Table 3 Comparison of proposed classifier with state-of-the-art classifiers

Classifier/Year	Accuracy (%)	FPR (%)
Reference [12]/2017	83.34	–
Reference [2]/2018	99.3	0.7
Reference [5]/2018	98.23	0.33
Reference [1]/2019	99.69	0.28
Proposed DAL	99.77	0.19

The proposed classifier was compared with four state-of-the-art deep learning classifiers. The reported results tabulated in Table 3 are for the experiments conducted using NSL KDD dataset. It is observed that the proposed classifier exhibits significant performance compared to the existing classifiers in terms of accuracy and FPR.

5 Conclusion

In this article, DAL classifier is proposed for on the fly classification of traffic in computer networks. The objective is to overcome the static nature of learning process in the existing deep learning classifiers. The features of network traffic were extracted and trained using DAL module. The performance of the proposed DAL classifier was analyzed using benchmark network traffic datasets by considering only the normal and DDoS attack records. It is evident from the results that the proposed classifier achieves promising performance for all the datasets. As part of the future work, the number of nodes in the hidden layers of FCN be optimized using evolutionary algorithms.

References

1. Amma BN, Selvakumar S (2019) Deep radial intelligence with cumulative incarnation approach for detecting denial of service attacks. Neurocomputing 340:294–308. https://doi.org/10.1016/j.neucom.2019.02.047
2. Amma NGB, Subramanian S (2018) Vcdeepfl: Vector convolutional deep feature learning approach for identification of known and unknown denial of service attacks. In: TENCON 2018-2018 IEEE region 10 conference. IEEE, pp 0640–0645
3. Amma NB, Selvakumar S, Velusamy RL (2020) A statistical approach for detection of denial of service attacks in computer networks. IEEE Trans Netw Serv Manag 17(4):2511–2522. https://doi.org/10.1109/TNSM.2020.3022799
4. Hinton G, Vinyals O, Dean J (2015) Distilling the knowledge in a neural network. arXiv:1503.02531
5. Idhammad M, Afdel K, Belouch M (2018) Semi-supervised machine learning approach for ddos detection. Appl Intell 1–16. https://doi.org/10.1007/s10489-018-1141-2
6. Istrate R, Malossi ACI, Bekas C, Nikolopoulos D (2018) Incremental training of deep convolutional neural networks. arXiv:1803.10232
7. Mishra P, Varadharajan V, Tupakula U, Pilli ES (2018) A detailed investigation and analysis of using machine learning techniques for intrusion detection. IEEE Commun Surv Tutor 21(1):686–728. https://doi.org/10.1109/COMST.2018.2847722
8. Moustafa N, Slay J, Creech G (2017) Novel geometric area analysis technique for anomaly detection using trapezoidal area estimation on large-scale networks. IEEE Trans Big Data 5(4):481–494. https://doi.org/10.1109/TBDATA.2017.2715166
9. NG BA, Selvakumar S (2020) Anomaly detection framework for internet of things traffic using vector convolutional deep learning approach in fog environment. Future Gener Comput Syst 113, 255–265. https://doi.org/10.1016/j.future.2020.07.020
10. Pratama M, Ashfahani A, Ong YS, Ramasamy S, Lughofer E (2018) Autonomous deep learning: Incremental learning of denoising autoencoder for evolving data streams. arXiv:1809.09081
11. Shone N, Ngoc TN, Phai VD, Shi Q (2018) A deep learning approach to network intrusion detection. IEEE Trans Emerg Top Comput Intell 2(1):41–50. https://doi.org/10.1109/TETCI.2017.2772792
12. Yousefi-Azar M, Varadharajan V, Hamey L, Tupakula U (2017) Autoencoder-based feature learning for cyber security applications. In: 2017 International joint conference on neural networks (IJCNN). IEEE, pp 3854–3861

Security Solution on KVM Hypervisor for Detecting DoS Attacks on Cloud Servers

Amar Khade and Jibi Abraham

1 Introduction

Cloud computing is a field that grows rapidly over time and it is widely used by private organizations and other sectors. In cloud computing, the resources are affordable, less in cost and can be managed from anywhere. Cloud computing services are delivered through a Hypervisor. While using cloud services, there are some concerns regarding vulnerability to security attacks that may exploit hypervisor vulnerabilities [1]. Denial of service (DoS) [1] is one such type of attack that might result in the unavailability of services provided by the cloud service when performed on an unsecured network. Several attackers try to send malicious packets to the victim at a high rate so that its computing resources or the network will get exhausted within a less time frame. When a system is getting under attack, some network traffic types that cause severe obstruction can be observed on the victim system. These malicious packets can be TCP, UDP, or ICMP types because the attacker should select the traffic type before launching an attack. Most of the hackings can trace for identifying the attacker. In contrast, it is challenging to discover the attacker's identity in DoS attacks due to spoofing the source addresses of IP packets.

Intrusion Detection System (IDS) keeps track of the network for signs of suspicious or malicious activities. It will pop up an alert if any suspicious/malicious activity is detected. With the huge amount of network traffic emerging from different kinds of dynamic and highly advanced attacks in characteristics, there is a need for more advanced and challenging Intrusion Detection Systems for the cloud. This clearly shows that the cloud IDS should check out a large number of network

A. Khade (✉) · J. Abraham
College of Engineering Pune, Pune, India
e-mail: khadear19.comp@coep.ac.in

J. Abraham
e-mail: ja.comp@coep.ac.in

© The Author(s), under exclusive license to Springer Nature Singapore Pte Ltd. 2022
U. P. Rao et al. (eds.), *Security, Privacy and Data Analytics*, Lecture Notes
in Electrical Engineering 848, https://doi.org/10.1007/978-981-16-9089-1_16

traffic to identify the characteristics of the new patterns of attack accurately and get a high accuracy rate with minimum false positiveness. In Cloud environments, to preprocess, analyze and detect intrusions with the help of traditional methods is of high cost as far as time, budget, and computation are considered. A new advanced intelligent way that uses techniques like Machine Learning techniques is required in the Cloud environments to achieve efficient intrusions detection.

After creating an attack scenario and analyzing the captured packet, it is observed that within a window of time the number of layer3 frames belonging to this packet is increasing rapidly, which made us include frame-based feature extraction into the learning module. It is observed that parameters like frame Epoch, frame Relative, and frame Delta time of tshark have an impact on the detection rate. So, if the relative time is very high and delta time is also high, then it is a normal scenario. But, if the relative time is high and delta time small between multiple packets within in same window time, then there is a possibility of an attack. This observation leads us to our proposed work to consider frame-level parameters during detection. In order to take care of the high volume of data arriving at the hypervisor, early detection of an attack based on machine learning will be of great help.

The major contributions in this paper include:

- Study the behavior of time frame in tshark and TCP, IP, Ethernet, and Frame layer contributing features toward detection of an attack.
- Identify a best suitable supervised machine learning technique to detect TCP, UDP, and ICMP-based DoS attack.
- Design a real-time packet sniffing module at the hypervisor level which uses LIBP-CAP library and tshark.
- Real-time process the network packets based on machine learning module and generate an early alarm toward attack detection.
- Select the impactful features for early detection of DoS attacks.

The remaining of this paper is organized as follows: Sect. 2 consists of the related work, and Sect. 3, describes the system's flow of the Proposed system. Section 4 includes implementation of an experimental setup and a comparison of it with and without DoS TCP, UDP, and ICMP flood attacks. In the end, we conclude this study and discuss future works in Sect. 5.

2   Related Work

Raneel Kumar et al. [1] describe a Denial of service attack on the hypervisor. Based on the attack, they proposed a DoS attack detection system. The proposed method consists of a packet sniffer, feature extraction, and Machine learning classifier for the detection system. A Network traffic dataset was generated and used machine learning algorithms like KNN and ANN to identify network traffic. The accuracy of KNN is 96.5%, and with the ANN, it is 99.98%. In [1], a Eucalyptus Cloud was set up for testing and a Denial of Service (DoS) attack is launched on the hypervisor. A custom build sniffer was developed by [1] using the LIBPCAP library. Only a TCP SYN flood attack was used for testing. Swathi Sambangi et al. [2] the author's objective is to study the problem of DDoS attack detection in a Cloud environment by considering the most famous CICIDS 2017 dataset and applying different regression to analysis for detection model for DDoS and Bot attack using traffic logfile.Also, in [2] CICIDS 2017 dataset was used to build the model, but the data is collected only for a single day. Reference [2] Feature selection was made using Information Gain. Pezhman Sheinidashtegol et al. [4] perform DDOS attack against hypervisor (XEN, KVM and Virtual Box). And Try to drench the victim resources and make them unavailable to the authorized user. They targeted resources like Network, CPU, Memory. Jason Nikolai et al. [5] author provides an architecture with an approach to virtualization technology in cloud computing and using Hypervisor performance metrics and they perform Intrusion Detection Security. Keunsoo Lee et al. [6] propose a method for proactive detection of DDoS attacks by exploiting its architecture which consists of the selection of handlers and agents, the communication and compromise, and attack. DDoS attacks were performed and select variables based on these features. The validation of the model is done on DARPA 2000 dataset.

In a cloud system, it is better to have an intrusion detection system as part of the hypervisor so all the servers running on top of the hypervisor will receive the protection. Also, in addition to [1], many more types of attacks like UDP and ICMP can be performed on a Hypervisor like KVM. The traffic log files for the DoS attacks from multiple days can be considered to make the system more efficient. Detection rate and computation time can be improved by considering various Machine learning algorithms for testing.

3 Proposed System

This proposed approach is designed to detect DoS attacks conducted from the external network, as shown in Fig. 1. Machine learning is an application of artificial intelligence that provides the ability to understand and analyze data. Machine learning is basically focused on data and data-related work based on computer program analysis systems. Machine learning techniques allow us to understand and learn devices or systems based on the data. For intrusion detection systems, machine learning plays a vital role in attack detection based on the behavior of the system the prediction is made. In the detection phase, the detection system collects the incoming packets in a time windows like 60 s. It is considered that the IP address of an attacker is spoofed. Then the incoming packets are sent to the packet analysis to extract the features of the packets. After analyzing the packets and extracting the features, those packets are passed to the test module. The test module will decide whether the packets are normal or abnormal.

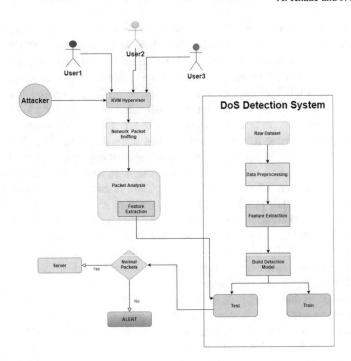

Fig. 1 Proposed system

3.1 KVM Hypervisor

The KVM kernel module turns the Linux kernel into a type 1 bare-metal hypervisor. At the same time, the overall system could be categorized to type 2 because the host OS is still fully functional and the other VM's are standard Linux processes from its perspective. KVM is an open-source hypervisor and it can be used as a type 2 hypervisor that is the reason for selecting KVM for experimentation. Every virtual machine has a local interface that is attached to the network interface in order to communicate with the external network.

3.2 Denial of Service (DoS) Attacks

TCP SYN Flood It is a type of DDOS/DOS attack which uses a 3-way handshake connection mechanism to consume resources and perform attacks.

UDP Flood It is a type of DOS attack in which a large number of UDP packets are flooded to the targeted server and makes the server overwhelmed. Nmap tool has been used for generating and sending legitimate traffic to the victim server.

ICMP Flood It is also known as a ping flood attack. In this attack, the targeted machine is overwhelmed by the Echo request. The attack involves flooding the victimÃ¢,¬â,¢s network with request packets, knowing that the network will respond with an equal number of reply packets.

3.3 Watchdog

The Watchdog is acting like a detection agent that has the capability of collecting and aggregating the data. It uses machine learning algorithms for the classification of datasets and the detection of DoS attacks.

3.3.1 Packet Capture Model

Whenever any DoS attack is executed on a network, the rates of packets transferring are very fast. The goal is to capture the packets in the network traffic at the hypervisor. This model is developed in C language using the LIBPCAP library for packet capturing in the Linux system. All types of network traffic coming to the destination address are observed using *tshark*.

3.3.2 Feature Extraction

Those packets are collected in the Packet capture model are sent to the Feature Extraction Model. This model is using an extraction script to calculate and extract time-based traffic flow features for each IP address that is communicated through the network interface. The features are shown in Table 1.

3.3.3 Detection Model

A training based on supervised learning is required to understand the attack pattern which is known as a signature database. Each instance of the database has features or characteristics associated with a label or a class. After features extraction from a network packet, the data is cleaned to remove values which are useless. If some feature attribute doesn't affect the output, it can be dropped from the database. The selected features will be given to multiple Tree-based Classifiers as an input that will further identify whether the track is legitimate or malicious. The flow of the model is shown in Fig. 2.

The machine learning classifiers generate a tree according to the algorithm. The algorithm takes the threshold value according to the pattern of data. Therefore each node has a condition based on the threshold value, which leads to the path for detection of TCP, UDP, and ICMP attacks. The T1, T2, and other values are described as

Fig. 2 Tree diagram for best
path

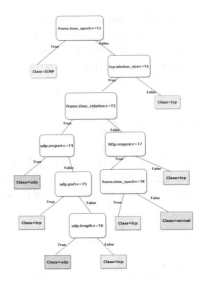

threshold values in Fig. 2. The tree is shown in the figure is based on the training
classifier. Based on the accuracy, the best classifier is chosen for the best path.

4 Implementation and Results

In this section, the attack approach was covered. First, set up the Network environment consisting tools needed to simulate users' activity in the network, performing
attacks and capturing the packets (Fig. 3).

Fig. 3 Experimental setup

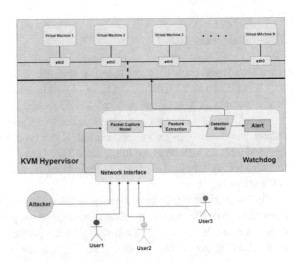

Table 1 Extracted packet features

No.	Feature name	Description
1	ip.src	Source IP address
2	ip.dst	Destination IP address
3	ip.len	Length of the incoming packet
4	ip.flags.df	Don't fragment
5	frame.time_epoch	Epoch time
6	udp.length	UDP packet length
7	tcp.flags.syn	TCP packet length
8	tcp.flags.ack	Acknowledgment
9	tcp.srcport	TCP source port
10	tcp.dstport	Destination port
11	udp.srcport	Source port
12	udp.dstport	Destination port
13	ip.ttl	Time to Live
14	ip.proto	Protocol
15	tcp.window_size	Calculated window size
16	tcp.ack	Acknowledgment number
17	tcp.len	TCP segment len
18	tcp.stream	Stream index
19	http.request	Request
21	frame.time_relative	Time since reference or first frame
22	frame.time_delta	Time delta from previous captured frame
23	tcp.time_relative	Time since first frame in this TCP stream
24	tcp.time_delta	Time since previous frame in this TCP

DoS Detection System TCP SYN Flood, UDP Flood and ICMP Flood attacks are performed using a tool like hping3 for a short period during experimentation. Then normal traffic is also generated. These malicious and normal packets combining make a common raw dataset. The sample dataset has instances of 797262 and results to 24 features. Some packets might be duplicates, or some of them are missing. To make the data clean and in an understandable format, data pre-processing is applied and the important features are extracted based on the headers of the packet (Table 2).

After extracting features, the dataset is trained under the detection model. This pre-processed data is then split into 90% for training and 10% for testing the dataset. Implementation of tenfold cross validation is also done using this dataset. Machine learning classifiers such as Random forest, Decision tree, and LogisticRegression are used. Cross-validation was used with machine learning algorithms like Random

Table 2 Applying tree-based classifiers on all features

Algorithm	Acc (%)	Incorrectly classified (%)	B.Time (s)
Decision tree	99.99975	0.00025	0.05
Random forest	99.999996	0.000004	0.20
Logistic regression	48.8408	51.1592	0.25

Table 3 Comparison of the frame layer performance

Classifier	Accuracy (%)	Time taken to detect an attack (s)
Random forest (without frame layer parameter)	99.9973	0.07161
Random forest (with frame layer parameter)	99.999996	0.04007

forest (RF), DecisionTree (DT), LogisticRegression. RF obtained highest accuracy while LogisticRegression obtained lower accuracy, as shown in Table 3. The DoS detection system is ready for testing of live packets. The RF, the best classifier out of our experimentation was chosen to understand the impact of frame layer features in the intrusion detection. Two experiments were conducted using random forest by including frame layer features and by excluding the frame layer features. As shown in Table 2, it is observed that the experimentation including frame layer features is having higher accuracy and early detection of intrusion detection in-comparison with the experiment which excluded the frame layer features. Below, Fig. 4 shows the impact of each feature on DoS/DDoS attack detection.

The impact of different features is analyzed on attack detection and we found that the most relevant features are frame.time_epoch, ip.length and tcp.ack in the descending order as shown in Fig. 4. To shed more light on the performance evaluation of our detection system in terms of scalability, the simulation is repeated with various number of users and increase in number of attackers. The graph in Fig. 5 shows the variation of time for detection with different users. This shows that our detection system is effective and stable in resisting both single-source and multiple-sources attacks.

Fig. 4 Impact of different features on detection

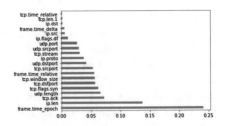

Fig. 5 Time for detection
the attack

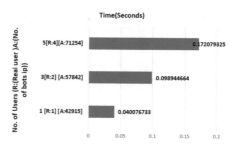

5 Conclusion

An intelligent intrusion detection system at the hypervisor level is designed and implemented to identify DoS/DDoS attacks on cloud servers. This system uses three types of machine learning classifiers to classify the network traffic captured by tshark by analyzing the features at transport layer, network layer, and frame layer. The experimentation shows that random forest outperforms all the other classifiers in terms of performance evaluations. In comparison to the existing research which considers only the network and transport layers, our results show that the frame layer features are having a high impact on the detection performance. The system is also stable in terms of scalable number of real and attack users. In future, this research can be continued for preventing DoS/DDoS attacks using a consensus-based machine learning model.

References

1. Kumar R, Lal SP, Sharma A (2016) Detecting denial of service attacks in the cloud. In: IEEE 14th international conference on dependable, autonomic and secure computing, 14th international conference on pervasive intelligence and computing, 2nd international conference on big data intelligence and computing and cyber science and technology congress (DASC/PiCom/DataCom/CyberSciTech)
2. Graziano M, Lanzi A, Balzarotti D (2013) Hypervisor memory forensic. In: International workshop on recent advances in intrusion detection. Springer
3. Shi J, Yang Y, Tang C (2016) The grid: hardware assisted hypervisor introspection. Springer-PlusDS
4. Szefer J, Keller E, Lee RB, Rexford J (2011) Eliminating the hypervisor attack surface for a more secure cloud. In: Proceedings of the 18th ACM conference on Computer and communications security
5. Sheinidashtegol P, Galloway M (2017) Performance impact of DDoS attacks on three virtual machine hypervisors. In: 2017 IEEE international conference on cloud engineering (IC2E)

Privacy Preservation Techniques and Models for Publishing Structured Data

Palak Desai and Devendra Thakor

1 Introduction

In today's era, everything is being digitized and this leads to generating an ample amount of digital data. These personal data are being generated and/or collected through the Internet, mobiles, social networking, sensors, and many such resources that are dependable for this huge data. This collected data is published for purpose of research and making business strategies that lead to the disclosure of sensitive and private information of users and due to that privacy of users are being bridged [1, 2].

Due to this digitization, individuals' privacy is more at risk than ever before. There are two aspects to protect the data: i. Security and ii. Privacy. The main focus of security is to protect the data from attack and provides data integrity, confidentiality, authentication, and access control whereas privacy focuses that data remains functional without disclosure of sensitive information of an individual [1–3].

The protection of the data maintained at the time of collecting data is known as input privacy whereas protection of data at a later stage of data mining is called output privacy. Very high privacy is achieved by applying cryptographic-based techniques but it will not address secured mining [4, 5].

The Privacy Preserving Data Publishing (PPDP) methods are used to protect along with maintaining the privacy of the individual's data by publishing it in such a way that data could be used in required research and data owner's privacy is also maintained [6].

Several organizations publish their data or records for decision-making practice or innovative development of problems through research and surveys. While providing protection to sensitive data by securing identity, it is equally important to have a utility of data for purpose of data utilization. This leads to the trade-off to the privacy of data

P. Desai (✉) · D. Thakor
C. G. Patel Institute of Technology, Uka Tarsadia University, Gujarat, India

D. Thakor
e-mail: devendra.thakor@utu.ac.in

© The Author(s), under exclusive license to Springer Nature Singapore Pte Ltd. 2022
U. P. Rao et al. (eds.), *Security, Privacy and Data Analytics*, Lecture Notes
in Electrical Engineering 848, https://doi.org/10.1007/978-981-16-9089-1_17

and its utility. Here, in this paper, the focus is on structured data, and various methods to provide privacy to the data are being discussed. Also, in various applications where privacy is required, benchmark methods to handle privacy with possible attacks are mentioned. As much research has been done in this field, various techniques to provide privacy have been reviewed.

In the paper, we will explore various methods to achieve data privacy, a comparison between them, and discuss possible attacks.

1.1 Applications

Many times, various organizations need to publish their data to find patterns out of it or for innovative solutions to the problems by surveys and research. In many domains, a huge amount of data is being generated and collected each day having private or sensitive information about the user. In such a case, a major concern is the need to provide privacy to sensitive data at the time of publishing it. Few such domains have been mentioned where data privacy perseverance is supreme [7–9].

Healthcare. Medical history and patient data can be collected from different sources. This medical data is very important for medical research but these data contain sensitive information regarding patients that patient is not willing to disclose.

Social Network. In the current era, most of the users on social networks publish their personal information, preferences, location history, etc. Due to this, private user information gets derived and user privacy gets compromised and misused.

IoT Applications. Extensive applications based on IoT such as smart watch, smart homes, intelligent transportation, smart city, etc. are being developed that collect the personal data of the user. If the privacy to this data is not provided, then an attacker may maliciously use the sensitive data of the user.

Government and Financial Companies. Periodically, the government needs to publish its citizen data publicly. These data usually work as external data and are used to identify sensitive information of a user in other applications. Apart from the government, financial organizations also have a lot of sensitive information regarding user financial status. So, it is necessary to publish this data as anonymized data.

1.2 Microdata Publishing

Raw data usually doesn't satisfy the privacy prerequisite for sensitive values of the user, so data must be modified before publishing. This procedure of modifying the data is either by eliminating personal key information, encrypting, or changing data to protect an individual's identity. This process is called data anonymization [6]. Microdata has records that provide information about an individual, organization, etc. Microdata has a table with the number of attributes that can be separated into four

Table 1 Medical microdata

Name	Age	Gender	Zip code	Disease
Riya	45	Female	444,805	TB
Shikha	25	Female	424,806	Diabetes
Miral	46	Male	424,806	TB
Rushabh	34	Male	444,806	Fever

categories: Explicit identifiers (Ex_ID), Quasi Identifiers (Q_ID), Sensitive attributes (SA), and Non-Sensitive Attributes (Non-SA) [4, 6, 10].

Explicit Identifiers (Ex_ID). It uniquely identifies individuals through a person's name, his PAN card, driving license number, voter ID, etc. Before publishing data, such attributes have to be removed.

Quasi Identifiers (Q_ID). This is a set of attributes that helps in the identification of the record owner. These will try to match its values with external data for the identification of an individual.

Sensitive Attributes (SA). It comprises of person-specific sensitive details such as CVV number, disease, or income.

Non-sensitive Attributes (Non-SA). These attributes have values that will not create any problem if its value is releveled to untrusted parties as it will not play role in the identification of the identity of a user.

In Table 1, the name is an explicit identifier, <Age, Gender, and Zip Code> are quasi-identifiers and Disease is a sensitive attribute.

1.3 Techniques of Privacy Preserving

Mainly, the methods used to calculate privacy use data transformation. To improve privacy, most of the methods decrease the granularity of representation. Due to this, there is a loss of effective data for research purposes [4, 10, 11]. The following are approaches that have been developed for PPDP.

Randomization. In this method, external noise is added to the original data for the protection of sensitive attributes from its disclosure. Because of high time complexity and less data utility, this method is not used on a large dataset.

Cryptographic Techniques. Higher privacy of data is achieved by applying encryption techniques to achieve the security and integrity of transferred data. Traditional encryption methods are highly difficult to encrypt large-scale data, also secure key management needs to be done between sender and receiver [12].

Anatomization. Anatomization also refers to Bucketization, and this will not change the value of quasi-identifiers or sensitive attributes but de-associate the relationship between the two. It will release two separate tables: Quasi identifier Table and Sensitive Table. Data is not modified in both the said tables which is the major benefit of anatomization [6].

Random Perturbation. In this method, it substitutes the original data with synthetic values which calculates statistical data from the perturbation of the original data in a way that will not have more variation between the statistical data and the original data.

Clustering. Clustering is a procedure to group entities in the dataset, and entities in the equivalent group are highly alike to each other compared to the further groups based on grouping criteria. Every cluster must have a predefined number of data values and anonymity applied to the clusters.

Currently, generalization, bucketization, and slicing are widely used. The major difference between the two techniques is that bucketization will not generalize the quasi-identifier attributes so there is higher utilization of data [13–15].

Generalization. It changes attribute values with a more general value than a specific one, due to which many attribute values for Q_ID have the same value. This process replaces the exact value with a more general description, making the quasi value less identifiable. If given data is numeric, it is likely to be changed with some range, and if categorical then transformed to another categorical value having wider category or higher-level concept of original categorical value [6].

Even though this method is popular, the constraint of this method is that because of the generalization of the data, it reduced data utility. Also, as every attribute is distinctly generalized, a correlation between attributes is mislaid. So, the data analyst needs to assume that all possible combination of the attribute value is identical.

Bucketization. Conceptually, it is related to generalization, and only it will not change Q_ID value or sensitive values. Rather this splits the records into numbers of partitions and keeps a unique identifier called G_ID to every partition. Every tuple of the same partition will be having an identical G_ID value. In the end, it forms two tables having the quasi-attributes and the sensitive attribute. Anonymized data contains a set of buckets having sensitive values that have been permuted.

Slicing. Slicing divides data either horizontally, vertically, or both. In horizontal division, records are clustered into buckets whereas, in the vertical division, highly associated attributes are grouped in a column. Columns are arbitrarily sorted for breaking the link between various column values [16, 17].

1.4 Comparative Analysis of Privacy Preserving Techniques

The following Table 2 describes different anonymization techniques and their comparison based on the two important comparison factors such as privacy and utility of data.

Among these slicing preserves better privacy and utility because it analyzes the data characteristics and uses them for anonymizing data [3, 6, 6].

Table 2 Comparison of anonymization techniques

Parameter	Bucketization	Generalization	Slicing
Privacy	– No change in the value of QI – Membership disclosure – Moderate level of privacy preserved	Good privacy perseverance, as each attribute is assigned to some less consistent but generalized value	Better privacy is preserved as in this technique uncorrelated attributes are partitioned in different columns
Utility	Data utility is better as compared to generalization	Higher information loss for High-Dimensional data decreases data utility	Data utility is much better because highly correlated attributes are grouped in a column

1.5 Attacks on Different Privacy Models

Privacy models can be differentiated as per the mode of attack on them. One such category where there is an attempt to create a link of the data table having owner's record and sensitive data by an attacker is called linkage attack. It can be record linkage where Q_ID values are used to identify a small number of record pairs in two separate tables, attribute linkage where the attacker attempt to retrieve sensitive values depends on the sensitive value linked with a group that the person belongs to, from the published data and table linkage where presence or absence of user information in a table reveals sensitive information of a user. In all these attacks, the attackers are aware of the Q_ID values of the owner. Another category is where, from the published records, an attacker has an aim to acquire more information with present background knowledge. It is called the probabilistic attack where dissimilarity of beliefs among post and prior is obtained [6, 18–20].

2 Privacy Models

There are two categories of privacy threat, one where an opponent can link to the owner's data with published data knowing quasi-identifiers, whereas the other category aims to achieve uninformative principle. The privacy of published data is said to be preserved if it can successfully prevent an opponent to perform any type of linkage between data. To do so, various privacy models are used [1, 4, 6].

k-Anonymity. In this model, every record is distinct from at the minimum k-1 very records compared with Q_ID. A table that satisfies said requirement is known as a k-anonymous table. To achieve that, usually suppression and generalization are used [9].

l-Diversity. The l-Diversity needs each Q_ID set to comprise at minimum l "well represented" sensitive data meaning that there exists at minimum l indistinguishable

Table 3 Privacy Model

Privacy model	Record linkage	Attribute linkage	Table linkage	Probabilistic attack
k-Anonymity	✓			
l-iversity	✓	✓		
t-Closeness		✓		✓
(α, k)-Anonymity	✓	✓		
(X, Y)-Privacy	✓	✓		
(k, e)-Anonymity		✓		
Distributional privacy			✓	✓
ε-Differential privacy			✓	✓

information for SA in every Q_ID set. This well-defined model of l-diversity also assures k-anonymity, given k = l as each Q_ID set contains at least l records.

t-Closeness. t-Closeness needs the division of the sensitive attributes in some group on Q_ID which is near to the division of the attribute in the whole table. To estimate the closeness between two distributive sensitive values, this uses the function called "Earth Mover Distance" (EMD). It requires closeness within t. Many other privacy models such as (α, k)- Anonymity, (k, e)- Anonymity, (X, Y)- Privacy, ε-Differential privacy, and Distributional Privacy are also available to address various privacy threats [6]. Here, Table 3 concise attack models addressed by the respective privacy model.

3 Threats to Privacy

At publication of private data, it is likely to suffer from several types of threats addressing privacy disclosure [17].

Membership Disclosure. Membership information may reveal the identity of a user from the published data. So, it is difficult to prevent an attacker from the identification that whether a specific person's record is available in a published table or not. It is essential to handle such cases when data or detail is integrated from an extensive range of populations having sensitive value. The said threat is known as membership disclosure.

Identity Disclosure. If an individual's identity is exposed, then his/her respective private sensitive attribute value will not remain private. For protection from disclosure of the identity of an individual, it is vital to protect the disclosure of membership when membership information is not known to an attacker. If an attacker is sure about an individual's membership in published records, then it is not sufficient to just protect membership disclosure of a person to protect a person's identity.

Attribute Disclosure. This disclosure may happen if the published records support exposing the details of a sensitive attribute of a specific person more compared to it would be probable from the unpublished data. Revealing the value of an attribute can be possible if the identity is exposed not because data of sensitive attribute is similar in all the alike records.

4 Related Work

As the world is moving toward digitization in every field, much research is being carried out by researchers in the field of privacy preservation of data as it is a need of an hour. The following Table 4 contains a survey of work done in the field of preservation of the privacy of structured data.

From Table 4, it has been observed that the technique in [29] is good for providing data utility whereas the technique proposed in [30] has high privacy preservation, also if the value of k decides appropriately, then high utility is also achieved. Apart from these, in a majority of techniques, there is a trade-off between data privacy preservation and data utility.

Table 4 Literature survey of related work

Paper	Data privacy	Data utility	Advantages	Limitations
[21]	Low	High	Authentication of requester and confidentiality to data are achieved	– Identity disclosure attack Requires more time as for each request to patient key generation and encryption-decryption is to be done
[22]	High	–	– Users have access control to give permission or not for each request – Authentication of the user is being done	– No data confidentiality as data transmission is in plain text form
[23]	High	Low	User authentication is done	– Data miner needs to take approval from each patient – Data is not confidential
[24]	High	–	– The integrity of data achieved – The system is scalable	– Privacy preservation is done manually as it is decided by users – No confidentiality of data
[25]	High	Low	– No need to have prior knowledge of threshold k – No need to identify the numbers of repetitions of values in columns	– Takes a higher time for bucket creation if a dataset is large – If data is less identical, then more buckets are generated

(continued)

Table 4 (continued)

Paper	Data privacy	Data utility	Advantages	Limitations
[26]	High	Low	For less value of k, Information loss is less	– Utility of data is less if high data anonymization is required – Data is not secured as data is transmitted in plaintext
[27]	Low	High	A high level of confidentiality and integrity is achieved	– Secure key distribution is required else data is exposed during migration – Need more time as encryption and hashing are needed to be done
[28]	Low	High	– Data transmission is done in a secure manner – User authentication and access are controlled	Less privacy is preserved as once access is granted; entire data is available for access
[29]	Less	High	Incremental Model	– Time complexity is higher for clustering and joining operation – A threshold value is critical to decide
[30]	High	–	Remove similarity and sensitivity attack	– Background knowledge is needed to decide sensitivity rank – Value of k decides the level of utility

There is also open research that if the data privacy and data utility are achieved but if not taken care of security aspects, then data loss is still there. As in the current era, even for a single application, data need to be collected/provided from/to various data sources or organizations which includes the requirement of data security aspects as well.

5 Conclusion

In today's digital era, in various domains, a massive amount of data is generated and accumulated for innovation, development, and research work. While analyzing of personal data of users, it is equally essential to protect the privacy of specific sensitive values of user data from being exposed. From the review of literature, it has been found that for privacy preservation, the trade-off is between data with higher privacy and utility. This needs much attention from researchers to achieve higher privacy without compromising much of the data utility.

References

1. Jadon P, Mishra DK (2019) Security and privacy issues in big data: a review, emerging trends in expert applications and security. In: Advances in intelligent systems and computing, vol 841. Springer, pp 659–665
2. Bhaladhare P, Jinwala D (2016) Novel approaches for privacy preserving data mining in k-anonymity model. J Inf Sci Eng 63–78
3. Singh A, Parihar D (2013) A review of privacy preserving data publishing technique. Int J Emerg Res Man-Agement Technol 2(6):32–38
4. Sangeetha S, Sadasivam GS (2019) Privacy of big data: a review. handbook of big data and iot security. Springer, pp 5–23
5. Terzi DS, Terzi R, Sagiroglu S (2015) A survey on security and privacy issues in big data. In: 10th international conference for internet technology and secured transactions (ICITST). London, pp 202–207
6. Fung BCM, Wang K, Fu AWC, Philip SY Introduction to privacy-preserving data publishing: concepts and techniques. CRC Press
7. Sharma S, Chen K, Sheth A (2018) Toward practical privacy-preserving analytics for iot and cloud-based healthcare systems, vol 22. IEEE Internet Computing, pp 42–51
8. Azeez NA, Van der Vyver C (2019) Security and privacy issues in e-health cloud-based system: a comprehensive content analysis. Egypt Inform J 20:97–108
9. Do Le Quoc MB, Bhatotia P, Chen R, Fetzer C, Strufe T (2018) Privacy-preserving data analytics. In: Sakr S, Zomaya A (eds) Encyclopedia of big data technologies. Springer, pp 1–8
10. Vaghashia H, Ganatra A (2015) A survey: privacy preservation techniques in data mining. Int J Comput Appl 119(4):20–26
11. Rao PRM, Krishna SM, Kumar APS (2018) Privacy preservation techniques in big data analytics: a survey. J Big Data 5. Springer
12. Stallings W (2005) Cryptography and network security principles and practices. Prentice Hall
13. Xu Y, Ma T, Tang M, Tian W (2014) A survey of privacy preserving data publishing using generalization and suppression. Appl Math Inf Sci Int J 8(3):1103–1116
14. Dubli D, Yadav DK (2017) Secure techniques of data anonymization for privacy preservation. Int J Adv Res Comput Sci (IJARCS) 8(5):1693–1696
15. Sriramoju SB (2017) Analysis and comparison of anonymous techniques for privacy preserving in big data. Int J Adv Res Comput Commun Eng (IJARCCE) 6(12):64–67
16. Li T, Li N, Zhang J, Molloy I (2012) Slicing: a new approach for privacy preserving data publishing. IEEE Trans Knowl Data Eng 24(3):561–574
17. Susan VS, Christopher T (2016) Anatomisation with slicing: a new privacy preservation approach for multiple sensitive attributes. Springer Plus 5(964):1–21
18. Hall R, Fienberg SE (2010) Privacy-preserving record linkage. In: Domingo-Ferrer J, Magkos E (eds) Privacy in statistical databases. PSD 2010. Lecture notes in computer science, vol 6344. Springer, Berlin, Heidelberg
19. Mane DB, Emmanuel M (2014) Review on privacy and utility in high dimensional data publishing. Int J Emerg Trends Technol Comput Sci (IJETTCS) 3(1):186–191
20. Lu Y, Sinnott RO, Verspoor K, Parampalli U (2018) Privacy-preserving access control in electronic health record linkage. In: 17th IEEE international conference on trust, security and privacy in computing and communications/12th IEEE international conference on big data science and engineering (TrustCom/BigDataSE), pp 1079–1090
21. Tembhare A, Chakkaravarthy SS, Sangeetha D (2019) Role-based policy to maintain privacy of patient health records in cloud. J Supercomput 75:5866–5881. Springer
22. Talat R, Obaidat MS, Muzammal M, Sodhro AH, Luo Z, Pirbhulal S (2020) A decentralised approach to privacy preserving trajectory mining. Futur Gener Comput Syst 102:382–392. Elsevier
23. Nortey RN, Yue L, Agdedanu PR, Adjeisah M (2019) Privacy module for distributed electronic health records (EHRs) using the blockchain. In: 4th international conference on big data analytics (ICBDA). IEEE, pp 369–374

24. Liang X, Zhao J, Shetty S, Liu J, Li D (2017) Integrating blockchain for data sharing and collaboration in mobile healthcare applications. In: IEEE 28th annual international symposium on personal, indoor, and mobile radio communications (PIMRC). Montreal, QC, pp 1–5
25. Ouazzaniand Z, Bakkalia HE (2018) A new technique ensuring privacy in big data: k-anonymity without prior value of the threshold k. In: The first international conference on intelligent computing in data sciences. Elsevier, pp 52–59
26. Li H, Guo F, Zhang W, Wang J, Xing J (2018) (a,k)- anonymous scheme for privacy-preserving data collection in iot-based healthcare services systems. J Med Syst 42, 56. Springer
27. Urmela S, Nandhini M (2018) Double-blind key-attribute based encryption algorithm for personalized privacy-preserving of distributed data mining. Int J Appl Eng Res 13(11):10048–10057
28. Aaro A, Usha S (2019) Data sharing and privacy preserving on personal healthcare information in cloud. Int J Adv Res, Ideas Innov Technol 373–377
29. Sudhakar RV, Rao TCM (2020) Security aware index based quasi–identifier approach for privacy preservation of data sets for cloud applications. Cluster Comput 23:2579–2589
30. Victor N, Lopez D (2020) Privacy preserving sensitive data publishing using (k, n, m) anonymity approach. J Commun Softw Syst 16(1):46–56

Ensemble Neural Models for Depressive Tendency Prediction Based on Social Media Activity of Twitter Users

Gurdeep Saini, Naveen Yadav, and Sowmya Kamath S

1 Introduction

Depression is a mental affliction that is often overlooked and is typically regarded as a non-serious condition in most countries. However, chronic depression causes the manifestation of various physical symptoms such as loss of appetite, reduction in attention and concentration, lack of self-confidence, and disturbed sleep. Many life experiences can trigger a bout of depression, such as losing a job, losing a loved one, family problems, health issues, and other tough situations such as COVID-19 outbreak. The pandemic has caused several punitive actions like the nationwide lockdown and physical distancing due to which many people have been leading isolated lives different from their normal life, making them feel lonely, emotionally distanced, and overwhelmed.

The World Health Organization (WHO) reports that 264 million people worldwide suffer from depression., while 1 in 13 globally suffers from anxiety [1]. Depression is often not diagnosed and is often attributed to other causes like fatigue or tiredness. Depression, at its worst, may lead to suicide, with the World Health Organization [2] reporting that approximately 8,00,000 depressed individuals commit suicide each year. Researchers have attempted to gather information on the problem through survey-based approaches using online question-answer and phone calls [3] However, the major limitations of these approaches are that the collected information is primarily incomplete dependent on the sampling processes used and due to the introduction of sampling bias.

In recent years, research studies have attempted to study mental health and mood using social media data [4–8]. Some approaches are based on supervised techniques [7, 9–12], while others have used lexicon-based methods [13, 14]. In supervised

G. Saini (✉) · N. Yadav · S. Kamath S
Department of Information Technology, Healthcare Analytics and Language Engineering (HALE), National Institute of Technology Karnataka, Surathkal, Mangalore 575025, India
e-mail: sowmyakamath@nitk.edu.in

© The Author(s), under exclusive license to Springer Nature Singapore Pte Ltd. 2022
U. P. Rao et al. (eds.), *Security, Privacy and Data Analytics*, Lecture Notes in Electrical Engineering 848, https://doi.org/10.1007/978-981-16-9089-1_18

learning-based approaches, machine learning algorithms such as support vector machine and decision tree have been used for sentiment analysis [15, 16], event analysis [17, 18], personalized recommendation [16], etc., with good results. In lexicon-based methods, researchers used the most important words, i.e., the words which have high frequencies compared to the rest of the words, for classifying the testing tweets.

These works, however, are limited due to a lack of consideration to an individual's forms of expression, followers and influencing network, user involvement, and emotion [15]. These aspects can serve as discriminating features to recognize depression-indicative posts very effectively. Social media networks like Twitter and Facebook have become very good outlets for sharing updates on one's life. Such social behavior on short messaging platforms like Twitter can be an excellent resource that can be used to generate insights into user behaviors, emotions, and feelings, that may be indicative of their mental health. For instance, consider the following news headlines – *"Twitter fail: Teen Sent 144 Tweets Before Committing Suicide & No One Helped"* and *"Jim Carrey's Girlfriend: Her Last Tweet Before Committing Suicide 'Signing Off'"*. These underscore the long-term depressive tendencies of the individual to a large audience on the respective social networks, which could have been used to prevent their eventual suicides. Several such works have shown that social media analysis is a good way to detect and address depressive tendencies. Challenges like low accuracy and labor-intensive methodology still persist, and in our work, we aim to address these limitations.

Our work focuses on identifying depressive tendencies based on users social media activity. To develop the proposed model, we utilized a large, public dataset called Kaggle Sentiment140, which contains 1,600,000 tweets with labels negative, neutral, and positive. First, we experimented with supervised learning models such as Support Vector Machine, Random Forests, and XGB for the task, while incorporating Term weight modeling techniques to boost prediction accuracy. We also present an ensemble model built on Convolutional Neural Networks and LSTM for further improving the accuracy of depression prediction. The rest of this article is organized as follows. Section 2 discusses several state-of-the-art methods for the tasks of depression detection. The details of the proposed machine learning models and deep learning model for the task of depression detection are discussed in detail in Sect. 3. The experimental evaluation and observed outcome are discussed in Sect. 4, later conclusion and future work is discussed.

2   Related Work

Studying social behavior for analyzing and understanding underlying patterns for enabling tasks like opinion mining, purchasing habits, bias estimation, and so on has become an increasingly popular research area. Several works exist that attempt to utilize social communication for identifying disease parameters for chronic illnesses like depression [19–22]. Choudhury et al. [9] state that successfully combating depression is a true measure of an individual's and society's well-being. A large number of people suffer from the negative symptoms of depression, but only a small percentage are diagnosed and receive adequate care. Researchers have explored social media platforms such as Twitter, Facebook, etc., and users' internet-based interactions to detect and assess the symptoms of serious depression in people. Through the use of text used by users in their posts, latent patterns associated with users' mindset, social contacts, emotional framework, self-esteem, hatred, etc., have been analyzed and studied.

Choudhury et al. [23] recognized online networking as a viable public-health tool, concentrating on the use of Twitter to develop statistical models for the impact of delivery on new mothers' behavior and temperament. They used Twitter posts to monitor 376 mothers' postpartum shifts in terms of social interaction, feeling, casual culture, and phonetic style. O'Dea et al. [24] found that Twitter is being increasingly studied as a means of detecting psychological well-being, such as stress and suicidal tendencies, in the general population. Using both human coders and a programmed computer classifier, They observed that the level of anxiety shown in suicide-related tweets may be detected accurately. Zhang et al. [25] showed that if people at high risk of suicide can be identified by online networking such as microblogging, a complex intervention mechanism to save their lives can be implemented. They used a dataset consisting of posts from 1041 Weibo users and NLP techniques like Latent Dirichlet Allocation (LDA) and Linguistic Inquiry Word Count (LIWC) were used to extract linguistic features. Their experiments showed that LDA outperformed all other models in the task of finding the topic that relates to suicide probability.

Paul and Dredze [26] developed a prediction model for modeling the occurrence of various diseases in the public based on the wordings used and emotion expressed in twitter posts. Sadilek and Kautz [27] proved the correlation between social media data and diagnostic influenza patient. Experiments performed on 2.5 million geo-tagged twitter messages, using Sadilek et al., showed interesting insights into the spread of influenza. They discovered that as the number of sick friends increases, the probability of falling ill increases exponentially. Billing and Moos [28] proved that users' stress levels can be predicted based on their twitter feed using various methods like linguistic analysis and emotion analysis.

Aldarwish and Ahmed [29] proposed a depression detection technique using Rapid-Miner. They used two classifier Naive Bayes classifier and SVM classifier. on two data sets containing 2073 depressed posts and social media posts. The limitations of the approach are that the models were manually trained, making it difficult to train and integrate into the model. Husain [30] used user generated content from Facebook, then they labeled the words from the post in the training phase. For testing, text classification algorithms are applied to detect the positive and negative class using SVM classifier. Biradar and Totad [31] proposed Sentistrength sentiment analysis and back propagation neural network for depression prediction. The advantage of using back propagation neural network is that it is fast, simple, and no other parameter is required except inputs. However, it cannot learn non-linearly tasks, which is a significant limitation of its approach.

3 Proposed Methodology

Different mechanisms outlined as part of the proposed strategy for depression prediction are discussed in this section.

3.1 Data Preprocessing

The Sentiment140 dataset containing 1,600,000 tweets was used for the evaluation. The dataset contains a target field—if the target is 0, it means the tweet is negative, if target is 2, then it means the tweet is neutral, and if the target is 4, then the tweet is positive. During data preprocessing, all URLs, unnecessary articles, punctuation, alphanumeric characters, and stopwords except first, second and third pronouns were removed. The NLTK tweet tokenizer was used to tokenize the messages. After tokenizing, we utilized the training dataset to create a final vocabulary which contains 242,660 unique tokens and is used to encode the sentences as series of indices.

3.2 Dealing with Multi-class Data

The dataset contains multiple classes, in order to categorize the preprocessed documents in the relevant classes, we adopt hyperplane- based concepts. The vocabulary is represented in an n-dimensional hyperspace using which classification can be performed. In the high-dimensional space, Support Vector Machine (SVM) is used to train and test the model. As it is a supervised learning model that maps two separate classes in a high-dimensional space, SVM has the potential to reduce overfitting difficulties to some level. To avoid the risk of overfitting [32], it may modify many features while maintaining great performance.

Let us consider datapoints $X_1, X_2, X_2 \ldots X_n$ that are to be mapped to a n-dimensional hyperspace. Equation (3) represents the hyperplane in n dimensions.

$$\alpha_0 + \alpha_1 * X_1 + \alpha_2 * X_2 + \alpha_3 * X_3 + \alpha_4 * X_4 + \cdots + \alpha_n * X_n = 0 \qquad (1)$$

where, α_0 is intercept, α_1 is coefficient of first axis and α_1 is coefficient of nth axis. To adjust this $n - 1$ dimensional plane in n dimensions, we need to adjust the weight such that for any point which belongs to output class, the value obtained with Eq. (2) should be less than 0. If the point (e.g. here point has n values in the n dimensional space, Tweet1 vector and Tweet2 vector are two points) lies in positive class, then Eq. (2) will give a value greater than or equal zero.

$$Weight = \alpha_0 + \alpha_1 * X_1 + \alpha_2 * X_2 + \alpha_3 * X_3 + \alpha_4 * X_4 + \cdots + \alpha_n * X_n \qquad (2)$$

Thus, we can conclude that if some feature maps to a negative class, its corresponding α value will be negative, and similarly for the feature which is inclined to positive class has corresponding α value as positive. During training, the SVM classifier adjusts the α values by using the maximal margin from the vectors, as per Eqs. (4) and (5), where M is the maximum achievable margin form the hyperplane to any of its side and m is the total training vectors, $Y = \{-1, 1\}$ depend on the class of vector, -1 for negative class and 1 for positive class, these two ensure that maximum margin is maintained between two classes.

$$M = \alpha_0 + \alpha_1 + \alpha_2 + \alpha_3 + \cdots + \alpha_n \tag{3}$$

$$Y_i(\alpha_0 + \alpha_1 * X_{i1} + \alpha_2 * X_{i2} + \alpha_3 * X_{i3} + \cdots + \alpha_n * X_{in} >= M \tag{4}$$

In the testing phase, we calculate the value of Eq. (5) for the testing vector. The vector belongs to the negative class if $F(X)$ is negative, and the testing vector belongs to the positive class if $F(X)$ is positive.

$$F(X) = \alpha_0 + \alpha_1 * X_1 + \alpha_2 * X_2 + \alpha_3 * X_3 + \cdots + \alpha_n * X_n \tag{5}$$

The process is performed as follows—firstly, we take the label data set which contain both positive and negative class, and split the dataset such that 80% is used for training and 20% is used for testing. After preprocessing, the data is fed into the SVM classifier, Random forest classifier and XGB Classifier for training/testing the model. The metric Social Media Depression Index (SMBI) is generated to measure the depression level of users in order to observe the performance of the trained ML models. The SMDI value is calculated for both men and women separately and comparative analysis of SMDI is undertaken in the night and day window. Performance obtained with ML models was lower in accuracy due to which we also experimented with deep neural models such as Convolutional Neural Networks (CNN) and Long Short-term Memory (LSTM).

4 Implementation Specifics

4.1 Depression Behavior Identification

For this task, we firstly identify specific keywords that are typically indicative of depressions, i.e., words that indicate unhappiness, negative or abnormal emotions in the post. Some such words are shown in Table 1. Time is also important factor to determine whether a user is in depression or not. To capture this aspect, we used a day and night window, to also model the fact that people are typically more depressed at night when compared to daytime due to factors like loneliness, darkness, hopelessness, isolation, fatigue, etc.

Table 1 Depression-indicative terms

Class	Type	Sample terms
1	Depression-indicative	hurts, escape, suck, loser, depress, lonely, sad, alone, weak, useless, worth, hate, uncomfortable, pressure, conversation, suicidal, imbalance, myself, blame, torture, safe, worry, intimidate, therapy, medication, break, mine, painful, nobody, shit, life, problems, unsuccessful
2	Non-depressive	football, favorite, sleepy, life, amazing, tips, beautiful, romantic, work, play, perfect, good, weekend, love, smile, hello, friends, follow, meet, team, movie, excited, great, night, brilliant, bored, awesome

4.2 Term Weighting

Term weighting is generally used for capturing the relevance of document terms in information retrieval and text mining applications. We evaluate the relative relevance of a word in relation to a specific document and across the entire corpus using term frequency and inverse document frequency (TF-IDF). Importance of a specific term/word directly depends on how many time a word appear inside the document. It can be understood by taking some example, in case of vectorization, we are giving equal preference to every word whether it is '*the*' or '*torture*', but we can easily say that word '*the*' don't have any importance in depression classification and it is present in most of the tweet so TF-IDF is used to penalize these kinds of words.

The number of times a word appears in the document divided by the total number of words in the document yields TF (Eq. 6). Every tweet is a document for our present work, and the occurrence of terms in a tweet is considered for this calculation. The relevance of an uncommon word in the corpus is captured by inverse document frequency (Eq. 7).

$$TF(t) = a/b \tag{6}$$

where, $TF(t)$ is the term frequency of term t, a is the frequency of particular word in the current document, and b is the sum of frequencies of all words in the corpus.

$$IDF(t) = log_e(TN/ND). \tag{7}$$

TN denotes the total documents and ND is the number of documents that contain a specific term t.

$$TFIDF(t) = TF(t) * IDF(t) \tag{8}$$

4.3   Measuring Depression

For this task, we adopted a standard metric called SMDI (Social Media Depression Index) [33] SMDI is used to measure the level of depression in the individual or population using statistical analysis of influencing factors. It is the standardized difference between the depression post and normal post in the given time t, where t may day, week, etc. In case of individuals, we take the tweets of the social media user, but in case of population, the entire tweet corpus is considered for computation of SMDI (Eq. 9).

$$SMDI = \frac{nd(t) - \mu d}{\sigma d} - \frac{ns(t) - \mu s}{\sigma s} \tag{9}$$

where, $nd(t)$ denotes the number of depression tweets, $ns(t)$ denotes total normal or standard tweets, μ_d is mean of numbers of depression tweets, μ_s is mean of numbers of non-depression tweets, σ_d is the standard deviation of numbers of depression tweets and σ_s is the standard deviation of numbers of non-depression tweets.

4.4   Prediction Models

For the task of depression detection and prediction, we employed an ensemble deep neural model consisting of Convolution neural network with LSTM. The model's architecture is seen in Fig. 1. The model uses a word embedding layer employing Word2Vec [34], which is a. neural embedding model trained on GoogleNews-vectors-negative300 dataset [35]. The first layer is a convolution layer using a liner filter, while the second layer is a max pooling layer, which is used to extract the important semantic knowledge, as all terms do not contribute equally important to the prediction task. The dropout layer is used to avoid overfitting challenges, in our work, we employed 20% dropout.

The LSTM is a recurrent neural network model that attempts to model past knowledge by 'remembering' it and 'forgetting' the information which is not relevant. There are different activation layers called gates for remembering the previous information and forgetting the irrelevant data. A Internal cell state vector is maintained in every LSTM recurrent unit. There are 4 gates in LSTM for different purpose—*Forget gate* (tells what information to be forgotten), *Input Gate* (writes the information to internal cell state vector), *Input Modulation Gate* (a subpart of input gate utilized to alter the information that the input gate writes in the internal cell state by introducing non-linearity and making information Zero mean, allowing for quicker convergence and reduces learning time.) and *Output Gate* (output is generated based on the information stored in the Internal cell state vector). After the LSTM layer, another Dropout layer is used, with a 20% dropout value. The final dense layer is set with the activation function as sigmoid, and the output is a two-class prediction, either 0 and 1. Here,

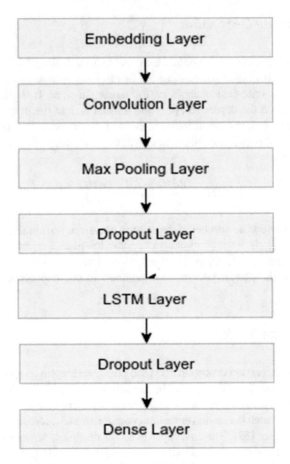

Fig. 1 Architecture of the Depression prediction CNN model

1 denotes the positive class, which indicates that a particular user shows depressive tendencies while 0 denotes that there is no evidence of depression in a given user.

5   Experimental Results and Discussion

We used Sentiment140 dataset which consists of around 1,600,000 tweets. The dataset contains 6 fields i.e. target, id, date, flag, user, and text. The target field indicates if a given tweet is negative, neutral or positive. Here, positive means the person is in depression, negative means the person is happy, and neutral indicates that the person is in normal condition. We trained and tested the proposed model on Google Colab using GPU processor.

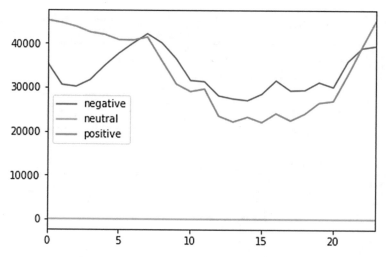

Fig. 2 Analysis of depression with time

5.1 Effect of Depression over Time

Time of social communication is an important factor in detection of depressive tendencies. To evaluate this aspect, we used the time stamp value of the tweet during the analysis, to determine whether the user is depressed or not. For this work, we have defined a day and night window as follows: Day window (6:00–21:00) and Night window (21:00–6:00). The results of this analysis are shown in Fig. 2, where it can be seen that the black line (Night window) is almost always above the black line (Day window). Based on this, we could conclude that the prevalence of depressive behavior is more at night time when compared to day because of feelings of loneliness and aloofness when alone at night time.

5.2 N-Gram Analysis Using SVM

Next, we conducted experiments to understand the contribution of terms used in the tweets by users, toward expression of depressive tendencies. For this, we considered various n-gram feature approaches for representing the tweet text. A contiguous sequence of *n* items retrieved from a text, dataset and speech is known as an n-gram. For our experiments, we considered different types of n-gram representations—unigrams, bigrams, trigrams, 4-grams, and 5-grams. Each of these characteristics is taken from user posts in order to account for normal language usage and to model the context. For the prediction, the SVM model trained on TF-IDF features is considered. Table 2 presents the observed performance of the model using various n-gram. We can observe that, the bi-gram representation outperformed all other models by a

Table 2 Observed performance of SVM classifier with TF-IDF and n-gram term representations

Features	Accuracy
Uni-gram	0.7075
Bi-gram	0.7200
Tri-gram	0.7085
Four-gram	0.7095
Five-gram	0.7090

Table 3 Effect of TF-IDF on performance of various classifiers

Approach	Classifier	Accuracy
No tf-idf	SVM	0.6905
	Random forests	0.6835
	XGB	0.6985
With tf-idf	SVM	0.7075
	Random forests	0.6985
	XGB	0.7092

small margin, while uni-gram, tri-gram, four-gram and five-gram also performed adequately.

5.3 Comparative Analysis of Three Classifiers

Comparative analysis of the performance of n-gram representations with other classifiers and when TF-IDF was not used, is presented in Table 3. First, we tested all three classifiers without TF-IDF then all three classifiers with TF-IDF. From the tabulated results, it is evident that TF-IDF increased the prediction accuracy of the SVM, while the XGB classifier achieved the best-in-class accuracy.

SVM [36] finds the Hyperplane in such a way that the margin between classes is maximum while the other algorithms, i.e., XGB, Random Forest don't care about the margin, that's why the accuracy of SVM is better as compared to XGB, Random-Forest.

We also used other metrics for assessing the goodness of the prediction of the classifiers. For this, precision and recall metrics were used. Precision is given by the number of true positives divided by the total number of true positives and false positives, where T_P denotes true positive, F_N denotes the false negative and F_P denotes false positive. The recall is calculated by dividing the total number of true positives by the total number of true positives and false negatives. After calculating the precision and recall, we can combine them to get F1-score. This is often used when there the data is imbalanced.

Table 4 Precision, Recall, and F-score performance for SVM classifier

Method	Class	Precision	Recall	F1-score
Uni-gram	Non-depressive	0.72	0.67	0.70
	Depressive	0.69	0.74	0.72
Bi-gram	Non-depressive	0.73	0.66	0.69
	Depressive	0.69	0.76	0.72
Tri-gram	Non-depressive	0.73	0.65	0.69
	Depressive	0.69	0.76	0.72

$$P = \frac{T_P}{T_P + F_P} \tag{10}$$

$$R = \frac{T_P}{T_P + F_N} \tag{11}$$

$$F1 - Score = \frac{2 * P * R}{P + R} \tag{12}$$

In terms of accuracy, recall, and F1-score, Table 4 shows the depression prediction performance using SVM for various n-gram encoding methods. When compared to the uni-gram representation, the bi-gram and tri-gram have greater accuracy, recall, and F1-score.

The ROC curve was also plotted to observe the Area Under the Curve (AUC). The larger the AUC, the better the model. ROC curve is shown in Fig. 3. The comparative

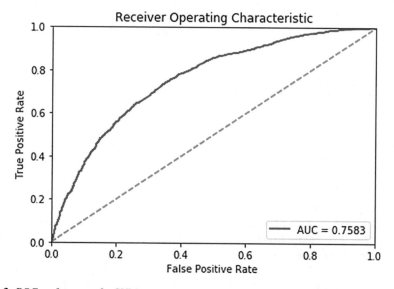

Fig. 3 ROC performance for SVM

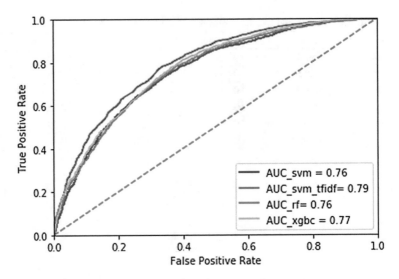

Fig. 4 Comparative AUC obtained for various models

ROC performance for the various classifiers is shown in Fig. 4. The PRC curve is plotted as a function of precision and recall. AUC determines the area under curve, the greater the value of the AUC, the better is the model. It can be seen that the black line has the highest area under curve, thus proving that SVM worked well for all model variants.

Most of the machine learning algorithms like SVM, XGB, Random Forest don't give good accuracy on complex dataset, therefore, we moved to deep learning algorithms like CNN, LSTM, etc., because they are able to learn complex structure inside the data, and hence give better accuracy as compared to machine learning algorithms.

5.4 CNN-LSTM Ensemble Model

During experiments, it was observed that the CNN-LSTM ensemble model outperformed SVM and all other ML models, with an accuracy of 97.1%. Figure 5 depicts the changes in testing and validation accuracy, it can be seen that as the number of epochs increases, both testing and validation accuracy also increases. Table 5 shows the CNN-LSTM model's observed performance in terms of accuracy, recall, and F1-score. When compared to the other machine learning models, the CNN-LSTM model achieved the greatest Precision, Recall, and F1-Score values. This shows that the deep learning model worked better when compared to machine learning models for the depression detection task.

To measure the depression in the population and for assessing the percentage of the population showing depressive tendencies, we used the SMDI (Social media

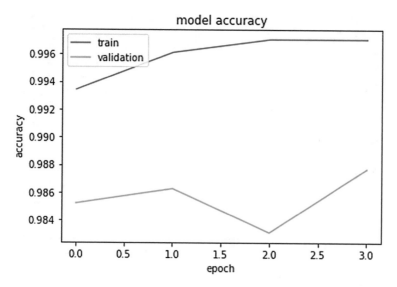

Fig. 5 Training and validation accuracy of the CNN-LSTM ensemble model

Table 5 Accuracy obtained with the CNN model

Class	Precision	Recall	F1-score	Support
0	0.97	1.00	0.99	2379
1	0.97	0.94	0.97	462
avg	0.97	0.97	0.98	2841

depression index) metric. The higher the computed value of this metric, the higher the prevalence of depression in the population. The overall SMDI value for the considered dataset was found to be −136.331764, which is quite low, which in turn shows that only a minority of the considered population exhibits depressive tendencies. Figure 6 shows a plot of the computed SMDI value during daytime and nighttime, it can be clearly seen that the SMDI value is higher for nighttime posts.

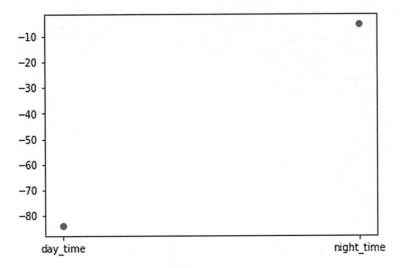

Fig. 6 SMDI value at day and night

6 Conclusion and Future Work

In this work, we presented an approach leveraging ML and DL algorithms for detecting and predicting the prevalence of depressive tendencies among social media users. The Sentiment140 dataset containing more than 1,600,000 tweets was used for the experiments. Term weighting and n-gram modeling approaches were adopted for representing the tweet corpus for feeding into the ML models. SVM, Random forests, XGB, and CNN were applied to the processed and modeled dataset. Experiments revealed that SVM model outperformed all other models when TF-IDF was used, as compared to count vectorization and with bi-gram approaches. The CNN and LSTM ensemble model outperformed all ML models and achieved 97% accuracy. Computation of SMDI metric for the tweet dataset showed that the percentage of depressed persons in the population is low, and the prevalence of depressive behavior is more at night when compared to daytime. In future, we intend to extend our work by using recurrent neural network for better accuracy and also adapt our approach for other social media platforms.

References

1. Depression in population according to WHO. https://www.who.int/news-room/fact-sheets/detail/depression
2. Suicide, prevention and control Strategy by WHO. https://www.who.int/news-room/fact-sheets/detail/suicide

3. Haselton MG, Nettle D, Murray DR (2005) The evolution of cognitive bias. The handbook of evolutionary psychology
4. Resnik P, Armstrong W, Claudino L, Nguyen T, Nguyen V-A, Boyd-Graber J (2015) Beyond lda: exploring supervised topic modeling for depression-related language in twitter. In: Proceedings of the 2nd workshop on computational linguistics and clinical psychology: from linguistic signal to clinical reality
5. Mitchell M, Hollingshead K, Coppersmith G (2015) Quantifying the language of schizophrenia in social media. In: Proceedings of the 2015 annual conference of the north American chapter of the ACL: human language technologies (NAACL HLT)
6. Benton A, Mitchell M, Hovy D (2017) Multitask learning for mental health conditions with limited social media data. EACL
7. Harman GCMDC (2014) Quantifying mental health signals in twitter. ACL 2014
8. Yazdavar AH, Al-Olimat HS, Banerjee T, Thirunarayan K, Sheth AP (2016) Analyzing clinical depressive symptoms in twitter
9. De Choudhury M, Gamon M, Counts S, Horvitz E, Predicting depression via social media. In: ICWSM
10. Nguyen T, Phung D, Dao B, Venkatesh S, Berk M (2014) Affective and content analysis of online depression communities. IEEE Trans Affect Comput 5(3):217–226
11. Coppersmith G, Dredze M, Harman C, Holling- shead K, Mitchell M (2015) Clpsych 2015 shared task:Depression and ptsd on twitter. In: Proceedings of the 2nd workshop on computational linguistics and clinical psychology
12. Coppersmith G, Dredze M, Harman C, Holling- shead K (2015) From adhd to sad: analyzing the language of mental health on twitter through self-reported diagnoses. In: NAACL HLT
13. Neuman Y, Cohen Y, Assaf D, Kedma G (2012) Proactive Screening for depression through metaphorical and automatic text analysis. Artif Intell Med 56(1):19–25
14. Karmen C, Hsiung RC, Wetter T (2015) Screening internet forum participants for depression symptoms by assembling and enhancing multiple nlp methods. In: Computer methods and programs in biomedicine
15. Pravalika A, Oza V, Meghana NP, Kamath SS (2017) Domain-specific sentiment analysis approaches for code-mixed social network data. In: 2017 8th international conference on computing, communication and networking technologies (ICCCNT). IEEE, pp 1-6
16. Ashok M, Rajanna S, Joshi PV, Kamath S (2016) A personalized recommender system using machine learning based sentiment analysis over social data. In: 2016 Ieee students' conference on electrical, electronics and computer science (SCEECS). IEEE, pp 1–6
17. Kaushik R, Chandra SA, Mallya D, Chaitanya JNVK, Kamath SS (2016) Sociopedia: an interactive system for event detection and trend analysis for twitter data. In: Proceedings of 3rd international conference on advanced computing, networking and informatics. Springer, New Delhi, pp 63–70
18. Chandra A, Mallya D, Chaitanya JNVK, Kamath S (2015) Ontology based approach for event detection in twitter datastreams. In: 2015 Ieee region 10 symposium. IEEE, pp 74–77
19. Holleran SE (2010) The early detection of depression from social networking sites. The University of Arizona, Tucson
20. Greenberg LS (2017) Emotion-focused therapy of depression. Per Centered Exp Psychother. 16(1):106–17
21. Haberler G (2017) Prosperity and depression: a theoretical analysis of cyclical movements. Routledge, London
22. Guntuku SC et al (2017) Detecting depression and mental illness on social media: an integrative review. Curr Opin Behav Sci. 18:43–9
23. De Choudhury M, Counts S, Horvitz E (2013) Predicting postpartum changes in emotion and behavior via social media. In: Proceedings of the SIGCHI conference on human factors in computing systems. ACM, New York
24. O'Dea B et al (2015) Detecting suicidality on Twitter. Internet Interv 2(2):183–8
25. Zhang L et al (2014) Using linguistic features to estimate suicide probability of Chinese microblog users. In: International conference on human centered computing. Springer, Berlin

26. Paul MJ, Dredze M (2011) You are what you tweet: analyzing twitter for public health. In: Proceedings of ICWSM '11
27. Sadilek A, Kautz H, Silenzio V (2012) Modeling spread of disease from social interactions. In: Proceedings of ICSWM '11
28. Billings A, Moos Rudolf H (1984) Coping, stress, and social resources among adults with unipolar depression. J Personal Soc Psychol 46(4):877–891
29. Aldarwish MM, Ahmed HF (2017) Predicting depression levels using social media posts. In: 2017 Ieee 13th international symposium on autonomous decentralized systems
30. Hussain J et al (2015) SNS based predictive model for depression. In: Geissbühler A, Demongeot J, Mokhtari M, Abdulrazak B, Aloulou H (eds) ICOST 2015, vol 9102. LNCS. Springer, Cham, pp 349–354
31. Biradar A, Totad S (2019) Detecting depression in social media posts using machine learning. In: Recent trends in image processing and pattern recognition. RTIP2R 2018. Communications in Computer and Information Science, Solapur
32. Mowery DL, Park A, Bryan C, Conway M (2016) Towards automatically classifying depressive symptoms from Twitter data for population health'. In: Towards automatically classifying depressive symptoms from Twitter data for population health, pp 182–191
33. Social media as a measurement tool of depression in populations. https://citeseerx.ist.psu.edu/viewdoc/download?doi=10.1.1.294.8952rep=rep1type=pdf
34. Distributed Representations of Words and Phrases and their Compositionality. https://arxiv.org/pdf/1310.4546.pdf
35. GoogleNews-vectors-negative300. https://code.google.com/archive/p/word2vec/
36. Cortes C, Vapnik V (1995) Support-vector networks. Mach Learn 20(3):273–297

A Simple and Effective Way to Detect DeepFakes: Using 2D and 3D CNN

Shraddha Suratkar and Purv Sharma

1 Introduction

Falsified videos created by Artificial Intelligence (AI) and Deep Neural Network (DNN) algorithms, specifically known as generative adversarial networks (GANs), are a recent twist to the displeasing drawback of online misinformation. The latest advancements in the domain have achieved a significant position in the creation of Deepfake videos. In the recent pandemic, people using and knowing Deepfake technology with the common name as 'Face Swap' has shown a high rise with the use of open-source applications like *Reface, FaceMagic, FaceApp, or SnapChat* and it's spread over social media. So, one of the aims of the Internet is information to all, this means that the information should be right and correct. In order to stop the spread of misinformation via Deepfake videos, detection for the same needs to be done. There are various methodologies and techniques already developed by using Convolutional Neural Networks (CNN), Long Short-Term Memory (LSTM), Recurrent Neural Networks (RNN), and Support Vector Machine (SVM) classifiers for spotting of different artifacts such as eye blinking, head poses, face geometry, lip/mouth movement and synchronization, background and likewise, or a combination of them.

When we speak of Deep Learning, CNN plays a very important role in identifying facial features. There are different types of CNN basically Conv1D, Conv2D, and Conv3D. These models work on various types of images like grayscale and RGB images generated for medical examinations or satellite images but have one different aspect that is the number of dimensions they work on. As the name suggests, Conv1D, Conv2D, and Conv3D work on 1, 2, and 3 dimensions, respectively. We are one of the first to introduce the use of Conv3D in the detection of deepfakes.

S. Suratkar · P. Sharma (✉)
Veermata Jijabai Technological Institute, Mumbai, India
e-mail: pgsharma_m19@ce.vjti.ac.in

S. Suratkar
e-mail: sssuratkar@ce.vjti.ac.in

© The Author(s), under exclusive license to Springer Nature Singapore Pte Ltd. 2022
U. P. Rao et al. (eds.), *Security, Privacy and Data Analytics*, Lecture Notes
in Electrical Engineering 848, https://doi.org/10.1007/978-981-16-9089-1_19

2   Related Work

Afchar, D. et al. in 2018 presented two methods which became popular to detect fake videos efficiently that is Meso-4 and MesoInception-4 which focuses on mesoscopic properties of the images [1]. Thereafter people started to use neural networks to extract and train the models based on different extraction features like Güera et al. in 2018 worked on the bases of frame-level features which was extracted by using a Convolutional Neural Network (CNN) and trained a Recurrent Neural Network (RNN) to evaluate a video as fake or real and tested for a large set of datasets which was collected from multiple video websites[3]. While Y. Li, M. Chang et al. in 2018 showed a new method which is based on Long-term Recurrent Convolution Neural Network (LCRN) where they focused on one physiological part of the face, i.e., blinking of the eye and showed a good performance on Deep Neural Network (DNN) generated fake videos [2]. Huy H. Nguyen et al. made a capsule network which detects different kinds of attacks, from presentation attacks to replayed attacks using printed images. The method uses many fewer parameters than traditional CNN with similar performance [15]. Yuezun Li et al. highlighted that their model doesn't require training on the negative images. The warping artifacts on the face can be detected using CNN [13]. Huy H. Nguyen et al. proposed a method that uses capsule networks for detecting different kinds of fakes, from replay attacks using printed images or computer-generated videos to recorded videos by using deep-CNN [14]. Hyeonseong Jeon et al. discovered a light and fast fine-tuned classifier based on neural network and named it as 'Fake Detection Fine-tuning Network (FDFtNet)', which is used to detect deepfake generation models by detecting new deepfake face image generation models and can be used with pre-existing image classification networks [17]. Joel Frank et al. ensemble different convolutional neural network models starting from the lowest/base model which is EfficientNetB4 and use them on huge datasets of video whose size is around 119,000 [18].

Researchers and developers also started seeing SVM classifiers as a part of detection like Yang et al. in 2019 performed detection using SVM classifiers based on head poses. These head poses are inconsistent when viewed in 3D [4]. F. F. Kharbat, et al. [2019] used Support Vector Machine (SVM) where they trained the classifier on different feature points and used the algorithms such as ORG, HOG, BRISK, FAST, KAZE, and SURF to get the results. Out of them, HOG showed some promising results [6]. Mattia Bonomi et al. analyze spatiotemporal features of the video by exploiting textural artifacts using Local Derivative Patterns on three Orthogonal Planes (LDP-TOP) and linear support vector machines (SVMs) which, being a low complexity, are able to get a comparable performance [19]. Armaan Pishori et al. propose three algorithms grayscale histograms, convolutional LSTM, and eye-blink recognition when they found that the grayscale histogram technique is more relevant than others [20].

Few researchers proposed unique models based on different features like X. Wu et al. in 2020 detected deepfakes using Spatial, Steganalysis, and Temporal features and called the model as SSTnet. Spatial features such as unnatural color, texture, and shape were extracted using DNN. Steganalysis features which are hidden arti-facts such as statistical characteristics of image pixels were extracted along with temporal features by using RNN. The outperformance of the model is observed on FaceForencis++ dataset [7]. M. A. Younus et al. highlighted that DeepFake generated outputs are not up to the mark as to fit the face to the source video the background needs to be blurred. This inconsistency adds to another clue which was later used in Haar Wavelet Transformation to analyze the sharpness and edges. The system accuracy was good on the UADFV dataset [10]. I. Amerini et al. in 2019 proposed a new forensic technique which is not like the common methods that are frame based, so they used optical flow fields to check differences between two consecutive frames which add to another clue and are used in convolution neural networks to detect videos. The detection was very well seen on FaceForencis++ dataset [5]. M. T. Jafar et al. design a deepfake detection model that focuses on the movement of lip/mouth (DFT-MF) [9]. Shraddha Suratkar et al. present DeepFake video detection methods using CNN with transfer learning. A comparative study of the various models is presented that are fine-tuned and tested on a custom dataset encompassing variations from benchmarks datasets from Google AI and FF++ datasets [28, 29].

The above-mentioned approaches had become common, and others tried to view things from a different angle and discovered methodologies that added to the detec-tion like E. Tursman et al. in 2020 propose a social video verification system that shows the truthfulness of the video by comparing a set of videos. They check for lip/mouth movement across different videos for detection [11]. S. Fernandes et al. [2020] propose attribution-based confidence (ABC) where it does not require to train the model and it can show results on previously trained models or the models which are trained only on original data [12]. Xu Zhang et al. propose classifying a Deep-Fake by using the spectrum rather than pixels of the image [21]. The Ricard Durall et al. method is based on a classical frequency domain analysis and then by using a classifier where they required only a few sets of training samples as compared to other systems. The results produced were good on the most commonly used datasets [16]. T. Jung et al. [2020] used DeepVision algorithm to analyze that when a human eye blinks, a pattern can be observed and if there's a change in it, it's taken as a clue which can be calculated on the basis of a number of eye blinks and to check if these blinks are short or long. But this will not be efficient to prove as eye blinking changes according to different aspects of the human body and is also different in each case [8]. Ning Yu et al. present a different approach and the first one is to detect DeepFakes by checking for the fingerprints that are left by the GAN models while generating the DeepFake [19].

While going through these proposed methods, we saw some common gaps which can be addressed as, most of the models are not applicable on all the datasets, i.e., they perform well only on the datasets that are mentioned or used by them. We can also note that there's a huge difference between the accuracy for different qualities of videos for example the performance for high-quality videos would be really good as compared to the lower ones or vice versa. Another aspect that can be looked upon is the accuracy, and it plays a vital role and most of the systems lack in that which in terms leads to the robustness of the system.

The major contributions of this paper are as follows: -

- We introduce a new approach in this segment wherein the use of 3D Convolutional Neural Network is done, which considers one more dimension for the video/image compared to the normal CNN or 2D Convolutional Neural Network.
- The difference between the performance of low- and high-quality videos is seen to be less than 1% which is not the case for most of the methods.
- As said, the better the data for training, the better are the results so we preprocessed the data in two steps rather than one and made the use of MTCNN.
- Our implementation and methods are simple but effective, which achieved performance accuracy for maximum tests above 90%.

Moving forward, we first define our proposed methods followed by the experiments performed on them with their results and a comparison table of the same for better understanding. And lastly, drawing a conclusion with the future scope.

3   Proposed Method

Figure 1 illustrates the overall architecture for proposed methods using 2D Convolutional Neural Network and 3D Convolutional Neural Network.

Preprocessing: Compared to the other state-of-the-art methods, we in this stage take a different approach of dividing this stage into two parts. First, given an input of videos, we extract frames out of it using the most common OpenCV library. Furthermore, we extract the faces from these frames using Multi-Task Cascade Convolutional Neural Network (MTCNN).

Multi-Task Cascade Convolutional Neural Network (MTCNN): In the next step of preprocessing, we use MTCNN which is one of the most popular and well-known neural networks for face detection due to its lightweight performance and

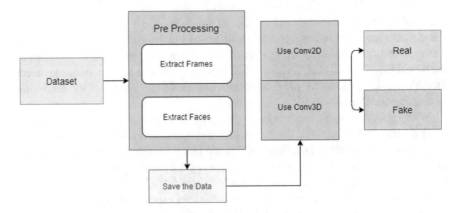

Fig. 1 The overall architecture for the proposed method

outperforming the other benchmarks. As the name suggests, it uses three networks that are connected in a cascade. It takes images as an input and marks/detects the faces followed by the facial landmarks on them. After the faces are detected, they are cropped into specified dimensions of $160 \times 160*3$, and the ones which don't have faces in them are ignored.

Training: Convolutional neural networks have been in use for a very long time. There are a lot of filters available for feature extraction. These features are used for a better approach in understanding and classification of different things. We in our methods have trained Conv2D and Conv3D models on the mentioned datasets in Sect. 4.1.

Conv2D: In Conv2D, the filters move in from left to right and from top to down. This will extract features from each frame and give the results accordingly. Here, seven layers in total are defined which includes input and output layers with maxpooling, flatten, and dense layers. While tuning the layers we take the kernel-size as 5×5 and pool-size as 2×2 in maxpooling with the activation function as Rectified Linear Unit (ReLU).

Conv3D: In Conv3D, the filters are the same like Conv2D, i.e., they move from left to right and top to bottom but there's also an addition to it, i.e., it moves from forward to backward which helps in understanding the depth also known as spatiotemporal features and adds up as another feature for the same. Here, seven layers in total are defined which includes input and output layers with maxpooling, flatten, and dense layers. While tuning the layers we take the kernel-size as $5 \times 5 \times 5$ and pool-size as also $5 \times 5 \times 5$ in maxpooling layers with the activation function as Rectified Linear Unit (ReLU).

Loss Function: For both the models, the use of Binary cross-entropy as loss function is done in order to define it as fake or a real video. The formula for it is stated below

$$H_p(q) = -\frac{1}{N} \sum_{i=1}^{N} y_i \cdot \log(p(y_i)) + (1 - y_i) \cdot \log(1 - p(y_i))$$

where y is the label of points, i.e., green (real) is noted as 1 and red (fake) is noted as 0, and p(y) is the prediction that the probability of the point is green for all the N points and (1-p(y)) is the prediction that the probability of the point is red for all the N points.

Limitations: The model Conv3D has one more filter added as compared to Conv2D, so the number increase in the filters is directly proportional to the use of computational resources, which means that for the given input shape, the use of computational resources is relatively very high compared to Conv2D.

4   Experiments

In this section, we'll first demonstrate the datasets that have been used followed by the implementation details and then the results obtained with a comparison table.

4.1   Dataset

For our experiments, we chose celeb-df v2 [22] a dataset which has 890 real and 5639 fake videos of celebrities taken from different Internet sources especially YouTube. The reason for selecting this dataset is because the maximum of the deepfakes is made on celebrities which creates a huge impact on society. Being a highly imbalance data, we took 500 videos from the dataset with a ratio of 1:1 for real and fake videos.

In addition to it, we also used VidTIMIT [24] as real video and DeepFake-TIMIT [23] for both High Quality (HQ) and Low Quality (LQ) for training and testing purposes. The reason for selecting this dataset is because unlike the state-of-art methods where there's a huge accuracy difference between low- and high-quality videos, we are able to achieve the accuracy difference of <1% for both HQ and LQ which can be seen in the results section.

In preprocessing, we first extract frames from the video using OpenCV which can be seen as the pictorial representation in Fig. 2a which represents frames extracted for real videos and Fig. 2b which represents frames extracted for fake videos. After this, the frames act as an input for face extraction. We use Multi-task Cascade Convolutional Neural Network (MTCNN) for face detection which is one of the best in

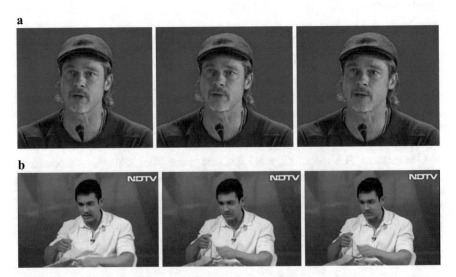

Fig. 2 a Frames extracted for a real video. **b** Frames extracted for a fake video

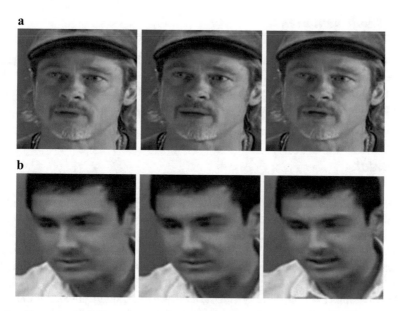

Fig. 3 **a** Faces extracted for a real video. **b** Faces extracted for a fake video

class. All the frames with no face detected are ignored and the output images are stored. This can also be seen as pictorial representation in Fig. 3a which represents faces extracted for real videos and Fig. 3b which is faces extracted for fake videos. For identification purposes, the dataset, i.e., celeb-df comes in two folders, real and fake, which has videos in it. After extracting the frames and faces from these videos, the final images are stored in two separate folders to differentiate between them for training.

Out of 500 videos from celeb-df dataset, we are able to get 10,922 faces and 13,630 for Deepfake-TIMIT HQ and 13,880 for Deepfake-TIMIT LQ datasets. An in-depth understanding of the same is mentioned in Table 1.

Table 1 Represents the total number of faces extracted from the frames

Dataset	Faces extracted		Total
	Real	Fake	
Celeb-df	5606	5316	10,922
Deepfake-TIMIT (HQ)	8398	5232	13,630
Deepfake-TIMIT (LQ)	8398	5482	13,880

4.2 Implementation

Both the models that are Conv2D and Conv3D are trained and tested on all the three above-mentioned datasets with taking the batch size as 50 and epochs as 64. Also note that the experiments are performed on an NVIDIA DGX—1 Deep Learning System with 8 V100 GPU accelerators given 16 GB of RAM to each GPU.

5 Results

We test our models on above-mentioned datasets and the results obtained are promising. The use of Adam optimizer is done here with the learning rate defined same for both the models, i.e., 0.00001.

For Celeb-df, our models Conv2D resulted in an accuracy of *91.86%* whereas for Conv3D, it showed us a bit low accuracy of *86.59%*. Also, our models are tested on Deepfake-TIMIT dataset and for Conv2D on High-Quality (HQ) videos, it is exhibited *99.81%* and for Low-Quality videos, it is 99.32%. Using Conv3D for the same, it is observed *95.17* and *96.37%* for High- and Low-Quality videos, respectively. Unlike the state-of-the-art methods which can be seen in Table 2. Our approaches are able to get a difference between the accuracies of Deepfake-TIMIT LQ and HQ with <*1%*, which, if compared, cannot be seen with many methods and they showcase a difference of *10–15%* between them (Table 3).

Table 4 represents a comparison between the other methods and it can be clearly seen that both our methods have outperformed the others. To break it down into visual representations, we plot graphs for each of the models toward their respective datasets. All these graphs illustrate training as well as validation accuracy with the x-axis representing the total number of epochs which is 64 for all cases and the y-axis representing the accuracy value for it. Figure 4a. illustrates the graphs for the models

Table 2 Represents a confusion matrix table for Conv2D

Datasets on Conv2D	TP	FP	FN	TN
Celeb-df	4537	779	153	5453
Deepfake-TIMIT LQ	5397	85	93	8305
Deepfake-TIMIT HQ	5217	15	13	8385

Table 3 Represents a confusion matrix table for Conv3D

Datasets on Conv3D	TP	FP	FN	TN
Celeb-df	4444	872	605	5001
Deepfake-TIMIT LQ	5399	83	318	8080
Deepfake-TIMIT HQ	4777	455	324	8074

Table 4 Represents a comparison between state-of-the-art methods with ours on the datasets used with the numbers representing accuracy in percentage

Methods	Celeb-df	Deepfake-TIMIT LQ	Deepfake-TIMIT HQ
DFT-MT [9]	71.2	98.7	73.1
Logistic regression MLP [25]	55.1	77.0	77.3
Head pose SWM [4]	54.6	55.1	53.2
Mesoscopic features [1]	54.8	87.8	68.4
Steganalysis + DL [26]	53.8	83.5	73.5
AE + Multi-task learning [27]	54.3	62.2	55.3
Capsule Network [15]	57.5	78.4	74.3
Conv2D (ours)	91.86	99.32	99.81
Conv3D (ours)	86.59	96.87	95.17

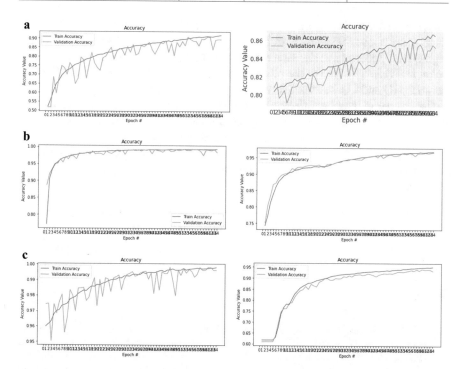

Fig. 4 **a** Performance accuracy for Conv2D and Conv3D, respectively, on Celeb-df dataset. **b** Performance accuracy for Conv2D and Conv3D, respectively, on Deepfake-TIMIT (LQ). **c** Performance accuracy for Conv2D and Conv3D, respectively, on Deepfake-TIMIT (HQ)

Conv2D and Conv3D on the celeb-df dataset which can be iterated as the highest accuracy obtained is *91.86, 86.59%,* and for validation *89.47, 85.26%* for Conv2D and Conv3D, respectively. Figure 4b represents models on Deepfake-TIMIT low quality (LQ) where the highest accuracy obtained is *99.32, 96.87%*; on the other hand for validation dataset, it is *99.08, 96.72%* for Conv2D and Conv3D, respectively. Figure 4c represents accuracies for Deepfake-TIMIT but for high-quality (HQ) videos, we can note that the highest accuracy obtained is *99.81, 95.17%* whereas for the validation dataset, it is observed as *99.63, 93.32%* for Conv2D and Conv3D, respectively. The models showed a really good performance on low-quality videos and the same can also be seen on high-quality videos.

6   Conclusion

The proposed models perform well with the highest accuracy of *99.81%* and most of them going above *90%*. The performance of models on Deepfake-TIMIT low- and high-quality videos have shown an improvement with the difference between them being less than *1%*. Unlike the other state-of-the-art methods where the difference between HQ and LQ was relatively very high at an average of *10–15%*.

This paper will add a different view of how people are looking at detection and creation of Deepfakes by considering the 3D face view. Another part that can be looked upon is implementing the system in real-time detection and analysis in web apps. Also, the model can be made more robust by focusing on different physiological aspects such as lip/mouth synchronization or eye blinking pattern or eyebrow movement.

Acknowledgements The authors are thankful to the CoE-CNDS lab, VJTI Mumbai, for providing them DGX-1 to train the models and obtain the results on the test dataset.

References

1. Afchar D, Nozick V, Yamagishi J, Echizen I (2018) MesoNet: a compact facial video forgery detection network. In: 2018 IEEE international workshop on information forensics and security (WIFS), Hong Kong, Hong Kong, pp 1–7.https://doi.org/10.1109/WIFS.2018.8630761
2. Li Y, Chang M, Lyu S (2018) In ictu oculi: exposing AI created fake videos by detecting eye blinking. In: 2018 IEEE international workshop on information forensics and security (WIFS), Hong Kong, Hong Kong, pp 1–7.https://doi.org/10.1109/WIFS.2018.8630787
3. Güera D, Delp EJ (2018) Deepfake video detection using recurrent neural networks. In: 2018 15th IEEE international conference on advanced video and signal based surveillance (AVSS), Auckland, New Zealand, pp 1–6. https://doi.org/10.1109/AVSS.2018.8639163
4. Yang X, Li Y, Lyu S (2019) Exposing deep fakes using inconsistent head poses. In: ICASSP 2019–2019 IEEE international conference on acoustics, speech and signal processing (ICASSP), Brighton, United Kingdom, pp 8261–8265. https://doi.org/10.1109/ICASSP.2019.8683164

5. Amerini I, Galteri L, Caldelli R, Del Bimbo A (2019) Deepfake video detection through optical flow based CNN. In: 2019 IEEE/CVF international conference on computer vision workshop (ICCVW), Seoul, Korea (South), pp 1205–1207. https://doi.org/10.1109/ICCVW.2019.00152
6. Kharbat FF, Elamsy T, Mahmoud A, Abdullah R (2019) Image feature detectors for deepfake video detection. In: 2019 IEEE/ACS 16th international conference on computer systems and applications (AICCSA), Abu Dhabi, United Arab Emirates, pp 1–4. https://doi.org/10.1109/AICCSA47632.2019.9035360
7. Wu X, Xie Z, Gao Y, Xiao Y (2020) SSTNet: detecting manipulated faces through spatial, steganalysis and temporal features. In: ICASSP 2020–2020 IEEE international conference on acoustics, speech and signal processing (ICASSP), Barcelona, Spain, pp 2952–2956. https://doi.org/10.1109/ICASSP40776.2020.9053969
8. Jung T, Kim S, Kim K (2020) DeepVision: deepfakes detection using human eye blinking pattern. IEEE Access 8:83144–83154. https://doi.org/10.1109/ACCESS.2020.2988660
9. Jafar MT, Ababneh M, Al-Zoube M, Elhassan A (2020) Forensics and analysis of deepfake videos. In: 2020 11th international conference on information and communication systems (ICICS), Irbid, Jordan, pp 053–058. https://doi.org/10.1109/ICICS49469.2020.239493
10. Younus MA, Hasan TM (2020) Effective and fast deepfake detection method based on haar wavelet transform. In: 2020 International conference on computer science and software engineering (CSASE), Duhok, Iraq, pp 186–190. https://doi.org/10.1109/CSASE48920.2020.9142077
11. Tursman E, George M, Kamara S, Tompkin J (2020) Towards untrusted social video verification to combat deepfakes via face geometry consistency. In: 2020 IEEE/CVF conference on computer vision and pattern recognition workshops (CVPRW), Seattle, WA, USA, pp 2784–2793. https://doi.org/10.1109/CVPRW50498.2020.00335
12. Fernandes S et al (2020) Detecting deepfake videos using attribution-based confidence metric. In: 2020 IEEE/CVF conference on computer vision and pattern recognition workshops (CVPRW), Seattle, WA, USA, pp 1250–1259. https://doi.org/10.1109/CVPRW50498.2020.00162
13. Yuezun L, Lyu S (2019) Exposing deepfake videos by detecting face warping artifacts. CVPR workshops
14. Nguyen HH et al (2019) Capsule-forensics: using capsule networks to detect forged images and videos. In: ICASSP 2019–2019 IEEE international conference on acoustics, speech and signal processing (ICASSP), pp 2307–2311
15. Nguyen HH, Yamagishi J, Echizen I (2019) Use of a capsule network to detect fake images and videos. (Cornell University). arXiv:1910.12467
16. Durall R, Keuper M, Pfreundt F, Keuper J (2019) Unmasking deepfakes with simple features. (Cornell University). arXiv:1911.00686.
17. Jeon H, Bang Y, Woo SS (2020) FDFtNet: facing off fake images using fake detection fine-tuning network. (Cornell University). arXiv:2001.01265
18. Bonettini N, Cannas ED, Mandelli S, Bondi L, Bestagini P, Tubaro S (2020) Video face manipulation detection through ensemble of CNNs. (Cornell University). arXiv:2004.07676
19. Bonomi M, Pasquini C, Boato G (2020) Dynamic texture analysis for detecting fake faces in video sequences. (Cornell University). arXiv:2007.15271
20. Pishori A, Rollins B, Houten NV, Chatwani N, Uraimov O (2020) Detecting deepfake videos: an analysis of three techniques. (Cornell University). arXiv:2007.08517
21. Zhang X, Karaman S, Chang S (2019) Detecting and simulating artifacts in GAN fake images. In: 2019 IEEE international workshop on information forensics and security (WIFS). pp 1–6. https://doi.org/10.1109/WIFS47025.2019.9035107
22. Li Y, Yang X, Sun P, Qi H, Lyu S (2020) Celeb-DF: a large-scale challenging dataset for deepfake forensics. In: 2020 IEEE/CVF conference on computer vision and pattern recognition (CVPR), pp 3204–3213. https://doi.org/10.1109/CVPR42600.2020.00327
23. Korshunov P, Marcel S Deepfakes: a new threat to face recognition? assessment and detection. Link to download: https://zenodo.org/record/4068245#.YOwvfegzbIU

24. Sanderson C, Lovell BC (2009) Multi-region probabilistic histograms for robust and scalable identity inference. Lecture notes in computer science (LNCS), vol 5558, pp 199–208. Link to download: https://conradsanderson.id.au/vidtimit/#downloads
25. Matern F, Riess C, Stamminger M (2019) Exploiting visual artifacts to expose deepfakes and face manipulations. In: Proceedings of the IEEE winter applications of computer vision workshops
26. Zhou P, Han X, Morariu X, Davis L (2017) Two-stream neural networks for tampered face detection. In: Proceedings of the IEEE/CVF conference on computer vision and pattern recognition workshops
27. Nguyen H, Fang F, Yamagishi J, Echizen I (2019) Multi-task learning for detecting and segmenting manipulated facial images and videos. arXiv:1906.06876
28. Suratkar S, Kazi F, Sakhalkar M, Abhyankar N, Kshirsagar M (2020) Exposing deepfakes using convolutional neural networks and transfer learning approaches. In: 2020 IEEE 17th India council international conference (INDICON), pp 1–8. https://doi.org/10.1109/INDICO N49873.2020.9342252
29. Suratkar S, Johnson E, Variyambat K, Panchal M, Kazi F (2020) Employing transfer-learning based CNN architectures to enhance the generalizability of deepfake detection. In: 2020 11th international conference on computing, communication and networking technologies (ICCCNT), pp 1–9. https://doi.org/10.1109/ICCCNT49239.2020.9225400

Decentralized Blockchain-Based Framework for Securing Review System

Suryansh Raj Singh, Harsh Mithaiwala, Nirav Chauhan, Parth Shah, Chandan Trivedi, and Udai Pratap Rao

1 Introduction

Lately with the advent of the internet and technology to each and every nook and corner of the world, a lot of things that were classically done offline have been shifted online as the availability of infrastructure improves [1]. Reviews are becoming an important aspect of such services. It helps the user and the service providers to incorporate changes in their business models and approaches for better outreach [2]. But, it has its shortcomings and advantages. This paper will predominantly focus on existing lacuna in the existing review systems and how upcoming disciplines such as blockchain help in addressing some of these issues.

A reviewer typically drops a review based on his experience with the product or service he opted for. He first differentiates what a product or service has to offer concerning his expectations [1]. He then makes up a mind to give a negative or positive review based on the fulfillment of that expectation [3]. But the service provider for his gain might masquerade to have positive reviews by deleting the reviews, adding

S. R. Singh · H. Mithaiwala · N. Chauhan · P. Shah · U. P. Rao
Sardar Vallabhbhai National Institute of Technology, Surat, Gujarat, India
e-mail: u17co040@svnit.ac.in

H. Mithaiwala
e-mail: u17co060@svnit.ac.in

N. Chauhan
e-mail: u17co067@svnit.ac.in

P. Shah
e-mail: u17co066@svnit.ac.in

U. P. Rao
e-mail: upr@coed.svnit.ac.in

C. Trivedi (✉)
Institute of Technology, Nirma University, Ahmedabad, Gujarat, India
e-mail: chandan.trivedi@nirmauni.ac.in

© The Author(s), under exclusive license to Springer Nature Singapore Pte Ltd. 2022
U. P. Rao et al. (eds.), *Security, Privacy and Data Analytics*, Lecture Notes
in Electrical Engineering 848, https://doi.org/10.1007/978-981-16-9089-1_20

fake reviews, and numerous other ways of fiddling with the original review dropped by the reviewer [3]. Therefore, a system is required which protects the consumers from such mala fide intentions by disabling any option of change or deletion of any review, rendering service providers unable to make changes. This would empower consumers and would act as a confidence-building measure between providers and consumers [1].

1.1 Motivation

Fraudulent reviews, review seeding, and deletion of negative reviews have turned review systems into a marketing gimmick rather than something considered by service providers to improve their services. Strides have been made in making these systems more reliable, some of them are as follows:

1. Revain is a review platform that filters out fake and low-quality reviews which can potentially skew the whole review system [4].
2. Amazon implements a blockchain-based review system by the name of Zapit [5].

This research paper focuses on building a tamper-proof review system that would provide reliability and transparency in recording reviews for future reference which are shortcomings of the existing review system [6]. This implementation provides the distinct benefit of the proposed model over the existing model, elaborated as follows:

1. Storing the reviews in a blockchain would result in distributed storage, thus making reviews tamper-proof [2].
2. The Ethereum blockchain used for implementing this is highly modular and thus provides us with the facility to write our own rules [7].
3. The blocks of blockchain are instances created by smart contracts written in solidity. These contracts once deployed cannot be modified.
4. It is next to impossible to change or delete the content of each block added in the blockchain [7].

The disturbing trends of review manipulation have made it even more important to incorporate decentralization in current review systems. Following are some of the recent cases of the same (Table 1).

1.2 Our Contribution

The research aims to provide a user-friendly and reliable review system by incorporating the latest development standards in a nutshell. The major objective to be looked for by this research is to:

Table 1 Realistic cases showing lack of trust in the centralized review system

Headlines	Source
Google deletes millions of negative TikTok reviews	BBC
Amazon third-party sellers pester customers who leave bad reviews	The verge
Google Deletes 100,000 Negative Reviews of Robinhood App From Angry Users	gizmodo.com
Yelp has removed thousands of "review bombing" attempts that target businesses' COVID-19 safety measures, such as vaccine requirements	Business Insider India
Amazon Hits Chinese Sellers With Crackdown on Fake Reviews	Bloomberg Business Week
Almost 4% of all online reviews are fake. Their impact is costing us $152 billion	The print

1. Removal of some of the most concerning disadvantages such as deletion of legitimate reviews with the help of facilities provided by blockchains such as distributed storage, tamper, and manipulation proof.
2. It also focuses on incentivizing the reviews by providing monetary gains to reviewers in the form of ethers [8].

The unique selling proposition of the solutions suggested in this paper, which is in in-congruence to the other case studies is that it would provide a scalable system at a minimal cost of deployment due to the use of IPFS [9]. Several options were available for a decentralized app such as Hash-graph, IOTA, and the blockchain. Also, in the blockchain itself, options such as Ethereum, Hyper ledger, Corda, Eos, and Quorum are available, but several of their grave disadvantages made it difficult to use them in the context of this research paper [10]. Hash-graph does not use the concept of mining to validate transactions. Hash-graph has several disadvantages such as its nascent stage, dissimilarity with other common programming languages, and not being open source [10]. Tangle also uses a directed acyclic graph (DAG), which resembles a distributed ledger. DAG is not under the control of any external authority such as a bank or any financial institution. The Tangle supports IoT (Internet of Things) [11]. This technology also due to its disadvantages was rendered unusable for our application. Some of the disadvantages are its less reliability due to incomplete development phase and its fewer security [9]. After examining other options, blockchain would be the most suitable option. Out of the blockchains mentioned earlier, 3 of them, namely, Hyper ledger, Corda [10], and quorum are private and henceforth were not used. Unlike other blockchains, Ethereum instills modularity and empowers the developer to write rules based on his choice [9]. The intention of building Ethereum itself came from the objective of mass consumption to run smart contracts and leverage blockchain technology. Whereas, Eos is comparatively less decentralized and not scalable [12].

1.3   Benefits of Shifting to Decentralized System

- **Organizational Benefits**

  1. **Storage problem solved:** Using decentralized storage, space can be very efficient and cost-effective compared to centralized data-centers or cloud environments, i.e., Filecoin (which is used as enterprise decentralized storage) charges only 0.38892% compared to aws s3.

     Also, a centralized system occupies a massive amount of space to keep the servers, and it becomes difficult to handle the mechanism. Also, the cost to maintain a centralized system would be very high. Decentralization can help us overcome the above-mentioned problems regarding space, storage, and maintenance.
  2. **Disaster recovery:** Failure of a centralized system can be catastrophic and could increase the downtime directly affecting the reputation of the company. Whereas in a decentralized system, multiple copies of data make failure recovery fast and economical, eradicating downtime.
  3. **Loosly coupled:** Change cost is low. The current review platforms stand to be very costly if any component requires any change. Whereas the proposed system tends to work on loosely coupled architecture where each component works individually. In this manner, the cost of upgrading can be minimized.

- **User Benefits**

  1. **Incentives:** The users are given incentives for reviewing in the form of coupons which can be redeemed for offers.
  2. **Trust, Reliability, and Genuine Review:** The system is taking some amount of ether as a token to reduce the fraud strategies acquired by some of the owners, in this manner, the trust and reliability can be developed, and also, this proposed system gives some of the parameters which help to reduce the flood of the reviews, which make it easier for a user to make a proper judgment for the product.
  3. **Transparency:** One can check their transactions and review data from www. etherscan.io, which makes the system crystal clear for anyone who raises any queries about genuineness.

The upcoming section would discuss various aspects of the existing review system and the proposed system, the literature survey section deals with the brief of technologies that can be useful for this research. The proposed system section includes various aspects such as design and architecture with relevant diagrams. The last section concludes the proposed system.

2 Literature Survey and Prerequisites

As modern society is moving more toward the virtual world, the importance of online review, feedback, or opinion is increasing. They have gained the power to make a product at the top list or destroy its reputation with a few negative reviews irrespective of whether the reviews are genuine or not. So, it is becoming necessary to have a structured, reliable, and trustworthy system for online review which is not currently available. Further, in this section, the loopholes of the existent systems would be discussed.

2.1 Centralized Review System

Today majorities of the websites are using Centralized Systems, which has their issues, which we can accept from a few incidents like:

- Deleting reviews and ratings given to the Tiktok app on Play Store Platform, also here comes the point of the rating given by fake users or accounts made for such sole purpose.
- European Union penalizing google for manipulating the users' view by decreasing or increasing the reach of a product or service [3].

From the above issues, we can note one thing that Centralized Systems have many issues that are needed to be eliminated to get a better online review system. Some major issues or challenges faced by centralized review system are listed under:

1. **Moderating product reviews:** Any merchandiser that provides product review features for purchasers on its website should settle for the chances that customers can post negative reviews. If a retailer seed out the unhealthy ones, the merchandise or service review board is no longer said to be "genuine" from a consumer law perspective [3].
2. **Seeding reviews:** Seeding reviews can be explained as, platforms or corporations hire paid groups or tie-up with other organizations to add positive reviews in their initial stages, so a good impression of the company can be made. Many big companies nowadays pull reviews from other review sites to make a fake impression in front of the public that they are in demand [3].
3. **The tendency toward negative reviews:** Generally people are more inclined to give negative reviews when they don't get a proper product or service but ignore to share a positive review for a good product or service [13].
4. **Fraudulent and Strategic Reviews:** AstroTurf can be done in online reviews means businesses telling their employees or itself pretending like a customer to give positive reviews to their product while marking out negative comments on the product of their competitor with only a single motive of acquiring the market with their product [3].

5. **Lack of negative reviews:** One common thing that most of the customers try to find out about a product is that if there is any problem faced by the previous buyers, and if the customer feels something fishy that they don't have many negative reviews so there are chances that he is viewing unreal reviews which sometimes leads to customer not purchasing that product or service.

For the above drawbacks, one of the solutions can be a decentralized system, and to carry out that, we can use a blockchain that provides the facilities to implement a distributed system. To build the proposed system, a publicly available chain, Ethereum is being used and also smart contract to carry out various functionalities which help to create a reliable system to resolve some of the issues found in the centralized review system [14].

2.2 Decentralized Review System

Today, centralized review systems are used worldwide. But full surety of trustworthiness and reliability cannot be given, which leads the customers to the wrong path. The blockchain is primarily a decentralized system that will help to increase the trustworthiness and reliability of the system and can also increase the relation of B2B and B2C [4]. As blockchain is in its early stage, so many of the systems are not much widely implemented. Still, some Tech Giants are looking forward to it as a solution to the centralized review systems. Many companies are working in the area of decentralized systems to give customers and businesses better services, here are some blockchain-based review systems that claim the use of Ethereum smart contracts to implement a review platform [8].

Lina
Lina is a blockchain-based platform, where users or companies can build their own domain system on the platform at no cost [15]. It is a platform that is used to store user-submitted reviews securely, compensating the user, and maintaining genuine reviews. However, while participation is of no cost, the system will be charged a maintenance fee by the platform, on the activities performed by the system, specifically, the participation of dealers, advertisers, and the reviewing activities [15]. There is no actual way to check that the user submitting the review has actually used the product or service that he is reviewing, and therefore, reviews can be falsely raised. In order to address the issues related to the economic credibility of storing reviews on Ethereum blockchain, the Lina platform utilizes a hybrid architecture, bridging between the Lina Core, and Ethereum, which is used to store detailed transactions [15].

Revain
It is a platform for reviews that are utilized by IBM. This Revain system is a combination of two components:

1. A token system using two tokens to make a stable coin [16].

2. An unchangeable blockchain is employed to record all reviews so they are never interfered, modified, deleted, or removed [4].

This approach enables the system to reward high-quality reviews, while also removing and penalizing fake reviews and companies that negatively affect their reputation [4]. Since quality reviews are rewarded, this acts as an encouragement for users to post good-quality reviews, as they will be compensated for their effort. These fees required are debited from the company of the reviewed product or service, which is already registered on the Revain platform which includes the user reward, and the platform fees, which is a fee paid to the platform as a means of profit margin [16]. Review Snapshots Storage, a smart contract is used to store essential parts of the reviews because it is economically costly to store all the review body into the ethereum blockchain [5].

SynchroLife
The first restaurant review platform is based on the Ethereum blockchain, which helps customers to check restaurant insights and share their experiences. It is based on the SynchroCoin token which will be rewarded to the user who provides good quality reviews making this platform more trustworthy and reliable [17]. The SynchroCoin token can be redeemed in another restaurant, restaurants can use these tokens as coupons or gift cards for the customer. Also, it provides a thread to connect one user to another, which helps an individual to explore various places in the globe rather than be attached to one location [17].

A common challenge in all the above-mentioned platforms is the storage of "genuine" reviews. So for storing review details on the blockchain, we make use of the distributed and decentralized file system—InterPlanetary File System (IPFS), which concludes that the Ethereum network will be used for storing transactions, while a peer-to-peer IPFS network is used to store all the review data with the content-addressable [8]. Table 2 shows the key comparison between centralized and decentralized review system.

Some of the essential components that are used for the implied online decentralized reviewing system are Ethereum, Blockchain, IPFS, which are discussed below according to requirements.

Table 2 Comparison between centralized and decentralized review system

Centralized review system	Decentralized review system
Low latency	High latency
Less storage required	Storage consumption is very high compared to centralized
Single point of failure	No single point of failure
Manipulation or tampering with data	No centralized authority to handle the data
Less transparent to end user	More transparent to end user
Examples: Yelp, Amazon, Play Store, Glassdoor	Examples: Revain, Lina, Synchrolife, Dentacoin

2.3   Blockchain

The digital way of recording transactions is called a blockchain. The name derived from its structure, in which blocks represent records and chains will be created when they are linked together in a single list. Blockchain is a public open-source digital ledger that is shared among peers in a decentralized network [14]. This public ledger cannot be manipulated, i.e., it cannot be altered once recorded. It carries a permanent record of transactions and interactions between the users in a decentralized network. Blockchain utilizes a shared ledger that is distributed among the users of the network. Blocks that are linked through a cryptographic hash [18], are recorded in a sequential chain [14]. Each block contains the information of the transaction and the asset exchanges that took place between the users. This technology became popular after the advent of cryptocurrencies, such as bitcoin [14].

2.4   Ethereum Smart Contracts

It is a decentralized open-source blockchain system having smart contract functionality. For creating decentralized applications, Ethereum is one of the most preferable programmable blockchain platforms [19]. It is easy to build a strong and compatible application with the help of Ethereum, also it is very easy and flexible to use rather than any other platform. It allows user to implement their own set of rules and definitions. Ethereum is the second-largest cryptocurrency platform by market capitalization, behind Bitcoin [19]. A smart contract is a self-executing contract that is directly written into a bunch of code and indicates the terms of the agreement between buyer and seller. The code and the agreements are distributed across the decentralized blockchain network. The execution is controlled by the code, and transactions are trackable and also cannot be reversed [19].

For storage and sharing of data in a distributed network system, the most common and easy-to-use protocol is the InterPlanetary File System (IPFS) which shares with peer-to-peer networks [20].

2.5   InterPlanetary File System

For individually identifying each data or review, IPFS uses content-addressing for each data in a universal name-space connecting all computing devices.

In the IPFS system, users not only get the data, but also can host their contents. In this decentralized system, user-operators are there, who carry a portion of the overall content for creating a flexible system of file storage and sharing [20]. IPFS will be a storage system in which reviews will be uploaded. Regarding the reviewer's Ethereum address, the IPFS hash of the review will be stored in the smart contract.

Fig. 1 Working of IPFS [5]

The smart contract will use token and IPFS hash to validate the review. Our solution utilizes a smart contract which is a code that captures the logic and algorithms for the online review dynamics and interactions [20] (See Fig. 1).

2.6 Web3 Browser or MetaMask Plugin

To work with Ethereum, end users need to have an Ethereum address. This leads to a condition that to interact with our application, end-users need to have a Web3 browser such as mist, status. Web3 Browser can open any website that the standard Chrome or Firefox can open, but in addition to that, it allows us to utilize and engage with Decentralized Applications (DApps) [5]. To allow you to fully utilize Decentralized Apps, it injects an object into the DOM of a given site, but before that, your permission is required for access, then it allows reference to your account on the blockchain [5]. And if a user does not want to install a specific web3 browser, then by adding the plugin MetaMask to a regular web browser [21], he can work with DApps.

Summary: The discussion of this section is mainly around the initialization of shifting focus from currently used centralized systems to a decentralized system. Currently existing Centralized systems are failing to build trust and reliability between the consumer and the retailer as consumers are not aware whether the reviews are genuine or not [8]. Also, the consumers feel less interested to review products as the efforts which they put into reviewing do not provide them comparative rewards. So, one of the solutions to this problem is using a decentralized online review system, which is going to be built using public chain Ethereum while smart contracts are used to build the logical functionalities for the system and validation [22].

Understanding the modern but under its early-stage decentralized online review systems makes it clear that it will help to remove some of the major challenges faced by online review systems.

From the above discussion, we can conclude that going through this research paper, we might be able to remove or moderate some key challenges faced by the online review system by utilizing the public chain ethereum, smart contract, and IFPS. The key issues which this research paper can pull over or control are:

- Removing false, fraudulent, and strategic reviews.
- Controlling seeding of the reviews or unethical practices from the Corporations [8].
- Taking control from Organizations themselves of removing or modifying reviews for their benefits or to change the market flow.
- By providing them an incentive, we can motivate users to give reviews so that it will balance the tendency of reviews. So, users can have all types of reviews whether it is for a good or bad product or service [13].

3 Proposed Work

This research aims to grant a decentralized review system utilizing Ethereum, Smart Contract, and IPFS (Decentralized file system) [23]. The further section shows the logical understanding of the system to overcome the issues happening with the current system and also, another aim to make a better trustworthy review platform that helps to build good relationships between the customer and Sellers. For the proposed work, the following functionalities can be used such as Ethereum to store the transaction, smart contracts to build the logical structure of the system, and IPFS is used to store all the reviews to reduce the heavy charges imposed by the Ethereum network [23].

3.1 System Overview and Design

The objective of this solution is to improve the trust between the customer and sellers by making the review more genuine and helpful. For this, one must have to first go through the logical structure of the system [7]. Figure 2 shows the actors diagram which helps developers to have a clear idea of users who are going to participate in the reviewing system.

For the proposed decentralized review system, actors can be categorized into four types of users who can carry out different types of interactions with the system:

1. Guest: This type of user can browse different products and check their reviews and also share their reviews on the products available on the platform.
2. Product Owners: They register their genuine products with proper details on the platform for getting reviewed by the customers or reviewers. If they want to modify the details of the products, this can also be considered by the platform [2].
3. Smart Contract: This is the backbone for the back-end management of the application. Which will handle the management of the products and their reviews so that it can provide a tamper-proof review system.

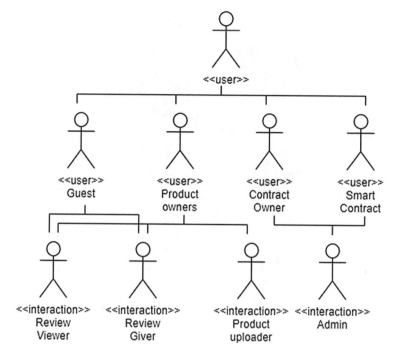

Fig. 2 Actors

4. Contract owner: The main task of the contract owner is to manage finance for the incentives for the reviewers and transaction charges (in ethereum) for the application [2].

The important point here is to notice that, unlike the centralized systems, the admin is consists of smart contracts so there is no direct interruption of centralized authorities.

3.2 User Interaction with System

Figure 3 illustrates the user interaction for the decentralized review system.

There are mainly three functions that help end users to interact with the proposed application and two extension functions to work with IPFS.

1. View reviews of specific products: This function is used to view all reviews of a given product [2].
2. Reviewing the specific product: This function is used to give the review to the given product.
3. Saving the new product on the blockchain: This function is used to upload new products to the platform.

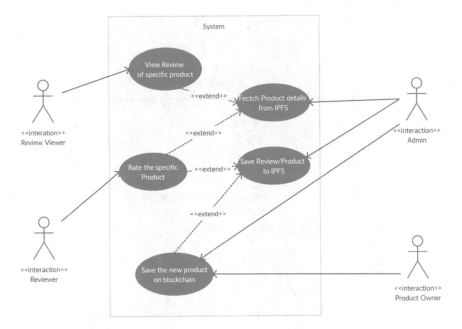

Fig. 3 User interaction Diagram

Two extension functions needed for IPFS are:

1. Fetch the file from IPFS: Using IPFS hash which is stored on ethereum, it will bring particular review/product details from the IPFS [23].
2. Save the file to IPFS: It will store the file to the IPFS blockchain and returns the hash(location) of the given file.

3.3 Flow of Control for Product Owner

Figure 4 shows the control flow diagram for the product owner uploading its new product on the system. The product owner sends a request to upload its product to the blockchain network. The system asks for the details of the product and then the product owner will give the necessary information related to the product. These details will be stored in a file by the system and sent to the IPFS network [24]. The IPFS network will store the file on their network and generate the hash value of length 46 bytes which will be used further to access the file to show the details of the product in the application. It returns the IPFS hash to the application [23]. The application will send the hash to the smart contract to store it in the blockchain network and the application will receive the promise from the network. The application will display a success message to the product owner after receiving the confirmation.

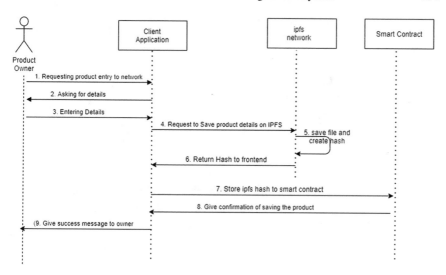

Fig. 4 Flow of control diagram for product owners

3.4 Flow of Control for Reviewers

The diagram in Fig. 5 illustrates the control flow for the reviewer to give a review to a specific product. Initially, the user will visit the website. On the website, products of different types would be listed. The reviewer will share their view for a specific product and the system would store these details in a file and forward it to the IPFS network [23]. The IPFS network will store the file on the network and create the hash value of length 46 bytes which will be used further to access the file to show that particular review of the product in the application [23]. The IPFS hash is returned to the front-end application. The application will send the hash to the smart contract to store the hash in the blockchain network. The front-end will receive the promise (i.e., confirmation) from the network. In the end, the application will give incentives to the reviewer.

3.5 Tracking and Verifying the Review System

Till now, the working process of the system is being illustrated. Yet the questions regarding the trust of end-user about the reliability of the system whether it is really a decentralized system would be raised [24]. As an answer to the raised query of the users that the review which individuals are writing, will never be deleted and tempered, the blockchain provides the facility of verifying the transactions [23]. Here are the steps to verify the transaction are being shown with few picturizations:

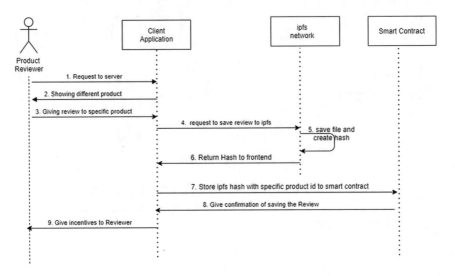

Fig. 5 Flow of control diagram for reviewers

1. Search your metaMask address in the search bar of etherscan.io.You will see all the transaction done with your metaMask address [24].
2. For viewing more details about the transition, the particular transaction should be selected which will open the window [23].
3. At the bottom of the details, "click to view more" can be seen. After clicking on it, the input data field which contains the coded data which was sent by the user from the system. The given coded text needs to be decoded. The mentioned tool would help individuals in decoding [24].
4. To decode the data, the only coded text is not sufficient. It also requires the contract-abi, which can be obtained from the git repository provided here: https://github.com/harsh9090/ blockchain-review-system-2021/blob/ main/ build/contracts/MyContract.json, ABI field provided in the file should be written in the ABI section on the preferred tool, then click on decode button [23].
5. Decoded input in JSON format can be visualized on the screen. In the output JSON, field input will give the hash of the review for verification on the IPFS server system.
6. To have the actual hardcode of the review, one needs to go to "ipfs.infura.io/ ipfs/your copied hash" [23].
7. Finally, the details of the reviews will be showcased here which shows every bit of detail about the review [23].
   As the whole process is shown in the above context, the system is totally transparent and at any point in time, and there is no inclusion of the central authority that can delete or temper the reviews. Also, it provides a way to check the review details anytime whether it is reliable or not [23].

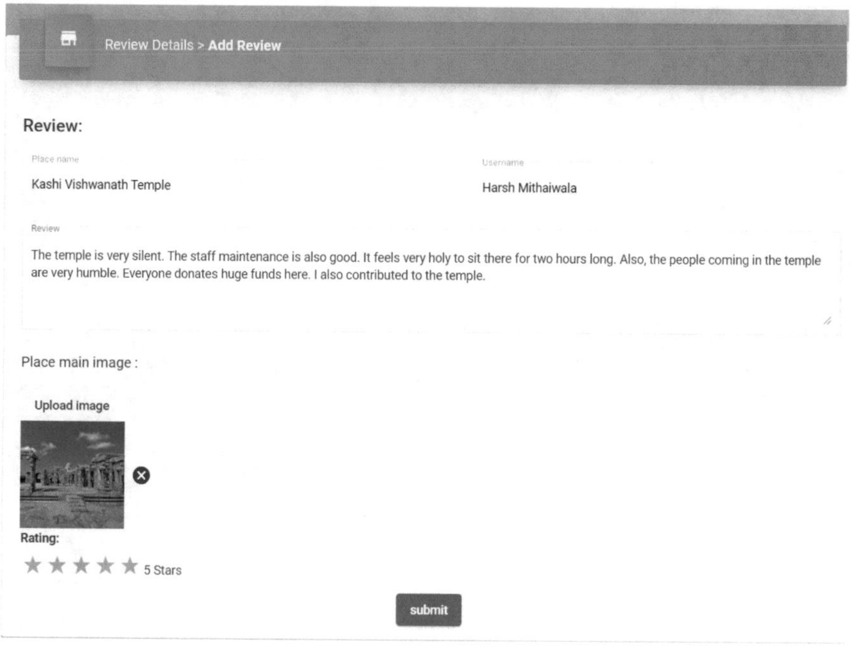

Fig. 6 Add Review Page

4 User Interface for the Web Application

In this section, the user interface part created by us would be briefly discussed.

4.1 Add Review

Only the registered users can write their feedback about the place in the form and can rate it as shown in the Fig. 6. The review will be stored in the form of an IPFS file and the hash of the file will be stored on the blockchain. The tempering issues can be solved using this technique [20].

4.2 View all Review

From the place detail page, view all reviews for the product can be seen as shown in the figure. The page also features a read more button. Through that button, a pop-up can be opened which shows a profile picture in a larger format with full remarks and

Fig. 7 View Review for a particular product page

ratings. This page requests the file of hashes of the reviews for that product from the blockchain (Fig. 7).

5 Conclusion

After going through many previous research papers and worldwide incidents, many loopholes in the current review system are being highlighted and that needs to be solved to provide proper guidance to the customers. As of now, due to central authority, owners can easily modify customer's genuine reviews. To mainly remove this drawback, the review system is being shifted to the decentralized structure. Using the mentioned different tools, the proposed system provides the facility to secure customer reviews without any tempering. Moreover, the contract of the system is also capable of overcoming the problems related to the flood of reviews as one user can review one product only one time. Thus, the review, which previously had security issues, is solved by the proposed system.

References

1. Cai W, Wang Z, Ernst JB, Hong Z, Feng C, Leung VCM (2018) Decentralized applications: the blockchain-empowered software system. In: IEEE Access, vol 6
2. Gutt D, Neumann J, Zimmermann S, Kundisch D, Chen J (2019) Design of review systems – a strategic instrument to shape online reviewing behavior and economic outcomes. https://ssrn.com/abstract=3162030

3. Jo-Anne M (2021) The pros and cons of online customer reviews. https://www.irpcommerce. com/en/gb/IRPStrategyCenter/The-Pros-and-Cons-of-Online-Customer-Reviews/sc-55. aspx. Accessed: 2021-03-20
4. What is revain: blockchain-based review platform. https://revain.org/about. Accessed: 2021-1-30
5. Le T, Kim Y, Jo J-Y (2019) Implementation of a blockchain-based event reselling system. In: 2019 6th international conference on computational science/intelligence and applied informatics (CSII), pp 50–55
6. Wu K, Ma Y, Huang G, Liu X (2019) A first look at blockchain based decentralized applications. Softw Pract Exp
7. Salah K, Alfalasi A, Alfalasi M (2019) A blockchain-based system for online consumer reviews. In: IEEE INFOCOM 2019 - Ieee conference on computer communications workshops (INFO-COM WKSHPS), pp 853–858
8. Lee S (2021) A decentralized reputation system: how blockchain can restore trust in online markets. www.forbes.com/sites/shermanlee/2018/-08/13/a-decentralized-reputation-system-how-blockchain-can-restore-trust-in-online-markets/. Accessed: 2021-1-18
9. Schueffel P (2017) Alternative distributed ledger technologies blockchain vs. tangle vs. hashgraph - a high-level overview and comparison. https://ssrn.com/abstract=3144241. Accessed: 2020-12-08
10. Brown R, Carlyle J, Grigg I, Hearn M (2016) Corda: an introduction
11. The tangle: an illustrated introduction. https://blog.iota.org/the-tangle-an-illustrated-introduction-4d5eae6fe8d4/. Accessed: 2020-09-20
12. LeewayHertz (2020) The complete guide to understanding EOS blockchain. www.leewayhertz. com/what-is-eos-blockchain/. Accessed: 2021-2-01
13. Quintero S (2019) Which rating system is best for your users? https://medium.com/enjoyhq/which-rating-system-is-best-for-your-users-9fddeeb455b5. Accessed: 2021-1-12
14. Ahram T, Sargolzaei A, Sargolzaei S, Daniels J, Amaba B (2017) Blockchain technology innovations. In: 2017 Ieee technology engineering management conference (TEMSCON), pp 137–141
15. Lina.Review: blockchain based review platform. https://lina.review/lina_whitepaper.pdf. Accessed: 2021-01-09
16. Revain: building a trustless, consumer review system on the blockchain. https://thebitcoinpodcast.com/release/-revain-building-a-trustless-consumer-review-system-on-the-blockchain/. (2017). Accessed: 2020-11-11
17. SynchroLife-decentralized restaurant recommendation platform. https://synchrolife.org/SynchroLife. (2020). Accessed: 2021-2-16
18. Lepore C, Ceria M, Visconti A, Rao UP, Shah KA, Zanolini L (2020) A survey on blockchain consensus with a performance comparison of pow, pos and pure pos. Mathematics 8(10)
19. Wang S, Ouyang L, Yuan Y, Ni X, Han X, Wang F-Y (2019) Blockchain-enabled smart contracts: architecture, applications, and future trends. IEEE Trans Syst Man Cybern Syst 49(11):2266–2277
20. Steichen M, Fiz B, Norvill R, Shbair W, State R (2018) Blockchain-based, decentralized access control for ipfs. In: 2018 Ieee international conference on internet of things (iThings) and ieee green computing and communications (GreenCom) and ieee cyber, physical and social computing (CPSCom) and ieee smart data (SmartData), pp 1499–1506
21. MetaMask documents. https://docs.metamask.io/guide/#why-metamask (2020). Accessed: 2020-12-13
22. Price C (2018) Introduction to quorum: blockchain for the financial sector. In: Medium, blockchain at berkeley. https://medium.com/blockchain-at-berkeley/introduction-to-quorum-blockchain-for-the-financial-sector-58813f84e88c. Accessed: 2020-09-12
23. Douglass C (2020) An introduction to IPFS (Interplanetary File System). https://blog.infura. io/an-introduction-to-ipfs/. Accessed: 2020-10-04
24. Ethereum input data decoder. https://lab.miguelmota.com/ethereum-input-data-decoder/example (2017). Accessed: 2020-11-15

White-Box Encryption Scheme for Resource-Constrained IoT Devices

Ankur Bang, Udai Pratap Rao, Pethuru Raj, and Alok Kumar

1 Introduction

The Internet of Things (IoT) has made the world more efficient, convenient, and human-friendly [1]. However, along with this gigantic growth in the IoT applications and the number of IoT devices, security in IoT remains a veritable minefield [2], [3]. Accordingly, huge efforts are being undertaken to ensure the security of IoT technology. Regrettably, the bulk of existing security systems are built and implemented to protect the black-box model/context [4]. Here, with no access to the systems where cryptographic operations are done, the adversary may be able to monitor and alter the ciphertext only [4]. However, there are two more security models or contexts that must be addressed [4, 5]. They are (i) Grey-Box model/context, in which the adversary has restricted access to the system, i.e., the attacker cannot see the keys but can obstruct the cryptographic method. (ii) White-Box (WB) environment, where the attacker has access to the whole cryptosystem and may monitor and change it. The majority of IoT applications need remote deployment of the involved embedded devices [5]. As a result, they are vulnerable to WB attacks [5]. Moreover, the WB model/context, as well as the grey-box and black-box models/contexts, must be addressed while designing a full security system [6]. The White-Box Cryptography (WBC) encryption method enables key concealment in the implementation code itself [6].

A. Bang (✉) · U. P. Rao · A. Kumar
Computer Science and Engineering Department, Sardar Vallabhbhai National Institute of Technology SVNIT, Surat 395007, GJ, India

P. Raj
Reliance Jio Platforms Ltd., Bangalore 560025, KA, India

© The Author(s), under exclusive license to Springer Nature Singapore Pte Ltd. 2022   257
U. P. Rao et al. (eds.), *Security, Privacy and Data Analytics*, Lecture Notes
in Electrical Engineering 848, https://doi.org/10.1007/978-981-16-9089-1_21

1.1 Related Work

The first WB Advanced Encryption Standard (AES) implementation was proposed by Chow et al. [4] in 2002. In addition, in 2002, they incorporated the WB Data Encryption Standard (DES) [7]. Despite the fact that Chow et al.'s implementations for DES [8] and AES [9] were not secure, their technique provided a structure known as the "CEJO framework" for the WB implementation using lookup tables. The CEJO framework has been used in the majority of WB implementations since Chow et al. [4]. Xiao and Lai [10] suggested implementing WB-AES with more thorough linear encodings than Chow et al. [4]. Karroumi [11] has changed the algebraic operations of each AES cycle. This technique made use of dual representations from the AES hardware to create a WB-AES implementation. Both of these ideas [9],[12], however, are considered insecure because the secret key may be easily recovered. Researchers have represented security principles for WB cryptography in [13–15]. Biryukovet et al. have suggested a novel symmetric Affine-Substitution-Affine-Substitution-Affine (ASASA) based block cypher with secret S-boxes that meet the WB security notations [16]. Estuardo et al. [17] recently elaborated on the WBC's security aims. The performance of the WB technique in terms of IoT has been discussed by Daniele et al. [18]. Jiqiang Lu et al. [19] have discussed the WB implementation of the "KECCAK Message Authentication Code (KMAC)" message authentication code.

However, minimal effort has been made to provide WB security for IoT devices with limited resources. Yang Shi et al. [20], and Arunima Saha et al. [21] have worked to resolve this issue. Both of them, have worked on symmetric-key block cyphers. Kwon et al. [22] employed a parallel lookups table to develop a secure WB Cipher. Shi et al. [23] employed state-dependent random replacements to defend against several WB cryptanalytic techniques. To our knowledge, just a few WB implementations for public key cryptography have been presented. Mizanur et al. [24] have discovered a hitherto way for protecting Elliptic-Curve Cryptography (ECC) keys. In [25], the authors suggest a strategy for WB multiplication over ECC. Zhang et al. [26] proposed the first WB implementation of an observable signature system in 2018. Jie et al. [27] have suggested a cloud-based solution for elliptical curve digital signature (ECDSA) algorithm WB implementation. However, neither the feasibility nor the usability of the proposed method in a resource-constrained device has been proven.

1.2 Motivation

Rapidly evolving IoT technology necessitates flawless privacy and security techniques. However, most of these approaches are being explored exclusively in the context of the black-box model [20]. This makes IoT devices susceptible to face security challenges in the WB context. Deployment of the resource-constrained devices in the WB IoT environments can be protected from the WB attacks by imposing WBC encryption [20]. Aside from that, there are some attacks, such as key whitening [28], code lifting [29], statistical analysis [29], data manipulation [29], and control flow manipulation [29], that need to be addressed in the existing WBC schemes. As a result, installing a safe WBC encryption system across specially developed and standardized IoT communication protocols is the need of the day [18]. All of the aforementioned limitations compelled us to propose a new, appropriate, and secure WBC encryption method.

1.3 Outline of the Paper

The remainder part of the paper is organized as follows. Section 2 describes the problem statement that we aim to resolve. Section 3 briefs about the proposed work. Discussion over the primary obtained results is made in Sect. 4. Further, Sect. 5 concludes the paper and states about our future work.

2 Problem Statement

We aim to design an efficient and secure WBC encryption scheme for resource-constrained IoT devices. The proposed scheme must have negligible overhead concerning memory and power usages. Besides this, the proposed scheme must be immune to the possible attacks on WBC. Further, it must provide a secure WBC encryption that can be easily used with the set of existing standard IoT communication protocols.

3 Proposed Work

In this section, we present the design rationales considered in the proposed work. Further, we provide a brief overview of the proposed WB-Elliptic-Curve Cryptography (ECC) implementation.

3.1 Proposed Architecture and Design Rationales

We depend on the following design rationales for the practical WB-ECC implementation. Figure 1 elaborates regarding the proposed architecture and workflow.

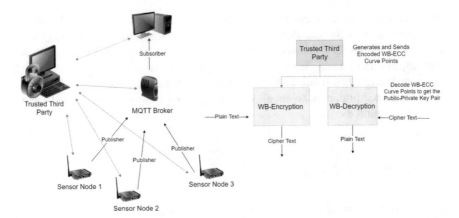

Fig. 1 Proposed architecture and work flow

1. To reduce the key size resulting in optimal use of the resources, our scheme depends on a public key WB implementation through a well known and proven ECC algorithm [30].
2. Along with this, we rely on a trusted third party that provides all the points on the elliptic curve using the curve equation in an encoded format when requested. Thus, before each encryption, the public-private key pairs are generated at the sensor node. This public-private key pair is used for performing encryption and decryption of the sensor node data on a one-on-one basis.
3. The existing WB-AES [31] implementation is made WB secure by mixing the key and bijections with the S-boxes. But, since in ECC there is no functional unit such as S-box, we decide to come up with a novel approach that seems to serve a similar purpose as the S-boxes in AES and also overcome the existing attack on the WBC schemes.

3.2 White-Box ECC Implementation Procedure

The proposed work follows the below mentioned functional steps:

1. A trusted third party, assumed to be secure, provides all the points on the elliptic curve using the curve equation [30] in an encoded form. The encoding is achieved with the help of randomization by performing an Exclusive-OR operation on all the curve points with a random value generated at the trusted third party. Points with the trusted third party are

$$Point.x \oplus Random Value$$
$$Point.y \oplus Random Value$$

2. Before each encryption, the public-private key pairs are generated at the sensor node. This is done by requesting the curve points from the trusted third party, which randomly selects an encoded curve point and sends it to the sensor node. As per our proposal, the trusted third party provides the sensor nodes with a random value and the S-Boxes. Now, the respective sensor nodes can choose the points at any random Index idx.

$$Point Third Party.x = Points[idx].x$$
$$Point Third Party.y = Points[idx].y$$

3. At the sensor node, the encoding is decoded, and the curve points are used in generating the public-private key pair. The sensor nodes will XOR it with the random value to get original points.

$$Original Point.x = Point Third Party.x \oplus Random Value$$
$$Original Point.y = Point Third Party.y \oplus Random Value$$

4. The public-private key pair is used for performing encryption and decryption of the sensor nodes data on a one-on-one basis.

Encryption and Decryption are shown in Figs. 2 and 3, respectively, and are performed as follows:-

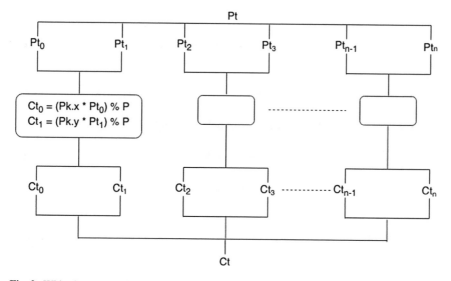

Fig. 2 White-box encryption architecture in ECC

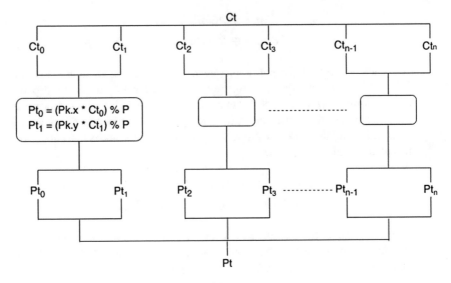

Fig. 3 White-box decryption architecture in ECC

- The plaintext message Pt is segregated into blocks as $Pt \rightarrow Pt_0 Pt_1 ... Pt_i ... Pt_{n-1} Pt_n$. This segregation is done in order to use both the x and y points for standard inception and decryption ECC process.
- The curve points obtained as per the above procedure are used to calculate the public-private key pair (Pk—public key, Pr—private key and P is prime modulo)
- The ciphertext blocks are calculated by performing:

$$Ct_i = (Pk.x * Pt_i)\% P \tag{1}$$

$$Ct_{i+1} = (Pk.y * Pt_{i+1})\% P \tag{2}$$

$0 <= i <= n$
- Thus, the ciphertext is obtained as $Ct \rightarrow Ct_0 Ct_1 ... Ct_i ... Ct_{n-1} Ct_n$ and it is sent to the receiver.
- At the receiver, the plaintext blocks are calculated by performing:

$$Pt_i = (Pr.x * Ct_i)\% P \tag{3}$$

$$Pt_{i+1} = (Pr.y * Ct_{i+1})\% P \tag{4}$$

$0 <= i <= n$
- Thus, the plaintext Pt ($Pt_0 Pt_1 ... Pt_i ... Pt_{n-1} Pt_n$) is obtained at the receiver.

4 Simulation Results and Discussions

To identify the efficiency of the proposed scheme, a weather monitoring IoT environment is simulated by establishing a publisher-subscriber system using the MQTT-SN [32] protocol in the Cooja simulator over Contiki OS. The motes in the simulation assume the roles of wireless sensor nodes that publish to the topics of weather data like light, temperature, humidity, pressure. The MQTT-SN broker subscribes to these weather data topics to receive the weather updates. Z1 motes [33] are used since they have a somewhat high memory of 96 KB. The data published by the motes is encrypted, and the data subscribed by the broker is decrypted using our WB-ECC implementation. We have also simulated the same for conventional ECC algorithm for comparison purposes. Other details of the simulation are as mentioned in Table 1. We consider end-to-end delay, throughput and average power consumption for the comparison purpose.

4.1 End-to-End Delay

From Fig. 4, it can be inferred that the end-to-end delay decreases in our WB-ECC implementation in comparison to the conventional ECC algorithm. When we considered 5 nodes, the end-to-end delay of WB-ECC was 852 Milliseconds (ms), and conventional ECC was 892 ms. This difference of around 40 ms was constant when the network of 10, 15 and 20 nodes was considered. With 10 nodes, the end-to-end delay of WB-ECC was 872 ms, and conventional ECC was 922 ms. Further, we got an end-to-end delay of 908, 931, and 972 ms with WB-ECC and 938, 971, 1001 ms with conventional ECC with the network topology of 15, 20, and 25 nodes, respectively.

Table 1 Simulation Parameters

Parameters	Value
Simulator	Cooja
Operating system	Contiki V 2.7
Node type	Z1
Number of nodes	5–25
Radio medium	Unit disk graph medium (UGDM): distance loss
PHY and MAC Layer	IEEE 802.15.4 with CSMA and ContikiMAC
ESMRF	Contiki V 2.7 default
Objective function	MHROF
Simulation duration	15 Min
Number of simulations	3 Per reading
Routing protocol	RPL (6LoWPAN)

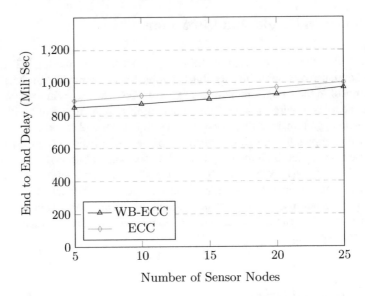

Fig. 4 End to end delay

4.2 Throughput

We consider the throughput in Bytes/Second over the network of 5, 10, 15, 20, 25 nodes. As shown in Fig. 5, the network throughput increases in our WB-ECC implementation in comparison to the conventional ECC algorithm linearly with the size of the network. The network throughput of WB-ECC was noticed as 4.94, 5.09, 5.25, 5.42, and 5.35, respectively, with the considered network topologies. At the same time, for the conventional ECC the network throughput in the respective order of considered network sizes was 4.41, 4.50, 4.95, 5.22, and 5.25.

4.3 Average Power Consumptions

Figure 6 shows the comparison of the proposed WB-ECC implementation over conventional ECC concerning average power consumption. The average power consumption of both the schemes was noted around 1 Milliwatt (mW) over the network

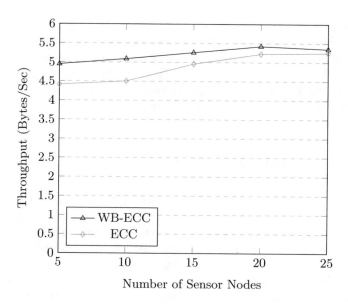

Fig. 5 Throughput

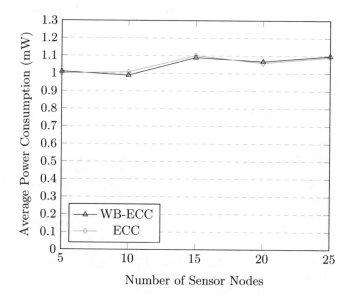

Fig. 6 Average power consumption

topology of 5 and 10 nodes. However, when the number of nodes was increased to 15 and then 20–25, the average power consumption of both the schemes was noted around 1.101–1.090 mW. Moreover, both the schemes have a similar amount of average power consumption. Moreover, WB-ECC have shown slight improvement.

The improvement over parameters like end-to-end delay, throughput and average power exhibited by our WB-ECC implementation can be best explained by the fact that in our WB-ECC implementation, the elliptic curve points are pre-computed and stored in a table in encoded form for direct use. Whereas, in the conventional ECC algorithm, there is a computation overhead since these points are needed to be computed first before the algorithm can commence.

5 Conclusion and Further Work

In this paper, we have proposed a WB implementation of a public key algorithm (ECC). This WB-ECC is implemented over MQTT-SN protocol and is used in simulating weather monitoring IoT environment to provide security to the data transmitted by the sensor nodes. This study is in progress, and primitive experimental results are positive. The proposed scheme has shown improvement over the parameters like end-to-end delay, throughput and average power consumption. We hope that our research will be helpful for other researchers working in the same area. However, creating a truly secure IoT ecosystem against WB assaults would still need a significant amount of further study. In the future, we would like to test the suggested security architecture in a practical situation.

References

1. Bang AO, Rao UP (2021) Context-aware computing for iot: History, applications and research challenges. In: Proceedings of Second International Conference on Smart Energy and Communication. Springer, pp. 719–726
2. Bang A, Rao UP (2021) A novel decentralized security architecture against sybil attack in rpl-based iot networks: a focus on smart home use case. J Supercomput 1–36
3. Patra L, Rao UP (2016) Internet of things–architecture, applications, security and other major challenges. In: 2016 3rd international conference on computing for sustainable global development (INDIACom). IEEE, pp 1201–1206
4. Chow S, Eisen P, Johnson H, Van Oorschot PC (2002) White-box cryptography and an aes implementation. In: International workshop on selected areas in cryptography. Springer, pp 250–270
5. Sanfelix E, de Haas J, Mune C (2015) Unboxing the white-box: Practical attacks against obfuscated ciphers. Presentation at Blackhat Europe
6. Wyseur B (2021) White-box cryptography: hiding keys in software. http://whiteboxcrypto.com. Accessed 25 06 2021
7. Chow S, Eisen P, Johnson H, Van Oorschot PC (2002) A white-box des implementation for DRM applications. In: ACM workshop on digital rights management. Springer, pp 1–15
8. Wyseur B, Michiels W, Gorissen P, Preneel B (2007) Cryptanalysis of white-box des implementations with arbitrary external encodings. In: International workshop on selected areas in cryptography. Springer, pp 264–277
9. Lepoint T, Rivain M, De Mulder Y, Roelse P, Preneel B (2013) Two attacks on a white-box aes implementation. In: International conference on selected areas in cryptography. Springer, pp 265–285

10. Xiao Y, Lai X (2009) A secure implementation of white-box AES. In: 2009 2nd international conference on computer science and its applications. IEEE, pp 1–6
11. Karroumi M (2010) Protecting white-box AES with dual ciphers. In: International conference on information security and cryptology. Springer, pp 278–291
12. De Mulder Y, Roelse P, Preneel B (2012) Cryptanalysis of the XIAO–LAI white-box AES implementation. In: International conference on selected areas in cryptography. Springer, pp 34–49
13. Delerablée C, Lepoint T, Paillier P, Rivain M (2013) White-box security notions for symmetric encryption schemes. In: International conference on selected areas in cryptography. Springer, pp 247–264
14. Saxena A, Wyseur B, Preneel B (2009) Towards security notions for white-box cryptography. In: International conference on information security. Springer, pp 49–58
15. Preneel B, Wyseur B (2008) "White-box cryptography," in Dagstuhl workshop on security hardware in theory and practice-a marriage of convenience, Date: 2008/06/18-2008/06/20. Dagstuhl Germany, Location
16. Biryukov A, Bouillaguet C, Khovratovich D (2014) Cryptographic schemes based on the asasa structure: black-box, white-box, and public-key. In: International conference on the theory and application of cryptology and information security. Springer, pp 63–84
17. Bock EA, Amadori A, Brzuska C, Michiels W (2020) On the security goals of white-box cryptography. IACR Trans Cryptograp Hard Embed Syst 327–357
18. Albricci DGV, Ceria M, Cioschi F, Fornari N, Shakiba A, Visconti A (2019) Measuring performances of a white-box approach in the IOT context. Symmetry 11(8):1000
19. Lu J, Zhao Z, Guo H (2019) White-box implementation of the KMAC message authentication code In: International conference on information security practice and experience. Springer, pp 248–270
20. Shi Y, Wei W, He Z, Fan H (2016) An ultra-lightweight white-box encryption scheme for securing resource-constrained IOT devices. In: Proceedings of the 32nd annual conference on computer security applications, pp 16–29
21. Saha A, Srinivasan C (2019) White-box cryptography based data encryption-decryption scheme for iot environment. In: 2019 5th international conference on advanced computing & communication systems (ICACCS). IEEE, pp 637–641
22. Kwon J, Lee B, Lee J, Moon D (2020) FPL: white-box secure block cipher using parallel table look-ups. In: Cryptographers' track at the RSA conference. Springer, pp 106–128
23. Shi Y, Wei W, Zhang F, Luo X, He Z, Fan H (2019) SDSRS: a novel white-box cryptography scheme for securing embedded devices in IIOT. IEEE Trans Ind Inf 16(3):1602–1616
24. Rahman SMM, Muir J (2016) System and method for generating and protecting cryptographic keys, 22 Nov 2016, US Patent 9,503,259
25. Hoogerbrugge J, Michiels W, Vullers P (2018) White-box elliptic curve point multiplication, 4 Sep 2018, US Patent 10,068,070
26. Zhang Y, He D, Huang X, Wang D, Choo K-KR, Wang J (2020) White-box implementation of the identity-based signature scheme in the IEEE p1363 standard for public key cryptography. IEICE Trans Inf Syst 103(2):188–195
27. Zhou J, Bai J, Jiang MS (2020) White-box implementation of ECDSA based on the cloud plus side mode. Secur Commun Netw 2020
28. Bhatia K, Som S (2016) Study on white-box cryptography: key whitening and entropy attacks. In: 2016 5th international conference on reliability, infocom technologies and optimization (Trends and Future Directions)(ICRITO). IEEE, pp 323–327
29. Biryukov A, Udovenko A (2018) Attacks and countermeasures for white-box designs. In: International conference on the theory and application of cryptology and information security. Springer, pp 373–402
30. Lauter K (2004) The advantages of elliptic curve cryptography for wireless security. IEEE Wirel Commun 11(1):62–67
31. Muir JA (2012) A tutorial on white-box AES. In: Advances in network analysis and its applications. Springer, pp 209–229

32. Cope S (2011) Introduction to MQTT-SN (MQTT for Sensor Networks). http://www.steves-internet-guide.com/mqtt-sn/. Accessed 25 June 2021
33. Meet the Z1 mote (2021) http://wiki.zolertia.com/wiki/index.php/Main_Page. Accessed 10 Feb 2021 [Accessed 25 June 2021]

Pay-Per-Byte for Block Reward: A Revised Incentive Mechanism in Bitcoin

Kunal Sahitya and Bhavesh Borisaniya

Abstract Since Satoshi Nakamoto introduced Bitcoin in 2009, there have been around more than 1600 other cryptocurrencies in the market [1]. However, only a handful of them can be compared with bitcoin as it still rules the cryptocurrency market. There are two types of incentives provided by Bitcoin for miners, namely Block Reward and Transaction Fees. For every miner, the block reward matters more than the latter one. Miners being the creator of the block and having received block reward have the moral obligation towards the system to give their best and to not be greedy while mining. However, it is found that around a quarter of the mined blocks until the start of 2017 are empty blocks and other blocks are also merely half-full from their allowed capacity. Thus, this work proposes a cerebral change in the block reward system. Being derived from pay-per-piece wage system, this revised mechanism imposes a policy of contributing best to the system on miners. This work comprises of theoretical discussion and experiment results analysis of the system with future extensions. Every Satoshi (smallest unit of bitcoin) being a scarce asset, miners should be rewarded in proportion to their better intentions towards the system.

Keywords Bitcoin · Blockchain · Cryptocurrency · Proof-of-work · Pay-per-byte

1 Introduction

In recent years, Blockchain has emerged as one of the greatest technological inventions of the twenty-first century. By solving the problem of double spending in digital cash, it has pushed the idea of digital finance and intellectual property to another level. Blockchain's widespread adoption in domains like finance, supply chain, energy trading, smart contracts, gaming, etc. has made it center of attraction for academic and industry research [2]. Though it looks "Immutable" solution at a quick glance from

K. Sahitya (✉)
Department of Information Technology, Dharmsinh Desai University,, Nadiad, India

B. Borisaniya
Information Technology Department, Shantilal Shah Engineering College, Bhavnagar, India

© The Author(s), under exclusive license to Springer Nature Singapore Pte Ltd. 2022   269
U. P. Rao et al. (eds.), *Security, Privacy and Data Analytics*, Lecture Notes
in Electrical Engineering 848, https://doi.org/10.1007/978-981-16-9089-1_22

a digital finance perspective, blockchain has its limitations and challenges like any other technology that needs to be addressed for its widespread success [3].

Initially, at the time of bitcoin creation, the existing reward mechanism was helpful to increase the user base and to distribute the coins in the community easily [4]. However, as the user base and popularity of the currency have increased immensely, still using the same old mechanism feels naive. Some selfish miners are playing smart to take advantage of this classic reward mechanism. Stats say around 25% of the total mined blocks till now are the empty blocks created by SPV mining [5]. "SPV Mining" term is used for the blocks which have only one transaction inside them, in which the miner pays himself the amount of block reward for creating that block. That singular transaction is known as coinbase transaction. Actually, such mined block is not totally empty, but in terms of transaction throughput, it doesn't contain anything. Hence, SPV mining blocks are known as empty mined blocks.

On the other hand, if one keeps the track of blocks created every day statistically, stats can show shocking results about block size. In real, blocks are on an average only 30–40% full [6]. Miners are not utilizing the full available block size to gain the advantage in the mining race over other miners by validating less transactions or no transactions at all as in the case of SPV mining. Hence, for the last considerable amount of time, there has been an overdose of waiting transaction in the mempool due to the low network throughput of bitcoin [7].

Pay-per-Byte for reward is the new incentive mechanism proposed in the research here for bitcoin blockchain. The main goal is to reinforce the network throughput for bitcoin by paying miners based on their devotion towards the system. This will lead miners to be more faithful towards the system as it pays them more than being reckless. We, as researchers, strongly believe that miners who work more for the system by filling block up to 90% must be paid accordingly. Moreover, transaction fees amount only up to 5–8% of the total reward for most miners. So their primary source of earning lies in block rewards, which is enhanced to be more efficient using this research.

The rest of the paper is organized as follows. Section 2 describes the incentive mechanism in Bitcoin network. Section 3 discusses the related work. Section 4 describes the revised incentive mechanism (Pay-Per-Byte) for bitcoin network in detail. It elaborates the structure of an entire block and a specific transaction for consideration into further research. Experiments and results are discussed in Sect. 5 with conclusion and references at the end.

2   Incentive in Bitcoin

Bitcoin is the first cryptocurrency to use the concepts of blockchain to solve the problem of double spending in the digital economy. Inventor(s) of blockchain implemented bitcoin as its application in early 2009 with an open source license. The very first node in the bitcoin network is known as "Genesis Block" mined by author Satoshi Nakamoto.

Bitcoin works on the consensus algorithm called Proof of Work (PoW). In which, special nodes called miners expend their electricity and CPU power to mine a number called the nonce. This nonce number helps in generating a desired block hash for the newly generated block. This unique hash is followed by some leading zeros in the same. These leading zeroes are known as block difficulty and which makes it tricky to find desired block hash with constraints. Miners have to conduct the validation of block hash, transactions inside it and find a new block hash suitable to block difficulty. Miners are paid for above-mentioned tasks in form of block reward and transaction fees, block reward being the primary source of income.

Bitcoin network compensates miners, special nodes in bitcoin network, in form of Block reward and transaction fees. Block reward is the miner's fee for mining every new block. However, if any transaction's output value is not adding up to the total of its respective inputs, that would be the transaction fee for a given transaction passed on to the miner. Block reward is the primary source of income for miners for their consumed electricity and CPU power. Block reward can also be considered as a way of generating new coins in the system analogues to printing new currency notes. But it has a limit of 21 Million BTCs, meaning more than 21 M BTCs cannot exist, due to its reward halving mechanism. Bitcoin block reward is halved after every 2,10,000 blocks are generated. In the beginning, Satoshi started with 50 BTCs as block mining reward, which has been reduced to 6.25 BTCs till now. The upcoming block reward will be halved after 8,40,000 blocks are mined by the miners, which is expected to be in midst of 2024 (for more details, refer Table 1 [8]). While announcing bitcoin to the real world Satoshi Nakamoto reacted, "Coins have to get initially distributed somehow, and a constant rate seems like the best formula" [4]. The above comment was done regarding the block reward mechanism in bitcoin blockchain, when a critique person asked Satoshi about the effect of inflation in bitcoin currency. One can analyze that rewarding miners was not a well-planned activity in bitcoin creation by the above comment and is still followed by almost all of cryptocurrencies created after bitcoin.

Table 1 Block reward halving statistics in bitcoin [8]

Reward Era	Year Range	Reward Amount	Annual Supply Growth	Daily Issuance Rate
1	2009–2012	50 BTC	2,625,000	7200 BTC
2	2012–2016	25 BTC	1,312,500	3600 BTC
3	2016–2020	12.5 BTC	656,250	1800 BTC
4	2020–2024	6.25 BTC	328,125	900 BTC
5	2024–2028	3.125 BTC	164,062	450 BTC

3 Related Work

Most of the related work in bitcoin research for the incentive domain conveys that transaction fees are the major point of concern assuming block reward might not be the primary income source in the near future which is critiqued by this study. Some work talks about self-interested mining techniques used by miners to increase their reward then fair share. But unfortunately, no subtle work is done related to bitcoin block reward. It is not relevant to discuss about the work related to change in block size or network throughput as bitcoin has already seen a number of hard forks related to the same. Moreover, such research either changes the underlying block structure or consensus algorithm for generating new blocks, which is out of scope in the case of this study.

There are empirical evidence that miners/mining pools are willing to attack others in order to maximize their own profits (e.g. by launching DDoS attacks against other mining pools) [9, 10]. Johnson et al. in [9] talk about a scenario where a mining pool plans a costly DDoS attack against its competing pool. In that case, the attacking pool checks all the trade-offs using a series of game-theoretical models for maximum profit. They concluded with the remarks of attacking bigger mining pools than a certain threshold to be benefited by costly DDoS attacks. Eyal in [10] talks about a Nash Equilibrium in bitcoin revenue where mining pools attack each other by corrupting miners of competitor pools. They describe how at Nash Equilibrium, either of the mining pool attacks will result in profit for them, but if both decide to attack at the same time, pools will earn even less than they would have without conducting such attacks. However, these types of attacks can encourage miners to join private mining pools rather than trusted public ones with less profit margins.

Eyal and Sirer in [11] claim that the bitcoin mining protocol is not particular enough to be compatible. They discuss some circumstances where miners can earn more than their fair share just by colluding with the network. With suitable experiment results and theoretical discussions, the authors suggest backward compatible modifications in bitcoin network regulations. Similarly, Bag et al. in [12] suggest that a "Sponsored Block Withholding Attack", a certain type of block withholding attack, can be more of a profitable choice than rational mining. Miners can use their CPU power wisely and not submit their job to the host pool. It will result in competitors being benefitted and corrupt miner would gain a stake from the same.

Work in [13–15] talks about advances in transaction fee or incentive regulations for the survival of bitcoin after block reward is ruled out of the picture. Talking about particulars, in [13], N. Houy designs a static partial equilibrium model for the economics of bitcoin transaction fees that directly relates network security with transaction fees. Kroll et al. in [14] survey economics of bitcoin mining. The authors suggest mining mechanism in bitcoin is an important aspect of bitcoin design and it protects the network from certain technical problems and adversary attacks. Moser and Bohme in [15] claim that transaction fee will substitute miners' minting rewards in long run. Authors identify several regime shifts while analyzing around 45 Million bitcoin transactions for transaction fees. Authors conclude with the thought that rules

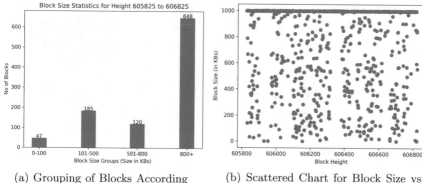

(a) Grouping of Blocks According to Size

(b) Scattered Chart for Block Size vs Block Height

Fig. 1 Block Size distribution

will dominate the existence of the bitcoin network if the transaction fee remains negligible.

Sompolinsky and Zohar in [16] pointed towards the fact that network throughput can be affected by two basic parameters for any chain: Block Creation Rate and Block Size. These both parameters unfortunately affect the security ratio of the bitcoin network. So unless a major change happens for the available processing power in the market, it is advisable to keep the security ratio of the system intact.

From the above discussion, it can be depicted that a novel solution is required that concerns the network throughput without affecting the security threshold of the bitcoin network. In simpler terms, changing block creation rate and/or block size will not be possible according to the former study. When we talk about increasing block size in the case of bitcoin, one would be thinking about the lack of space to fill in more transactions inside the block. However, Fig. 1 portrays total contradictory behavior to that.

Given Fig. 1a shows the statistics for 1000 blocks from block height 605825 to 606824. The maximum transaction size was 992388 bytes and the minimum transaction size was 266 bytes for an empty block. The resultant average transaction size is only around 701279 bytes. From Fig. 1a, it is clear that 352 blocks are under filled or partially empty. It supports the earlier stated fact that 30–40% blocks of bitcoin blockchain are partially occupied. Moreover, 26.3% of the analyzed blocks were less than 50% filled. The above graph can be drawn as a scattered chart and will yield the following resultant Fig. 1b.

Figure 2a states the analysis for no of transaction per block. Minimum being 1 transaction for empty blocks and maximum being 3736 transactions included inside a single block, these 1K blocks averages around 2100 transactions per block. Scatter graph shown in Fig. 2b clarifies density of blocks in a particular transaction count group for same data.

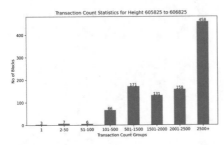
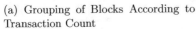

(a) Grouping of Blocks According to Transaction Count

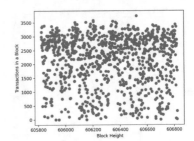

(b) Scattered Chart for Transaction Count vs Block Height

Fig. 2 Transaction count per block

Table 2 Bitcoin block structure [18]

Field Size (in bytes)	Field Name	Description
4	Block size	Total block size in bytes
80	Block Header	Multiple fields described in Fig. 4
1–9	Transaction count	Number of transactions included in body part
Variable	Transaction data	Definite transaction details for every transaction

4 Pay-Per-Byte

The main idea behind the proposed solution is to bridge the gap of information that network throughput for bitcoin can't be increased without affecting its security parameters. As discussed earlier in Fig. 1, stats suggest that miners are not utilizing the maximum allowed capacity of block size, which is 1 MB. Every day blocks are being added to the blockchain that merely averages just above half of its allowed size. That suggests that 30–40% remaining space is just going into vain at every block creation that is under filled. SPV mining is also conducted by the miners often just to increase their profit without working much for the system. This greedy approach, which is mostly followed by solo miners, is not avoidable at all for the network.

Pay-per-Byte for block reward, a novel incentive mechanism, is proposed here for efficiently utilizing block space. Prior task strongly reinforces the network throughput based on the policy imposed on the miners. This study doesn't require a single change in the background and/or the underlying structure of the bitcoin network. Bitcoin blockchain structure is described in Fig. 3 [17]. A block carries details like the previous block's hash, version, timestamp, nonce, Merkel root hash and difficulty in the block header. Apart from that, in its body part, a block is filled with transaction hashes and related data bits (coinbase transaction is also part of the same). Block structure with its properties can be listed as per Table 2 [18].

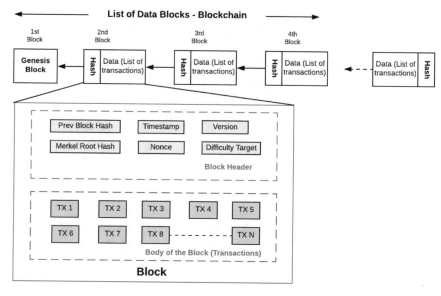

Fig. 3 Structure of bitcoin blockchain [17]

Chunk 1						Chunk 2	
Block header							Padding
Block header candidate						Nonce	
Version	Previous hash	Merkle root		Time stamp	Bits (difficulty)		
		Head	Tail				
4 bytes	32 bytes	28 bytes	4 bytes	4 bytes	4 bytes	4 bytes	48 bytes
		Message²					

Fig. 4 Bitwise structure of block header [19]

As shown in below Fig. 4, block data is followed by block header + padding (48 bytes). Block header can be further broken down into candidate properties & nonce. Block header candidate properties consist of blockchain version (4 bytes), previous hash (32 bytes), Merkel root (32 bytes), timestamp (4 bytes) and difficulty bits (4 bytes). Merkel root can be divided into head (28 bytes) and tail (4 bytes) parts.

The maximum allowed block size is currently 1 MB in bitcoin blockchain. So it is obvious that transactions that can fit inside the blocks will have to manage in less than 1MB size. If one wants to calculate the maximum available space for miners to fit in transactions inside the bitcoin block, it can be calculated using the equation below.

Table 3 Coinbase transaction bitwise structure [18]

Field Size (in bytes)	Field Name	Description
32	Hash (Strictly Null)	No previous UTXO hash (newly mined coins)
4	Index	0xffffffff
≥ 4	Height	Block height
Variable	Script_sig Count	No of bytes to be included in Script_sig
Variable	Script_sig Bytes	Actual Script_sig data included by miner (≤ 80 bytes)
4	Transaction sequence	Sequence number of transaction included in block

Available Transaction Space = (Maximum Block Size Limit) -
                              (Block Header + Padding) - (Actual Block Size)
                              - (Transaction Count) - (Coinbase Transaction)
                            = 1 MB – (80 bytes + 48 bytes) – (4 bytes) –
                              (3 Bytes) – (65 bytes)
                            = 999800 bytes

In the above calculation, block header padding and coinbase transactions are considered to be redundant and not available for storing actual transactions. So those bytes are simply removed from available space. Another noticeable thing is fixing two variable sizes of transaction count and coinbase transaction as a whole. Here, 3 is the minimum bytes needed to specify any transaction count. Coinbase transactions generally contain variable fields called script_sig count and actual script_sig bytes up to count of 80 as described in Table 3. Here, it is assumed to be no script_sig bits in coinbase transaction ideally. The above assumptions are further discussed in [18]. Moreover, details about coinbase transaction fields is mentioned in below Table 3.

The remaining work after finding the maximum available transaction size for miners is to reward them in such a manner that honest miners get their fair share of reward compared to greedy miners. Till now, it was believed that miners expend their electricity and CPU power to apply PoW consensus to the newly generated block. So the existing reward system is designed in such a way that every miner gets constant rewards for working equally hard towards finding nonce. The constant reward mechanism doesn't take into consideration that honest miners have actually included maximum possible transactions for healthy transaction throughput. On the other hand, greedy miners got away with it just by filling the block partially or not filling it at all (SPV mining). This behavior is categorized as greedy because miners don't want to waste their time in verifying transactions inside the block and just want to jump into calculating the next block's nonce for greater earning purposes. The above behavior affects the bitcoin network's transaction throughput.

Pay-per-Byte design for block reward helps in solving the above miner's greedy behavior problem by rewarding miners based on their productivity towards the network rather than electricity and CPU time. This study also proposes linearly variable reward instead of constant. It suggests that miners, which make most of the available transaction space, should be paid with the maximum block reward, and those who show irresponsibility towards available block space for transactions should not be paid for expended electricity and CPU time as it was of no use to the bitcoin network. Miners should be rewarded variably based on included transactions inside the block as per the following equation.

$$B_{RM} = \frac{B_{RX}}{(1e+6) - B_H - C_{Tx} - Tx_C - BS_C - B_P} \times B_S \qquad (1)$$

where B_{RM} = Block Reward for given mined block, B_{RX} = Maximum Current Bitcoin Reward (As per halving countdown), B_H = Block Header Size, C_{Tx} = Coinbase Transaction Size, Tx_C = Transaction Count, BS_C = Count of Actual Block size as whole, B_P = Padding to block header and B_S = Transaction space utilized by miner from available transaction space. For the record, denominator of given equation 2 as a whole just specifies actual available transaction space for miners (inherited from equation 1). On the other hand, BS is the actual space used by miner from maximum available space for transactions.

As depicted from Eq. 1, B_{RM} is a linearly growing variable depending on other block properties. As other block properties are bound by the rules of bitcoin block formation, miners can only focus on increasing B_S. As B_S represents the space used by the miner to store actual productive transaction, increment in it will simply tend to reinforce the network throughput. Here, miners will have to work towards maximizing B_S to increase their share of reward. As the honest miners are simply getting more rewards according to the above mechanism, there is a very rare possibility of them infecting system health in an adverse manner.

This change of variable reward mechanism for miners will impose a policy of producing possible best for the network to get rewarded in a better manner. Putting into simple words, they will try to include as many transactions as they can into the available block space, to gain most of the possible reward. As the method yields more for honest miners, it is unlikely to be rejected by the mining pools and dedicated solo miners. We are not affecting any block structure parameters for the proposed mechanism, hence it won't have to deal with any new blockchain security concerns. This reward mechanism for miners resembles with pay-per-piece wage system, in which workers are paid variably according to their share of yield to the company rather than lump-sum amount depending on their energy consumed.

The proposed hypothesis is able to achieve the following gains as system features, which are mainly focused on promoting rational mines, working on system throughput and avoiding inflation in cryptocurrency, etc.

Rational miners will earn better:As per the new reward mechanism, miners will be rewarded based on their yield towards the system rather than their expended electricity and CPU time. This policy will help towards the betterment of the honest miners, who spend considerable time including more transactions inside blocks and verifying them. Miners will be paid null for SPV mining as it depicts no productivity towards network throughput.

Dependency on block rewards will be extended: This variable reward distribution mechanism helps in saving those extra rewards that are being distributed to the greedy miners now as per the constant reward formula. This helps in pushing reward halving away on the timeline, which is a good thing for the overall bitcoin blockchain. If reward halving is pushed in the future by paying variable reward, it will basically extend the dependency on block reward for miners as a source of income.

Encouragement for better block syncing:Miners will have to include as many transactions as possible to gain up to full reward in this mechanism.

If a miner wants to include more transactions in its block creation, he will have to be connected to the maximum possible peers for receiving that amount of transactions. Now, a good peer count in any P2P network leads to good synchronization of the system as a whole. Hence, this will help bitcoin network in achieving better block synchronization and will reduce the fork occurrences.

Help reducing inflation: Satoshi Nakamoto mentioned in his critique conversation that if coin generation rate is backed up by the increasing number of users, the currency will be inflation-free [4]. Provided the former fact, very less has been done towards controlling coin generation and distribution in bitcoin. This specific study will control the distribution of coin to miners and will in turn help the currency to be less affected by inflation.

5   Experiments and Results

For the experiment purpose, we have created scripts to mimic the miners' behavior. We also focused on the script to calculate block incentive or reward based on block size and keep a count on transaction throughput based on actual blockchain data. Our script is written in Python language and runs very efficiently on Google Colab. As the manual script was mimicking miners' behavior on actual blockchain data, we had to have full blockchain downloaded on our machine. So we synced the bitcoin core module without pruning to its latest block. It had massive weighed data around 246GB at the time of conducting these experiments.

Moreover, we have divided our approach to be checked for three different types of miners: honest/ideal miners, greedy/dishonest miners and random miners. These miners' will be filling blocks according to their behavioral aspect and will be rewarded according to blocks filled (or created block's size). More emphasis on wallet functionality is not depicted in the script as it is merely a coinbase transaction where miners reward themselves which can be calculated easily. It was also necessary to check our approach at different block heights to prove its optimality. We have experimented on three different block heights (299999, 399999 and 499999) for 25 blocks in each of the miner's behavioral experiments.

Ideal/Honest Miner's Behavior: One of the key types of miner that benefits the system most is known as an ideal or honest miner. The foremost aim of honest miners is to maximize the system's throughput of transactions by validating and adding the maximum amount of transactions into the block from mempool waiting area. So it is

Table 4 Ideal/Honest Miner's Behavior at Different Block Heights

Parameters	Conventional Approach			Pay-Per-Byte		
	299999	399999	499999	299999	399999	499999
Block space (No. of Blocks)	152.26	28.68	25.53	25	25	25
Throughput (Txs/Block)	303.62	1426.46	2637.02	1849.16	1636.44	2692.95
Reward (Bitcoins)	1912.5	362.5	325	312.0185	312.3424	312.3629

Table 5 Random Miner's Behavior at Different Block Heights

Parameters	Conventional Approach			Pay-Per-Byte		
	299999	399999	499999	299999	399999	499999
Block space (No. of Blocks)	104.03	20.31	21.43	25	25	25
Throughput (Txs/Block)	336.42	1432.55	2623.75	1399.92	1163.8	2249.08
Reward (Bitcoins)	1312.5	262.5	275	227.537	223.6542	262.1529

desirable that these miners should tend to earn most among the other type of miners as they are thinking about the system. Table 4 show results for honest miners' block size, transaction throughput and incentive at respective height.

Random Miner's Behavior: If the system was to contain all the honest miners, it was never supposed to face any difficulty at all. Hence, we evaluate the behavior of random miners. These miners do not care about the system much and just sweep through the minimum available transaction that has been already checked while trying to create the last block. They just check for the transaction included in recent blocks to deduct them and avoid time for more transaction validation. They throw whatever they have in temporary block to actual block mining them. Their sole purpose is to just participate in the mining process and earn without worrying about system throughput. Table 5 shows the results for random miner's behavior at different block heights.

Greedy/Dishonest Miner's Behavior: There also exists a type of miners who deliberately tries to harm the system despite earning their fair share from it. Such miners can be classified as greedy/dishonest miners and such mining is known as SPV mining. In SPV mining, the miner doesn't have the last block's header, they just start mining empty blocks, having no transaction to earn their reward and adversely affect the system. One of our approach's objectives is to prevent the system from SPV mining so that we can save bitcoins from going into the hands of greedy miners. As greedy miners just create empty blocks, it is not possible to test their behavior at a particular height in the blockchain. However, for SPV mining conventional approach provides rewards per mined block, our approach will not provide any reward.

From the results, it is apparent that the Pay-per-Byte approach for miners is not only promoting honest mining, but also saving bitcoin by rewarding greedy miners/random diggers as per their contribution to the system. Apparently, we haven't changed the original maximum allowed block size into consensus protocols. Apart from that results shown depict that network throughput was enforced and honest miners were rewarded with more bitcoins for helping the system in achieving better results. As we have rewarded miners based on the number of transaction bytes, they have ben included in the block, we can mark down the objective of implementing the pay-per-wage system. Furthermore, we are paying NIL to the miners mining empty blocks, which suggests that it will have a major impact on SPV mining by removing them to the most possible extent from the bitcoin mining scenario. Similarly, that thing will help the system to depend on block reward for a longer period of time as we are distributing it cautiously. The objective of achieving better syncing can be justified by the miner's urge to include maximum earning for better transaction inclusion.

6 Conclusion

Pay-per-Byte is the new incentive mechanism for block reward in bitcoin blockchain, a solution by design, just like its underlying blockchain technology. Apart from making the system lucrative for honest miners, this idea also backs up the message of the founder about mining that "If miners ought to find it more profitable to play by the rules, they will never undermine the system" [20]. Hence, this proposed change will help the bitcoin network to reinforce its lacking throughput and delay the expiration of mining activity to a considerable extent by distributing coins to the miners efficiently. New technological inclusion in any solution brings its own positive as well as negative aspects unlike this novel proposal. This solution is merely a design change in the bitcoin network which does not disturb its security aspects. Efficient utilizing of already existing limits will give rise to secure blockchain solutions.

References

1. Hileman G, Rauchs M (2017) Global cryptocurrency benchmarking study. Camb Centre Altern Financ 33:33–113
2. Zile K, Strazdina R (2018) Blockchain use cases and their feasibility. Appl Comput Syst 23(1):12–20
3. Lepore C, Ceria M, Visconti A, Rao UP, Shah KA, Zanolini L (2020) A survey on blockchain consensus with a performance comparison of POW, POS and pure POS. Mathematics 8(10). https://www.mdpi.com/2227-7390/8/10/1782
4. Nakamoto S, Cryptography mailing list. https://satoshi.nakamotoinstitute.org/emails/cryptography/5/#selection-5.0-5.25
5. Sina A (2019) Investigating the Bitcoin blockchain through the analysis of empty blocks. BS thesis, Università Ca'Foscari Venezia
6. Andresen G, Why increasing the max block size is urgent. http://gavinandresen.ninja/why-increasing-the-max-block-size-is-urgent
7. Saad M, Njilla L, Kamhoua C, Kim J, Nyang D, Mohaisen A (2019) Mempool optimization for defending against ddos attacks in pow-based blockchain systems. In: 2019 IEEE international conference on blockchain and cryptocurrency (ICBC), pp 285–292. IEEE

8. Meynkhard A (2019) Fair market value of bitcoin: halving effect. Invest Manag Financ Innov 16:72–85

9. Johnson B, Laszka A, Grossklags J, Vasek M, Moore T (2014) Game-theoretic analysis of ddos attacks against bitcoin mining pools. In: International conference on financial cryptography and data security. Springer, pp 72–86

10. Eyal I (2015) The miner's dilemma. In: 2015 IEEE symposium on security and privacy. IEEE, pp 89–103

11. Eyal I, Sirer EG (2014) Majority is not enough: bitcoin mining is vulnerable. In: International conference on financial cryptography and data security, pp 436–454. Springer

12. Bag S, Ruj S, Sakurai K et al (2015) Revisiting block withholding attack in bitcoin cryptocurrency. Comput Secur Symp 2015(3):1167–1174

13. Houy N (2014) The economics of bitcoin transaction fees. GATE WP 1407

14. Kroll JA, Davey IC, Felten EW (2013) The economics of bitcoin mining, or bitcoin in the presence of adversaries. In: Proceedings of WEIS. vol 2013, p 11

15. Möser M, Böhme R (2015) Trends, tips, tolls: a longitudinal study of bitcoin transaction fees. In: International conference on financial cryptography and data security. Springer, pp 19–33

16. Sompolinsky Y, Zohar A (2015) Secure high-rate transaction processing in bitcoin. In: International conference on financial cryptography and data security. Springer, pp 507–527

17. Kumar A, Is blockchain a linked list like data structure? https://hbr.org/2017/01/the-truth-about-blockchain

18. Georgiadis E (2019) How many transactions per second can bitcoin really handle? Theoretically. IACR Cryptol ePrint Arch 2019:416

19. Technologies P, Parity-bitcoin github. https://github.com/paritytech/parity-bitcoin/tree/master/chain

20. Nakamoto S (2019) Bitcoin: a peer-to-peer electronic cash system. Technical report, Manubot

Blockchain-Based Drug Regulation System

Yash Solanki, Soumya, and Reema Patel

1 Introduction

Drugs, intended to be developed as a boon to serve the right to good health for every human being, have now transgressed to become a bane for millions of families worldwide. According to WHO, around 31 million people suffer from drug use disorders due to the use of illegal drugs like cocaine, opioids, and other similar products. Also, several readily available drugs or chemicals are directly or indirectly used to produce illegal drugs, if not regulated. In India, unauthorised easy access to strongly concentrated acid causes about 300 acid attacks every year, destroying the lives of several young girls [1]. The Overuse of drugs and alcohol also results in millions of deaths worldwide. According to WHO, 3.3 million deaths are caused every year due to alcohol abuse as no purchase limit exists for these products. These phenomena of unauthorised access to drugs are widespread in areas where regulation and surveillance of restricted products need improvement or are lacking, which poses a significant concern for public health and safety.

However, due to the absence of a single track record of the drug product among the stakeholders in the system, the supply chain becomes unsafe and difficult to handle. The possibility of the access of drug products to unlicensed people and the entry of false products in the supply chain becomes relatively easier. As health and safety are the factors of major concern, many organisations and several researchers referenced blockchain as a transformative technology with the capacity to manage a supply chain, regulate their sales, and detect counterfeit drugs through verification of supply chain participants [4, 5, 8, 9, 14, 15, 17, 19].

As the supply chain's complexity increases, affecting the costs of products and their access to consumers, the need for cheap, reliable, accessible, and secure supply

Y. Solanki (✉) · Soumya
Pandit Deendayal Petroleum University, Gandhinagar, GJ, India
e-mail: yash.sce16@sot.pdpu.ac.in

Soumya
e-mail: soumya.ce16@sot.pdpu.ac.in

R. Patel
Indian Institute of Information Technology, Surat, GJ, India

© The Author(s), under exclusive license to Springer Nature Singapore Pte Ltd. 2022   283
U. P. Rao et al. (eds.), *Security, Privacy and Data Analytics*, Lecture Notes
in Electrical Engineering 848, https://doi.org/10.1007/978-981-16-9089-1_23

chains becomes increasingly essential. The recent advancement in blockchain technology has provided a potential solution to convert the existing drug supply chain practices to more robust and secure systems that are fully automatic. To build such a software-based platform that can be utilised without involving a trusted central entity, Ethereum blockchain [24] provides the best option. Ethereum provides smart contract infrastructure which helps in solidifying transactions between various actors in the system. Various properties of ethereum like decentralised architecture, smart contracts, security, proof of work, etc. make it the best candidate for our supply chain implementation.

In this work, the major focus is the implementation and design of a secure and trustworthy drug supply chain system and regulating the sales of drugs based on specific rules codified using smart contracts deployed on the Ethereum blockchain network. The structure of the work is organised as follows: Sect. 2 enlists and describes some of the related work on drug supply chain solutions, which are based on blockchain. Section 3 deals with participants involved in the overall scenario of the drug supply chain system, system design, structure of smart contracts in the system, and overall sequence of transactions within the proposed system. Section 4 provides information about the deployment of the proposed architecture, elaborating on implementations, and smart contract modelling. Section 5 consists of the interfaces of the developed system. Section 6 shows the outcome of the system elaborating on the system's tests and its cost in terms of computation and ether.

2 Literature Review

Blockchain is poised to be the most disruptive and world-changing technology of the future. Several research studies about the development of blockchain systems in various fields and the numbers are increasing exponentially [6, 7, 23–25]. In this literature review study, our primary goal is to cover several proposed and existing drug supply chain solutions in the blockchain and compare their merits and demerits with respect to the proposed solution (Fig. 1).

3 Proposed Solution

In this section, we first explain the actors present in the system followed by system architecture and finally conclude with how smart contracts are structured into the proposed architecture.

Table 1 Comparative study of various existing solutions

Author	Technology used	Merits	Demerits
Jamil et al. [11]	Hyperledger Fabric	Prescription Handling and tracking of the drug sold by pharmaceuticals avoiding unauthorised access to drugs	Doesn't resolve the drug counterfeit issue occurring during the supply of the drug from manufacturer to retailers
Khatoon et al. [12]	Ethereum	Prescription Handling and tracking of the drug sold by pharmaceuticals avoiding unauthorised access to drugs	Doesn't resolve the drug counterfeit issue occurring during the supply of the drug from manufacturer to retailers
Ijazul Haq et al. [10]	Permissioned Blockchain	Handles counterfeit drug issue by keeping track of supply chain from manufacturer to consumer	Lacks implementation details
Tseng et al. [22]	Bitcoin-based Proof-of-Work Approach	Handles counterfeit drug issue by keeping track of supply chain from manufacturer to consumer	Does Not resolve the issue of unauthorised access to drugs and also Proof-of-work approach leads to the problem of scalability
Schöner et al. [18]	Bitcoin-based Proof-of-Work Approach	Handles only counterfeit medicine issues by keeping track of the supply chain from manufacturer to customer using an unambiguous identification tag	Lacks implementation details
Sylim et al. [20]	Ethereum (Proof-of-work consensus algorithm)	Handles counterfeit drug issues by keeping track of supply chain from manufacturer to customer using DApp	Does not resolve the issue of unauthorised access to drugs and also Proof-of-work approach leads to the problem of scalability
Toyoda et al. [21]	Ethereum	Prevent counterfeits of RFIDattached products in the post-supply chain	Does not solve the issue of unauthorised access
Kumar et al. [16]	Bitcoin-based Proof-of-Work Approach	Handles counterfeit drug issue by keeping track of supply chain from manufacturer to consumer using DApp	Proof-of-work approach leads to the requirement of high computational power and issue of scalability. Also, it doesn't resolve the issue of unauthorised access
Kaid et al. [13]	Hyperledger Fabric	Prevents unauthorised access by implementing automated payments under specific conditions among manufacturers, wholesalers and retailers	Does not solve the issue of unauthorised access of customers with respect to age, prescription, etc
Azaria et al. [3]	Bitcoin-based Proof-of-Work Approach	Easy access to patients medical records and avoids fragmented data by enabling the sharing of medical data by patients and doctors among different parties using distributed ledger technology. Also prevents unauthorised access data as only patients could buy the drugs.	Does not prevent the problem of counterfeit drugs

3.1 Actors Present in the System

Blockchain technology has the power to revolutionise the governance of a country. This research proposed a Blockchain-based drug regulation system for effective implementation of regulation rules in sales of drugs and also to help the elimination of drug counterfeit.

The proposed system develops a decentralised blockchain solution that supports a consortium blockchain network. The proposed Blockchain DApp is capable of managing and updating the complete supply chain by transferring the ownership of drug; paying through the Blockchain network; storing data related to drugs, manufacturer, wholesaler, retailers, and consumers; authenticating the consumers before their purchase; tracking the purchase limit of drugs; adding additional restriction rules for the purchase; etc. Figure 1 represents the actors of the proposed solution, namely Regulatory Committee, Quality Certifier, Manufacturer, Wholesaler, Retailer, and Consumer.

The roles of the actors in the proposed system are given below:

- Regulatory Committee: The governing body responsible for regulating drugs by creating authentication and authorization rules in form of smart contract implementation.
- Quality Certifier: This entity is responsible for providing quality certificates which ensure that product produced by various manufacturers falls within the rules set up by the regulatory committee.
- Manufacturer: This entity manufactures products and sells to various wholesalers or retailers.
- Wholesalers: This entity sells products to various retailers after buying them from manufacturers.
- Retailers: This entity sells products to consumers after buying them from wholesalers.
- Consumer: This entity buys products from various retailers after providing proper authentication as required by the defined contracts.

3.2 System Architecture

The actors are the nodes that use a drug supply chain system. The government assigns the regulatory committee. They act as the admin of the developed system and have the responsibility to set up regulatory rules and add or manage all the manufacturers. They can also trace the whole batch progress from upstream manufacturers to downstream consumers. The drug supply chain begins with the regulatory committee examining and registering a manufacturer in the system. Manufacturers then need to get their product certified by a recognised certification firm acknowledged by the regulatory committee. This certifier then assigns a production limit based on the product quality

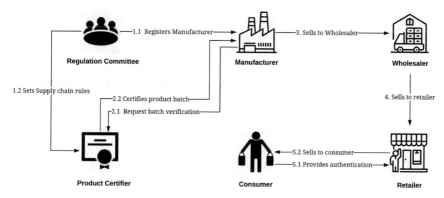

Fig. 1 The architecture of Drug Regulation System

and other rules laid by the committee for a specifically requested product to the manufacturer. The manufacturer then produces different sets of batches of drugs and requests a regulatory committee to register this fresh set of batches in the system. If approved, the manufacturer registers the wholesalers in the network to whom they wish to supply the drug products. The wholesaler can place purchase requests to the manufacturer, who can approve/disapprove the request accordingly. If the request is more than the number of products present with the manufacturer, the request gets automatically rejected.

Similarly, the wholesaler can register retailers and can change the ownership of the drug products to the retailers. Finally, when the consumer arrives to buy a drug product at retailers, they are first authenticated using their identification card (e.g., Aadhar Card) and their biometrics. Once authenticated successfully and verified to satisfy all the regulation rules (such as age, purchase limit, etc.), the drug product is sold to the consumer by again changing its ownership in the network. The retailers can verify citizen's identification data (for example, Aadhar card data in India), which contains his name, image, and biometrics through APIs provided by the government organisation responsible for that identification (for example, UIDAI for Aadhar). The consumer can also check the originality of the drug products by scanning the barcode and checking its supply chain journey. This solution would help prevent drug counterfeit. Figure describes the complete scenario of the proposed drug supply chain system.

3.3 Smart Contracts Structure in the Proposed System

A Smart Contract adds more features to a vanilla blockchain network, as it is a self-executing program that contains conditions of a trade agreement between two parties involves in the trade, and it is written with some simple programming language like Solidity. It can access blockchain blocks and the history of previous transactions and can execute transactions whenever needed. The code and the agreements contained within the contract are stored in a distributed database across the decentralised blockchain network [2]. The smart contract contains rules for entry, execution, and exit of the entire contract and has different functions responsible for different operations/transactions within the contract. The proposed solution implemented the smart contracts in a relatively newer programming language called Solidity on the Ethereum network.

The proposed system contains three contracts, namely "ContractFactory", "SupplyTrack", and "QualityCertifier". These contracts contain methods that allow the actors/users to interact with the Blockchain data. For example, methods to register manufacturers, wholesalers, retailers, and customers; accept payment; and keep track of the registered products.

The "ContractFactory" contract is responsible for registering the manufacturers and processing requests from manufacturers to register their product batch to the network and creating a new contract instance "Supply Track" per batch. The "SupplyTrack" contract is responsible for registering wholesalers, retailers, and customers and keeping track of a particular set of batches down the supply chain. The "QualityCertifier" contract is responsible for verifying the manufacturer's requests and also setting production limits of the particular products to be produced by the manufacturers.

These contracts provide specific access control of all the operations and only let the actor, who is authorised to use the information, query the information. For example, only manufacturers can request a ContractFactory instance to generate a SupplyTrack instance for their certified product batch, and further, all the buying and selling of the batch would be locked in this particular SupplyTrack instance. Actors can retrieve information by doing a function call in the smart contract (hence carrying out a transaction). The blockchain-based DApp performs the transactions and updates the data on the blockchain by adding the transactions in different blocks. This updated outcome is then sent to the application as acknowledgement.

4   Drug Regulation System Implementation

In this section, we first talk about the implementation environment and then see how smart contracts are modelled to support the application.

4.1   Implementation Environment

The proposed system's development environment is grouped into two parts: a React-based front-end and Ethereum powered back-end. The back-end implementation for the Blockchain-based drug regulation system uses smart contracts made in the solidity programming language. The entire back-end is supported by Intel(R) Core(TM) i5 6200U CPU @ 2.40GHz CPU with 4.00 GB of primary memory. Ethereum was run on Rinkeby Test Network and Smart Contracts written in solidity were compiled using solc.

4.2 Smart Contracts Modelling

The proposed system model consists of three working contracts: "Quality Certifier," "Contract Factory," and "Supply Track." The owners and users of the contracts might be different actors according to the access control policy set up in the system. The descriptions of each contract are shown below.

4.2.1 Quality Certifier

"Quality Certifier" is a contract that is owned by the quality certifier actor of the system. With this contract, they can take requests from manufacturer actors for certifying their products. They create certificates for different products of each manufacturer in the system. This contract also enables the certifiers to set production limits to products based on their quality and other parameters pre-decided by the regulatory committee.

4.2.2 Contract Factory

This contract is a master contract managed by the regulatory committee. Manufacturers use this contract after they are registered as actors by the regulatory committee. Registered manufacturers can request this contract to register batches of products in the supply chain. Each set of product batches have their own "Supply Track" contract instance spawned by the contract factory. Manufacturers would be required to get their products certified and get a production limit before requesting the contract factory for the registration of batches. Each time the manufacturer sends a request, the contract verifies if the product is certified, and the requested batch size is under the production limit.

4.2.3 Supply Track

A Supply Track contract instance is created only through a master contract instance of a contract factory. Each supply track instance is associated with some specific set of batches. The entire flow of this batch from manufacturer to consumer will be logged in this instance. The manufacturer made the manager of this contract and is responsible for registering wholesalers/distributors in the contract instance. Wholesalers are responsible for registering new retailers in the instance. The transaction between manufacturers and wholesalers or wholesalers and retailers takes place in three steps:

1. The buyer sends the request of products to the seller with appropriate details like name, universal product code, quantity required, and other relevant details.
2. The seller checks his inventory and accordingly accepts or rejects the request. In case of acceptance, he sends the invoice with the total outstanding amount to the buyer.
3. The buyer then pays the amount received as part of the invoice and gets the product transferred under his ownership.

The above-mentioned steps are implemented in the functions mentioned below: requestToBuy(), handlePurchaseRequest(), and payAndFinalizeTransaction(), respectively. This contract mandates any retailer to authenticate and log customers before they buy any product to ensure proper regulation.

5   Execution Results

The contracts were tested with the Mocha test framework on the Ganache network. Table 2 tabulates the resulting timing for every function of all contracts.

Table 2 Mocha test results for the proposed blockchain-based drug regulation

Contract	Function	Time (ms)
Quality Certifier	constructor()	183
Quality Certifier	registerRequest()	5050
Quality Certifier	processRequest()	1049
Quality Certifier	verifyRequest()	172
Contract Factory	constructor()	1615
Contract Factory	registerActor()	345
Contract Factory	processRequest()	12694
Supply Track	constructor()	2154
Supply Track	registerWholesaler()	482
Supply Track	registerRetailer()	542
Supply Track	requestToBuy()	2570
Supply Track	handlePurchaseRequest()	3267
Supply Track	payAndFinalizeTransaction()	7864
Supply Track	logCustomer()	8946

6 Conclusion

Thus, we implemented a Drug Regulation Supply Chain on Ethereum Blockchain which is capable of detecting counterfeit or substandard drugs and also removes the possibility of Unauthorised access to restricted drugs. This system can prevent many cases of drug overdose, acid attacks, and fake drug rackets and if implemented uniformly can help eradicate these types of crimes to a great extent.

References

1. Number of convictions in acid attack cases across India between 2016 and 2018. https://www.statista.com/statistics/1103125/india-conviction-in-acid-attack-cases/. Accessed 19 Nov 2020
2. Smart Contracts. https://www.investopedia.com/terms/s/smart-contracts.asp. Accessed 08 Oct 2019
3. Azaria A, Ekblaw A, Vieira T, Lippman A (2016) Medrec: using blockchain for medical data access and permission management. In: 2016 2nd international conference on open and big data (OBD), pp 25–30. https://doi.org/10.1109/OBD.2016.11
4. Azzi R, Kilany R, Sokhn M (2019) The power of a blockchain-based supply chain. Comput Ind Eng 135. https://doi.org/10.1016/j.cie.2019.06.042
5. Bell L, Buchanan W, Cameron J, Lo O (2018) Applications of blockchain within healthcare. Blockchain Healthc Today. https://doi.org/10.30953/bhty.v1.8
6. Casino F, Dasaklis TK, Patsakis C (2019) A systematic literature review of blockchain-based applications: current status, classification and open issues. Telemat Inf 36, 55–81 (2019). https://doi.org/10.1016/j.tele.2018.11.006, http://www.sciencedirect.com/science/article/pii/S0736585318306324
7. Davidson S, De Filippi P, Potts J (2016) Economics of blockchain. SSRN Electron J. https://doi.org/10.2139/ssrn.2744751
8. Dujak D, Sajter D (2019) Blockchain applications in supply Chain, pp 21–46. https://doi.org/10.1007/978-3-319-91668-2_2
9. Fu Y, Zhu J (2019) Big production enterprise supply chain endogenous risk management based on blockchain. IEEE Access 7:15310–15319. https://doi.org/10.1109/ACCESS.2019.2895327
10. Haq I, Muselemu O (2018) Blockchain technology in pharmaceutical industry to prevent counterfeit drugs. Int J Comput Appl 180, 8–12. https://doi.org/10.5120/ijca2018916579
11. Jamil F, Hang L, Kim K, Kim D (2019) A novel medical blockchain model for drug supply chain integrity management in a smart hospital. Electronics 8. https://doi.org/10.3390/electronics8050505
12. K, A (2020) A blockchain-based smart contract system for healthcare management. Electronics 9:94. https://doi.org/10.3390/electronics9010094
13. Kaid D, Eljazzar M (2018) Applying blockchain to automate installments payment between supply chain parties, pp 231–235. https://doi.org/10.1109/ICENCO.2018.8636131
14. Kakavand H, Sevres N, Chilton B (2017) The blockchain revolution: an analysis of regulation and technology related to distributed ledger technologies. SSRN Electron J. https://doi.org/10.2139/ssrn.2849251
15. Kshetri N (2018) 1 blockchain's roles in meeting key supply chain management objectives. Int J Inf Manag 39:80–89. https://doi.org/10.1016/j.ijinfomgt.2017.12.005
16. Kumar R, Tripathi R (2019) Traceability of counterfeit medicine supply chain through blockchain. In: 2019 11th international conference on communication systems networks (COMSNETS), pp 568–570. https://doi.org/10.1109/COMSNETS.2019.8711418

17. Montecchi M, Plangger K, Etter M (2019) It's real, trust me! establishing supply chain provenance using blockchain. Bus Horiz 62. https://doi.org/10.1016/j.bushor.2019.01.008
18. Schöner M, Kourouklis D, Sandner P, Gonzalez E, Förster J (2017) Blockchain technology in the pharmaceutical industry. FSBC Working Paper
19. Siyal A, Junejo A, Zawish M, Ahmed K, Khalil A, Soursou G (2019) Applications of blockchain technology in medicine and healthcare: challenges and future perspectives. Cryptography 3:3. https://doi.org/10.3390/cryptography3010003
20. Sylim P, Liu F, Marcelo A, Fontelo P (2018) Blockchain technology for detecting falsified and substandard drugs in the pharmaceuticals distribution system (preprint). JMIR Res Protoc 7. https://doi.org/10.2196/10163
21. Toyoda K, Mathiopoulos PT, Sasase I, Ohtsuki T (2017) A novel blockchain-based product ownership management system (POMS) for anti-counterfeits in the post supply chain. IEEE Access 5:17465–17477. https://doi.org/10.1109/ACCESS.2017.2720760
22. Tseng JH, Liao YC, Chong B, Liao SW (2018) Governance on the drug supply chain via gcoin blockchain. Int J Environ Res Publ Health 15:1055. https://doi.org/10.3390/ijerph15061055
23. Vokerla RR, Shanmugam B, Azam S, Karim A, Boer FD, Jonkman M, Faisal F (2019) An overview of blockchain applications and attacks. In: 2019 international conference on vision towards emerging trends in communication and networking (ViTECoN), pp 1–6 (2019). https://doi.org/10.1109/ViTECoN.2019.8899450
24. Wood D (2014) Ethereum: a secure decentralised generalised transaction ledger
25. Zhao J, Fan S, Yan J (2016) Overview of business innovations and research opportunities in blockchain and introduction to the special issue. Financ Innov 2. https://doi.org/10.1186/s40854-016-0049-2

ShoutIMEI: Ultrasound Covert Channel-Based Attack in Android

Keval Pandya, Bhavesh Borisaniya, and Bharat Buddhadev

1 Introduction

Android is an open-source and Linux kernel-based operating system developed by Google [1]. Android is a widely used operating system by the second quarter of 2021 [2]. There are over 28,93,806 Android apps on Google Play Store by the second quarter of 2021 [3]. Android is a permission-based operating system. Hence, to access any resources or complete any task, it requires permissions [4, 5].

Applications downloaded from Google Play Store may have been developed by untrusted developers. These applications may have lots of permissions granted by user. Based on these permissions, applications can access private data of the user, which leads to information leakage.

Nowadays, users are aware about the information leakage through applications with potential permissions. However, privilege escalation attack can take place when two applications communicate with each other requesting minimal set of permissions to leak private information even though the user carefully checked their permissions.

To communicate with each other, both applications require a communication channel. There are two types of communication channels. One is overt channel, which is a visible way to transfer data [6], whereas the second is covert channel, which works as a hidden communication channel by exploiting shared resources [6].

Many research have revealed various covert channels by which privilege escalation attacks can take place. In this paper, we are proposing an attack based on ultrasound covert channel. With the help of ultrasound covert channel, private information can be leaked covertly from the sender application to receiver application residing on the same or different devices. However, ultrasound also has a limitation. It only works if both devices are in a range of 10ft. To overcome this limitation, we propose a combination of the ultrasound and network-based covert channel to leak private information over the Internet.

K. Pandya (✉) · B. Borisaniya
Shantilal Shah Engineering College, Bhavnagar, India

B. Buddhadev
Government Engineering College, Gandhinagar, India

© The Author(s), under exclusive license to Springer Nature Singapore Pte Ltd. 2022   293
U. P. Rao et al. (eds.), *Security, Privacy and Data Analytics*, Lecture Notes
in Electrical Engineering 848, https://doi.org/10.1007/978-981-16-9089-1_24

This paper is organized as follows. In Sect. 2, we present a literature review and related work. In Sect. 3, we describe architecture of ShoutIMEI. In Sect. 4, we describe an implementation strategy of ShoutIMEI. In Sect. 5, we evaluate experimental results and finally, we conclude the paper with references at the end.

2 Related Work

In this section, we will discuss the related work found in the literature related to covert channel-based attacks.

Bushra Aloraini et al. [7] proposed an attack based on cellular voice channel. This attack leaks private information in the form of "speech-like" signals in a voice call. To achieve this, a custom FSK-based software audio modem has been designed.

Ahmed Al-Haiqi et al. [8] proposed a covert channel based on sensors. Vibration pattern is generated based on the information gathered by an application residing on the victim's device. When the device starts vibrating, the attacker's device near the victim's device starts reading Accelerometer data. Based on the graph generated by the Accelerometer, information can be extracted.

Mengchao Yue et al. [9] proposed a covert channel based on CPU Frequency. To leak the information, the sender application varies the speed of the CPU, while the receiver application monitors the variation in CPU speed. Based on the speed variation, information can be extracted.

Wen Qi et al. [10] proposed a user-behavior-based covert channel. The sender application forces the user to tilt the phone right or left based on private information gathered. The receiver application starts reading Gyroscope. Based on the readings of the Gyroscope, information can be extracted.

Nikolay Matyunin et al. [11] proposed a covert channel based on magnetic field. Sender application residing on a laptop computer generates a magnetic field based on private information. Receiver application activates EMF meter on the other device. Based on the readings of the EMF meter, information can be extracted.

Luke Deshotels [12] proposed a covert channel based on ultrasound. Private information is converted into an ultrasound in MATLAB and played on a computer speaker. Meanwhile, the receiver application on the other device records this ultrasound and extracts information.

Roman Schlegel [13] proposed an attack that records private information during a phone call and leaks it via different covert channels.

Riccardo Spolaor et al. [14] proposed an attack that uses a USB charging cable at the public charging station that manipulates the power consumption of the smartphone's CPU and sends out bits of data in a form of power bursts without using the data transfer functionality.

Ed Novak et al. [15] proposed a covert channel based on flash and camera in which sensitive data is sent out via flash and captured by another application via camera.

Some of the above covert channel-based attacks need very specific and/or sophisticated environments to leak any private information, e.g., Vibrator and Accelerometer, Flash and Camera, or Gyroscope-based covert channels. On the other hand, few approaches uses another application or device to send the private information e.g., CPU or EMF-based attacks. However, inference from another application or device can populate incorrect data causes failure in decoding private information on receiving side. Hence, we present our attack based on an ultrasound covert channel which has a higher throughput for privacy leaks.

3 Proposed Work

ShoutIMEI is a covert channel-based attack which extracts an IMEI number from the smartphone and transmits it to the attacker. Figure 1 shows the architecture of ShoutIMEI attack. There are 4 components in the ShoutIMEI attack.

3.1 Victim

Victim application resides within the victim's device. This application has only one permission (2) shown in Table 1 to extract an IMEI number from the device. This application maps an IMEI number on ultrasound frequency with the help of Frequency Shift Keying (FSK) Encoder and transmits sound packets through the device's speaker. Speaker and microphone of the smartphone do not support frequency greater

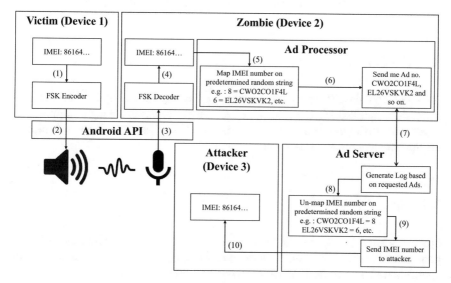

Fig. 1 ShoutIMEI architecture

Table 1 List of all permissions used by ShoutIMEI attack

No.	Permission	Description
1	INTERNET	Allows an application to access the Internet
2	READ_PHONE_STATE	Allows an application to access cellular network information, phone number of the device, status of ongoing calls, etc.
3	RECORD_AUDIO	Allows an application to record audio

than 22 kHz. Hence, ultrasound covert channel uses 15–22 kHz range of frequency (near-ultrasonic frequency) which is nearly inaudible to humans.

3.2 Zombie

Zombie application resides within the victim's device or device of the victim's colleague, family, or friend who stay together most of the time. This application has two permissions (1)(3) shown in Table 1. This application uses the microphone to record the sound played by the Victim application. FSK Decoder retrieves an IMEI number from the recorded sound.

To leak an IMEI number to the attacker over the Internet, Ad Processor is used. This application maps each digit of an IMEI number on a random string predetermined by Zombie and Ad Server. Once the mapping is done, this application requests Ad Server to send ads based on a series of predetermined random strings.

3.3 Ad Server

Ad Server contains different ads to be displayed on applications and websites. It logs and sends requested ads to the Zombie application. It parses the log to un-map and retrieve an IMEI number and stores it in the database. It also sends a notification to the Spy application about new data arrival.

3.4 Spy

Spy application resides within the attacker's device. This application has only one permission (1) shown in Table 1. Once an IMEI number is fetched by Ad Server, this application gets a notification and displays the stolen IMEI number.

4 Implementation

As discussed in the previous section, we have implemented a prototype of ShoutIMEI for Android devices. Table 2 shows the list of tools, services with their description, and their usage to implement ShoutIMEI.

4.1 Victim

The victim application extracts the IMEI number and plays the ultrasound accordingly. For the implementation, we chose to use the 17.5–18.25 kHz (750 Hz) range of ultrasound, because the speaker and microphone of the smartphones can only support frequency below 22 kHz. Chosen frequency range is still inaudible to humans, i.e., it is stealthy. Victim application generates data segments 441 samples long. Each segment is the sum of many modulated sub-carrier frequencies. There are 10 sub-carriers for 0–9 digits. This application reserves four sub-carrier frequencies (17.7, 17.9, 18.1, 18.3 kHz) to reduce the error rate when recovering data. So, in summary, we used the following parameters for implementation:

- Frequency Range: 17.5–18.25 kHz (750 Hz)
- Packet Size: 441
- Sample Rate: 44.1 kHz
- Sub-Carrier Frequencies: 17.7, 17.9, 18.1, 18.3 kHz

Table 2 List of tools and services required in ShoutIMEI

Tool	Description	Usage
Android studio	IDE for building Android applications	Victim, Zombie, and Spy application development
APKTool	APK file reverse engineering tool	Reverse engineering trusted application to hook Victim and Zombie code
Firebase (Notification)	Cloud service by Google for sending notification to smartphones	Sending notification to Spy application from Ad Server
Genymotion	Android Emulator	Testing Victim, Zombie, and Spy applications
IIS	Web Hosting Server	Hosting Ad Server
Microsoft Azure	Cloud service by Microsoft	Provides Virtual Machine for hosting Ad Server
Microsoft SQL Server	Database Management System by Microsoft	Storing stolen IMEI number, parsed from generated log by IIS
Microsoft Visual Studio	IDE for building .NET framework-based applications	Ad Server development
SignAPK	APK file signing tool	Signing trusted application containing Victim and Zombie code

4.2 Zombie

As mentioned in Sect. 3.2, Zombie application uses a predetermined random string to map each digit of an IMEI number. Table 3 contains that list of predetermined random string. If an IMEI number starts from 861, then mapped random string based on Table 3 is CWO2CO1F4L, EL26VSKVK2, and NWVE8XCP4K. Zombie application requests Ad Server to send ad number CWO2CO1F4L to display on application, then ad number EL26VSKVK2, and so on. Strings SHLT7ZO59F and 3GMJT32OL5 indicate starting and ending of an IMEI number to Ad Server, respectively.

4.3 Ad Server

We chose Microsoft Azure cloud service to host a virtual machine. This virtual machine has IIS-enabled Windows Server 2012 R2 Datacenter operating system. IIS is used for hosting ad service which has 12 ads listed in Table 3. It is configured to store generated log in database table of Microsoft SQL Server 2012. When an ad is requested by the Zombie application, IIS logs the details of the request as shown in Fig. 2.

We have developed a desktop application called Spy Server to parse the log generated by IIS to retrieve the IMEI number and store it on another table in Microsoft SQL Server 2012. With the help of the Firebase notification service, Spy Server can send a notification to the Spy application about the newly retrieved IMEI number.

Table 3 List of mappings of data on predetermined random string

Data	Predetermined random string (Ad No.)
Start	SHLT7ZO59F
0	86F5H7HHGK
1	NWVE8XCP4K
2	WLHYWG7G7O
3	VKD5OYOSWI
4	W8N37W9UUU
5	HX3EGI8BWA
6	EL26VSKVK2
7	8GQXHZ3UM4
8	CWO2CO1F4L
9	NL1C7GIU5C
End	3GMJT32OL5

	userna...	service	processingti...	bytesrec...	bytesse...	servicestat...	win32stat...	operati...	target	paramet...
1	-	W3SVC3	0	0	0	200	0	GET	/SHLT7ZO59F.png	-
2	-	W3SVC3	0	0	0	200	0	GET	/CWO2CO1F4L.png	-
3	-	W3SVC3	0	0	0	200	0	GET	/EL26VSKVK2.png	-
4	-	W3SVC3	0	0	0	200	0	GET	/NWVE8XCP4K.png	-
5	-	W3SVC3	0	0	0	200	0	GET	/EL26VSKVK2.png	-
6	-	W3SVC3	0	0	0	200	0	GET	/W8N37W9UUU.png	-
7	-	W3SVC3	0	0	0	200	0	GET	/HX3EGI8BWA.png	-
8	-	W3SVC3	0	0	0	200	0	GET	/86F5H7HHGK.png	-
9	-	W3SVC3	0	0	0	200	0	GET	/VKD5OYOSWI.png	-
10	-	W3SVC3	0	0	0	200	0	GET	/NL1C7GIU5C.png	-

Fig. 2 Log generated by IIS in Microsoft SQL server 2012

4.4 Spy

When the Spy application gets installed for the first time, it registers itself with the Firebase notification service to get a notification from Ad Server.

5 Results

Results gathered by experiments and testing suggest that the ultrasound covert channel-based attack is practical. We measured bit-rate and transmission range by performing various experiments.

5.1 Bit-Rate

We tested ShoutIMEI Victim and Zombie applications on Xiaomi Redmi Note 3 device and measured the bit-rate for transmission which is 50–55 bits per second. We even tested both applications on Genymotion emulator and measured the bit-rate for transmission which is 40–45 bits per second.

5.2 Transmission Range

We measured the transmitting range of ultrasound as a channel in smartphones is around 10ft. Even though the device is in the pocket, transmission can be done successfully. However, the device in the pocket requires a range of 5ft or less to transmit data accurately.

Conclusion

In this paper, we have proposed and implemented an attack based on ultrasound covert channel, and proved that this type of attack is practical. Not limited to IMEI numbers, this type of attack can also leak any small amount of data very efficiently, e.g., credit card details, login credentials, and OTPs. There is no explicit permission required to play a sound on Android. Hence, an ultrasound-based communication channel is more stealthy than network or any other communication channel. However, ultrasound-based attacks are only effective for devices in a shorter range. This research work leads to an open issue for mitigating such types of attacks.

References

1. Android (operating system) (2021) https://en.wikipedia.org/w/index.php?title=Android_ (operating_system)
2. Mobile Operating System Market Share Worldwide (2021) https://gs.statcounter.com/os-market-share/mobile/worldwide/
3. Google Play Store: number of apps (2021) https://www.statista.com/statistics/266210/number-of-available-applications-in-the-google-play-store/
4. Marforio C, Francillon A, Capkun S (2011) Application collusion attack on the permission-based security model and its implications for modern smartphone systems. Technical report, ETH Zurich. https://doi.org/10.3929/ethz-a-006720730
5. Fang Z, Han W, Li Y (2004) Issues and countermeasures, Permission based Android security. Comput Secur 43:205–218. https://doi.org/10.1016/j.cose.2014.02.007
6. Marforio C, Ritzdorf H, Francillon A, Capkun S (2012) Analysis of the communication between colluding applications on modern smartphones. In: Proceedings of the 28th annual computer security applications conference on—ACSAC '12, p 51, Orlando, Florida, ACM Press. https://doi.org/10.1145/2420950.2420958
7. Aloraini B, Johnson D, Stackpole B, Mishra S (2015) A new covert channel over cellular voice channel in smartphones. arXiv: 1504.05647
8. Al-Haiqi A, Ismail M, Nordin R (2014) A new sensors-based covert channel on android. Sci World J 2014:1–14. https://doi.org/10.1155/2014/969628
9. Yue M, Robinson WH, Watkins L, Corbett C (2014) Constructing timing-based covert channels in mobile networks by adjusting CPU frequency. In Proceedings of the third workshop on hardware and architectural support for security and privacy. Minneapolis Minnesota USA, ACM, pp 1–8. https://doi.org/10.1145/2611765.2611768
10. Qi W, Ding W, Wang X, Jiang Y, Xu Y, Wang J, Lu K (2018) Construction and mitigation of user-behavior-based covert channels on smartphones. IEEE Trans Mob Comput 17(1):44–57. https://doi.org/10.1109/TMC.2017.2696945
11. Matyunin N, Szefer J, Biedermann S, Katzenbeisser S (2016) Covert channels using mobile device's magnetic field sensors. In 2016 21st Asia and South Pacific design automation conference (ASP-DAC). Macau, IEEE, pp 525–532. https://doi.org/10.1109/ASPDAC.2016.7428065
12. Deshotels L (2014) Inaudible sound as a covert channel in mobile devices. In: Proceedings of the 8th USENIX conference on offensive technologies, WOOT'14. USENIX Association, San Diego, CA, p 16. https://www.usenix.org/conference/woot14/workshop-program/presentation/deshotels
13. Schlegel R, Kapadia A, Xiaofeng Wang X Soundcomber: a stealthy and context-aware sound trojan for smartphones. https://citeseerx.ist.psu.edu/viewdoc/summary?doi=10.1.1.363.1699

14. Spolaor R, Abudahi L, Moonsamy V, Conti M, Poovendran R (2017) No free charge theorem: a covert channel via USB charging cable on mobile devices. In: Gollmann D, Miyaji A, Kikuchi H (eds) Applied cryptography and network security. vol. 10355. Springer International Publishing, Cham, pp 83–102. https://doi.org/10.1007/978-3-319-61204-1_5
15. Novak E, Tang Y, Hao Z, Li Q, Zhang Y (2015) Physical media covert channels on smart mobile devices. In: Proceedings of the 2015 ACM international joint conference on pervasive and ubiquitous computing—UbiComp '15. ACM Press, Osaka, Japan, pp 367–378. https://doi.org/10.1145/2750858.2804253

A Review of Machine Learning-Based Intrusion Detection Systems on the Cloud

Nishtha Srivastava, Ashish Chaudhari, Nidhi Joraviya, Bhavesh N. Gohil, Suprio Ray, and Udai Pratap Rao

1 Introduction

Due to the electronic transmission of data, the use of computer systems and the Internet have resulted in significant privacy concerns. Despite significant progress made in improving computer systems' privacy, many issues remain unresolved. In reality, no system is safe. The interaction among the cloud actors such as consumer, provider, auditor, broker, and carrier makes the system more vulnerable. Network attacks come in a variety of flavours. All such attacks occur when a signature with abnormalities is added to the signature database. As a result of the advent of various types of attacks, many techniques are built and utilized in multiple network attacks. IDS can detect and track attacks aimed at compromising a system's security features (confidentiality, availability, and integrity).

As technology advances, hacking incidents are becoming more common. In such a dynamic technological world, security concerns pose major challenges. The cloud providers and consumers both record attacks on a daily basis. According to a Symantec report, during the year 2020, more than 600 major companies became victims of security attacks. More than 95% of cyber security professionals are concerned about cloud security.

N. Srivastava (✉) · A. Chaudhari · N. Joraviya · B. N. Gohil · U. P. Rao
Sardar Vallabhbhai National Institute of Technology, Surat, India
e-mail: d20co005@coed.svnit.ac.in

A. Chaudhari
e-mail: ds19co003@coed.svnit.ac.in

N. Joraviya
e-mail: d20co002@coed.svnit.ac.in

B. N. Gohil
e-mail: bng@coed.svnit.ac.in

U. P. Rao
e-mail: upr@coed.svnit.ac.in

S. Ray
University of New Brunswick, Fredericton, Canada
e-mail: sray@unb.ca

© The Author(s), under exclusive license to Springer Nature Singapore Pte Ltd. 2022
U. P. Rao et al. (eds.), *Security, Privacy and Data Analytics*, Lecture Notes
in Electrical Engineering 848, https://doi.org/10.1007/978-981-16-9089-1_25

Researchers have discovered a new vulnerability on the Amazon cloud computing platform using the Elasticsearch [1] distributed search engine method. Hackers were able to obtain access to the search engine and use it to launch a battalion of botnets on Amazon's cloud, according to analysis. Because it has the potential to be used to DDoS attacks against tens of billions of websites, the vulnerability should be taken seriously and brought to the attention of businesses. Elasticsearch, an open-source search engine server built on Java, allows Amazon cloud users to search different documents using a representational state transfer API. Recently, insider attacks/abuse accounted for 55% of events according to Verizon [1]. Malware developers use web browser addons to distribute malware and unauthorized applications, according to Cisco.

The rest of the paper is organized as follows: Sect. 2 gives a brief overview of the various attacks in the cloud environment and a comparative study of the IDS techniques. In Sect. 3, some light is shed on the various machine learning techniques used in IDS. Section 4 gives a summary and discusses the open issues of IDS approaches based on ML.

2 Cloud-Based IDS

The cloud computing paradigm is increasingly expanding in the world of information technology. Furthermore, the continuous availability of cloud computing services encourages intruders seeking access to the cloud service provider's services, tools, and resources.

2.1 Cloud Attacks

There are many types of cloud attacks, but a few major types of attacks are listed as follows:

- Insider attack
- User-root attack
- Port scanning
- Virtualization attack
- Side-channel attacks
- Backdoor channel attacks
- Denial of Service (DoS) attack
- Privilege's escalation attacks
- Cross-VM Row Hammer attack.

2.1.1 Insider Attack

In an insider attack [2], the attackers try to obtain and abuse privileges that have been assigned to them. As a result, they can defraud others, deliberately alter data, or expose secrets to competitors. This is a substantial breach of confidentiality. As an example, an inner DoS attack was performed that targeted Amazon (EC2) [3].

2.1.2 User-Root Attack

In a user-root attack [4], the user gains unauthorized access to the user account because of the malicious code (password sniffer, a dictionary). Buffer overflow attacks, perl, xterm, and other user-root attacks are just a few examples.

2.1.3 Port Scanning

The attackers scan the ports to find out the vulnerable ports. Examples of this include the open ports, the close ports, and the ports that are filtered. Port Scanning could be used by attackers to detect ports that are vulnerable and the services operating on them. Existing port scanning techniques include SYN, ACK, TCP, Windows, FIN, and UDP scanning. This method of scanning the port displays all the network packets, including MAC addresses, IP addresses, router and gateway filters, and firewall rules, among other things. A port scanning attack in the cloud environment could jeopardize the cloud's secrecy and integrity.

2.1.4 Virtualization Attack

By exploiting the hypervisor, an attacker can gain access to a VM. Virtual layer attacks such as SubVir [5], BLUEPILL [6], and DKSM [7] are well-known. As a result, hackers can get access to the hypervisor and take control of the host. By targeting zero-day attacks in VM, attackers can simply target and get access to them, potentially resulting in the damage of numerous websites that rely on virtual servers [8].

2.1.5 Side-Channel Attack

A side-channel attack, as defined by Ainapure [9], is one that relies on the data collected from a computer system's application rather than defects in the algorithm alone. Timing data, power usage, electromagnetic leaks, and sometimes even sound are used to provide an additional source of information. VMs running on the same core as the OS can be targeted by malicious or anomalous attacks, which includes side-channel attacks. Cache is a resource that may be shared between several VMs running simultaneously on the same core as of the OS. The attacker can use the victim's cache functionality to launch a (cache-base) memory side-channel attack.

2.1.6   Backdoor Channel Attack

The attacker attacks via the backdoor. It is a passive attack in which hackers attain remote access to a compromised node in order to compromise user privacy. Hackers can monitor a victim's resources and turn them into a malicious entity for a DDoS attack by using backdoor channels. It could be utilized to obtain sensitive information about the victim [10]. As a result, the infected device may have trouble executing its routine tasks. In the cloud environment, an attacker could utilize a backdoor channel to acquire access and control of a user's resources, as well as turn a VM into a "zombie" to launch a DDoS attack.

2.1.7   Denial of Service (DoS) Attack

The attack is also known as a flooding attack, which tries flooding a VM by delivering massive amounts of packets over the network from unsuspecting hosts (zombies). UDP, TCP, ICMP, or a combination of these protocols may be used to send packets. The goal of this attack is to prevent legitimate users from accessing the cloud services and then hacking them. An attacker may be able to make the intended service unavailable by focusing on a single server that provides it. It is referred to as a direct DoS attack. The flood requests deplete the physical resources of the server to the point where future service instances on the same physical device are unable to perform their required tasks. This is referred to as an indirect relationship [11].

2.1.8   Privilege's Escalation Attack

An attacker aims to find additional permissions or access to an already compromised account or tends to increase their privileges by gaining control of some other example. An adversary might induce memory errors and escalate privileges remotely by embedding malicious JavaScript code into the target's web traffic [12].

2.1.9   Cross-VM Row Hammer Attack

The attack exploits a flaw in the design of dynamic random-access memory (DRAM). Since present-day high-capacity DRAM has a high storage cell density, there is a greater electrical connection between surrounding cells, which can lead to the usage of malicious programs or vulnerabilities, as well as abuse of the legitimate rights granted to other users [12]. In light of the aforementioned attacks, a number of researchers have proposed IDS for cloud computing. Figure 1 depicts an overview of IDS.

An IDS is a protection tool that collects and tracks network traffic along with scanning the system/network for suspicious activities. The system or the cloud administrator is further warned of attacks.

There are three different types of IDS:

- Host-based IDS (HIDS)
- Network-based IDS (NIDS)
- Hypervisor-based IDS.

Individual hosts are monitored by HIDS. It sends a message to the user if it senses unusual behaviour, including the modification or deletion of system files, an abrupt pattern of system calls, or an unexpected setup specification shift at a VM. NIDS are installed at network nodes such as gateways and routers to track network traffic for anomalies. A Hypervisor-based IDS is installed at the hypervisor level or on the monitor of VM or on a privileged VM and can capture all state information for the VMs running on top of the hypervisor. This can monitor and implement different security policies to other VMs according to their requirements.

There are two broad classifications of IDS techniques: signature and anomaly-based IDS. However, apart from signature and anomaly, there are other IDS tech-

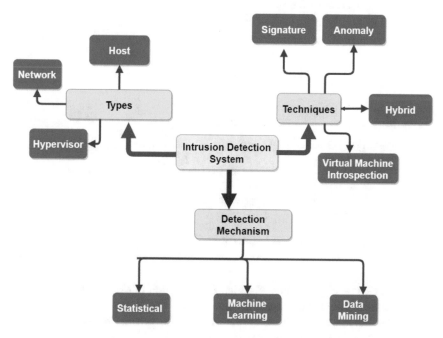

Fig. 1 An overview of IDS

Table 1 Comparative study of IDS techniques

Parameters	Signature/misuse-based IDS	Anomaly-based IDS	Virtual machine introspection	Hybrid
Attacks and vulnerabilities	Contextual analysis is used in identifying known attacks	Contextual analysis is used in identifying known and unknown attacks.	Detecting vulnerabilities and assaults by monitoring the run-time status of a system-level virtual machine (VM)	Contextual analysis is used in identifying the attacks as well as monitoring the run-time status of a system-level VM
Detection of attack and Recognition of attack techniques	Techniques preserve attack pattern in terms of signature and compare monitored observation against the same	Detects the anomaly based on abnormal behaviour observed in the monitored system	Virtual machine monitor provides the low-level information which is then converted pattern for detecting the vulnerabilities and attacks	Checks the abnormal behaviour as well as the preserved patterns to detect the attacks
Use of IDS	Signature-based IDS provides a basic understanding of protocols	Protocol analysis is used by the anomaly-based IDS to investigate packet data	It is used for debugging or forensic analysis	Provides security as a combination of the other approaches to achieve better results

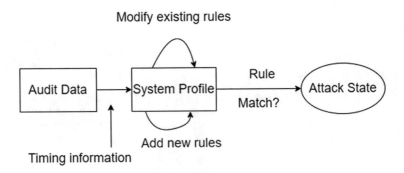

Fig. 2 The operation of the signature-based IDS

niques that exist such as Virtual Machine Introspection (VMI) and hybrid. Table 1 summarizes the different IDS approaches.

For IDS, the signature/misuse approach looks for specific patterns [13]. Basic working of the signature technique is shown in Fig. 2.

Information acquired from a network or device is compared to a signature database in signature/misuse-based IDS. A signature is a set of patterns or rules linked to a

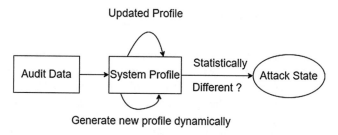

Fig. 3 The operation of anomaly-based IDS

certain attack. This technique is also known as misuse identification. These signatures are made up of a variety of components that allow the traffic to be recognized. Pattern recognition techniques are used by this IDS to determine if network traffic matches a known signature. Snort and Network Flig [14] use this technique in their IDS. Network Flight Recorder, Network Security Monitor, and Network Intrusion Detection, among others, use this method. It is capable of detecting known attacks with minimal false alarms. Network managers with ordinary security understanding can use the signature-based technique to appropriately identify breaches. It is a versatile method because fresh signatures are included in the dataset without interfering with current ones. However, it is incapable of detecting patterns having unknown attacks [14].

Anomaly detection systems look for deviations from the system's expected behaviour [15]. An anomaly-based IDS looks for unusual behaviour. This method compares actual user behaviour to user or network profiles in order to identify suspicious or potential activities which would represent intrusions. Profiles of users can be dynamic or static, and they should reflect the actions they intend to take. In order to generate a profile, daily behaviours of users, network links, or hosts are watched for a set amount of time, termed as the training period [16]. Failed login attempts, the amount of incidents a file is viewed by a certain user over a specific time period, CPU usage, and other factors are used to generate profiles.

The detection based on anomalies is effective against unknown attacks. To assess what constitutes normal behaviour, the researchers employ a variety of detection techniques that include Intrusion Detection Expert System (IDES) [17], which is a knowledge-based system, ISA-IDS [18], which is based on statistical methods, Audit Data Analysis and Mining [19], which is based on automatic/ML methods, and so on. The basic working of the anomaly-based IDS detection technique is shown in Fig. 3.

3 Cloud IDS Using Machine Learning (ML)

ML is a branch of computer science that allows computers to learn without having to be programmed first [20]. Network security employs ML to do a variety of computations and analyses in order to determine which packets should be dropped and which should be allowed into the system. A crucial prerequisite for any technique to function, according to [21], is a thorough understanding of the method. The most critical criterion for creating a useful tool for any system is a deep knowledge of the system's operation, capabilities, and limitations.

Chandola et al. [22] investigated the majority of the known anomaly detectors and their applications. For intrusion detection, ML provides both supervised and unsupervised learning options. Supervised learning uses classifiers to identify unknown instances based on training data that have been labelled. Because of this, it is an excellent option for detecting misuse-based IDS. Unsupervised learning data, on the other hand, do not have user-defined (labelled) categories because it aggregates related data. As a result, it is often used in anomaly detection. However, as with other methods, they have drawbacks, which should be carefully considered when designing IDS. Semi-supervised classification is the third type of classification in which a portion of the data is classified during the analysis.

3.1 ML Techniques Used in IDS for the Cloud

Many ML frameworks have been proven helpful in IDS, but each has its limitations. The effectiveness of the technique used in IDS is due to a variety of factors, including feature selection, the number of samples utilized in the model training, number of instances being utilized for model evaluation, and optimization of algorithm.

Figure 4 shows a classification of the IDS into two based on the techniques, anomaly and misuse/signature which are discussed in Sect. 2. Further, different ML techniques are elaborated with details as used in different approaches.

3.1.1 Naive Bayes

In IDS, Naive Bayes is applied for classifying attacks by selecting important features. In a study conducted by Singh et al. [23], experiments were performed on the KDD dataset and 24 features were selected. Experiments were conducted to measure the relevance of each feature. This strategy is based on precision, actual positive rate, and the system's false positive rate. The only limitation which can be pointed is the size of the feature set which is big.

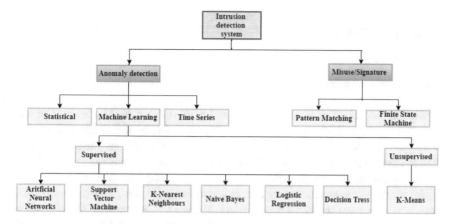

Fig. 4 Classification of ML-based IDS algorithms

3.1.2 Support Vector Machine

It is widely used in comparison to other approaches of ML. It is a method of classification, which divides data using a hyperplane by maximizing the margin between the data points and hyperplanes. The efficiency and feasibility of intrusion detection can be improved through feature selection. It is one of the most popular ML methods in IDS, but it has advantages and disadvantages with other algorithms [24]. SVM is an extensively used ML technique in the IDS area, which also has the overall best accuracy in all ML algorithms [25]. Overfitting is one of the important issues that ML algorithms need to address, and this is easily remedied in SVM via combinatorial optimization [26]. It handles high-dimensional feature vectors as well. Hence, large intrusion datasets like KDDCUP99 [27] utilize SVM. In a study conducted by Ullah et al. [28], a lightweight attack detection strategy using an SVM-based classifier was implemented. Real-time traffic data was used with 41 features and out of those, 23 features were selected. Alshammari et al. [29] and Naser and Jaber. [30] applied SVM with classifiers.

3.1.3 Deep Learning-Based Techniques

Large datasets may lead to several categories based on data classifications and the efficiency of the IDS model may decrease. In addition to this, the in-depth study of high-dimensional datasets is not possible with shallow learning. Deep Learning (DL) approaches, by contrast, are capable of handling high-dimensional data. Due to the growth in computational resources, DL techniques such as Recurrent Neural Networks (RNNs) and Convolutional Neural Networks (CNN) have gained recognition. These techniques have been used by Mishra et al. [31] for building efficient

IDS models. Chiba et al. [32] and Hajimirzaei et al. [33] also applied DL-based techniques as classifier.

3.1.4 Tree Classifiers

It is a prominent classification strategy for estimating the outcome by interacting with variables of the underlying dataset. Tree classifiers follow the divide and conquer strategy. The tree-like structure with a root node, leaf nodes, and branches is constructed iteratively. Two main criteria are taken into account for creating an optimum classification model: the selection of a dataset for assessment and the selection of a model for data assessment. As the data can contain partly noisy data or non-relevant data, it is important to choose appropriate attributes. Therefore, in Alshammari et al. [29] two different approaches for selecting features from the dataset, namely chi-square and IG were implemented. Misra et al. [34] and Patil et al. [35] applied Random Forest (RF) as classifier.

3.1.5 Logistic Regression

A supervised learning classification technique used to estimate the likelihood of a target variable is known as logistic regression. Because the nature of the target or dependent variable is binary, there are only two potential classes. It is one of the most basic ML algorithms that may be used for a variety of categorization tasks. However, the non-linear data cannot be handled by LR, which is a limitation of LR. Ghosh et al. [36] and Mishra et al. [37] used LR as classifier and Besharati et al. [38] used feature selection for their proposed IDS.

3.1.6 Clustering-Based Techniques

The method of grouping the entities represented in a dataset based on their similarity is called clustering. The efficiency of these algorithms is enhanced when data is scaled linearly. In IDS, clustering is used as an unsupervised ML method to group similar data. Unsupervised learning tries to extract useful information from data without class labels. Clustering is used as a classifier and feature selection in IDS. The k-means and k-Nearest Neighbours (k-NN) are the commonly used clustering techniques for IDS. Balamurugan et al. [39] applied k-means as classifier and Naser et al. [30] have used fuzzy c-means as initial classification in their system.

The details of the ML-based IDS are summarized in Table 2. Over the years, machine learning and deep learning-based approaches have also proven their utility in the fields of security and intrusion detection. This table represents an exhaustive summary of the applicability of ML-based intrusion detection technologies.

Table 2 Summary of ML-based IDS for the cloud

Author(s)	Technique/approach	Implementation details	Merits	Limitations
Partha Ghosh et al. [36] 2015	Logistic Regression (LR)-based classifier	Python 2.7.10; dataset: NSL-KDD	Best Feature Selection Set (BSFS) selects best features to reduce storage space and time	LR Classification accuracy depends on features provided in the system
Mishra et al. [37] 2016	Ensemble of neural network, Naïve Bayes, and Decision Tree C 4.5	Windows 32 GB RAM, 1 TB HDD and Core i7 processor, WEKA 3.7 tool; dataset: KDD99	Speed of detection is improved	For better accuracy, implement GPU-based techniques
Misra et al. [34] 2017	Random Forest (RF) LR as classifier	Python 2.7.10, Xen 4.6 as hypervisor; dataset: UNSW-NB, CAID	Proposed IDS provides Low false alert rate due to two-layer security	Unable to detect stealthy activities that hide their behaviour from IDS
Gautam et al. [23] 2018	Ensemble approach using Naive Bayes	R-Programming language, WEKA 3.7 tool; dataset: KDD-99	Emphasis made to optimize classifier model for two-class attack	Feature set can be reduced with help of better classifiers
Jan et al. [28] 2018	Lightweight attack detection strategy using SVM-based classifier	Matlab version 2018b simulation tool, traffic dataset	Better security provided for resource-constrained IoT devices	Change in Internet traffic intensity is not clearly masked by intruders
Bahram Hajimirzaei et al. [33] 2018	Neural Networks: The multi-layer perceptron (MLP) network, artificial bee colony (ABC), and the clustering method are used in combination as model	WEKA 3.7 tool for classification algorithms; dataset: NSL-KDD	The use of two algorithms with ANN is leveraging the overall detection accuracy	Initial values of the system define the accuracy of FCM and ANN. Each layer of ANN is affected by the weighted inputs and active function
Chiba et al. [32] 2019	Self-adaptive genetic algorithm (SAGA) to build automatically a Deep Neural Network (DNN) based on Anomaly Network Intrusion Detection System (ANIDS)	Windows 10 Core-i7, CloudSim simulator 4.0; dataset: CICIDS2017	The model generates low false warnings	CloudSim lacks GUI. Experiments can be performed on other simulators for better results
Besharati et al. [38] 2019	Logistic regression with three different classifiers: neural network, decision tree, and linear discriminant analysis	CloudSim software; dataset: NSL-KDD dataset	Logistic Regression selects different features for each class of dataset instances which increases detection accuracy	Proposed approach fails for a higher amount of data; feature selection depends on the regularized factor value
V. Balamurugan et al. [39] 2019	Enhanced IDS/IPS using hybrid classification and OTS generation, K-means clustering algorithm, RNN	WEKA 3.7 simulator, Lab generated dataset	Provides extra layer of security with cloud data access control by one time signature for cloud user	Unable to identify internal intrusion attacks K-means clustering requires higher execution time to form clusters

(continued)

Table 2 (continued)

Author(s)	Technique/approach	Implementation details	Merits	Limitations
Mishra et al. [31] 2019	Applies deep learning-based machine learning techniques for detecting attacks at VM layer in cloud environment	Performs the two-layer classification, L1-Convolutional neural network (CNN) L2-Bi-Directional Long Short-Term Memory (LSTM); dataset: University of New Mexico (UNM)	System cannot be easily bypassed by anti-detection methods such as obfuscation and encryption techniques	There is processing overhead due to two-layer classification
Muhammad Ash et al. [40] 2020	Convolutional auto encoder (Conv-AE)	4-bit Ubuntu14.04 OS, Java 1.8 (JDK), Scala 2.11.8; dataset: heterogeneous-CIC-IDS2018	Designed IDS system detects attacks for heterogeneous data, which is a major research problem	Model has potential to be applied on real-time streaming image data for better results
Patil et al. [35] 2020	Random Forest Classifier (RF) and Binary Bat Algorithm (BBA)	Executable file tracker (EFT): Python script, VirusTotal API; dataset: ClaMPIntegrated, ClaMPRaw	Proposed system design reduces the communication overhead and provides low false alerts	The suggested AMD framework can be used to detect encrypted malware (such as Ransomware), which is difficult to detect without running it
Naser Jaber et al. [30] 2020	Three phase—clustering using fuzzy c means, training with SVM, and evaluating with SVM classifiers	Intel Xeon E3, Debian OS; dataset: NSL-KDD	The system detects a wide range of attacks with excellent detection accuracy and a low percentage of false alarms	FCM fails to create accurate clusters when huge request arises from user on cloud environment
Alshammari et al. [29] 2021	Ensembled model of SVM, decision tree, and neural networks	Python 3.7.12; dataset: SOT-CID	This model records the differences between the data instances	This model damages the necessary speed in real-life networks because of the large dataset

4   Summary and Open Issues

Although excellent research has been carried out in the field of IDS, its performance depends heavily on realistic data. In contrast to other domains, ML algorithms have excelled and demonstrated that manual data rendering inspection does not allow it when the volume of data is high.

Despite the fact that machine learning approaches have made significant progress in the field of intrusion detection in cloud, there are still some open issues and we outline them as follows:

- ML algorithms can identify intrusions to some extent, but they frequently fail to do so while dealing with unlabelled data. Even if the models attain high accuracy on test datasets, good performance in real-world situations is not always guaranteed [33][38].

- The necessity for real-time detection in IDS is critical. As a result, improving the efficiency of ML models is one of the major issues. It is also important to minimize the time it takes to gather and store data [30][38].
- The false alarm rates and missed alarm rates of ML algorithms are often high, while rule-based detection approaches have a low rate of false alarms [35].
- Various features must be retrieved for particular kinds of intrusions, such as DoS and phishing, based on attack characteristics that may be abstracted using domain expertise [23].
- ML-Based IDS heavily rely on detection performance, therefore, they frequently use complex models and intensive data preparation procedures, resulting in low efficiency [32]. IDS, on the other hand, must identify intrusions in real time to minimize harm as much as to obtain feasibility [28].

5 Conclusion

In this paper, we have explored IDS for the cloud. We have first examined the attacks in order to address the need for IDS for the cloud. Further, various IDS techniques, types, and detection methods have been presented. We have focused on ML that includes some of the most promising detection techniques used in IDS for the cloud. The comparative study and summary of various existing ML approaches have been discussed. Research gaps are also provided for new research directions.

References

1. Smith J (2012) Cloud security incident reporting: framework for reporting about major cloud security incidents
2. Duncan A, Creese S, Goldsmith M (2015) An overview of insider attacks in cloud computing. Concurr Comput: Pract Exp 27(12):2964–2981
3. Mishra P, Pilli ES, Varadharajant V, Tupakula U (2016) Black hat presentation demo vids: amazon. In: 2016 international conference on advances in computing, communications and informatics (ICACCI). IEEE, pp 56–62
4. Fields T, Graham J (2016) Classifying network attack data using random forest. CATA, Dec
5. King ST, Chen PM (2006) Subvirt: implementing malware with virtual machines. In: 2006 IEEE symposium on security and privacy S & P'06). IEEE, pp 14–pp
6. Rutkowska J (2006) Subverting vistatm kernel for fun and profit. Black Hat Briefings
7. Bahram S, Jiang X, Wang Z, Grace M, Li J, Srinivasan D, Rhee J, Xu D (2010) Dksm: subverting virtual machine introspection for fun and profit. In: 2010 29th IEEE symposium on reliable distributed systems. IEEE, pp 82–91
8. Kene SG, Theng DP (2015) A review on intrusion detection techniques for cloud computing and security challenges. In: 2015 2nd international conference on electronics and communication systems (ICECS). IEEE, pp 227–232

9. Ainapure BS, Shah D, Rao AA (2017) Understanding perception of cache-based side-channel attack on cloud environment. In: Advances in intelligent systems and computing. Springer Singapore, pp 9–21, Aug 2017
10. Munir K, Palaniappan S (2012) Security threats/attacks present in cloud environment. IJCSNS 12(12):107
11. Modi CN, Patel D (2013) A novel hybrid-network intrusion detection system (h-nids) in cloud computing. In: 2013 IEEE symposium on computational intelligence in cyber security (CICS). IEEE, pp 23–30
12. Xiao Y, Zhang X, Zhang Y, Teodorescu R (2016) One bit flips, one cloud flops: cross-vm row hammer attacks and privilege escalation. In: 25th USENIX security symposium (USENIX Security 16)
13. Barbabra (2002) Applications of data mining in computer security
14. Mehmood Y, Shibli MA, Habiba U, Masood R (2013) Intrusion detection system in cloud computing: challenges and opportunities. In: 2013 2nd national conference on information assurance (NCIA). IEEE, pp 59–66
15. Garcia-Teodoro P, Diaz-Verdejo J, Maciá-Fernández G, Vázquez E (2009) Anomaly-based network intrusion detection: techniques, systems and challenges. Comput Secur 28(1–2):18–28
16. Scarfone K, Mell P (2007) Guide to intrusion detection and prevention systems (IDPS). NIST Spec Publ 800(2007):94
17. Denning DE (1987) An intrusion-detection model. IEEE Trans Softw Sng 2:222–232
18. Ye N, Emran SM, Li X, Chen Q (2001) Statistical process control for computer intrusion detection. In: Proceedings DARPA information survivability conference and exposition II. DISCEX'01, vol 1. IEEE, pp 3–14
19. Barbara D, Wu N, Jajodia S (2001) Detecting novel network intrusions using bayes estimators. In: Proceedings of the 2001 SIAM international conference on data mining. SIAM, pp 1–17
20. Samuel AL (1967) Some studies in machine learning using the game of checkers. II'recent progress. IBM J Res Dev 11(6):601–617
21. Sommer R, Paxson V (2010) Outside the closed world: On using machine learning for network intrusion detection. In: 2010 IEEE symposium on security and privacy, pp 305–316
22. Chandola V, Banerjee A, Kumar V (2009) Anomaly detection: a survey. ACM Comput Surv 41
23. Kumar Singh Gautam R, Doegar EA (2018) An ensemble approach for intrusion detection system using machine learning algorithms. In: 2018 8th international conference on cloud computing, data science engineering (Confluence), pp 14–15
24. Kuang F, Xu W, Zhang S (2014) A novel hybrid KPCA and SVM with GA model for intrusion detection. Appl Soft Comput 18:178–184
25. Salo F, Injadat M, Nassif AB, Shami A, Essex A (2018) Data mining techniques in intrusion detection systems: a systematic literature review. IEEE Access 6:56046–56058
26. Tao P, Sun Z, Sun Z (2018) An improved intrusion detection algorithm based on GA and SVM. IEEE Access 6:13624–13631
27. Alavikia Z, Ghasemi A (2018) Overload control in the network domain of lte/lte-a based machine type communications. Wirel Netw 24(1):1–16
28. Jan SU, Ahmed S, Shakhov V, Koo I (2019) Toward a lightweight intrusion detection system for the internet of things. IEEE Access 7:42450–42471
29. Alshammari A, Aldribi A (2021) Apply machine learning techniques to detect malicious network traffic in cloud computing. J Big Data 8(1):1–24
30. Jaber AN, Rehman SU (2020) FCM-SVM based intrusion detection system for cloud computing environment. Clust Comput 23:1–11
31. Mishra P, Khurana K, Gupta S, Sharma MK (2019) Vmanalyzer: malware semantic analysis using integrated CNN and bi-directional lSTM for detecting VM-level attacks in cloud. In: 2019 twelfth international conference on contemporary computing (IC3). IEEE, pp 1–6
32. Chiba Z, Abghour N, Moussaid K, El Omri A, Rida M (2019) A clever approach to develop an efficient deep neural network based ids for cloud environments using a self-adaptive genetic

algorithm. In: 2019 international conference on advanced communication technologies and networking (CommNet). IEEE, pp 1–9

33. Hajimirzaei B, Navimipour NJ (2019) Intrusion detection for cloud computing using neural networks and artificial bee colony optimization algorithm. ICT Exp 5(1):56–59

34. Mishra P, Pilli ES, Varadharajant V, Tupakula U (2016) Nvcloudids: a security architecture to detect intrusions at network and virtualization layer in cloud environment. In: 2016 international conference on advances in computing, communications and informatics (ICACCI). IEEE, pp 56–62

35. Patil R, Dudeja H, Modi C (2020) Designing in-VM-assisted lightweight agent-based malware detection framework for securing virtual machines in cloud computing. Int J Inf Secur 19(2):147–162

36. Ghosh P, Mitra R (2015) Proposed GA-BFSS and logistic regression based intrusion detection system. In: Proceedings of the 2015 third international conference on computer, communication, control and information technology (C3IT), pp 1–6

37. Mishra P, Pilli ES, Varadharajan V, Tupakula U (2016) Efficient approaches for intrusion detection in cloud environment. In: 2016 international conference on computing, communication and automation (ICCCA), pp 1211–1216

38. Besharati E, Naderan M, Namjoo E (2019) LR-hids: logistic regression host-based intrusion detection system for cloud environments. J Ambient Intell Hum Comput 10(9):3669–3692

39. Balamurugan V, Saravanan R (2019) Enhanced intrusion detection and prevention system on cloud environment using hybrid classification and OTS generation. Clust Comput 22(6):13027–13039

40. Khan MA, Kim J (2020) Toward developing efficient conv-ae-based intrusion detection system using heterogeneous dataset. Electronics 9(11)

Printed in the United States
by Baker & Taylor Publisher Services